Unproductive Labour in Political Economy

Contemporary mainstream economists see social wealth as the sum of individual incomes, but for three centuries many economists saw wealth as consisting of the public and private resources of a nation. This led them to explore the idea of unproductive labour, which provides a nation with an individual income, but does not contribute to an increase in social wealth or help to foster development.

This book analyses the evolution of ideas surrounding unproductive labour, offering an unprecedented history that guides readers from the work of Petty through to the present economic crisis. This volume explores the work of several key scholars, including Smith, Petty, Marx, Ricardo, Mill, Say and Schumpeter.

This book is suitable for scholars and researchers with an interest in the history of economic thought, labour economics and economic philosophy.

Cosimo Perrotta is a retired Professor of the History of Economic Thought at the University of Salento, Italy.

Routledge Studies in the History of Economics

203 Asia and the History of the International Economy
Essays in Memory of Peter Mathias
Edited by A.J.H. Latham and Heita Kawakatsu

204 The Economic Thought of Henry Calvert Simons
Crown Prince of the Chicago School
G.R. Steele

205 The Economic Thought of William Petty
Exploring the Colonialist Roots of Economics
Hugh Goodacre

206 Greed in the History of Political Economy
The Role of Self-Interest in Shaping Modern Economics
Rudi Verburg

207 Aristotle's Critique of Political Economy
A Contemporary Application
Robert L. Gallagher

208 Otto Neurath and the History of Economics
Michael Turk

209 A Brief Prehistory of the Theory of the Firm
Paul Walker

210 Unproductive Labour in Political Economy
The History of an Idea
Cosimo Perrotta

For more information about this series, please visit www.routledge.com/series/SE0341

Unproductive Labour in Political Economy

The History of an Idea

Cosimo Perrotta

Routledge
Taylor & Francis Group
LONDON AND NEW YORK

First published 2018 by Routledge

2 Park Square, Milton Park, Abingdon, Oxfordshire OX14 4RN
52 Vanderbilt Avenue, New York, NY 10017

Routledge is an imprint of the Taylor & Francis Group, an informa business

First issued in paperback 2020

British Library Cataloguing-in-Publication Data
A catalogue record for this book is available from the British Library

Library of Congress Cataloging-in-Publication Data
Names: Perrotta, Cosimo, 1942– author.
Title: Unproductive labour in political economy: the history of an idea / Cosimo Perrotta.
Description: London; New York: Routledge, 2018. |
Series: Routledge studies in the history of economics; 210
Identifiers: LCCN 2018002788 | ISBN 9781138658325 (hbk) | ISBN 9781317218326 (pdf) | ISBN 9781317218319 (epub) | ISBN 9781317218302 (mobi)
Subjects: LCSH: Labor productivity. | Labor. | Wealth.
Classification: LCC HC79.L3 .P47 2018 | DDC 331.11/8—dc23
LC record available at https://lccn.loc.gov/2018002788

ISBN: 978-1-138-65832-5 (hbk)
ISBN: 978-0-367-66644-6 (pbk)

Typeset in Bembo
by codeMantra

Contents

Preface

"Le travail producteur commence par être purement physique dans les premières phases de l'industrie et finit par être complètement intellectuel dans les dernières" ("Productive labour begins by being purely physical in the first phases of industry and ends by being completely intellectual in the last phases").

(Gustave de Molinari, 1846, 1.II)

"Every economic theory includes—or, at least, is haunted by—the distinction between productive and unproductive labor".

(David Ruccio, 2016)

This volume follows on from my previous book *Consumption as an Investment – I. The Fear of Goods from Hesiod to Adam Smith*, published by Routledge in 2004. It begins by reviewing – in summary – the issue of productive/unproductive labour and consumption from the 16th century up to Quesnay and Smith (chs. I–II), dealt with in the 2004 book. Then it goes on to examine the subsequent treatment of this issue from Quesnay and Smith up to the 1970s (chs. III–XVIII). Finally, we will, from the same viewpoint, be looking into the welfare state, its decline and the present crisis (chs. XIX–XXI). The analyses of unproductive labour and consumption also entail considerations on accumulation, crises, technical progress, unemployment, the tendency towards immaterial wealth, increasing investment in human capital, class transformations, etc.

This book is not a collection of essays, but the result of long-planned research. The list of *References* is not a bibliography. It contains only works I have personally examined, selected from the many more writings I examined for this research. Many of the texts read in the early 1980s are cited/quoted here in the online version, which I have recently tracked down.

None of the chapters has been published previously, except some parts of Chapter 4. Since the 1970s, I have been publishing provisional comments on some aspects of the unproductive labour/consumption issue. All of these deliberations have been radically rethought and reworked. Some material used here has also been used in the following publications of mine (in brackets are the chapters in the present book where they are used):

- *Consumption as an Investment – I*, Routledge 2004, Chapters 9 and 11 (Chapter II);
- "The four 18th century streams on productive labour", *Iberian Journal of the History of Economic Thought*, vol. 1, no. 2, 2014: 1–13 (Chapters III–IV);
- "The Stationary State: Deadlocks and New perspectives", in G. Bitros and N. Kyriazis, eds., *Essays in Contemporary Economics. A Festschrift in Memory of A.D. Karayiannis*, Springer, 2015 (Chapters XIX–XX);
- "Classical Underconsumption Theories Reassessed", in J. Kregel, M. Corsi, and C. D'Ippoliti, eds., *Classical Economics Today. Festschrift in Honour of Alessandro Roncaglia*, Anthem Press (Chapter IX).

Acknowledgments

As follows are listed the libraries where I spent more time working on this subject, mainly in the 1980s (I am grateful to their staff, who showed great competence and kindness, especially in the first three listed):

Goldsmith's Library, London
Fondazione Einaudi, Torino
Dipartimento di Filosofia, Storia e Scienze Sociali, Univ. di Lecce
L. Robbins Library, London School of Economics
British Library, London
Biblioteca Civica, Torino
The libraries of the Faculties of Economics of Firenze; Modena; Bologna
The libraries of the University of Lecce (now, Univ. of Salento).

Many books were examined directly online, mostly through the Internet Archive, Google Books and the Library of Economics and Liberty.

I am very grateful to Salvatore Rizzello and Claudia Sunna for helping me track down a number of books and articles. I am also grateful to all those who have encouraged me in pursuing this project. Particular mention here goes to the late Giacomo Becattini, Umberto Cerroni and Bob Coats (my "mentors"). I also owe thanks to Peter Groenewegen, Bertram Schefold, Katsuyoshi Watarai; and to Michele Alacevich, Cristina Marcuzzo, Estrella Trincado; the representatives of the Hiberian Association for the History of Economic Thought (AIHPE) and of the Italian Association for the History of Political Economy (STOREP); the anonymous referees of the book project; and the supervisor of my English, Graham Sells, for his accurate and valuable work. Of course, I alone am responsible for any mistakes.

A grateful thank you to all my family, particularly my wife Anna, my son Paolo and my daughter Susanna, for their constant support.

C.P. – December 2017

Notes on the text

- In the text, the numbers in parentheses, alone or after the semicolon, indicate the pages of the work in question.
- Quotations from texts not written in English are in my translation.
- Italics in quotations are by the author quoted.
- In the citations and the References, the date after the name usually indicates the year of the first edition. If the publication is posthumous or much later, the date indicates the last year of composition and is usually in square brackets.
- The author's name in square brackets means that his/her work originally appeared anonymously.
- The author's names, when first appearing in a section or paragraph, are stressed in italics.

I Introduction

What is unproductive labour

Background

This book is the continuation of C. Perrotta, *Consumption as an Investment: I. The Fear of Goods from Hesiod to Adam Smith*, Routledge, 2004. The "I" implied a "II", which is the present work.

The 2004 book describes the hostility (which dominated pre-modern economies) towards the pursuit of enrichment through economic activities. In that static context, social wealth only increased by despoiling or exploiting other societies. Only in modern times has the hostility towards enrichment through economic activities to some extent been contested by humanists and disregarded by mercantilists. Finally, the Enlightenment legitimised the pursuit of wealth at both the individual and the social level. Moreover, the Enlightenment authors theorised a policy based on high wages and growing skills. Indeed, they saw the increase in consumption as an investment, and development as both economic and social process. The industrial revolution wiped out the Enlightenment approach.

In the present book we examine the authors who analyse capitalist accumulation through the productive/unproductive labour distinction and also through the consequent productive/ unproductive consumption distinction. Such distinctions are relevant to economic thought from the 16th–19th century, but linger on, as a marginal issue, to the present day.

1. The concept

a. Definitions

Labour is a planned activity. It produces something useful for us, which we call wealth. The economists who speak of unproductive labour are usually referring to the labourer who produces less wealth than – or just the same wealth as – he consumes. They refer to social wealth regardless of the revenue that a certain occupation yields to the individual who performs it. Other economists – like the neoclassical authors – consider the concept of unproductive labour as meaningless, given that labour only exists if it yields a revenue to the labourer. But in this case, their reference is to the individual, not society.

In the modern age economists began seeking to identify which labour contributes most to the national wealth. The proportion in which social labour is distributed between more and less productive activities is decisive for the final production. The quantity of social wealth produced determines the level of social consumption, but it is also determined by it. The skill and productivity of labourers depend on the comfort, education and culture that society can provide to them.

The concept of unproductive labour is relevant only to the theories that consider the economy not as a mere series of exchanges between individuals, but as the organisation of society for the production of social wealth.

b. Why it appears only in modern economy

Pre-modern economies are static: wealth grows neither endogenously nor constantly, and occupations are normally inherited, together with the social status acquired by birth. Labour is not a free choice, nor is it motivated by self-interest. Often it is even forced labour, as in slave or serf systems. In principle, there can be no conflict between individual and collective interests, because the former are hardly acknowledged.

Pre-modern culture reflects this context. The pursuit of enrichment through labour and trade is morally condemned. The basic canon of all pre-modern authors is this: the enrichment of one is the impoverishment of another. It was theorised by *Aristotle* and repeated over and again for two thousand years, up to *Alberti* (1437–41) and *Montaigne* (1580).[1]

The modern economy has shaken up this state of affairs, albeit gradually. After several centuries of fierce social struggles – often experienced by the protagonists as religious conflicts – the choice of labour has become free, although to a very limited extent and only for a few social categories. The pursuit of own self-interest is to a certain extent legitimised. The mercantilists expressed the new values. They were aware that their aim – a rich and powerful nation – could only be pursued by linking two factors: a strong state policy favouring the country's own merchants and respect for individual self-interest (see *Montchrétien* 1615).[2]

The 16th-century authors began to think about the production sectors or occupations that are particularly important for the growth of national economy and deserve to be supported. They considered two features: first, the nature of the occupation; second, whether or not that occupation is overcrowded for the specific need it meets. Note that the idea of more or less productive occupations implies the possibility of conflict between collective and individual interests. Any such conflict was in reality excluded, not only by pre-modern culture, where the collective dimension dominated, but also by neoclassical economics, dominated by individual interests.

Thus the productive/unproductive labour distinction can only have sense in an approach where collective interests and individual interests are both recognised, and where they can collaborate, albeit at times coming into conflict. This approach was shared by the mercantilists, the authors of the Enlightenment and the classical economists in all their branches, and it is by today's so-called heterodox economics.

2. Two centuries of literature ignored

Before Smith, there are over two centuries of literature on unproductive labour (see ch. II), which, however, historians of economic thought usually ignore. For the 19th century, we have found only five historians aware of the debate on unproductive labour before Quesnay and Smith.[3] Even *McCulloch*, the untiring editor of pre-Smithian texts, ignores such reflections. For the 20th century, we can add another eight historians.[4] *Garbero* (1980) has the merit of providing a systematic account of the pre-Smithian theories on productive labour.

Almost all the best-known general histories of economic thought – from *Gonnard* (1921) to *Cannan* (1929) and *Schumpeter* [1949] – ignore this aspect of the pre-Smithian literature. Except for *Johnson* (1937), even the best studies on mercantilism ignored this issue (see *Sewall* 1901; *Furniss* 1920; *Morini-Comby* 1930; up to *Viner* 1937, 1948, 1968; etc.). *Bevan* (1894) is the best example of how the prejudices can blind historians. In his monograph on Petty, he speaks at length of labour, how important the issue was for Petty and how indebted Smith was to him. But not a word is spent on Petty's numerous reflections on unproductive labour.

We have insisted on this point, because the issue of unproductive labour is the only apparent thread of continuity between the mercantilist and subsequent economic thought. Had Smith not so accurately concealed his mercantilist sources, had he and his contemporaries been less extreme in despising the previous economists, the mercantilist heritage would not have been lost, and the productiveness of labour would have been recognised as central to the economics of accumulation and development.

3. Private and public interest

Helen *Boss* (1990) rightly notes that the authors of the Enlightenment considered it obvious that individual and social interests can come into conflict (24). However she disregards the mercantilists, who had the same attitude. Many of these authors were opposed to the high prices of exports, which enriched the merchants but hindered the growth of national trade.[5]

Many other authors attacked the importation of luxuries or goods substituting internal products, since they enriched the respective merchants but damaged the nation.[6] Others stated that competition in general enriches the nation but damages some individuals.[7] Finally many authors recognised in general the conflict between individual and collective interests.[8] Josiah *Tucker* (1750) wrote that every merchant must pursue his own interests, but this did not always coincide with the interests of the nation or of other merchants.

It was the government that had to defend the general interest (316–18). Self-interest, he writes elsewhere, is the driving force of human progress. However, it is narrow-minded. It does not conceive of legitimate competitors. Thus, it must be governed; otherwise the mutual exclusion will produce common poverty and the negation of self-interest itself (T. 1755: 56–8).

Several historians have noticed this attitude in the pre-Smithians.[9] Some maintain that the attitude has hindered the progress of economic theory.[10] By contrast, others maintain that it expressed an elementary truth.[11]

Conclusions

In its original form, the concept of unproductive labour implied, first of all, that the productiveness of labour was relative. Unproductiveness often derives from an excessive number of people employed. Second, it implied possible conflicts between private and public interests. Third, it also implied identity between the usefulness and productiveness of labour. All three of these features were to be denied later.

Notes

1 Aristotle (*Politics*, I, 1258b.1–2). Alberti (1437–41, III: 315). Montaigne (1580, ch. 22).
2 Montchrétien (1615: 133, 285–8).
3 These are: Roscher (1854: section 59, fn); Marx (1859, I.I.A: 64–7; *Theory*, I, 4.2, 4.6.b and *Appendix* 1–2); Heyking (1880: 75fn); Ingram (1888: 49); Schmoller (1900, 39: 130).
4 Johnson (1937: 215–16, 245–6, passim); Tagliacozzo (1937: LX); Pribram (1983: 77); James (1959: 47–8); Spengler (1960: 31, 33fn); Rima (1967: 26–7); Deyon (1969, I.2.3: 56–7); Garbero (1980).
5 See e.g. Mun [1623, III.8, VII]. Child (1693, IX: 176–8). Cary (1695, Intr.: 2; II.4: 132–3). Postlethwayt (1757: 369–70). Harris (1757, 15: 362).
6 See e.g. Roberts (1641: 76). Forbonnais (1753: 695b).
7 See Child (1693, 9: 187). Martyn (1701: Ch. 4–5).
8 See Fortrey (1663: 218–19). Becher (1668: 4). Petyt (1680: 287–9, 457). Jansenn (1713: 1).
9 See e.g. Cole (1931: 224). Johnson (1937: 307). Buck (1942: 72–3, 103–4, 107–13, 215). S. Hollander (1973: 45–6). See also Heckscher (1931, V.3).
10 See Schatz (1907: 15–30). Gregory (1921: 49). Viner (1935: 409; 1948: 277–86).
11 See Furniss (1920: 39–40). Morini-Comby (1930: 134–8).

II Unproductive labour before Smith[1]

Background

All the authors of the 16th–17th centuries interested in the social or economic problems are obsessed with the vagabonds, gamblers and various charlatans who thronged the cities and fairs of Western Europe. There were also fierce social struggles and great political initiatives endeavouring to transform the poor and beggars into productive labourers.[2]

This issue is connected with that of unproductive labour, but there is a significant difference between the two issues. The attitude towards the poor is a moral and social issue that is dealt with in different ways by all societies. The problem of unproductive labour derives from the capitalist tendency to economic development. In what follows we will treat only the second issue.

1. The emergence of the issue

The first authors who raised the problem of unproductive labour were the modern utopians. According to Thomas *More* (1516), the rich, the noble, priests and religious orders, together with their servants and clients, consume without producing. The occupations that afford them luxury consumption are useless (I: 44–5). In the "City of the Sun", by *Campanella* (1602), all people work. All engage in both practical and speculative activities. This allows them to work only four hours a day. In the real city of Naples of his time, Campanella noted that only 50 thousand people out of 300 thousand worked and so their work was extremely hard (20–1, 28).

But the economists, too, soon became aware of the problem. John *Hales* (1549) wrote that some fields of work damage the balance of trade by importing wares. Others, like handicrafts, are neutral. Yet others, which export wares, are useful, because they improve the balance of trade (123–6). Luis *Ortiz* (1558) called for the idle and the rich, soldiers, menial servants, vagabonds, students, jurists and scholars to be put to productive work (i.e. manufacture). Ortiz's list of the unproductive (128–9) is much like the lists compiled by Petty and Smith.

Some of the best authors (*Botero* 1589, *Serra* 1613) compare the different sectors of production, affirming that manufacture is more productive than agriculture.[3] *Roberts* (1641) maintains that, without trade, a country can never become rich (61–5). *Appleby* (1978: 116) referred to the thesis of John Keymor, who wrote in 1650 that two-thirds of the English population were mere consumers of wealth.

Montchrétien (1615) reversed the pre-modern idea that nobles and the clergy are the more productive members of society (an idea that Gregory *King* 1696 still maintained at the end of the century: 424–5). He stated that the most important classes in society were farmers, artisans and merchants, who enable the others to survive. It was they who preserved the state.[4]

The Cameralist *Becher* (1688) provided the most organic analysis before Petty. He said that the "community servants" – i.e. nobles, the clergy, intellectuals, soldiers and professionals – run society, providing it with culture and safety. On the other hand, farmers, artisans and traders provide material wealth. Each of these groups must maintain a certain numerical proportion with respect to the others. The community servants were not to grow in number too much and were to be a minority; otherwise the state would fall into ruin (Introduction, II: 4–11).

2. Petty

Like Botero and Serra, Petty set out to identify which occupations produce more wealth and which produce less or no wealth at all. In general, the former are those whose products are relatively easy to store, like durable goods. Petty persevered in his endeavour to list the more productive occupations through a hypothetical census of the British population. In the most complete of his lists of the productive population, he included a quarter of the women over seven (namely, those who cook, make bread, beer and milk; sew and weave; grow corn, etc.); then artisans, seamen, farmers, hirelings, labourers and errand boys.[5]

Petty would often also draw up lists of the unproductive members of society: landowners; theologians and those who "uselessly waste their time studying Latin and Greek"; doctors, pharmacists, lawyers; all the administrative apparatus of the state; plus gamblers, cheats, prostitutes and beggars.[6] Elsewhere he added philosophers, menial servants and people engaged in entertainment. However, he deemed research on nature highly productive.[7] Note that Petty seems to have considered as unproductive not these occupations as such, but only the supernumeraries present in them.

Soldiers, traders and retailers were unproductive, although they were among the "pillars" of the nation. Traders simply transported the goods produced by others. They were like gamblers playing with the others' work.[8]

Petty deemed that taxes should be levied above all on the consumption of superfluous foodstuffs and other perishable luxuries. For the purpose of enriching the country, the proceeds from such taxes should be transferred, in order of priority, to those who bring into the country gold and silver (the most durable goods); those engaged in the improvement of land, mines and fishing; and those who purchase houses, furniture and, lastly, clothes. By contrast, if these proceeds are transferred to workers in the field of entertainment, those who study metaphysics and those who are in any case not involved in the production of material or useful things, then the country will be so much the poorer. Only once we have a clear idea of how many people are needed in production and in the direction of it can the supernumeraries be employed in pleasurable activities. But the most important of these activities is the study of nature.[9]

Note that, in these lists, the foodstuffs for workers are included among the top items. This means that, although Petty started from a physical idea of accumulation as storing up, he then went on to an economic idea of accumulation, regarding activities that are useful for the increase of production. This shows that Petty's approach to the issue was flexible and empirical. He was able to acknowledge the real needs of social accumulation and even to suggest the modern concept of disguised unemployment (see XIV.3). He observes that trade was the most lucrative activity. Then there was manufacture and, third, agriculture.[10] On this basis, he called for the transfer of some labourers from agriculture, where they were poor despite working hard, to manufacture and trade. Moreover, he stressed that, if we increase agricultural productivity, we can transfer some workers to more productive activities without reducing agricultural production.[11] *Boss* (1990) is one of the few historians who note the advantages of Petty's approach over that of Smith (17–22).

3. After Petty: proportion among sectors

After Petty, there were authors who simply repeated some of his arguments,[12] while others sought to go deeper into the question. These reflections show two particularly recurrent features. One is the classification of the different occupations as productive or unproductive. The other is the conviction that the most important thing is to keep a proportion among the different occupations. The supernumeraries are understood to be unproductive or less productive. However, a few authors apply this principle to all kinds of occupations, while others apply it only to non-material activities.

Petyt (1680), the author of *Britannia Languens*, gives Petty's arguments more coherence. But, in so doing, he also introduces a rigidity that was bound, in the long run, to distort the concept of unproductive labour. All material occupations and export activities are productive, while retailers and shopkeepers are unproductive. The latter live off buying cheap and selling dear, and if they import their commodities, they also export wealth (III: 301). Also unproductive are professionals of all kinds, officials, scholars and the clergy. Here, Petyt formalises a distinction, which sometimes implicitly appears in Petty. He states that these occupations are useful and honourable but unproductive.[13] This distinction between useful and productive – although contrary to common sense – was to have great fortune. It was to be adopted by the major authors concerned with such issues, including Quesnay, Smith and Marx.

Petyt adds that also unproductive are those who love luxuries and impoverish the nation by importing them (VIII: 376–7). Although unproductive activities grow along with the increase in population, they should not increase beyond a certain proportion, whilst manufacturing and large-scale trade can increase indefinitely (292, 302).

Dalby *Thomas* (1690), contesting the alleged chrysohedonism in the mercantilists (namely the confusion of wealth with money),[14] makes it clear that money is only a measure, not the true substance of wealth. True wealth consists of land, natural resources and, above all, labour. He writes that "labour, inventions, trade and negotiations" are the only cause and support of wealth (406). As for the gentry, clergy, lawyers, serving men and beggars, although some of them are necessary, "yet the fewer such the better" (407). Thomas distinguishes between those who add nothing, or less than they consume, to the nation, those who add the same wealth they consume through services or intellectual labour, and those who add more. The latter are the only cause of wealth (408).

Locke (1691) includes among the unproductive scholars of all kinds, women, gamblers and menial servants. He then foreshadows a distinction between labour spent on production (productive) and labour spent on consumption (unproductive). Smith was to transform the idea into a distinction between labour exchanged with capital and labour hired for private consumption. Manufacturers, Locke writes, are the most productive, while retailers and traders are less so, since they make money at the expense of the workers and landowners (28–9).

Cary (1695), while largely repeating the views of Petyt, adds that agricultural products increase national wealth only if they are exported. If they are consumed internally, they are part of the nation's expenses.[15] The importance of *Pollexfen* (1697) lies in stressing that intellectual labourers are necessary like the others, although if their number exceeds social needs they are hands subtracted from the more useful jobs (43–6). *Child* (1694: 12) affirms the same thesis. *Davenant* (1698), like Petty and others, include scientists – and traders – among the productive (I: 139–41). *Bellers* (1699) insists on the due proportion in the numbers of workers in each sector although, he observes, the manual workers are never too many (10). In his considerations on investment projects, Littleton ironically observes: "there is nothing easier than finding jobs which give no profit" (see *Appleby* 1978: 154–5).

Cantillon (1730) holds that the people who produce wealth are a quarter of the total population. Another quarter is made up of non-active population, like landowners and businessmen. The remaining half consists of soldiers, menial servants, churchmen and producers of luxury goods. The latter in particular come in for criticism by Cantillon. If they produced useful goods, instead of luxuries, the country would not only appear but actually be richer. The productive workers are the ones who produce essential goods, either for survival or for accumulation. From the latter derives the stock of wealth that exceeds the annual consumption.[16] Entertainment or production of luxuries can only be admitted if there is no possibility of employing those workers in productive activities, while churchmen are completely useless.[17] *Vanderlint* (1734) insists on the numerical proportion among sectors. Scant agricultural production can render the number of manufacturing workers excessive (53ff.).

4. The Enlightenment

a. Critique of the privileged classes

The authors of the Enlightenment intensified the attacks on the wastefulness of the aristocracy. About to lose their politically dominant role once and for all, this class could no longer justify its habitual consumption of luxuries. *Tucker* (1750) lamented the excessive number of French nobles (331–2), while *Hume* stated that landowners are unproductive.[18] Similar reflections can be found in other authors.[19]

Some authors called for limitation of the number of churchmen and putting them to useful work.[20] The unproductiveness of doctors and lawyers was a recurrent argument,[21] as well as scholars, secretaries, artists and professionals in general (*Faiguet* 1763: 66–7, 123–6, 140–2) and of people of entertainment (*Rousseau* 1755: 726). The need was also expressed to keep public administration at the minimum indispensable.[22]

On the productiveness of commerce – always a much debated issue – *Harris* (1757) held trade to be useful (sections 13–14). *Hutcheson* (1733–37) maintained that, in the exchange value of goods, not only is the labour of production included but also the labour of storage and marketing (II.12: 63). Finally the mercantilist *Forbonnais* (1753), while admitting that domestic trade also has a value (against the conviction of the 17th-century economists), was confident that a developed export commerce could absorb the redundancy of labourers caused by technical progress (697–9). The Spanish *Ward* (1762) admits the productiveness of commerce, but states that material production is more productive because, besides profits, it also creates employment.[23] On the contrary, according to *Muñoz* (1769), wealth is not produced by trade, but by production (89–92). Tommaso *Vasco* (1773) takes a middle way: trade is "indirectly productive" (a category taken up from Genovesi) because it raises productivity by saving time and labour for the producers. He is also doubtful about reducing the number of intermediaries (another eternal question). Such a reduction, he notes, could lead to the very monopoly they want to oppose (II.5: 398–9).

Hume (1752d) favoured a balanced proportion between producers and idle people in general. The latter should never be too many (366). He also noted that traders and entrepreneurs were the most productive categories, because their pursuit of profit was the driving force of production.[24] *Plumard* (1752) maintained that the rural classes, being the very basis of the national economy, are "never too numerous", and yet in France they are oppressed by taxes and are the most miserable. Consequently, the endeavour is made to enter professions, public administration or the clergy, while they "produce less" and should not grow beyond a certain limit. Lastly, the third class, the idle who consume what others have produced, forms – for Plumard – a list of occupations similar to those of Ortiz, Petty, Smith, etc. It includes pimps, solicitors, frivolous writers, preachers and theologians, and servants kept out of vanity.[25]

Griselini (1766) gives one of the best description of the benefits of a proportional distribution of workers: "The more precise the placement of workers in trades, with regard to the greater or lesser importance of each trade and of its relation to the common good, the more will wealth spread among workers themselves" (143). And *Beccaria* (1769–70) provides the basic motivation for the pursuit of productive labours: the general aim of political economy is to stimulate the greatest possible amount of useful labour, which produces the greatest quantity of goods (I.17: 35).

b. Two analytical lines

In the second half of the 18th century, the introduction of the surplus, by Quesnay, as the basic category of economic analysis, divides the literature on unproductive labour into two streams. One line conceived of productive labour as that labour which adds to social wealth by increasing the surplus. This approach was initially confined to the physiocrats and Smith, who formulated the categories of what is called the birth of "scientific economics", namely value, surplus, capital, investment, accumulation and the relationship between production and consumption. The new approach resulted in the issue of unproductive labour becoming better structured, but also more rigid, but it was destined soon to become the only way to deal with the problem. We will examine its origin in Chapters III and IV.

The other line, by contrast, retained the empirical approach inherited from Petty and its flexible nature. It conceived of wealth as mere use values and was based on the proportion among sectors. This line was analytically weaker, because it did not use the above-mentioned new categories and as such was destined to rapid decline. However, in its final phase, it appears even more far-reaching that that of Quesnay and Smith. It developed a dynamic interpretation of the equilibrium among sectors, resulting in an evolutionary view of the division between productive and unproductive work and an evolutionary view of labour as such (see also *Díez* 2001: 28–42). Subsequently, this view was never again to see the light (apart from some allusions), whilst today it would be of great help in understanding what is going on. We examine this approach in the following section.

5. The evolutionary approach

Evolutionary ideas were quite widespread in the 18th century, thanks to the broad historical view of the Enlightenment authors. Elsewhere, we have already tried to show that the so-called theory of stages was by no means confined to the "discovery" made by Smith and Turgot. It was rather a very old idea, revived by the humanists and mercantilists and given a good airing time and again during the Enlightenment.[26] The stages theory describes a succession of periods, each with a prevalent type of production (breeding, agriculture, manufacture, trade). Human civilisation advances by going through these stages.

In this context, some authors realised that the succession of stages also implied an evolution in productive labours. The more advanced production systems led to intellectual labour being increasingly involved in productive activities. Joseph *Harris* (1757), an expert in monetary questions, first approached this view, writing that "as a country grows in wealth, the candidates for genteel employments may become more numerous in proportion to the rest" (2: 348fn). But the evolutionary conception of unproductive labour found most cogent expression in Antonio *Genovesi*, an abbot from Naples and an author unfairly neglected in the history of economic thought. Genovesi was influenced by – apart from the culture of the Enlightenment – his fellow citizen Giambattista Vico, a visionary philosopher who had recently developed a powerful theory of the evolution of mankind through the stages of sensations, emotions and reason.

In his *Economia civile* (G. 1765–67), Genovesi writes that only one third of the population is productive (I.11.6) and describes society as a pyramid (an image frequently used at that time). In the lower part of the pyramid there are the most numerous categories of manual workers. First those of the primary sector, then artisans and manufacturers. Above are the traders. All of these perform the most necessary work, and their number is never excessive. The upper ranks progressively diminish in number. We find the producers of luxury goods and then the overseers and directors, etc. The usefulness of their occupations progressively diminishes towards the top. At the top, there are the arts and research. In the various versions of this list, the distinction remains between necessary and useful production.[27]

Thus, no occupation is productive or unproductive in an absolute sense. They are more or less productive, according to their usefulness. The author also introduces a new category: professional, administrative and intellectual occupations – he writes – are "indirectly productive", because they are necessary for the production of material goods, which satisfy our needs. Indirectly productive activities are science, trade, management, protection, healthcare.[28] These occupations must be prevented from becoming too numerous. Workers in excess must be discouraged, not forbidden (I, 11.3, 12.1). Some of these occupations are restricted by the market itself (traders, doctors and, indeed, artisans); whilst in the case of lawyers, churchmen and scholars, the state must intervene to discourage excessive numbers (12.9).

Genovesi's most important principle is that the intellectual and more skilled occupations show varying degrees of productiveness according to the level of economic development. In the primitive stages, intellectual labour is hardly productive, because consumption goods are elementary and the productive structure of society is simple. However, this labour becomes productive along with improvements in techniques and increase in the demand for refined consumption (I, 11.3, 12.1). Besides, the new goods, which initially appear as luxury goods, gradually enter into daily use and are eventually considered necessary.[29] Genovesi tirelessly repeats that, along with the growth of civilisation, new occupations emerge and the economic need for them also grows.[30]

Finally, Genovesi outlines the concept of social investment in human capital (as distinct from individual investment in human capital; see XII.1.a). He affirms that research and education have a fundamental role in the process, which enhances both wealth and civilisation. Leaving education in the hands of private individuals, he adds, is characteristic of primitive peoples.[31]

6. Its decline

Genovesi's analysis, although so insightful, had little success, except in Italy and Spain. Even less appreciated were his considerations on unproductive labour. In the final year of his major publication, 1767, three important authors discarded this issue. James *Steuart* (1767), the last great mercantilist, ignored the issue of unproductive labour, calling only for a numerical proportion between nobles and workers. The former should account for little luxury consumption and should not be too numerous (I.XI: 67–73).

Graslin (1767), opposing the physiocrats, stressed the importance of industry, which "adds value" to natural goods.[32] He then provided a very tortuous and contradictory, although sometimes brilliant, analysis in which he proposed a subjective conception of value and wealth (probably he influenced Condillac). Trade, says Graslin, causes an inversion of values between parties: it brings goods wherever there are unsatisfied needs and takes them away where, being in excess, they are valueless. Thus, the "relative values" of goods are determined by their marginal utility, with reference to the total amount of the goods possessed by an individual (I.2, I.5). In this view, all types of goods make up wealth – not only the products of agriculture and crafts, but also the products of the researcher, the artist, etc. Even security, defence, glory and honour, and the idleness of useless servants – although withholding wealth from reproduction – are wealth for those who appreciate them.[33] This bizarre conclusion is symptomatic of Graslin's strictly individual approach.

The penetrating analysis by *Ferguson* (1767) is more rigorous. A measure of national wealth, he writes, should calculate profits and losses, national income and national spending. It should also divide people between the industrious and the idle and include under the losses every superfluous member of the state and of the military apparatus, plus the forensic, scientific and theological professions, the idle rich, and those scholars whose work does not improve lucrative professions. The value of each person should be calculated according to his work and its capacity to procure the means for survival. On the other hand, all activities that produce superfluities should be prohibited, except those for export. However, privileged people should be exempted from work because their status constitutes a goal that encourages the industriousness of workers. Thus, some superfluous people are needed (IV.1; VI.2).

The sense of Ferguson's analysis derives from the Enlightenment tendency to create a welfare society. What is the sense, Ferguson asks basically, of building such a society by subtracting well-being from those who already enjoy it? His contemporaries implicitly answer this objection pointing out that it is precisely excessive luxury and the idleness of some people that, by wasting social wealth, stands in the way of welfare for all. However, Ferguson maintains, the rich represent the prize for the industriousness of the poor. He seems to be reviving the pre-modern justification of social inequalities when he suggests that the classes are complementary. The aims of each spontaneously concur in the harmony of the others' interests (IV.1: 270). *Salvucci* (1972) appears too condescending towards Ferguson's position.

Beccaria's (1769–70) static view of unproductive labour is less interesting than that of his sources, Cantillon and Genovesi. "The growth of the inferior arts, he writes, gives strength to the superior arts", but the reverse does not happen. The state must keep the proportion among arts and prevent the luxury of personal services from reducing manpower in the production of material goods.[34]

Even more static is *Ortes* (1774), representative of the stagnant economy of the later Republic of Venice. Ortes called for limitation of professional, administrative and intellectual classes, which are necessary but produce little wealth. They are dominant in barbarous and servile nations, whereas in civilised nations most of the population are employed in industry and trade.[35] However, he states that the numerical proportion between classes must always remain the same and must be equivalent to the quantity and quality of the goods produced.[36] His aversion to growth and change leads him into contradiction. He states that there will never be too many churchmen, philosophers or magistrates: the greater their number, the more civilised the nation (III.22: 348–9).

7. The Enlightenment on consumption

The views of the authors of the Enlightenment on unproductive labour were closely connected with their views on consumption, as can be seen in ch. 11 of Perrotta (2004), which is entitled "The Enlightenment theory of development: consumption as an investment". Let us recall here some essential points, dealt with in that chapter, without which the successive debate would be hard to follow.

The 18th century saw a great revolution in the attitude towards consumption. Increase in both individual and social consumption was seen as positive for the first time. Preceded by Bayle, Mandeville, Barbon, Defoe and a few others, the authors of the Enlightenment finally demolished the Aristotelian canon that the enrichment of one is the impoverishment of another. Here, too, it was *Genovesi* who best expressed the new attitude. He denied Aristotle's distinction between natural and artificial goods, by saying that all goods are at the same time natural, since they are dictated by nature, and cultural, i.e. the result of human evolution.[37]

Consequently, the authors of the Enlightenment (except for the physiocrats) condemned the landowners who wasted their rents in ostentatious luxuries. But at the same time, they (except for the utopians) defended the increase in comfort of the productive classes, with regard to which they referred to "moderate luxury". The waste made by the landlords, they underlined, was the cause of excessive inequalities, because it impeded productive investment. On the other hand, the vast majority of the authors observed that a moderate inequality should exist, since – as an incentive for the people to improve their condition – it encourages industriousness. Wages, moreover, should be kept high, in order to encourage the industry and skill of the workers. As *Schumpeter* [1949] recalls, according to Smith the "liberal reward of labour" is at the same time "the necessary effect" and "the natural symptom of increasing national wealth". Thus, Smith's attitude on wages – Schumpeter notices – is very different from Ricardo's (II.3.4.e).

This attitude explains why the Enlightenment concept of subsistence wages is exactly the opposite of the classical one. For example, *Steuart* (1767) states that subsistence level means workers being granted holidays and being well-fed, well-clothed, protected from the elements and, above all, protected from excessive competition, which drives wages below the subsistence level.[38]

Finally, many pre-Smithian authors outlined the concept of human capital. The latter was born together with the modern economy. The guilds of artisans were well aware of the importance of their professional knowledge, to the extent that this knowledge was a closely guarded secret. Since the 16th century, economists had attributed much importance to skill in enhancing productivity.[39] For example, *Serra* (1613) had a precise idea of what he called the quality of the people, as a decisive factor of growth. This quality included not only industriousness but also professional skill.[40]

Petty's writings are full of references to specialisation. *Petty* (1672) places the know-how among the factors of production. He also explains that if one, for a certain period, studies new techniques instead of ploughing, in the end he will produce more (XV: 182). For some interesting passages by Mandeville on education as a factor which enhances productivity, see *Prendergast* (2010: 15–16). Many authors of the Enlightenment analysed increase in consumption as a means to enhance skills and productivity through education.[41] For these reasons we can say that the authors of the Enlightenment, while referring to the productive classes, conceived of "consumption as investment".

Conclusions

The evolutionary interpretation of unproductive labour fell away quite soon, because it did not make use of the modern economic categories. Besides, the confrontation between the physiocrats and Smith monopolised the post-Smithian debate and wiped out even the memory of the evolutionary approach. The result of this loss has been devastating. Not only the classical economists and their successors, but even the historians have ignored the very existence of a literature on unproductive labour which was developed for more than two centuries before Smith. This is why even today most historians find it strange that Smith paid attention to this issue.

Notes

1 A part of this chapter is a summary, completely reworked and revised, of ch. 9 of Perrotta (2004).
2 See Perrotta (2004, ch. VI–IX).
3 Botero (1589, VIII.3: 247–8). Serra (1613, I.3).
4 Montchrétien (1615: 170, 276, 400–1).
5 Petty [1671: 238–9]. See also Petty [1644–45: 185, 190–1. —1647. —1672, 2. —1676, 8: 307. —1685. —1686].
6 Petty (1662, II.15–33: 23–9). —[1676, 2: 269–71].
7 Petty [1672, 2: 144].
8 Petty (1662, II.32: 28). —[1676,1: 259]. For erroneous interpretation of these passages, see Marx (*Theory*, I, 4.6.b) and Johnson (1937: 245). For apt interpretation, see Pasquier (1903: 167–70).
9 Petty (1662, II.27: 26). —[1676, 2: 259–60, 269–71].
10 Petty [1676, I: 256, 259, 267].
11 Petty [1664, X: 118–19. —1676, 1267–8; 4: 289].
12 See e.g. Briscoe (1696: 68–9, 116).
13 Petyt (1680, I: 292; III: 301–2).
14 See Perrotta (2004, 8: 163–5).
15 Cary (1695: xxxvi–xxxix, 8–12, 49, 137–8).
16 Cantillon (1730, I.16: 87–95).
17 Cantillon (1730, I.12: 47; I.16: 91–2).
18 Hume (1752b: 326–30); —(1752c).
19 See D'Arco (1771: 55–9, 74–7, 121–3); Dubuat-Nançay (1773, I: 221 and ch. 18); Sénac (1787: 116ff).
20 See e.g. Dupin (1745, I: 214). Tucker (1750: 331–2). Plumard (1752: 14–15). Faiguet (1763, II: 116–19, 146–51).
21 E.g. Hume (1752b: 324–5).
22 See Plumard (1752: 30–1, 36). Justi (1755, sections 275–88). D'Arco (1771: 58–9, 137, 141–3).
23 Ward (1762: 96–7, 157, 164–7, 212–25).
24 Hume (1752b: 322–5).
25 Plumard (1752: 23, 41–3, 254–7, 268–9).
26 See Perrotta (2004, 11: 195–8).
27 Genovesi (1765–67, I, 3.5, 3.7, 5.12. See also G. 1757c, sections 6–8).
28 Ibid, I, 7.6, 11.1.
29 Genovesi (1757a. —1757b. —1765–67, I, 9.11, 10.10–13, 10.22; II, 1.5).
30 G. (1765–67, I, 5.12, 7.8, 8.15, 9.15–16, 11.1).

31 G. (1765–67, I, 6.1, 6.8). On Genovesi's theory of development the following studies are important: Rosario Villari (1970) and Venturi (1969, ch. 8). See also Demarco (1957). De Luca (1968) grasps the novelty of Genovesi's theses and links them to the 1960s theories of development (ch. 7–12).
32 Graslin (1767, I.1, I.4, I.10).
33 Graslin (1767, I.1: 25; I.10: 111).
34 Beccaria (1769–70, I.23–27; IV.33. See also I.19ff).
35 Ortes (1774, III.22: 343–4; IV.15).
36 Ibid, III.14–19; III.24; IV.3–7.
37 Genovesi (1765–67, I, X.10, X.13, XIX.8; II, I.17.4).
38 Steuart (1767, II.21: 273–5).
39 See Perrotta (2004, 8:173–5).
40 Serra (1613: 123–5, 155, passim).
41 See e.g. Josiah Tucker (1755: 125ff; —1757: 239–42). Postlethwayt (1757, I: 18–19). Butel-Dumont (1771, II: 122–6, 132–4).

III Physiocracy

Labour productive of surplus – Condillac[1]

Background

Quesnay invented neither the concept of unproductive labour – introduced by Petty – nor the concept of surplus, foreshadowed by Botero, Serra and Montchrétien, and given expression by Petty, Cantillon and some Enlightenment authors.[2] However, it was he who transformed both concepts into analytical tools. Quesnay connected the surplus with investment and with the distribution of wealth. He also defined productive labour as the labour that produces a surplus. Due to this approach, the concept of labour productiveness became logically strong but lost its flexibility. This connotation was to remain in all the successive authors who wrote on unproductive labour.[3]

1. Unproductiveness of non-agricultural labour

As we know, *Quesnay* provided for the first time a rational explanation of the general process of production, exchange, distribution and reproduction of wealth. He also defined the social classes according to the role each of them has in the reproduction cycle. The increased wealth generated in every cycle is the surplus. Only the labour that produces the surplus can be called productive. This, for Quesnay, is agricultural labour, because the surplus is generated only in agriculture by applying human labour to land.

Quesnay borrowed from Boisguilbert and Cantillon the idea that landowners' consumption is the very basis of the distribution process. However, his main concern was to introduce capitalist modernisation in agriculture. This, according to him, is the only way to develop the economy. The farmers' initiative is the starting point of the production process. Quesnay made the separation between productive and useful jobs yet more distinct. Manufacture and commerce are certainly useful, he says, but they are sterile, because they can only reproduce what artificers or merchants consume during their performance. He explains:

> One must distinguish the value of products that are reborn (*productions renaissantes*) from the value of expenditures which are a mere cost. Actually, spending is not an act of production; and the reimbursement of

> this spending, when it is not done for the rebirth (*renaissance*) of the riches produced by nature, is itself a new expenditure.
>
> (Q. 1766a: 753)

And, in *Grains*:

> the value of manufactured goods is proportional to the value of the goods consumed by the workers and the merchants. Thus the artisan destroys [consumes] as much as he produces with his work.
>
> (Q. 1757: 496)

The physiocrats were aware that investments and profits are also present in manufacturing (see Quesnay 1766c: 888), but the latter only transforms wealth. "Producing and shaping (*façonner*) – said *Baudeau* (1767–70) – are two different operations" (847); and intellectual labour is mere consumption (846). *Le Trosne* (1777) writes: "industry does nothing but adding shape to raw materials while the earth provides substances that from inexistent become existent" (V.1: 574). He also stated that spending on commerce is a loss for the nation, not an increase in wealth.[4]

Baudeau (1771) made this argument finally clear: agricultural labour activates the productivity of the earth. It stimulates the production of wealth, but does not create it (I: 657–63).[5] *Dupont de Nemours* (1815–16) still wrote in capital letters to Jean-Baptiste Say: "*Dieu seul est producteur*" ("Only God is producer": 399). Non-agricultural activities can yield a profit, because of the increase in the price of their products; but they cannot generate a surplus, because they only transform the products generated in agriculture.[6]

Manufacturing labour is only an expense, says Quesnay (1766a: 753–5). He gives the example of the shoemaker: in his activity,

> is there not, one will ask, the production of a pair of shoes? No, because if you distinguish the raw material of this pair of shoes from the form of the product, you find only the processing carried out by the shoemaker, the value of which is pure expenditure made for his subsistence.
>
> (753–4)

Thus, the artisan's labour is merely exchange between present and future goods: "the workman does not produce the raw material of his product; he buys it and resells it with the product, so he can only be seen as a merchant who resells" (754). Like the merchant, the artisan makes an exchange. However, since the exchange is "between equal values (*de valeur pour valeur égale*)", "it produces nothing" (753). It causes "no loss or gain on one side or the other".[7]

Le Mercier (1767) devotes an entire chapter to the exchange between equal values (10: 536–43). *Le Trosne* (1777) confirms it against Condillac (II: 521– 8). As *Cannan* (1893) observes, Quesnay considers all the labourers in non-primary sectors "as exchangers and not producers" (I: 20). *Higgs* (1897) recalls Simon Gray's objection to the physiocrats' thesis that only agriculture is productive: the fact that a certain factor is necessary to produce wealth does not mean that it is the only factor. Otherwise, we should mention first heat or human reason as the only cause of wealth (VI: 133).

Thus, Quesnay contests the time-honoured mercantilist tradition that sees manufacture as the driving force of development (expressed in France by Laffemas, Montchrétien, Colbert). He explicitly associates himself with the opposite French tradition, which believes in development driven by agriculture. The latter view was first expressed by Olivier des *Serres* (1600) and subsequently by Maximilien de Bethune, duke of Sully, who – like Laffemas – had been Minister of Henri IV (1589–1610). *Sully* (1638 and [1662]) inspired Boisguilbert and in part Cantillon, the main sources of Quesnay. He also inspired Vauban, Fénelon and many others.[8] Quesnay considers him the founder of the anti-mercantilist stream of thought and pays him a warm tribute.[9]

Quesnay's attitude was encouraged by the great importance that 18th-century authors attached to agriculture. In the previous centuries, agriculture had progressed very little, due to the strong opposition of landlords to any modernisation. However, the attention to agriculture, for most of the Enlightenment authors, by no means implied disregarding manufacture. Not even Turgot shared Quesnay's attitude. He was very keen on the development of industry and reproached Dupont and the other physiocrats for not caring about it enough (see Hector *Denis* 1904: 140–1).

Actually there is a connection between Quesnay's view on unproductive labour and his attitude towards the increase in consumption (which is caused by manufacture). He writes:

> The discovery of America has been for Europe what the conquest of Asia was for the Romans. From the wealth of individuals, a great quantity of needs derived; and the facility of satisfying them has transformed them into necessities. Were we less happy before the commerce with the West Indies? Are we stronger? Have our customs gained from it?
>
> (Q. 1759: vi–vii)

Furthermore, Quesnay praises Cicero, who best expresses the ancient view that agriculture is the only proper production, since it derives from nature.[10] He also praises China and the Inca Empire. He affirms that in these states, which are governed by "enlightened despotism", the economy is static and the *produit net* does not grow; it is reproduced in the same quantity every year (Q. 1767b; —1767c).

Thus, unlike the other Enlightenment authors, Quesnay revived the pre-modern hostility towards increase in consumption goods. The same attitude we find in Aristotle and his followers, in Roman culture, in the Christian Fathers and in the scholastic authors and, finally, in the late humanists.[11]

2. Condillac: productiveness of all labour

In the same year as Smith's *Wealth of Nations*, the abbé de *Condillac* published *Le Commerce et le Gouvernement.* The basic theory of this book is physiocratic: land is the only source of wealth; the farmer is the only worker who produces more than he consumes; the artisan produces only what he himself consumes.[12]

However, this view refers only to elementary needs. Condillac is not really concerned with surplus or exchange value, but with utility. Although artisans do not add new value to the product, they add wealth because the latter depends on utility. There is no doubt, says the author, that artificers add utility to raw materials and enhance the potential of these materials to satisfy our needs. The wealth that derives from agricultural labour (landed wealth) refers only to our natural needs and cannot be extended beyond them. On the contrary, mobile wealth, which is produced by manufacture and trade, satisfies our artificial needs. Since artificial needs have no limits, mobile wealth can be accumulated.[13]

Here Condillac, under the influence of Graslin, takes a path that leads him very far from Quesnay. In exchange – he says – we give a good less useful to ourselves for a more useful good. Thus, although the relative values of the goods exchanged do not vary, the respective utilities do. Indeed, they increase for both exchangers. Thus, exchange increases the general utility (i.e. wealth) of society.[14]

Condillac draws important consequences from his thesis. First, trade as such acquires great importance in his analysis (not only trade of agricultural goods, as in the physiocrats' view). Trade is the stream that carries goods from the place where they are superfluous to another place where they have more value.[15] On the other hand – he writes in another of his works – financial merchants get rich without enriching the state.[16] Besides – being a utopian, like his brother Mably – Condillac criticises luxury goods. They, he states, subtract wealth from the production of necessaries.[17] This view is in contradiction with his idea that the utility that derives from "artificial" needs has no limits.

Condillac had previously stated that only agricultural occupations are productive.[18] But in 1776, influenced by Graslin, he maintained that all jobs are productive "when all things go on properly", whilst, in the periods of disorder, great riches are wasted.[19] With the exception of landowners who do nothing, all citizens get their wages from one another, i.e. from those to whom they sell their products (C. 1776: 259b). Also merchants and artisans contribute to the production of wealth. A society that lives on agriculture alone is poor. Even the public administration and the clergy contribute to the growth of wealth. The richest nations are those that have every kind of occupation.[20]

Thus, Condillac adopts a subjective concept of value. Due to this fact, he has been highly praised by the neo-classical authors. See *Schumpeter* [1949], who reports the comments made by Jevons and McLeod.[21] See also *Gide and Rist* (1909: 52). Subjective value was by no means new in the 18th century.[22] However, Graslin's and Condillac's versions were to be the most influential in the following literature.

3. Debate on physiocracy

a. Supporters and sympathisers

As early as the 1760s, a keen confrontation began between followers and critics of physiocracy, including the question of unproductive labour. *Steiner* (1995) affirms that physiocracy was discredited during the French Revolution but was later revived (221).

Solera (1785) was a committed follower of the physiocratic school, as appears from his analyses of value, money and trade.[23] The Russian prince *Golicyn* (1796) extended the "accusation" of being sterile to the entire "third state", taking issue with Sieyès and the French Revolution (227). John *Gray* (1797) – not to be confused with the homonymous Ricardian socialist, who wrote some decades later – maintained that artificers and manufacturers are sterile (although less sterile than menial servants), like a barren field that returns only the seed sown into it (10–12). Manufacture does not increase national income, although it increases the country's goods (37–8). Gray repeats the physiocratic thesis that the only valid tax is that on rents (64–5). According to *Meek* (1951a), Gray uses the physiocratic theory "not to defend but to attack the landed interests". Indeed, he states that, while manufacturers are in any case useful, landlords are a burden on society, because land rent is now separated from the original purpose of defending the state. Meek adds that Charles Hall, Piercy Ravenstone and Thomas Hopkins also applied the physiocratic principles to attack landowners' parasitism (355–6).

Hall (1805), although not referring to the physiocrats, fiercely attacked industry (and civilisation) as the cause of the terrible conditions of the poor. He maintained that the remedy lies in a great number of agricultural workers. William *Spence* was a follower of the physiocrats, but – contrary to John Gray – he took physiocracy as a basis to defend landed interests. His approach was highly orthodox: agriculture is the only productive sector and manufacture, like commerce, is mere exchange of equivalents. Manufacture does not produce more wealth than that consumed by its workers.[24] Spence came in for severe, detailed criticism from Robert *Torrens* (1808).[25]

Schmalz (1808) provides tortuous and contradictory statements about unproductive labour, but ultimately says that both artisans and menial servants save the labour-time of the master.[26] He even maintains that, according to Smith, wages are equal to what workers consume (122ff, 305–6). In conclusion, Schmalz excludes from the computation of national revenue all incomes except agricultural rent, since all wealth derives from nature, as the physiocrats stated (299–331).

The Scottish moral philosopher Dugald *Stewart*, the first biographer of Smith, while apparently conceding something to Smith, effectively repeats Quesnay's arguments. He states the "pre-eminence" of agriculture.[27] The latter feeds all labourers and "reproduces a surplus in addition to its value" (264). On the contrary, the artificer, however useful, "adds nothing to the materials of his labour but the value of his own subsistence" (260–2). The same holds for the manufacturer and the merchant. Their wages "are a mere transference of wealth" (265). The manufacturer only gives "a greater exchangeable value"; "the portion of that produce which he is continually consuming being always equal to the same value which he is continually producing" (261). Finally, "The corn which the farmer produces is the free gift of nature and costs nothing to society; [whilst] the manufacturer only changes the form of his commodity" (263).

Again:

> the gains of the merchant are but a transference, not a production of riches. The same thing may be said of every species of industry, the object of which is to modify the productions of the earth, without increasing their quantity.
>
> (266–7)

This holds independently of the utility or necessity of a certain labour, so that even the ploughwright is sterile, as Baudeau states, no less "than a lace-maker or an embroiderer" (S. 278).

b. Critics of physiocracy

Arriquíbar [1764–70] criticises Mirabeau's *L'Ami des Hommes*, because – he says – not only agriculture but also industry is productive.[28] Like all the 18th- century Spanish authors,[29] Arriquíbar was obsessed with Spain's age-old backwardness, caused by the lack of manufactured production, and argued the need to industrialise the country.

Later on, *Storch* (1815) was to remind the physiocrats of Graslin's objection: if land is the only source of wealth, how could industrial and commercial countries survive? Turgot replied to Graslin distinguishing between productive nations and waged nations. This is a childish distinction, comments Storch.[30] Pietro *Verri* (1771), too, defends the productive nature of both agriculture and handicraft (3: 21–6). However, Verri believes that not only public administration but also commerce and transports – although very useful – are unproductive, being activities of pure mediation. On the other hand, he defends the landlords and their "utility" for society.[31]

Longo (1773) – like Boisguilbert, Cantillon and Quesnay – places the proprietors' surplus at the basis of the economic process. However, he uses pre-physiocratic categories: all occupations are "necessary" insofar as they produce either things, as do peasants and artisans, or services, as do merchants and professionals (340–2). Longo considers professionals, the clergy and the learned to be productive, while only vagabonds, prostitutes, usurers, gamblers, etc. are unproductive (II.1.1–14). The productive nature of industry, in contrast with the physiocrats, was also asserted by *Isnard* (1781: XIII, passim). *Biffi Tolomei* (1792) criticised those who believe that value is produced only by agriculture, not by manufacture (61).

David *Buchanan* (1814) severely criticised the physiocrats. Given their idea that the net surplus in agriculture is granted by high prices, surplus goes to the detriment of consumers, who would benefit from lower prices. Moreover, if the surplus depends on price, manufacturers, too, can be productive thanks to high prices of their products on the market, while agriculture would be unproductive with a low price on its goods (134–6).

According to *Steiner* (1995), in 1819 interest in physiocracy abruptly died out, at least in France, subsequent to publication of Ricardo's *Principles*. The same authors who had compared Quesnay and Smith (G. Garnier, Ganilh, J.-B. Say) were now comparing Smith with Ricardo, while physiocracy, from being a theory, became a doctrine of the past (24–7). A few years later, Say was able to state that physiocracy "est maintenant complètement abandonné[e], et je ne connais plus une seule personne qui [la] soutienne" ("is now completely abandoned, and I don't know one single person who supports it": 27). For a survey of German authors on physiocracy and Smith in the 18th and early 19th century, see *Cossa* (1892: 295–325).

Conclusions

Like the other authors of the Enlightenment period, the physiocrats were convinced that economic development could not proceed without agricultural development. However, they took this position to the extreme. In contrast with their great merit in elaborating the basic analytical categories and analysis of the circular process of the economy, confining productive labour to agriculture was a failure, and Smith took on the task of proving it.

Notes

1 Some materials in this chapter have already been used in "The four 18th century streams on productive labour", *Iberian Journal of the History of Economic Thought*, vol. 1, no. 2, 2014: 1–13; online. The present chapter has been completely reworked.
2 See Perrotta (2004, 8: 176–8).
3 See also Bradley and Howard (1982: 3–6).
4 See also Quesnay (1766c: 892); Mirabeau (1769–71, vol. I: 38). Compare Weulersse (1910, I: 272–7).
5 See also Le Mercier (1767, 17: 597–607) and Le Trosne (1777, V.3–10: 577–92; VI.5: 609–13).
6 See Quesnay (1766c: 892); Baudeau (1767–70: 847). Le Trosne (1777, V.1: 574). See also Mirabeau (1769–71, I: 38). Cp. Weulersse (1910, I: 272–7).
7 Quesnay (1766c: 897). This concept was often repeated by Quesnay (see for ex. Q. 1756: 455; —1766b: 806).

8 See Weulersse (1910: 1–2, 5).
9 Quesnay (1767a, Note to Maxim IX: 964–5).
10 Ibid.
11 See Perrotta (2004: 24–5, 29–30, 37–9, 79; ch. 5).
12 Condillac (1776: I.6: 255a; I.9: 261b–2a).
13 Ibid., I.1: 244b–6a.
14 Ibid., I.6: 254b–7a; I.9, 262b. See Graslin (1767, I.2: 13.27; I.5: 48–58). See also Lebeau (1903, ch. 1) and Meoli (1961, ch. 2).
15 Condillac (1776, I.6–7: 256b–8b; I.30: 318b).
16 Condillac (1758–65a, X.4: 169b).
17 Condillac (1758–65a, X.4: 168a–9b; —1758–65b, IV.9: 113b–6a; —1776, I.27: 309b–10b).
18 Condillac (1758–65a, X.4: 169b).
19 Condillac (1776, I.7–10: 258b–63b. Cp. Graslin 1767, I.2: 25; I.10: 111).
20 Condillac (1776, I.7: 258a; I.29: 314b–5a).
21 Schumpeter [1949, II.3.4.c: 175–6].
22 See the survey of Tagliacozzo (1937, XL–LI).
23 Solera (1785: 265–9, 296–301, 355–63).
24 Spence (1807: 27–37; —1808: 105–8, 135ff).
25 See VIII.1. See also *Robbins* (1958: 11–18).
26 Schmalz (1808, I: 2–3, 20–1, 31–2).
27 Stewart (1809–10: 255, 260).
28 Arriquíbar [1764–70, I.3.6–7: 106–10].
29 See these authors in Perrotta (2004: 142–4, 191–2).
30 Storch (1815, vol. I: 116–17fn).
31 Verri (1771, 24: 204–5; 29: 238–9).

IV Adam Smith

The struggle against rent[1]

Background

Smith overhauled the issue of unproductive labour so thoroughly that he doomed the earlier debate to oblivion, except the physiocratic position. His analysis proved decisive in all subsequent treatments of the issue. Petty and the other 17th-century authors saw the subject as a typical mercantilist problem: what occupations produce more wealth and boost profits more than the others? Quesnay brilliantly associated productive labour with the production of surplus. Smith did not fail to take up these points but channelled them towards a precise goal: fighting the waste of social wealth made by the pre-modern dominant classes and transforming the unproductive consumption of rent into capital investment.

1. Productive and unproductive labour

a. Redefinitions

In the "Introduction" to the *Wealth of Nations*, Smith presents the contents of the second book with these words:

> Whatever be the actual state of the skill, dexterity, and judgment with which labour is applied in any nation, the abundance or scantiness of its annual supply must depend, during the continuance of that state, upon the proportion between the number of those who are annually employed in useful labour, and that of those who are not so employed. The number of useful and productive labourers, it will hereafter appear, is every where in proportion to the quantity of capital stock which is employed in setting them to work, and to the particular way in which it is so employed.
>
> (S. 1776, I.I.6)

In the footnote, the editor (E. *Cannan* 1904) writes: "This word [productive] slips in here as an apparently unimportant synonym of 'useful', but subsequently ousts 'useful' altogether, and is explained in such a way that unproductive labour may be useful". *Bowley* (1975) replies to Cannan that Smith, first, draws a contrast between the idle and the labourers and then between productive and unproductive labourers. Bowley rightly notes that, in Chapter 3 of book II, Smith brings into close connection, even in the title, the quantity of productive labourers and accumulation of capital (363–4).

In this chapter, entitled, "Of the Accumulation of Capital, or of Productive and Unproductive Labour", Smith writes:

> The labour of some of the most respectable orders of the society is, like that of menial servants, unproductive of any value. For example, the sovereign, public officers and soldiers "are maintained by a part of the annual produce of the industry of other people. Their service, how honourable, how useful and how necessary so ever, produces nothing for which an equal quantity of service can afterwards be procured". In the same class – he adds – must be ranked "some of the gravest and most important, and some of the most frivolous professions.

Here, Smith very closely echoes Petty's lists of unproductive occupations (see II.2), without citing the source. His own list contains "churchmen, lawyers, physicians, men of letters of all kinds; players, buffoons, musicians, opera-singers, opera-dancers, etc." (S. 1776, II.3.2). Thus, some occupations are very useful but unproductive, since they do not produce value.

On the other hand, productive labour is the labour "which adds to the value of the subject upon which it is bestowed". Such is the case of the manufacturer, whose labour adds "to the value of the materials which he works upon, that of his own maintenance, and of his master's profit". The labour of the manufacturer "fixes and realises itself in some particular subject or vendible commodity, which lasts for some time at least after that labour is past". It is "a certain quantity of labour stocked and stored up" (II.3.1). For this reason, also, artisans are productive.[2]

On the contrary, the services of the menial servant, like those of the actor, the orator or the musician, "generally perish in the very instant of their performance" (II.3.1). The same holds for public professions. Here, the effect of the labour of one year – in terms of protection, security and defence – "will not purchase" the same things for the next year, for, "like the declamation of the actor [...] or the tune of the musician", "the work of all of them perishes in the very instant of its production" (II.3.2). Note that Smith repeats, probably unawares, the Christian Father St. Basil (4th century), who prefers labour applied to material transformation rather than dance and music, because – he says – the result of the former lasts after its performance (see B. *Gordon* 1989: 106). Besides, Smith ignores the category of "indirectly productive", proposed by Genovesi. He probably was not acquainted with Genovesi, whose book was not present in his library (see *Mizuta* 1967).

b. Influences of Petty and the physiocrats

Most historians are convinced that Smith borrowed the concept of unproductive labour from physiocracy and see the concept as erroneous (see as follows). In fact, Smith knew the British economic literature too well to be unaware that such a concept had been largely used.

However, Smith failed to register two important aspects of Petty's approach: the idea of unproductiveness as excess of labourers employed, and the basic identity between useful and productive. In Smith, on the contrary, not only are usefulness and productiveness separated, but the difference between productive and unproductive labour is absolute and unchangeable, depending on the very nature of a certain occupation.

According to *Cannan* (1893), there is an inconsistency in the *Wealth of Nations* between the first book and the following. In the first book, Smith sees professional and intellectual occupations as important as any others, whilst in the second book he considers non-material labour as unproductive. Cannan explains this discrepancy by saying that Smith wrote the first book before coming into contact with the physiocrats, while the other books were written after the influence of the French authors (I: 19). The discrepancy was also noted by *Ingram* (1888), *Patten* (1899) and *Schumpeter* [1949].[3] These authors, too, attribute Smith's idea of unproductive labour to the influence of physiocracy.[4]

Cannan is right in saying that Smith's treatment was influenced by the physiocrats. But this does not mean that Smith learned of the issue from them. The physiocratic influence, on the one hand, strengthened the theoretical foundation of Smith's distinction. As *Groenewegen* (1994) notes, Smith rejects Quesnay's idea that only agriculture is productive, but takes up his view that only the labour that produces surplus is productive (135). On the other hand, most probably the physiocrats were behind Smith's choice to give a rigid definition of the distinction.

In the chapter devoted to physiocracy, Smith makes his view even clearer. Having perfectly summarised physiocratic theory (IV.9.1–28), he goes on to observe that its main error lies in the belief that artisans, manufacturers and merchants are sterile (IV.9.29). Note, by the way, that in this chapter Smith always mentions these three categories together. Probably he considers merchants productive in that they intervene on material commodities in many ways, and not because they produce a profit, as *Garbero* (1980: 23n) maintains.

Smith concedes that agricultural labourers are more productive because, he says, they produce a rent as well as the funds for wages and profit.[5] He has been criticised for this idea (by *Gide and Rist* 1909: 69–71). But, adds Smith, this does not mean that the other labourers are sterile, as a marriage that produces only one son and one daughter is not sterile (S. 1776, IV.9.30). Artisans, manufacturers and merchants are not to be confused with menial servants, whose product vanishes as soon as their activity finishes. Actually, the labour of the former fixes and realises itself in some vendible commodity. They increase social wealth, because their products are durable, whilst the consumption of a menial servant or a soldier only subtracts wealth from society (IV.9.31–32).

2. Material labour and service labour

a. Smith's double definition

Marx writes that Smith gives two different definitions of productive labour as if they were only one. On the one hand, productive labour is the labour exchanged with capital; on the other, it is the material labour that produces durable modifications in matter. But, Marx objects, if a teacher yields a profit to his entrepreneur without producing any physical object, his labour is no less productive than that of a manufacturer.[6]

Germain *Garnier* (1802) had already made the same case about a theatre manager (176). *Rubin* (1929) affirms that Smith confuses the technical-material aspect of production with its social form. He adds that the minor classical authors pay attention only to the second of Smith's definitions (material labour) while neglecting the first (214–15). *Myint* (1948) reshapes Smith's double definition in the value version and the storage version of the productive/unproductive labour distinction. The storage version (material labour) praises the consumption that is delayed to the future (73–8). Smith's aim is to outline a policy of economic development (60–1, 78–9).

Smith even repeats and illustrates at length the thesis – first expressed by Petty – that durable goods are preferable to "things which are consumed immediately" (II.3.38–42). *Meek* (1951a: 351–2) and *Roncaglia* (2001: 132) observe that accumulation in Smith's time was essentially based on material production. Meek also acutely examines the relationship – ascertained by Smith for the first time – between the three theories of surplus, productive labour and value. However, Smith's position on material labour is a step backward from the earlier authors like Petty or Genovesi. It was later to be severely criticised by his own supporters (see section 4; Chapters VI and VII). Actually, Smith's approach is extremely effective against his critical targets (the waste represented by the aristocracy, parasitism and physiocratic analysis), but it depends too much on the polemics of his time. By excluding immaterial labour from accumulation, Smith fails to explain long-run development.

b. Historical reasons for preferring material labour

Most commentators have neglected the historical context in which Smith approached the issue of unproductive labour, while also failing to recognise the Enlightenment authors' scathing indictment – Smith's first and foremost – of the parasitic customs of the aristocracy which hindered European development. Deprived of these basic elements and unaware of the long pre-Smithian debate on unproductive labour, historians have often reduced the question to little more than a logical puzzle.

In the feudal economy, Smith says, the part of produce invested as capital was very little, while the greatest part of it was wasted in ostentatious luxury consumption, which is why the feudal economy was so poor. The vast majority of labourers employed by the aristocracy in various services were unproductive. By contrast, in modern economies a great part of the produce is invested, and the majority of the population are productive labourers. The latter produce material objects – which can be accumulated – and a growing surplus. What decides on the wealth of a country is the proportion in which the produce is employed as capital or consumed as income, i.e. the proportion between productive and unproductive labourers (II.3.4–8). The author insists in particular on the unproductive nature of the numerous menial servants maintained by the rich out of their income (II.3.1, II.3.7). Note that Smith uses the term "revenue" in the sense of income (see *Cannan* 1929: 47).

The vast majority of Enlightenment authors shared Smith's opinion on the ostentatious luxury of aristocracy. The latter, says *Verri* (1771), subtracts wealth from the annual reproduction process.[7] Enhancing these authors' stringent analyses of this aspect is the moral tone with which they are delivered. The host of voices raised against waste found their champion in Smith. Smith contrasted the moral quality of a frugal and affluent society, with great investments and numerous productive labourers, with the corruption of aristocratic society, living in luxury and idleness, while surrounded by poverty (II.3.9–13). The inhabitants of the cities with extensive trade are active and industrious, he writes, whilst those of the cities where a court resides become "idle, dissolute, and poor" (II.3.12). Prodigality makes society poor, while parsimony makes it rich (II.3.14–20).

Patten (1899: 239–42) writes that although Smith never cited James Steuart, he greatly appreciated his treatment of the balance between demand and production, which leads to the same conclusion as Smith.[8] As *Groenewegen* (1977) explains: "the division of the labour force into productive and unproductive labour is synonymous of the division of output into saving and consumption" (401, fn. 20). See also *Oakley* (1994: 95–6). *Dumond* (1977) stresses Smith's commitment to development (87).

Bladen (1960) complains that historians have lost sight of the real problem that Smith was addressing, because they take his text too literally. Today, Bladen explains, Smith's distinction is not useful, because we know that national revenue is formed with a flow of goods and services. What interests us here is that the composition of this flow matches individual preferences (but see XX.3). However, Smith's problem was how to shift capital from idle consumption, still so widespread in his times, to investment. From a neoclassical viewpoint, shifting workers from services to industry does not make sense, but in underdeveloped economies – as in Smith's times – it does. Today, Bladen concludes, the issue appears not so much a problem of unproductive labour as a question of more or less productive labour (625–8).

3. The two factors of growth: skill and extension of productive labour

a. Acquired talents

Before addressing unproductive labour, Smith discusses fixed capital, observing that it is also made

> of the acquired and useful abilities of all the inhabitants or members of the society. The acquisition of such talents, by the maintenance of the acquirer during his education, study, or apprenticeship, always costs a real expense, which is a capital fixed and realised, as it were, in his person. Those talents, as they make a part of his fortune, so do they likewise of that of the society to which he belongs. The improved dexterity of a workman may be considered in the same light as a machine or instrument of trade which facilitates and abridges labour, and which, though it costs a certain expense, repays that expense with a profit.
>
> (II.1.17)

Besides Cannan (see section 1.b), other historians have noted a contradiction on this point. *Bonar* (1893) writes that Smith, although acknowledging that "capacities and skill" are part of national wealth, confines productive labour to the production of material objects, since durability and the possibility of diffusion is proper of physical goods (161–2). *Catlin* (1962) tellingly comments: why talents and skill are part of the social stock but not of social wealth is a mystery. He accounts for this inconsistency with the fact that Smith and the classical school had a "materialistic" idea of wealth (173). A similar observation is made by J. *Young* (1978: 77). *Dankert* (1974) maintains that Petty had already expressed the view of social intellectual capital. Anyway, he adds, Smith and the classical authors never formulated the idea of education as an intentional means of development (235).

b. Division of labour and education

Cannan (1893) interprets the passage from Smith's *Introduction* quoted before (IV.1) in the sense that the national product depends on two factors: on the skill and dexterity of the workers and on the proportion between productive and unproductive labourers. He analyses in depth both factors and their effects; nevertheless, for the first factor, he nearly always focuses on the skill acquired during the production process, through the division of labour, while neglecting the skill due to study and specialisation (IX: 379).

Blaug (1962) writes that Smith's storage version – as Myint puts it – implies that knowledge is unproductive. But knowledge too can be accumulated and affects economic growth (57, 83). Blaug also describes Smith's productive/unproductive labour distinction as "probably the most maligned concept in history of economic doctrines". However, he acknowledges that Smith's concern about the waste of saving represented by luxury is right. He also admits that even now Smith's distinction still makes a sense in a state of war (56).

Increase in labour productivity, Smith notes, derives from either increase in the worker's ability or mechanisation. He adds:

> But the labour of artificers and manufacturers, as it is capable of being more subdivided, and the labour of each workman reduced to a greater simplicity

> of operation than that of farmers and country labourers, so it is likewise capable of both these sorts of improvements in a much higher degree.
>
> (IV.9.35)

However, Smith neglects the fact that, beyond a certain limited expansion, not only does the increase in the division of labour depend on technical progress, but the latter, in turn, requires higher education and new skills.

4. Germain Garnier: the first critic

After the *Wealth of Nations*, the progressive attitude of the Enlightenment began to decline. The cultural climate and in particular the attitude towards the worker changed sharply. Denunciation of high wages, already severely expressed by Benjamin *Franklin* (1760; —1768) and others, became more frequent. Apart from Tommaso *Vasco* (1773: I.1–7) and *Sénac* (1787: 116ff), who attacked frivolous luxury, the others' arguments were no longer against the aristocrats' luxury but against "too high" wages.[9] This trend set in further after the beginning of the French Revolution.[10]

However, other authors continued to repeat the typical Enlightenment theses. *Tramontani* (1792) supported manufactures, which – unlike agriculture – can feed an unlimited population. He also defended luxury production and sciences, which are not – he said – in the lowest ranks of economic activities (293–4). Unlike Garnier, Josef Alonso *Ortiz* (1794), who translated the *Wealth of Nations* into Spanish, seems to agree with Smith's concept of unproductive labour (97fn).

On the contrary, the best-known of Smith's first followers, Germain *Garnier* (1796), is sceptical about this concept. Also, non-material products, he writes, are sold and yield a "profit", although in their case there is no entrepreneur's mediation. Thus, the labour that produces them is productive.[11] But Garnier goes on to develop a more radical argument, in which the difference between capital and revenue – which is the very core of Smith's analysis – disappears. In 1802 he published his French translation of the *Wealth of Nations*, accompanied by extended comments. In Note XX, devoted to our subject, Garnier restates – contrary to Smith – that it is not the proportion between capital and revenue in society that determines the proportion between productive and unproductive labour. The latter depends on custom and on industrial development (177).

Garnier mixes up arguments of different natures. All occupations are productive insofar as they yield pleasure (171). Domestic work, too, is productive because it prevents goods from deteriorating (172). And then, why should the violin-maker be productive and the violin-player unproductive? The same holds for the confectioner who satisfies my taste and the musician who satisfies my ears, or indeed the road-builder and the magistrate in charge of roads (172–4). Again, why should the maker of ornaments be more productive than a professional figure who provides an aesthetic enjoyment (178–9)?

Thus, Garnier inaugurated an approach – the casuistry of productive or unproductive occupations – which was to become widespread in the 19th century.

He often confuses individual utility and social utility. Then, he goes back to the physiocratic thesis that agricultural labour is more important because it produces a surplus (G. 1802: 183ff. See also his Preface in the first volume of the 1802 edition). In the second edition of his translation (G. 1822), Garnier completely rewrites the Note on productive labour (now the 49th). He repeats his casuistic arguments. Many menial servants focus their work on material objects, while many wage-earners do not. Many non-material activities are linked to the manufacture of material products (132–5). Not all material products can be accumulated (131). And so forth. His basic idea is that any product has value if there is a consumer who pays for it (132). In the end, he states, both types of labour (productive or unproductive) are limited by the extension of needs. Thus, society does not gain by extending one of them at the expenses of the other (127). Germain Garnier was the model for most of the critics who rejected Smith's distinction.

Conclusions

Paradoxically, Smith's shortcomings, in the treatment of unproductive labour, derive from his innovative views, including the idea that Petty's vague approach should be superseded and the concept made more rigorous. He also aimed to eradicate the unproductive consumption of rent – consumption mainly regarding services and non-durable things, like food. In pursuit of both aims, Smith made his conception excessively rigid and ill-suited to explain the complexity of industrial economy. In the long run, these limitations discredited his own interpretation. Since Smith's treatment had swept away all the earlier reflections, the discredit that befell it also implied failure on the entire issue.

Notes

1 Some materials in this chapter had already been used in "The four 18th century streams on productive labour", *Iberian Journal of the History of Economic Thought*, vol. 1, no. 2, 2014: 1–13; online. The present chapter has been completely rewritten and revised.
2 Smith (1776, II.3.18; II.3.41).
3 Ingram (1888: 97, 103). Patten (1899: 239). Schumpeter (1949, II.3.4.e: 192; III.6.5.a: 630).
4 The same idea is to be found in Hector Denis (1904: 234); Rist (Gide and Rist 1909: 68–9); Scott (1937: 125–6); Bowley (1975: 369); Skinner (1979: 123–4) and many others.
5 Smith (1776, IV.9.30). See also the first lines of II.5.12.
6 Marx (*Theories*, I, IV.3; Addenda, 12.D). See also XI.2.
7 Verri (1771, 26: 217). See also Perrotta (2004, 11: 235–7).
8 See *Steuart* (1767, 2, ch. 10 and 15).
9 See Perrotta (2004, 11: 230–1).
10 See e.g. *Burke* (1795, 4.4.17–21).
11 Garnier (1796, 38–9). See also G. (1802: 175–6).

V Supporters of Smith on unproductive labour

Background

In the twenty years that lay between the *Wealth of Nations* and Germain Garnier's observations, a radical change occurred in Western culture through the two great revolutions that dominate the end of the 18th century and the first decades of the 19th. One was French revolution, which saw the bourgeoisie prevailing over the aristocracy. In economic terms, it meant that investment and productive consumption prevailed over rent and waste. This was the change so eagerly invoked by Smith. However, the success of the bourgeoisie broke the solidarity among the productive classes. By then, the proletariat was no longer perceived by the new dominant class as an ally, but as an adversary.

The second radical change came with the industrial revolution, when the bulk of production shifted from manufactures and agriculture to the factory and mechanised production. Skilled manual labour was no longer the driving force behind increase in productivity, but rather machines. Mass labour became increasingly basic and high wages were no longer required for the progress of accumulation. On the contrary, the rapid substitution of labour with machines provoked keen competition among the unskilled workers. Such a competition saw wages falling to subsistence level and led to dreadful working conditions in the factories. The two revolutions converged in their final result.

1. The classical approach

The classical economists took a great interest in development, and the issue of unproductive labour became a widespread concern. Preoccupation with the wastefulness of the aristocracy diminished. Luxury was considered a secondary phenomenon. Nevertheless, all the goods and services that were not part of wage-goods were considered luxuries by definition. *Winch* (1966: 14) reports a eulogy of the middle classes by James Mill. Like the Scottish authors of the Enlightenment, Mill observed that these classes are the product of civilisation. And yet, how could J. Mill reconcile this observation with the idea that only material workers are productive?

Of course, the growing complexity of fixed capital required an extension of skilled labour and of the ability to invent, design, build up, control and maintain the new machines. Skilled labour was in great demand (and highly rewarded). Skilled labourers belonged to the new dominant class. However, they accounted for a very small percentage of total labour, while the skill of mass labour was declining.

We can distinguish three tendencies among the authors of the period. The first accepted Smith's productive/unproductive labour distinction and also – more or less – his distribution of the various occupations between the two fields. The second tendency did not deny the distinction, but rejected Smith's idea that intellectual and service labour is unproductive. Finally, a third group of authors rejected the distinction as such, maintaining that all occupations are productive insofar as they are useful. For most of the latter authors, value only depends on utility. However, our classification is by no means rigid. Authors often escape any taxonomy.

Neither of these approaches succeeded in building a non-contradictory theory of accumulation. The crux of the question lay in the subsistence wage principle. Once aristocratic luxury had been marginalised, the problem of feeding the accumulation process with a sufficient quantity of investments was solved. But the opposite problem now arose. How would the growing surplus be employed? According to the capitalist logic, it should be employed productively. This could only be in three ways: either absorbed by rapid increase of population or increase in wages, or otherwise by an increase in the means of production. The first way clashes with the limited natural resources, asserted by both Malthus and Ricardo. The second was unanimously considered impossible, because it violates the principle of the subsistence wage level. The third, which is Marx's solution, simply postpones but does not solve the issue of the excess of surplus.

Myint (1948) writes that the theory of productive labour is the keystone of classical welfare economic policy. He also insists on the fact that the classical economists conceive of wealth and accumulation as increase in physical production. Myint links the physical approach with the idea of the economy as a permanent struggle of man against nature – which provides us the resources we need.[1] However, not all the classical authors stick to the material conception of wealth and production.

Here we will examine the first of these streams. The second and the third will be examined in the following two chapters.

2. Restatement of Smith's position

The authors in this group, in general, accept Smith's division between production of material goods, which is productive, and production of services (non-material products), which is unproductive. They also accept the idea that the labour exerted in the first type of production is exchanged with capital and yields a profit, while the labour of services is exchanged with revenue and only yields personal utility. Accumulation can be made only with material goods, since they are durable and can be stored and exchanged. Services, on the other hand, cannot be accumulated, because even when they are exchangeable they are not durable.

In turn, these authors can be subdivided into groups focusing on different aspects of the issue. The authors in the present section simply repeat Smith's views.

The German *Sartorius* (1796) – whose book is a sort of summary of the *Wealth of Nations*, as the extended title itself declares – simply repeats Smith's ideas (§§ 46 & 47). *Bentham* distinguishes four kinds of occupations: those totally unproductive (menial servants in excess, musicians, etc.); producers for fast consumption (luxury food, etc.); producers of durable goods; and producers of means of production, regardless of their durability.[2]

Lüder (1800–04) recalls the Fuggers, who had been rich as merchants and poor as Counts.[3] He effectively describes the luxury and idleness of the city capitals: Warsaw; "the new and the old Rome"; and Naples, where "pomp and ostentation live together with extreme poverty" (264). The export of money (to buy foreign luxuries) is the effect, not the cause, of a country's decadence (268–70). However, it is preferable to spend on durable luxury goods – which give work to the poor, according to the old idea – than on immediate consumption (271–9). *Colquhoun* (1806), an applied statistician, proposes a detailed project – which reminds us of that of Queen Elisabeth I – to convert the begging poor into productive labourers. Colquhoun (1814) uses Smith's distinction in his classifications of social groups.[4]

David *Buchanan* (1814), to the objection that excessive (i.e. unproductive) labourers can also have a part in manufactures, responds that private employers and competition check any such increase (131–4). *Du Bois Aymé* (1823) devotes his entire book to criticising Ferrier (see as follows) on all aspects, our subject included (40–56, 156–81). The anonymous *An Essay* (1821), while not mentioning Smith, closely follows his classification of the unproductive occupations (I.1: 4, 6, 8–9). *Read* (1829) states that Smith's distinction is essential to understand the effects of an undue increase of unproductive workers (35–7). On Read, see also *Bowley* (1937: 74). *Ramsay* (1836), although writing about productive and unproductive consumption (see Chapter VIII), closely follows Smith's distinction (I.2: 30–2).

The faithful followers of Smith on unproductive labour included not only Malthus (see as follows), but also *James Mill* (1821, IV.I.13) and *Ricardo*. In the 3rd edition of his *Principles* (1821), Ricardo introduced the qualification of "productive" or "unproductive" in several passages. Unproductive consumption, he says, when it grows more than reproduction, diminishes capital. On the contrary, when diminishing, it increases national capital.[5]

> It must be understood – he adds in a footnote – that all the productions of a country are consumed; but it makes the greatest difference imaginable whether they are consumed by those who reproduce, or by those who do not reproduce another value.

When the revenue is consumed by productive labourers, it is saved and added to capital; when it is consumed by unproductive labourers, it does not add to capital (ibid.). The same concepts are expressed in the *Notes on Malthus*.[6]

The Portuguese author *Ferreira-Borges* (1834) distinguishes between labour that produces material objects, which is productive of wealth, and labour that produces inner goods, which only contributes to civilisation. Only wealth, i.e. material goods, is exchangeable (45–7, 56–7). The Polish count *Skarbeck* (1829) accepts Smith's view that only material labour adds to national wealth, but he considers service labour equally important for the economy (vol. 2, I.3: 67–8). His tortuous considerations on consumption make no substantial distinction between productive and unproductive consumers (68–73). However, at the general level, he endorses Smith's distinction between productive consumption, which derives from investment, and unproductive consumption, which derives from revenue (III.1: 220–1).

3. Critics of the aristocracy's wastefulness

Of Smith's closest followers, some lay particular stress on condemnation of the aristocracy's wastefulness, and especially on unproductive servants. *Schlötzer* (1804) is favourable only to a reasonable degree of luxury, which encourages industry without damaging society (123). *Predaval* (1807), although still taking a pre-Smithian approach, severely criticises the nobles because they do not work (207–12). James *Mill* (1808) draws attention to the double sense of the word consumption: "One is consumption for production, either for means of production or for wages". The other is unproductive consumption – for example, for "the maintenance of dogs, of horses for pleasure, and of livery servants". If the latter is great, then the national product will be little.[7] *Isola* (1811), who cites only Genovesi, not Smith, states that reproduction and society are poor when inequalities are excessive (94). For other criticisms of aristocratic luxury, see *Dawson* (1814: 78–9) and *Foster* (1815: 14–15).

Rau (1826–27) has the merit – together with Malthus – of reviving Smith's historical analysis, where he explains why the production of material goods is preferable to that of services. Rau stresses that, when landed property was concentrated in great estates, the few owners supported a great many idle people, to the detriment of the production of goods. This made society poor. When the production of material goods started increasing, national revenue also increased. Only then was it possible to put many people to the production of services (148–9).

In this respect, the French Count *Destutt de Tracy* (1817) was an outsider, but an interesting one. He defines production as the activity that confers utility to things and also changes things in form or in place (20, 25). Destutt also maintains that productive consumption is that of the entrepreneurs, in which the consumption of their employees is also included (170–4). Accordingly, the author argues that all the working classes are productive. Idles, on the contrary, are the true sterile class, the "drones of the hive". To quote Virgil, they are *fruges consumere nati* (born to consume the land products). Destutt expresses the genuine spirit of Smith and of his severe indictment of the unproductive consumption of the rich. It is true that the rich who consume for their own satisfaction give work, he says, but it is a sterile work (168–9). On the other hand, for a dull, moralistic criticism of luxury, see *Raymond* (1820).[8]

4. Smith corrected on some occupations

Jakob (1805) maintains that labour productiveness cannot be measured in quantitative terms (§ 486). He also states that all labourers can be productive, directly or indirectly, if they add something to the national wealth in excess of what they consume (§§ 486–96). *Kraus* (1808–11) has some difficulty in explaining why services like healthcare and teaching help productive labourers, but, as such, they are unproductive (vol. 1: 13–29).

Other authors affirm the productiveness of some occupations that Smith considers unproductive. The anonymous author of the *Political Economy* (1810) entry in the *Encyclopaedia Britannica* is inclined to accept Smith's distinction on the basis of durability, but he admits that the most eminent authors of the time consider the distinction "nugatory". He affirms that, for them, wealth is the sum of conveniences and pleasures of life and that whoever contributes to their increase is a productive labourer (112–13). However, the author maintains that public administration is productive, being part of the fixed capital of society (120b).

Curiously enough, *Cagnazzi* (1813) also includes rentiers among the productive because they lend money for investment or land and buildings for production (IX.2). He also notes that those unproductive labourers who are useful should not in any case exceed in number. There must be a proportion between productive and unproductive labourers, and between agricultural workers and the others (IX.4–6). Cagnazzi also stresses in capital letters "an ignorant nation never becomes rich" (107). Mrs. *Marcet* (1816) – in her universally praised book, which aimed at disseminating knowledge of political economy – repeats Smith's theses, but she is careful not to refer to material labour. She also reproaches the economists for confining Smith's distinction to this aspect (291–4).

Malthus (1820) states that the expenses for education can be considered productive only when they help workers to acquire dexterity in their labour. But general education for professionals, not being paid for with capital, is unproductive (37–8). The anonymous *Inquiry* (1821) shares Smith's view (117–18fn), but states that the clerks of private enterprises are productive (58). *Rau* (1826–27), too, considers public work indirectly productive, but admits that there can be too many intellectual or public workers.[9] He is dubious about the productive nature of commerce and says that, in personal services, it is difficult to distinguish between productive or unproductive activities (140–8).

The Americans authors *Putnam* (1834) and *Newman* (1835) diligently repeat Smith's distinction. However, Putnam declares that public labour is productive when it increases the utility of public property (I.10). Newman states that researchers are in any case productive, because – directly or indirectly – they help production (I.1; I.12–13). Newman shares the classical idea that wages always tend to the subsistence level (II.2). Much later, Henry *Fawcett* (1863) revived Smith's assertion that only material labour is productive. However, he extends productiveness to all occupations that increase or maintain the efficiency of the workers: teachers, the police, even entertainments (6–16). His wife, Millicent *Fawcett* (1870), repeats the same concepts, in a more taxonomic way (14–25). She arranges them like a catechism for children.

5. Sismondi and Malthus on material production

Sismondi (1819) defends Smith against G. Garnier's criticism. Smith, he notes, makes it clear that the market selects the occupations more necessary to society by paying them more. This expression of individual interest coincides with the general interest (I, I.7: 49). The author repeats time and again that saving is the only way to accumulate wealth. But he also wrongly attributes to Smith his conviction, shared by the majority of the classical school, that labour is the only source of wealth (51, 85, 90).

Sismondi shares Smith's idea about material jobs, because productive labour must be accumulable. Musicians, lawyers and servants do not leave anything as a product, while the watchmaker does. Sismondi gets entangled in his own reasoning by confusing the performer who is paid with the payer. It is true, he writes, that also immaterial labourers receive payment and can spend it, but the purchaser of the watch can use it for future work (can invest its value) whilst those who pay non-material labourers are left empty-handed.[10]

The same applies to the professions that guarantee security. They do not consume capital, but incomes. As time goes by, public managers will tend to take advantage and govern "too much". They are expected to conserve wealth, but they end up wasting it. Sismondi adds that, certainly, society needs occupations that produce "spiritual enjoyments" or provide health and welfare. However, the results of these occupations are not accumulable.[11] Sismondi's arguments are rather weak. He too includes landowners among the "productive classes", together with productive workers and capitalists (Ibid.: 90–1). He adds the bizarre view that scholars and musicians are productive when they publish their works, but are unproductive when they perform or give lessons (93fn).

Even weaker, if not disastrous, is the author's attempt to defend Smith against Quesnay, in an apparently impromptu text. Quesnay had motivated his conviction that commerce and manufacture are sterile by maintaining that both activities accomplish mere exchange between equal values, with no surplus. Sismondi replies using – inappropriately – Condillac's argument that any exchange increases utility for both parties. Moreover, he maintains that in exchange both parties can save the increment of utility.[12] Thus, he concludes, also manufacture workers are productive. Earlier on, the author had used Condillac's argument, but – more prudently – had admitted that the reciprocal advantages cannot be expressed quantitatively (S. 1803: 190–1).

Thus, Sismondi confuses Condillac's subjective utility with the value in the Smithian sense. The further he takes his argument, the more he gets tied up in inextricable contradictions. He ends up begging the question: enjoyments provided by productive workers can be saved, while those provided by the unproductive – although equally useful – cannot (S. 1810: 124). He even adds that soldiers, judges and the government protect production, so they can be considered productive, like the factory worker who organises the others' work (126).

The most insightful defence of Smith's distinction comes from *Malthus*. He states that such a distinction is essential to understand capitalist accumulation.[13] Material capital is the basis of the main factors of accumulation, namely production of profit, division of labour and technical progress (36). Without the productive/unproductive labour distinction, we could not see the difference between parsimony, which makes a country rich, and profligacy, which makes it poor (38–40).

Smith has taught us that the balance between annual production and annual consumption is crucial to understand where a country is going (41–2). If all personal services (in Smithian terms: unproductive labour) were to be included in production, the resulting balance would not explain the historical process that European societies have undergone. We started growing, economically, only when the personal services of idle servants were gradually substituted with the production of material objects. The latter production requires saving and accumulation of capital. It generates the new classes, industrious and autonomous, i.e. the middle classes, who live on profit. It is this process that has caused the division and alienation of those immense landed estates, which were based on primitive personal services (42–3).

In his *Definitions*, Malthus writes that in a country where landlords mainly consume material goods production increases, while in a country where their consumption goes mainly into menial servants this does not happen.[14] Here Malthus restates the difference between labour paid with capital (which is productive) and the same labour paid with revenue (which is unproductive), a distinction that the critics of Smith – like McCulloch – have forgotten (93–4).

In the *Principles*, against the physiocrats, Malthus states that agriculture cannot "alone determine the national wealth". He repeats Smith's argument in other terms: two countries with the same number and dexterity of agricultural labourers can have the rest of the population devoted to manufacture and commerce, and grow rich, or devoted to the tasks of menial servants and soldiers, and grow poor.[15] Malthus refuses to endorse the indirect productiveness of personal services, because this would blur the distinction and legitimise any inclusion among the productive occupations (45).[16]

As for the productiveness of intellectual labour, Malthus admits it is accumulable. Economic wealth, he says, must have a certain duration in order to be accumulated. No doubt "the law of the legislator, the precepts of the moralist and the conclusions of the natural philosopher" are susceptible of accumulation and "of receiving assistance from past labour". But it is impossible to say how much they have contributed to the wealth of a country through the "gross calculations" of national wealth (M. 1820: 46, 49).

Malthus tries to answer to Garnier's principal objections (Ibid.: 46–7). He acknowledges some incoherence in Smith's approach and admits that a number of public employees or even some menial servants are not unproductive (34–5, 47–8). However, these are very minor aspects with respect to the general theory. Malthus also notes a contradiction in McCulloch. The latter had criticised Lauderdale's definition of wealth (all things that man desires as useful or delightful). This way, says McCulloch, political economy should include all human activities, and so he confines wealth to material goods. But why, then, Malthus asks, does McCulloch reject the concept of productive labour as that which produces material goods?[17] *Cazenove* (1832), one of Malthus's followers, shares the concept of unproductive labour, above all on the basis of the division between material and non-material products (XV: 87–90).

Thus, Smith and Malthus maintain that capital accumulation was borne thanks only to the shift from wealth wasted in unproductive services to wealth invested in material production. However, in the period of the industrial revolution, the context had changed. That argument no longer had a great importance.

6. Ricardian socialists

In the mid-1820s, the first works of the Ricardian socialists appeared (see also *Lowenthal* 1911). These authors adhered to Smith's productive/unproductive labour distinction in order to denounce the exploitation of material workers, who perform productive labour.

Ravenstone (1821) was an alleged Ricardian socialist, but also an apparent late physiocrat. In fact, he was a bizarre but by no means banal author. He states that only land cultivators are productive. They produce the surplus from which both rents and profits derive, industrial enterprises being unproductive.[18] Capital, like uncultivated land, is sterile. "Great capital is no proof of the wealth of a country, its existence only proves a disordered state of its institutions" (311). In turn, the incomes of lawyers and merchants derive from rent and capital (303–7). "Since trade consists always in an exchange of equal values, the profit of the merchant can add nothing to the wealth of a country" (298). Lawyers and merchants "inasmuch as they grow rich, others must grow poor" (303). On the other hand, Ravenstone concedes that, if productivity increases, unproductive labour that produces comforts can increase. Actually the aim of society is to increase comforts by diminishing the labour that is needed to produce necessaries (313–4).

William *Thompson* (1824) published an enormous treatise on political and social issues. Labour – he states – is the father of all wealth, as it was to be repeated time and again throughout the 19th century (6–17). Inequality is the cause of all evils (ch. 2). Wealth in excess is entirely consumed by unproductive labourers, who do not produce material objects. This wealth is lost to accumulation. On the contrary, productive labourers never consume but by reproducing (195–8). Thompson (1827) repeats the same ideas. Here, the author also attacks merit and competition – when it is totally free – as the causes of inequalities and low productivity. He contrasts with them voluntary cooperation between productive workers. Education, healthcare and comforts are the best incentive to productivity. It is possible to secure workers the whole product of their exertion only in a collective dimension, not at the individual level.[19]

John *Gray* (1825) writes that landowners, professionals and capital-owners are unproductive. They are a tax burden for the productive workers. They are also useless, unless they provide an equivalent of their consumption. Gray attempts a list of the unproductive categories according to their uselessness. He declares totally useless: the nobility, landowners, big merchants, capitalists, most of the public employees, half of the army, three quarters of the professionals and all the workers (although productive) who produce luxuries. Among the useful he puts the royal family, the navy, judges and doctors, artists and also small landowners and farmers, provided they are not too many. He goes on with this minute and extravagant list (15–30). Later on, Gray defended Smith's distinction against McCulloch. However, he says, it is important to avoid too many productive or too few unproductive labourers. We should not look at the results – as McCulloch maintains – but at the kinds of occupations. Gambling or working as a lawyer can provide bread, but it does not produce the bread. McCulloch confuses producing with obtaining.[20]

The pamphlet by *Hodgskin* (1825) is based on the Ricardian principle that capital derives from labour. Workers are the only source of wealth and the only productive class. Only they confer utility on capital (5–18). However, according to Hodgskin, it is impossible to say whether material labour is more productive than immaterial labour. He cites G. Garnier, who had written that it is like asking which of the two legs is useful to walk. Hodgskin adds that a worker is productive, not when he yields a profit to the capitalist, but when he produces what he consumes.[21] Later on, Hodgskin provided a brilliant, although utopian, analysis of the social transformation of labour and society. Due to technical progress, unskilled labour tends to disappear. A middle class rapidly grows up, which retains the features of both workers and capitalists. This fact foreshadows a society where men are all equal and free.[22]

Bray (1839) repeats that all occupations have the same dignity, because all of them are necessary. However, he states that wage-labourers form the productive classes. It is an insult, he exclaims, to recommend these workers to accumulate, because they simply cannot do so. On the other hand, they are necessary for the accumulation achieved by the others (44–7). The idle classes are a burden on the labouring classes (66–79).

Conclusion

However faithful to Smith, these authors cannot help opening the issue of unproductive labour, a veritable Pandora's box. Since the services and intellectual labour are steadily increasing, in order to employ the surplus productively, as the theory requires, authors have only three possibilities: they may deny the Smithian thesis that intellectual labour is unproductive (see next chapter), or indeed radically deny the Smithian productive/unproductive labour distinction (see Chapter VII), or they fail to find a productive outlet to the surplus (as was the case with Ricardo, J. S. Mill and Marx).

Notes

1 Myint (1948: 84–8, 231–3).
2 Bentham (1800: 237; —1801a: 138–9; —1801b: 285).
3 Lüder (1800–04, vol. I, 4: 256–67).
4 Colquhoun (1814: 89, 109, 126, passim).
5 Ricardo [1951–73, vol. 1: 150–1].
6 Ricardo (1820, notes 215 and 289).
7 J. Mill (1808: 68–74. See also —1821, ch. 4, sections 1 and 4).
8 Raymond (1820, I.19: 407–18).
9 Rau (1826–27, I, §§ 94–5 and 332–9).
10 Sismondi (1803; I: 28–34 and fn.: 90–6).
11 Sismondi (1819, vol. 1, II.9: 141–8).
12 Sismondi (1810: 118–19).
13 Malthus (1820, I.1.2: 34–5).
14 Malthus (1827, VII: 73–5).
15 Malthus (1820, I.1.2: 43).
16 This thesis is effectively repeated in Malthus (1827, VII: 96–8).
17 Malthus (1827, VII: 71–3).
18 Ravenstone (1821: 298–314, passim).
19 See e.g. Thompson (1827: 36–9, 44–8, 114–21).
20 Gray (1831: 237–45).
21 Hodgskin (1827: 49–52).
22 Hodgskin (1931: 85–101).

VI Critics of Smith on services and intellectual labour

Background

Smith maintains that services, however useful, are unproductive because they are not durable and so not accumulable, and moreover because they exchange labour for revenue (i.e. wealth used for personal consumption), not for capital (wealth used for investment). The authors of this group do not deny Smith's concept of unproductive labour but attack the weakest point of his approach, namely the idea that only material labour is productive. They also claim that intellectual labour and services are useful for the production process.

Rightly, these authors see the separation between social utility and productiveness as unfounded and contrary to the common sense (see also *Boss* 1990: 6–7). However, they unwittingly overlook Smith's basic distinction between labour paid with capital and labour paid with revenue. Without that distinction, the very issue of unproductive labour becomes meaningless. Thus, the authors described here start by accepting Smith's distinction, but lose track of it on the way.

1. Indirectly productive labour

The concept of indirectly productive labour, clearly stated by Genovesi (see II.5), re-emerges from time to time throughout the entire debate on our subject. It refers to those occupations that in one way or another help in the production of wealth achieved with material labour.

According to *Boileau* (1811), means of production and personal services – although the product of the latter is hard to measure – are indirectly productive. But if these services produce more than what they cost, they are productive *tout court*. Labour is productive only when it produces more than the producer's consumption, i.e. when it yields rent, interest or profit. When labour is neither directly nor indirectly productive, it simply subtracts wealth from others. As for the physiocrats, Boileau states that it is wrong to think that only nature is productive and not man too. On the other hand, like Say and Ricardo, he observes that industrial labour is helped by nature even more than agricultural labour (II.8: 190–5).

The concept of being indirectly productive is used by *Storch* (1824, Preface, III). One of Storch's followers, *Fuoco* (1825–27), writes that, strictly speaking, no social class is unproductive. Those who do not affect production directly do so indirectly. Those who do not work make the others work. Thanks to this, their sterility "partly" disappears, provided they maintain the right proportions with the productive classes (I.2: 321–3).

McCulloch's (1824) attack on Smith with regard to services is particularly important, since it comes from one of Ricardo's closest pupils. The author forcefully argues that services do in fact produce wealth, like material labour. Wealth – he writes – does not consist in matter; it consists in the utility produced by labour (231b, 275a). Even the menial servant produces utility, and so wealth. If making a coat is productive, no less productive is it to keep it in good condition. If mining coal is productive, it is also productive to transport it from the cellar to the house. The doctor does not procure comfort directly, says Smith. But what is the difference if he procures it indirectly? If the worker who produces a locomotive is productive, why should the doctor who saves the life of Watt (the inventor of locomotive) be unproductive (275b)?

McCulloch (1845) finds the concept of unproductive labour in Smith incongruous, because it does not fit with his conception of the invisible hand, i.e. the harmonious convergence of private interests with general interest (1: 12–13). In his edition of the *Wealth of Nations*, McCulloch recalls Ricardo, who defines as productive any worker who procures, directly or indirectly, the same or greater produce than that which he consumes, but also any work which yields an income, without diminishing the revenue of society. Ricardo, stresses McCulloch, unlike Malthus, looks at the result, not the kind of occupation.[1]

McCulloch adds that menial servants produce utility by enabling merchants etc. to do their work.[2] The latter argument is used by many other authors referring in particular to entrepreneurs, who can dedicate themselves fully to their professional work thanks to the work of their menial servants (*Rossi* 1836–37: 69a; *Meynieu* 1839: 54; etc.).

The American Rev. *McVickar* (1825) argues somewhat superficially that all classes contribute to the production of wealth, either with labour or with capital. Thus, no one is unproductive, except for Roman Catholic priests, beggars and gamblers. He repeats once again the argument of the doctor and wonders why making a product for sale should be different from making it for one's own consumption (160–8fn). He endorses McCulloch's assertion that unproductive labour can be found in an excessive number of workers, not in the nature of an occupation (164).

Flórez Estrada (1828), much better qualified, defines as a "producer" of wealth whoever adds value or utility to material goods, whether directly or indirectly. All the others – like holders of capital – are not producers of wealth (it is absurd, Flórez notes, to say that someone produces wealth while being idle). He then includes among the productive labourers also researchers and professionals, too. Smith is contradictory when he defines intellectual occupations as unproductive and, at the same time, includes them in the national capital (XVII: 260–3). J.B. Say – writes Flórez Estrada – is inconsistent when stating that services, although useful and even essential to society, produce goods that are not accumulable. They do produce accumulable goods, like books or paintings (263–4). Against the argument that service products disappear very soon, he notes that all goods sooner or later disappear (265). Finally, services contribute to making material jobs more productive (266). The author concludes that the more education people have, the greater wealth they produce (266–7).

Mrs. *Martineau* (1832), very popular in divulging political economy, accepts Smith's distinction in principle but defends the utility of professionals, politicians and menial servants. They are necessary to society, just like material labourers. There is no negative sense in the word "unproductive", she says a bit paradoxically. The best thing is a mixture between the two types of labour (vol. I: 48–54). *Urbain* (1833) states that value only derives from demand and supply, and thus the wealth of a nation is variable; it is not measurable in physical terms like that of the niggard. The source of wealth lies in the facility of exchange, as mercantilists had understood (109–10). Besides the material production of industry, only the "intellectual communication" of the banks is productive labour. The other communications can only be "indirectly productive" (119–21).

The concept of indirectly productive can be found in many other authors. *Pautet* (1835) complains that often the public services do not equal the value of the private products exchanged with them (27–30). Pellegrino *Rossi* (1836–37: 67b) – who was murdered while leading the government of the Papal States – writes: even if my servant's work were unproductive for me, certainly it is not so for him. The same confusion between social and individual utility can be found in *Twiss* (1847) when criticising Smith's distinction (VI: 171–90). Moreover, Rossi also confuses the utility deriving from a service and that arising from income.

As for public officers, *McCulloch* (1824) writes that they are the most productive class because they create secure conditions for economic activities (275b). Like menial servants, there may be too many of them, but this does not change the nature of their occupation (McC. 1828: 114). On the other hand, he repeats time and again a commonly shared view: it is necessary to verify the number of public employees and the effectiveness of their performance. While the other service workers are verified – in number and efficiency – by the market, public work is not and is therefore susceptible of an excessive quantity of unproductive labour.[3]

Read (1829) puts forward the same argument (38–9, 40–1fn). *Sanfilippo* (1828) adds that, not only may public workers be in excess, but the price of their work is not regulated by free competition. Moreover, some of them are paid more, some less than what they deserve (130–1). The book of the American author *Cooper* (1826) is rather poor. He condemns occupations that are not – even indirectly – useful for social welfare. Among these he includes many public employees, gamblers, people who do not work or whose labour is useless (38–46, 111–19). And he actually believes that according to Smith merchants and even manufacturers are unproductive (45–6)!

2. Intellectual labour and new needs

Several authors have cogent arguments to offer revealing the contradiction Smith falls into. Services, they rightly maintain, cannot be unproductive since they are the result of the social division of labour (e.g. *Boileau* 1811: 193; *Bosellini* 1816: 7).

Dutens (1804) defended the productive nature of professionals and of intellectual labourers with contradictory arguments. He considered the activities regarding the law, taxes and defence unproductive, since they only protect the given order (28–31). However, Dutens (1835) later on insisted that landowners are productive, as well as menial servants, since they save their masters time.[4]

Lord *Brougham* (1804), in a long review of Lauderdale's book, criticises Smith's criterion of the durable nature of products to define productive labour. Against both the physiocrats and Smith, he effectively deploys the argument of the universal cooperation of labours in a market economy. Brougham's basic point is that people cannot confine their consumption to mere survival; thus, we cannot say that the only productive labour is the production of material goods or – even worse – the production of agricultural goods (355–64). Very similar ideas will be expressed much later by *Hamilton* (1830, 3: 35–7) and *Cannan* (1893, I: 24). *Soden* (1806) acutely argues that without intellectual labour factory production would not go beyond a medium level of productivity. This holds not only for the contribution of scientific research but also for that of humanistic culture and even of the fine arts (sections 208–10: 3–7).

Implicitly, *Hauterive* (1817) seems opposed to Smith's distinction. He insists on the social and cooperative spirit of labour, stressing that not only are services and professionals a necessary part of production (*industrie*), but they also augment both the sum of common labour and the mass of human needs (18– 20, 29ff). *McCulloch*, too, uses this argument (see XII.1.b). The Spanish author *Colmeiro* (1859) has a well-balanced approach to the question. Services are "more or less productive". By unproductive labour, Colmeiro simply means labour ill-performed. Working skill, he adds interestingly, grows along with industry and experience. It is transmitted to new generations through practical and theoretical teaching (67–8).

These authors also attack another pillar of Smith's construction, namely the idea that labour which produces durable goods is more productive, and the associated conviction that durability can only refer to material goods. In Smith's view, this is a crucial point, because he believes that the bulk of capital accumulation can only be realised with material, durable goods. Many authors try to show that non-material products can also be durable. See for instance *Longfield* (1833: 261) and P. *Rossi* (1836–37: 69b).

The oft-repeated example of the doctor who heals someone and is therefore productive is introduced by J.B. *Say* in his comment on Storch.[5]

John *Gray* (1831: 243–4) reports McCulloch's reference to Watt (see VI.1). Mention of great personages, to show that their work is far more productive than material work, was a tactic imitated by many. See, for example *Senior, Sedgwick* and *Scialoja*.[6] Sedgwick also states that artists are productive (231).

According to *Chalmers* (1832), durability is not an argument in favour of material products: the effects of material products finish, too, and often the effects of immaterial work last longer, as in the case of doctors, lawyers and priests (243). Much later, *Toniolo* (1908) implicitly agreed with the Smithian view that wealth is made of material goods, but he conceived the production of wealth as involving intellectual as well as material work. Moreover, the former is more important because it directs the second (II: 14–20).

3. "Moral capital"

a. Inner goods

Less convincingly, many authors – while supporting the productive nature of intellectual labour – use concepts like "spiritual goods", "moral capital", "inner goods", etc.

Probably the most successful analysis in support of the so-called inner goods was proposed by *Storch* (1815). This work was republished and commented upon in 1823–24 by J.B. Say, who was already famous by then. In the third volume, mainly devoted to inner goods, Storch's analysis is too far-reaching. As *Say* comments in a long footnote,[7] Storch mixes up different things. He includes in this category of goods, besides dexterity, culture and health, also taste, religion, safety and entertainments. Say adds ironically: why not also love, friendship, cheerfulness and so on? Marx, too, has some sarcastic comments to make on this view.[8] Say and Marx could not imagine that one day many authors would see relational goods (i.e. the emotional relationship with one's own environment) as economic goods. This improbable connection derives from the analyses by Daniel Kahnemann, a psychologist who was awarded the Nobel Prize in economics.

Say explains that Storch's inner goods cannot be said to be economic because they have no exchange value and do not enrich people economically, nor are they measurable (see note 3). He also states that productiveness does not depend on whether labour is material or not. Services can be consumed either in a reproductive or in a sterile way, like material goods.[9] The weakness of Storch's analysis also appears when he shows some nostalgia for the agricultural society of the past. He suggests that common people were then better off thanks to more positive "relational goods".[10] Storch (1824: *Preface*) answered to Say's criticisms scathingly. Here he maintains that, according to Say, immaterial goods contribute directly to national revenue, while he (Storch) believes they contribute only indirectly (*Preface*, III).

Lotz (1821) follows Storch and effectively shows how important intellectual work is for the general progress in the production of wealth (§ 38: 181–6).

Lotz also defends the productiveness of commerce (§ 39: 186–91). Like Storch, *Fuoco* (1825–27) includes not only education, science and administration but also religion, ethics, etc. among the economic goods (II.5, 181). However, Fuoco – like other authors – maintains that material and immaterial production require and foster each other. In this way, they cooperate to create development and civilisation (II.5: 171–3).

The Rev. *Chalmers*, who earned sarcastic comment from Marx, trivialised G. Garnier, Lauderdale, J.B. Say, etc. He defines the productive/unproductive labour distinction as useless and also harmful because it suggests an opposition between moral and economic goods. Besides, the distinction between material and non-material activities is often impossible. The clergy and the other professions are useful to society.[11] A similar attitude is expressed by the French Christian philosophers *Droz* (1829, 5: 28–9) and *Villeneuve Bargemont* (1841, II: 188–91).

The acute and well-informed Portuguese author *Silveira Pinto* (1837), although a follower of Smith, believes in immaterial wealth. The latter can be natural, like human faculties (both intellectual and sensitive), or social, like the action that the mind exerts on itself, for example in education (56–7, 177–8). Only the labour that adds utility to something is productive. Intellectual and managerial activities belong to the first type of labour (84–6, 104). They can enjoy the advantages of the division of labour (99–100).

b. "Spiritual" approaches

In some authors, the idea of moral goods leads to an attitude of vaguely spiritual and holistic attitude, hostile to the idea of the division of labour. The authors taking such an approach end up by supporting the status quo, including social privileges, or even the pre-modern economic system. A typical example of the latter case is Adam *Müller* (1809). This author shows an organicistic vision of the economy, derived from the medieval corporate society, where both the state and social classes each have a specific role in supposedly harmonious collaboration.[12]

Müller – says Luigi *Cossa* – was considered by Roscher a follower of the anti-modern Möser – author of *Patriotische Phantasien* (1750–60s) and founder of the Romantic German School.[13] *Spann*'s history of economic thought (which was much praised under the fascist regimes of the 1930s) includes a great eulogy of Müller (Spann 1910: 134–5). Another example of this attitude is offered by the less known Johann *Wagner* (1815).[14] There is also a Catholic version of this approach. *Coux* (1832), for example, in all his lectures complains that Smith neglects "spiritual wealth", "moral virtues" and science.

4. Doubts on the productiveness of immaterial labour

From the opinion that only material labour is productive, an extreme idea derived, opposite to the human capital approach: the conviction that only labour which produces necessities is productive. *Canard* (1801) states that the part of labour that produces more wealth than that usually consumed is labour in excess (that is unproductive). He also defines productive labour as that which increases the sources of incomes – not simply incomes (15–16). *Edmonds* (1828) even fits intellectual labour into this logic: it is productive only if it is directed to improving the production of necessaries. He adds, inconsistently, "Knowledge is power" (27–8, 162–6). However, *Craig* (1814) criticises such views.[15]

Later on, many authors appeared uncertain about the productiveness of services, on which they appear rather confused. *Courcelle Seneuil* (1858) maintains that wealth is only made up of material goods. He divides labour (services included) and consumption between industrial and non-industrial.[16] But his reflections are as weak as they are pretentious. Later he wrote that no one can judge the real productiveness of any occupation (C.S. 1862: 97–8).

Cherbuliez (1862) stated that work on research, education, public administration, defence, circulation and distribution contributes only indirectly to the production of wealth. But soon after, he maintained that all occupations are productive. He then stated that wealth is only made of material goods, because the utility of services vanishes as soon as its production finishes (vol. 1: 60–6). Like Say, he stated that we cannot include in the concept of wealth that we cannot measure. If we eliminate the barrier between material and non-material goods, we should call wealth all human faculties: health, morality, pity, etc. (65–9).

Cauwès (1881) too denies that services can be considered wealth, although they are "productive of utility".[17] In Cauwès, the real problem disappears behind nominal questions. The American author John Bates *Clark* (1886) asserts that personal faculties – like knowledge and skill – are not part of wealth because they cannot be alienated like commodities (2–4). Clark does not agree with Say on the concept of the indirectly productive. Any labour is productive of wealth and each class contributes to the production of wealth. One class (public officials) confers on the products the attribute of appropriability, while the other class creates the attribute of utility (13–16). Clark (1907) repeats that all occupations are immediately productive of wealth (17–18).

Conclusions

The authors referred to here accept Smith's concept of unproductive labour in principle but often they make an empty box of it. However, albeit amid much confusion, they raise a difficult question, not yet properly defined, namely the economic nature of moral faculties, natural or acquired. Many authors have the merit of showing that these "goods" can be durable (see VI.2.b), accumulable (VII.3) and transmissible (XII.5). For example, healthcare, education and the transmission of them show that this is by no means a trifling question (see Chapter XII).

Contrary to many of the viewpoints examined here, the exclusion of these goods from the economic field cannot be based on the fact that they are not exchangeable or not measurable. There are factors that do not always have a market price and yet are important for economic growth – for example, certain particular attitudes or abilities. Other economic factors are hard to measure, beginning with productivity potentials.

Notes

1 McCulloch (1827: 4. See also —1828: lxxi; and *Notes* to b. II.3: 95).
2 McCulloch (1827: 5. —1828, *Notes*: 97).
3 McCulloch (1824: 276a–78b).
4 Dutens (1835: 7–14, 100–4, 207–16).
5 In Storch (1815, vol. 3, I.6: 258–9fn).
6 For Senior, see Marx (*Theories*, I.4.17) and his sarcastic comment (see XI.5). Sedgwick (1836–39, I: 159–60). Scialoja (1840: 121–4).
7 Say (1823–24, in Storch 1815, ed. 1823–24, vol. 3, II.1.1: 223–9).
8 Marx (*Theories*, I, IV.16: 410).
9 Say (1823–24, in Storch 1815, ed. 1823–24, vol. 3, II.1.1: 237–8 and fn).
10 Storch (1815, vol. 3, II.3: 337–45).
11 Chalmers (1808: 199–226; 1832: 240–53).
12 See Müller (1809, vol. 3, lecture 26: 31–57).
13 See L. Cossa (1892: 298, 320–1).
14 Wagner (1815, §§ 200–202, 223–6).
15 Craig (1814, vol. 2, 4.3: 93–120).
16 Courcelle Seneuil (1858, I: 37, 60–118).
17 Cauwès (1881, sections 150–1: 250–2).

VII The subjective approach (all labour productive)

Background

The third group of classical authors was radically sceptical about the existence of unproductive labour. They held Smith's distinction to be meaningless, since all labours are productive insofar as they are useful. Often these authors failed to make a clear-cut distinction between social and personal utility, although the distinction dates back to Petty and lies behind the whole issue. Once the distinction is lost, the concept of unproductive labour becomes a logical error (as was later the case with the neoclassical approach). However, in the analyses of this group of authors, we find an idea of the importance of immaterial labour for the creation of wealth. Productiveness is partly freed from the coercive bond of material production and can open new prospects for growth.

1. Individual and social utility

Condillac (1776) can be considered the starting point of the modern utility-value approach. As we have seen (III.2), he stated that, in exchange, utility increases for both parties. It is this utility, not labour, that is the real measure of value. Actually, in the 19th century, no one shared Condillac's idea that exchange produces value.

Even J.B. *Say* (1803), while maintaining that commerce increases the value of commodities through transport, criticised Condillac's thesis (39–40). However, Condillac showed an alternative to the objective approach, based on labour and on the cost of production. In turn, Say (1803), in contrast with Quesnay, stated that production does not consist in creating something material because it is creation of utility (36). *Rist* maintained that Say provided the definitive confutation of the physiocrats, which Smith had not managed to complete.[1]

On the basis of the three original incomes indicated by Smith – wages, profit and rent – Say then went on to elaborate the notion of the three factors of production: respectively labour, capital and nature. According to *Cannan* (1893), it was the first time that these three factors had appeared in economic literature (40–2). Natural agents, Say specified, help production not only in agriculture but also in industries. All three factors are necessary for production.[2] Thus, the question of being productive or not concerns not only labour, but all the production factors.[3] Say sometimes seems to be midway between the idea of accumulation based on the cost of production and the idea based on personal utility. However, this apparent uncertainty derived from his careful consideration of the real economy and constitutes an element of strength rather than weakness in his analyses.

Lauderdale (1804) attacked Smith's idea that wealth consists mainly in durable objects. Wealth, he wrote, is given by "the abundance of objects of man's desire" (135–53). He stated that utility and rarity, not labour, are the source of value; and that demand and supply are the source of exchange value (ch. 1: 12–13). According to *Ferrier* (1805), there are no unproductive occupations. Any useful labour is productive (140–2). Ferrier maintained that Smith did not differ from the physiocrats in his conclusions (378–89). He also defended the importance of money as a source of wealth (55, 384–9).

Simon *Gray*, alias Purves (1815), proposed a subjective theory of value, more radical than that of Say. While, according to Say, value depends on the quality of goods, for Gray it depends on the level of demand (xii-xiv). Gray repeated some of G. Garnier's arguments against Smith's distinction. He could not understand why the musician is unproductive and the scene painter productive, etc. (III.2: 59). Finally, he exclaimed: "*It is happiness* [i.e. satisfaction of one's own needs], *that is the true standard of the value of things*".[4]

Melchiorre *Gioia* (1815–17) made detailed criticism of Smith's distinction. First, he wrote, productive labour is that which produces utility. Second, it is absurd to place honourable professions like those of lawyers, doctors or professors at the same level as prostitutes or gamblers. Indeed the former ones are much more productive than artisans, because they have reached perfection in their art (tome I: 276–96). Commerce, too, increases wealth (tome II: 119). *Ressi* (1817–19) repeated that wealth consists in utility and that all labours are productive. He also wrote (with what evidence one can only wonder) that Smith sees only agriculture as productive, as it is for the physiocrats, and that G. Garnier had hidden this fact. Moreover, Ressi runs into a number of contradictions.[5]

Daniel *Raymond* (1820) is considered the founder of American economics and was a model for the subsequent American authors. He put forward a particularly naive interpretation of unproductive labour, imbued with moralism, in which the classical categories disappeared. Any useful labour – that is, any labour that provides "innocent enjoyment" – is productive. But if labour is perverted and disseminates immorality, it becomes unproductive. Some jobs are unproductive *per se*, such as those of the speculator, stockjobber, gambler or sharper. However, Raymond mixed this criterion with another one, taken up from J.B. Say (see as follows): if we have an excessive number of physicians or lawyers, the supernumeraries are unproductive (I.18: 400–5).

Ganilh (1821) criticised Malthus for accepting Smith's distinction (284–97) and Say for being inconsistent in stating that there should not be too many priests, musicians or clerks, for otherwise they would hinder accumulation (280–4). However, Ganilh rejected Lauderdale's assertion that wealth does not derive from saving (297–310). Against Malthus, he also noted that the increase in wealth depends on population growth and on the increase in agricultural production, which feeds the new population.[6] In his *Dictionnaire*, Ganilh (1826) repeated all his theses on labour and production (*Travail*: 415–26). Nevertheless *Blanqui* (1837) judged him caustically for the weakness of his arguments (235, 344).

Louis Say (1822) rejected Smith's postulate on material labour, because services too have utility. Value is only given by utility.[7] Labour, he maintained, can be productive but also destructive, since it often destroys houses or natural beauties, or subtracts work from useful production in order to produce luxuries.[8] It is worth recalling the author's observation that the incomes of public employees do not add, as such, to national revenue.[9] This assertion is only apparently obvious. Actually the modern public budget is organised on the contrary criterion. Louis Say was kept at a distance by his brother Jean Baptiste (see L. Say's 1822 dedication to his brother and the latter's rejoinder).

Carrion-Nisas (1825) repeated that all jobs which yield utility are productive (ch. 8: 18–9). *Cantalupo* (1825: 121–2) saw in utility the source of value. *Riflessioni* (1824) is an entire book against J.B. Say and his view on non-material labour. The only problem is that this book maintains the same theses as Say (22–7, 75–9).

2. Towards economic individualism

a. Exchangeable labour is always productive

This title is a simple variant of the thesis that any useful labour is productive. J.B. *Say* (1803) remarked a contradiction in Smith's definition of productive labour, very similar to that stressed by Marx (see XI.2). Smith – Say wrote – rightly substitutes the physiocratic idea of material surplus with the abstract concept of value. But then he makes the same mistake as the physiocrats by stating that only material production can be productive. The utility (i.e. productiveness) of doctors, lawyers or musicians is not less real than that of material labour. Indeed they earn an income from their labour and can acquire objects, making this wealth circulate (I, ch. 12 and 13: 78). However – Say added – the latter occupations, although productive, cannot increase indefinitely (as G. Garnier believes) because non-material products cannot be accumulated (78–9).

Ganilh (1809) produced one of the earliest histories of economic thought, in which he also addressed our topic (he added a series of considerations on this issue in the 1821 edition). Wealth, he stated, is produced by all occupations, insofar as they have an exchange value (97–126). Simon *Gray* (1815) stated that productiveness is the same as reciprocal dependence: since the circulation of goods makes social classes dependent on, and necessary to, each other, all classes are productive, although at different levels (5). In his title, Gray (1817) proclaims: "All classes productive of national wealth".

Nassau *Senior* is seen as marking transition from the concept of utility as source of value to that of utility based on the demand-supply relationship. While demand depends on utility, Senior wrote, supply depends on scarcity. But supply also depends on labour and on nature, or in other words on the cost of production.[10] Senior changed the concept of profit, considering it the result of abstinence (185). Another of Senior's features, typical of the neoclassical approach, is the supposed neutrality of political economy, given its scientific nature (S. 1852, lecture 3). Thus, there are all the conditions to reject the concept of unproductive labour. Consequently, Senior stated that labour is productive if its produce is vendible.[11] The concept of productive labour as exchangeable labour is also present in Mary *Meynieu* (1839: 51) and in *Carey*.[12]

b. Economic harmony

From the 1830s on, the view that useful labour means productive labour found ever wider circulation.[13] *De Augustinis* (1840) repeated that utility is the source of value (20, 29–32). *Blanqui* (1843), one of J.B. Say's pupils, re-proposed Say's approach on several occasions. He effectively summarised it by saying that any useful labour is productive (414–15fn).

In the second half of the century, the view that useful and productive labour coincide became dominant. Two (rather undeservedly) famous authors, Bastiat and Carey, put an "easy" approach to the issue into circulation. In his *Harmonies économiques*, *Bastiat* (1850) depicted the economy as entirely smooth and positive. Production is creation of utility. Demand is the driving force of production and exchange (ch. 11). Wealth is measured by the amount of utility at disposal (ch. 6). Men work on the sole basis of their self-interest and satisfy their needs reciprocally (ch. 3). Normally, services are paid for in proportion to their real utility (ch. 5). Unproductive labour is not even mentioned.

Another populariser, Charles *Knight* (1855, chs. 20 and 22) admired and followed Bastiat, while stressing the decisive importance of knowledge and skill for economic progress. *Macleod* (1872) stated that wealth must be exchangeable, but it does not need to be produced by labour or be material or durable (IV.11: 152–3). He even denied that labour produces wealth or value. The proof, according to the author, is this: if there is no demand for the goods produced by labour, these goods have no value. It is demand, he wrote, which creates value.[14] Significantly, Macleod believed Bastiat to be "the brightest genius who ever adorned our Science" (p. V).

Carey (1858–59) repeated, much more superficially, Germain Garnier's paradoxes against Smith's material postulate (III: 44–6). Productive labour, he said, is that which governs the forces of nature (47. See also, I: 186). He stated that every act of consumption is also an act of production (III: 19). A popular book by the American author George *Tucker* (1859) contains a chapter on "mental industry" (i.e. intellectual labour), but Smith's distinction finds not so much as a mention in this chapter (ch. 11). Again, *Amasa Walker* (1866) repeated that all labours are productive insofar as they are useful. He conceded that some occupations are directly useful to production (teaching included) while others are only indirectly useful (like that of priests), but this does not change the basics (II.12: 71–6). According to *Périn* (1880), labour of the "moral order" contributes to the production of wealth like labour of the physical order (48–51). Charles *Gide* (1883) included services among the productive occupations. He added that in any case services are indispensable even for the production of material goods because of the necessary cooperation among the different types of labour in modern production.[15]

c. Scarcity

Auguste Walras (1831), Léon's father, wrote that Say's distinction between material and non-material utility is so obvious that it is of no importance. It is the last trace of Smith's erroneous productive/unproductive labour distinction. By now, wrote A. Walras, it has been perfectly proved that all labours are productive (83). Also useless is Say's statement that material goods are durable and so can be transferred, while non-material goods, being non-durable, cannot. For instance, there is nothing more transferable than a piece of curative advice.[16] Besides – he noted, together with many others – some material goods are consumed as soon as they are produced (like services). Their physical life is different from their economic life (W. 1831: 86). A. Walras also stated (204) that the glory of Smith lies in the principle that labour is the source of value (but Smith never said this) and added that most probably Smith was referring to exchangeable value. Walras stated that value does not derive from utility, but from rarity (*rareté*. 91ff, 172ff; also W. 1849: 21). The latter assertion raised the resentful sarcasm of Say (whose comments appear in the edition of Walras we have used). Rarity is utterly nothing, Say maintained (Ibid.: 302).

Both authors seem unaware that rarity, together with utility, was a component of the "just price" in the Middle Ages.[17] We can say that the term rarity is the way of expressing scarcity in a static economy. A. Walras showed insight with his observation that the demand-supply relationship expresses rarity. This is exactly the neoclassical approach, in which endowments are given. But we should not forget that, for the classical authors, scarcity has another meaning. It is the natural context with which economic activity contends. Production is precisely the struggle to decrease scarcity and achieve abundance.

In the mid-19th century, the whole debate arising over Smith's concept of unproductive labour seemed superseded by the theory of the three factors of production (nature, capital and labour) all receiving remuneration proportional to their contribution. So much has to be seen, for example, in *Molinari* (1854, vol. 1, leçon 8).

3. Accumulation of immaterial wealth

"Social capital", "immaterial capital" and similar expressions were used by several authors of the period (see XII.1). But these expressions must not be confused with today's concept of "social capital", which, although vague, refers to social cohesion, civic sense, etc.

In the classical school, the author who revived the concept of investment in personal education was once again J.B. *Say*. Many authors had already stated that education is an investment intended to render labour more productive (see II.2–3; IV.3). But Say, under the influence of Smith, gave the process a social dimension (see XII.1.a). He first stated that some non-material occupations (professions in general) require an investment. The product of this investment becomes a social capital, of knowledge and skill, which – Say maintains, contradicting his observations in other contexts – can be accumulated. By contrast, there are other services (courtesans, porters, etc.) that require no training or investment, although they, too, have some utility.[18]

Simon *Gray* (1817), while criticising Quesnay and Smith, stated that the skilled are the most productive workers (96–7). *Ganilh* (1815), too, saw intellectual occupations as the most productive (with the exception of the clergy and the government). They are the main source of wealth and regulate the other work. However, Ganilh attributes their greater productivity to the fact that they earn more.[19] *Blanqui*, too, insisted on the great importance, for progress, of "moral capital", namely the skill of professionals. This skill forms a capital that is accumulated, above all, through education.[20]

In his enormous treatise, dedicated entirely to extolling economic liberty, Charles *Dunoyer* (1830) devoted a chapter to unproductive labour (tome 2, b. 5: 1–33). He criticised the major authors, from Smith to Say, for thinking that non-material goods cannot be accumulated and cannot expand indefinitely. Dunoyer attributed much importance to the distinction between labour and the results of it: in the case of services, when the labour finishes, its results do not. The latter can be stored up, accumulated and sold exactly like material goods (11–3). *Fuoco* (1825–27) maintained the same thesis (II.5: 171fn).

Senior (1847) joined these authors, stating that teaching is productive, because it creates professional knowledge (14). *Banfield* (1845) expressed the general view of his time when he wrote: "The most productive labourer is he who, by extending the bounds of knowledge, multiplies the general fund at our disposal" (I.22: 27). According to *Roscher* (1874), also, Frederick Bülau believes in the productive nature of immaterial labour and in the "spiritual capital" of society (§ 184: 905).

Baudrillart (1883), too, expressed the common opinion when writing that all production is non-material insofar as it is production of utility. He added that utility always vanishes after a short time but can be fixed in humans, for example through education. Thus, it is accumulable (lecture 11: 157–60). There is also a non-material capital, made of ideas and culture, which is perfectly accumulable (lecture 12: 177–8). *Valenti* (1892), too, stated that immaterial labour is accumulable (IV: 241).

Conclusions

There is some truth in the argument by *Meek* (1950a), who stated – taking up Marx's view – that Ricardian political economy frightened most academic economists, after 1830, because it had been used to criticise capitalism. However, this was not the real reason for the theoretical change. Ricardian economics was not able to explain the growing importance of intellectual and service labour in accumulation. The authors illustrated in this chapter stress the interconnection between increase in refined consumption (comfort, education, culture), increase in skill and research and increase in productivity. They rendered immaterial wealth a familiar concept when it was still rejected by most authors (see XIV.2). They paved the way to the concept of accumulation centred on human capital. A few of them – like J.B. Say and Dunoyer – elaborated some concepts that might be called investment in human capital. However, they did not go so far as to construct a theory of accumulation based on this kind of investment.

Notes

1 See Gide and Rist (1909: 119).
2 Say (1803, I, chs. 3, 4, 7; —1820: 32–8).
3 Say (1803, I, chs. 12 and 13).
4 S. Gray (1815, I.2: 5; see also II.3: 47–69). This book, the author wrote, was already finished in 1804: iii–iv.
5 Ressi (1817–19, see respectively II: 330–1; III: 14–26, 231–86; III: 28–42).
6 Ganilh (1815, II: 307–8).
7 L. Say (1822: 95–8, 260–1. See also —1836: 80–1).
8 L. Say (1822: 261–3; S. —1827: 35–7).
9 L. Say (1827: 299–300).
10 Senior (1836: 173–9). See also Myint (1948: 36).
11 Senior (1847: 10–13). See also —1836: 6–12; —1852, lecture 4.
12 Carey (1837, ch. 1: 3–6; —1858–59, III: 44–5).
13 See, for instance, *Poulett Scrope* (1833: 44fn–46), Pellegrino *Rossi* (1836–37: 66b–67a), *Pinheiro-Ferreira* (1840: 20–1), *Joseph Garnier* (1846, I.1.3, VI: 43–7), *Scialoia* (1848: 21) and finally, the popularising authors John *Wade* (1833, II.5: 178–80) and Mary *Meynieu* (1839: 55). For later authors, we will mention just a few examples, like *Ferrara* (1853: 28; 1855: 470–3; 1859: 377–8, 416–7), *Metz-Noblat* (1853: 41, 353–4), *Trinchera* (1854, VII: 131–8), *Leroy-Beaulieu* (1895, tome I, II.1.3: 152–9), etc.
14 Macleod (1872, V.25–6: 337–8; IX.6: 652).
15 Gide (1883, II.3: 111–13).
16 A. Walras (1831: 84–5. See also —1849: 11–12).
17 See e.g., Roncaglia (2001, 2.5: 39–40).
18 J.B. Say (1803: 79–80; III, chs. 3 and 4).
19 Ganilh (1815, I: 271–3; II: 28–48).
20 Blanqui (1825, 19: 39–41, 104–10; —1837: 116–17, 233, 271–2; —1843: 414–15fn).

VIII The deadlock of unproductive consumption

Background

It took some time for 19th-century economists to realise that consumption – not only labour – is an essential factor of accumulation. Many authors neglected this aspect,[1] due to two complementary postulates of the classical school. One is that wages are fixed at the subsistence level. The other is that comforts are luxuries; thus, they are excluded by definition from accumulation. These assumptions reflect a polarisation and raise a question which no one had asked at Smith's time: how will the growing surplus be employed?

1. Demand as the driving force of accumulation

We have seen before (II.7) that, in the 17th century the conspicuous consumption of the upper classes was defended with the argument that the luxury of the rich gives the poor work. In contrast, in the 18th century, most of the economists opposed this argument as harmful to saving and investment. On the other hand, they defended the increase in consumption by the productive classes, i.e. the comfort of the bourgeoisie and the high wages of workers.

In the early 19th century, as we have seen (V.3), many authors continued to censure the waste and ostentatious luxury deriving from rent, and yet some continued to defend it. The defence survived in the thought of the moralists and the later physiocrats. Continuing in this line, some early 19th-century authors were still opposed to Smith's insistence on saving and investment. They believed that the real fuel of accumulation is consumption, not saving.

The Earl of *Lauderdale*, one of the most representative authors of this tendency, attacked Smith, showing a radical aversion towards saving and thrift. Saving, he states, is not the basis of accumulation. An excess of it can even lead to stagnation and generate both excess of investment and lack of demand. Moreover, the increasing use of machinery diminishes capital returns. The driving force of accumulation is increase in consumption. Demand should be supported even with public debt.[2] The author also attacked the sinking fund.[3]

Lauderdale's main argument was that economists (especially Smith) confused private and public wealth, since they considered the latter as the sum of private riches. This is wrong, Lauderdale held, although both types of wealth have the same three sources: land, capital and labour.[4] Private wealth is measured by its value, which is determined by scarcity. For an individual, the greater the scarcity, the greater the value of a good and the greater the owner's wealth. On the contrary, public wealth depends on its utility for society. Otherwise we should think that the less water a society disposes of, the richer it grows, which is absurd. Lauderdale went on to present a series of amusing paradoxes to prove that thrift or prodigality produce different effects for individuals and society (L. 1804: 40–3). Private thrift makes a man richer, because it increases his income. But general thrift makes society poorer.[5] Every prodigal man, he complained, referring to Smith, is regarded as a public enemy, and every thrifty person as a public benefactor (L. 1804: 41).

Malthus largely borrowed from Lauderdale, without acknowledging the fact.[6] However he rejected Lauderdale's view that consumption, and not saving, is the driving force of accumulation.[7] A similar anti-saving attitude appears in *Ferrier* (1805: 130–40). *Spence* (1807) used Quesnay's defence of landlords' luxury to support his own underconsumptionist view (30fn).[8] *Quesnay* and *Mirabeau* had approved of the *luxe de subsistance*, because – by consuming land products – it fosters agricultural production, while they condemned the *luxe de décoration*, involving manufactured products.[9]

Spence (1807) also attacked Smith's defence of parsimony. If everyone saved, he writes, no one would consume the products of industry. The rule of thrift does not hold for landlords' consumption. Without the latter, incomes and the consumption of the other classes would diminish. However, Spence admitted that excessive consumption reduces reproduction (29–36. See also S. 1808, —1822). Unlike Quesnay, he preferred the luxury of durable goods, which increases national wealth (S. 1807: 35). As *Meek* (1951b) explained in his refined analysis, Spence and Chalmers recalled physiocracy because they still had a pre-industrial mentality, while Sismondi's and Malthus's thoughts at times inhabited the pre-industrial world, and at times the Ricardian world.

M. *Gioia* (1815–17) criticised Smith and Say at length for their praise of thrift and condemnation of profligacy. To Smith, he objected that consumption encourages production and that, in order to enhance production, it is not necessary to employ more workers. Accumulation can advance thanks to technical progress and the consequent increase in productivity (tome IV: 77–97). Contesting Say, Gioia insisted that ornaments and luxury are necessary to gratify people and drive them to emulate one another. Thus, they do not harm production (ibid: 87–98).

Many 19th-century authors even revived the pre-modern idea that the luxury of the rich is necessary because it gives work to the poor. As *Attwood* (1817) put it: "The more numerous and affluent are the rich, the more comfortable and happy are the poor" (24). The same view was expressed by *Solly* (1814: 28–9) and *Martineau* (1832: 50–1); by *Flury* (1833: VII: 196–7), a follower of Lauderdale; and *Lechevalier* (1834), a follower of Fourier (V.I.7: 446–7). This timeless attitude had, in the modern age, been widespread among the Free Thinkers and the 17th-century mercantilists.[10]

Ganilh (1815) contested Malthus's view that industrial nations have a short life. On the contrary, he writes, these nations are richer than agricultural economies (I: 321–3). Production, he repeated time and again, adapts to demand.[11] On the other hand, Ganilh (1826) rejected Say's law (see IX.3) and believed that overproduction was possible ("Consommations": 159–61). He always seems to waver between the thesis that individual saving is necessary for investment and the view that consumption supports production in any case.[12]

Simon *Gray* (1817) scathingly attacked Smith, whose theory on unproductive labour – he states – has damaged the aristocracy, together with the professionals and the bourgeoisie. Smith's theory has put the masses in the hands of the demagogues (viii–ix). It sets the social classes one against the other, while his (Gray's) theory reconciles them (II.11: 227–37). According to Gray, the existence of the rich is necessary because there is no other way to augment wealth. Without them, the others would be poorer (S. Gray 1815: 67). Consumption, he says, plays an essential role in development: "In sum, an increase of population, though it be an increase of sellers, is an increase of buyers also; and …, instead of tending to diminish the capability of buying …, operates powerfully in increasing that capability" (1815: 32).

Gray also criticised the distinction between labours that produce necessaries and labours that produce luxuries. Such a division, he says, serves to hide the unsustainable distinction between productive and unproductive labour (65–6). Gray also stated, contesting Malthus, that it is population that regulates the quantity of subsistences, not the other way around. He also anticipates to some extent the much later theory of demographic transition: "excess" of produce reduces the fertility of society, and so the population decreases (S. Gray 1818: 10–11).

Like Lauderdale, *Ressi* (1817–19) saw the danger of insufficient consumption and thought that Smith's defence of parsimony was excessive (vol. 2: 320–1; vol. 4: 447–56). *Wheatley* (1822) enumerated eight social classes and maintained that they should not grow beyond their present proportions if prosperity was to be preserved. However, he writes, workers do not reproduce with moderation. He put landowners among the productive classes (7–13). *Saint-Chamans* (1824) was entirely devoted to the following thesis: multiplying needs, i.e. increasing demand (and public spending), is the only way to foster production. All consumption is then productive. Saving impoverishes the state (101–21, passim). *Louis Say* (1822) graphically commented on Saint-Chamans's thesis: it is like Harlequin, who maintains that salty food quenches thirst because it makes one drink (364–5). Mary *Meynieu* (1839) came up with a very naive argument: the presence of "futile goods" means that society already has enough necessaries (51). Meyneiu was unaware that luxuries exist even in the poorest and most primitive societies.

The Rev. *Chalmers* (1832) bravely stated that the consumption of landlords and the clergy supports accumulation. But the clergy goes further, because it also provides a service to society (252). He criticised both Smith and J.B. Say for believing that capital can expand indefinitely (249; ch. 1–5. See also —1808). This is not true, he says, due to the diminishing returns, discovered by Malthus and Ricardo (60–5, 249fn, passim). Chalmers goes on to observe that machinery, too, can be in excess, because it brings down the rate of profit. Excessive saving has the same effect (65–9ff).

Longfield (1833) maintained that we cannot speak of workers' productive consumption. Human consumption is always unproductive, because it destroys the wealth consumed. On the other hand, wages are higher than the consumption that is strictly necessary to exert labour, to the extent that the banks hold a great quantity of workers' savings (164–5, 258–61). Longfield was already using the concept of marginal productivity (59–60).

2. Consumption above subsistence wages is unproductive

a. The subsistence wage level

We have seen (II.7) that the 18th-century concept of wages at the subsistence level was used to grant workers protection from excessive exploitation. The classical authors not only overturned the sense of this concept, but even lost the memory of the original meaning. The subsequent economists, too, remained oblivious of it. What brought about such a radical reversal? Here we must look to the new features of accumulation. The radical mechanisation of the first industrial revolution reduced mass labour to elementary levels. Meanwhile the huge unemployment caused by mechanisation fired such keen competition among the workers that wages effectively dropped to subsistence level and even below (see ch. X).

Some early authors still echoed the Enlightenment attitude. *Canard* (1801) takes a positive view of "superfluous consumption". He first defines the labour that goes beyond the production of bare necessities as "superfluous". This labour produces luxuries, the consumption of which is also superfluous, i.e. unproductive. According to Canard, *ceteris paribus*, the level of luxury is proportional to the industry of a people. We need – he wrote – a balance in the advantages provided respectively by the three sources of income (land, capital and labour). The sum of the advantages provided by one of these sources is always proportionate to the sum of exigible (i.e. exchangeable) superfluous labour that has created it. When luxury consumption exceeds what is produced by superfluous labour, it means that it is wasting the very sources of incomes (15–16, 80).

Boileau (1811) is among the very few who escaped the trap of the subsistence wage level. Like James Steuart, he maintained that the wage level must be adequate in order to keep up productive capacity, ensure protection from calamities and provide "some conveniences". Wage level must also allow some small undertakings to make workers more motivated (IV.4: 366–7). The consumption made by those employed for personal services derives from the labour of productive workers. If the latter produce a great surplus and the services are useful to society, all goes well (373). On the other hand, public services are necessary, but must be obtained with the least possible expense (IV.5, 377–8).

In general, however, the new version of the subsistence wage held. One point all the authors concurred upon was to consider the subsistence level as determined not by biological survival but by customs. This means that it could increase over time (see *Stirati* 1994: 172–7). But this awareness did not render their idea of accumulation really dynamic; because customs – and so the wage level – change too slowly in relation to accumulation (see also *Myint* 1948: 32). The result is a substantially static view, where wages and profits were not conceived as growing together.

In his *Principles*, *Ricardo* considered unproductive any consumption by the workers that exceeded what is merely necessary to perform their work:

> If the price of labour should rise so high, that notwithstanding the increase of capital, no more could be employed, I should say that such increase of capital would be still unproductively consumed.[13]

In a letter to Malthus, he confirmed:

> if the labourer receives a large proportion of the produce as wages, all that he receives more than is sufficient to prompt him to the necessary exertions of his powers, is as much unproductive consumption as it were consumed by his master, or by the state - there is no difference whatever.[14]

Marx took note of this conception and attributed it to all classical economists.[15] Ricardo also "rigidly" distinguished between wage goods and luxury goods (see also *Blaug* 1962: 95). The former are only necessary goods, not susceptible of improvement, while the latter are the goods that will never enter into the reproduction process. This is why, even when Ricardo acknowledges that wages can remain above the subsistence level for a long time (ch. 5.8), he sees it as a condition that never increases productivity, nor fosters accumulation. On the contrary, a rise in wages should slow down accumulation because it depresses profits.

The Ricardian inverse relationship between profit and wages derived from this static viewpoint. Such a relationship, as *Sleeman* (1837) pointed out, has little to do with reality: it only holds if we imagine that no other consumers exist apart from capitalists and wage earners. Actually, Ricardo did not take other consumers into account because in his view all the other incomes derived from profits or wages. However, this position was contested by Sleeman (22–4, 63).

Later on, *Peshine Smith* (1868) came up with an acute analysis of the issue. He held the popular interpretation of the Ricardian inverse relationship to be wrong (due also to some ambiguity in Ricardo's phrasing). He argued that the relationship does not refer to absolute amounts, either in money or in goods, but to the proportion of wages in the total cost of production. This viewpoint leads to a conclusion exactly opposite to the first one. The wrong interpretation suggests that high wages are incompatible with high profits. On the contrary, high wages and the consequent high consumption in comfort and education raise labour productivity and profits, while the *proportion* of wages out of the entire produce diminishes (V: 103–37). However, Peshine Smith's interpretation seems far from Ricardo's original ideas. Samuel *Hollander* (1983), contesting Stigler, has interpreted Ricardo's wage model as a variable-level model rather than a fixed-level one. Nevertheless, in Ricardo, wages are kept at the subsistence level by the law of diminishing returns.

b. The wage fund doctrine

The subsistence wage level led *Senior* (1830: Preface) and J.S. *Mill* (1848: II.11.4) to theorise the wage fund doctrine. According to these authors, the annual fund devoted in advance to wages cannot be enlarged in the same year. This view gave an interpretation of capitalist accumulation completely static with regard to productive consumption. However, the vigorous development of the following decades cast serious doubts on this thesis. *Longe* (1866) and *Thornton* (1869: II.1: 43–87) criticised it with excellent analyses. After J.S. Mill's recantation (in his "Thornton on Labour and its Claims", *Fortnightly Review*, 1869), the doctrine came in for further criticism from Francis Amasa *Walker* (1876).[16]

On this doctrine, see *St. Clair* (1957: 80–103). *Bowley* (1973) unconvincingly maintained that, while Ricardo and J.S. Mill shared the wage fund theory, other classical authors, like MacCulloch, Senior and Longfield, had a dynamic view of wage growth, similar to Smith's (183–208, 217–18). On the other hand, Samuel *Hollander* (1979) attributes to Ricardo a view similar to Smith's (548–9). *Stirati* (1994), too, rightly maintains that Ricardo has nothing to do with the wage fund doctrine (ch. 6.3).

However, historians seem to have exaggerated the differences on wages among the classical authors. In general, the latter did not believe in steady increase in workers' consumption.

3. Productive and unproductive consumption

J.B. *Say* is probably the first critic of the view which sees consumption as the central factor of accumulation. He criticised Lauderdale, who believed that saving can damage production. Lauderdale – Say maintained – is in favour of waste.[17] Say, while rejecting Smith's concept of unproductive labour, developed his own criticism of waste. He did so mainly in three ways. First, he set limits to expansion of the sector of professionals and services in general (see VII.2.a). He then elaborated the concept of unproductive capital (see XIII.2). Finally, Say substituted the productive/unproductive labour antithesis with that of productive/unproductive consumption (S. 1803, III, ch. 2–4). Unproductive consumption, he wrote, can satisfy the highest needs (like intellectual needs) as well as the crudest (4: 446). He added that slow is preferable to rapid consumption (449–51), which reminds us of Petty's and Smith's preference for durable goods.

Many authors unconvinced by the concept of unproductive labour preferred to substitute it with Say's productive/unproductive consumption distinction.[18] However, there was much confusion in the use of the latter distinction. At times it is taken to refer to the difference between the necessary consumption of workers and their consumption above the subsistence level. At other times, unproductive consumption refers to final consumption, as distinct from the productive consumption of the means of production. At yet other times, it is referred to unproductive labourers and non-labourers. In some cases, the same author may even attribute different meanings to it in different contexts.

James Mill (1808) scathingly criticised Spence, who defended the luxury of landlords (75–80). Spence, Mill wrote, does not even distinguish between the unproductive consumption of landlords and the productive consumption of entrepreneurs (68–9). Mill (1821) also stated that productive consumption is either the consumption of machinery and raw materials or the necessary consumption of productive labourers (ch. 4.I). According to *Patten* (1899), James Mill fiercely attacked landowners, whom he considered parasitic, on the basis of Ricardo's defence of profit. However, once the bourgeoisie had marginalised the aristocracy, his support of profit went to the detriment of wages (316–17).

Wade (1833) used the concept of unproductive consumption, but criticised Smith's concept of unproductive labour (II.5: 178). Andrew *Young* (1841) pointed out that unproductive consumption caused the production of unnecessary goods (§ 994: 321–2). *De Augustinis* (1840) maintained that all kinds of consumption were reproductive, but some directly, some indirectly (182, 191ff). *Lawson* (1843) simply denied that such a distinction had any sense. No type of consumption can be said to be unproductive because each class consumes by giving something in exchange: workers give their labour, landlords give the use of their land and capitalists give the use of their money (V: 111–12).

J.S. Mill (1848) used both distinctions – regarding labour and consumption – in close connection, in order to better explain the rationale of accumulation (see also XII.2). He stated: "The only productive consumers are productive labourers; the labour of direction being of course included" (I.3.16). Physical luxuries, although belonging to unproductive consumption, derive from productive labour, as long as the latter is paid to produce these luxuries (I.3.17). But even more important than the distinction between productive/unproductive labour is the distinction between labour that is employed for productive consumption and labour that is employed for unproductive consumption. The former enriches the nation, while the latter, should it prevail, tends to impoverish society (I.3.18; see also I.4.9–14). J.S. Mill harked back to Ricardo's concept with a subtle distinction: a part of the consumption made by productive labourers is unproductive, namely that part that does not increase their productivity. It then consists in luxuries (I.3.16; I.4.7). Luxuries are defined as what is useless for accumulation.

Cournot (1863) repeated this distinction, but he also distinguished between the unproductive consumption that is connected with accumulation (education, services for protection, welfare services) and that which is totally unconnected (55–6). A similar view was expressed by *Henry Fawcett* (1863), who also stressed that luxuries are not exchanged with capital and so cannot be employed productively (16, 20–1). His wife *Millicent Fawcett* (1870) also expressed this view (22–4).

Baudrillart (1883) affirmed the same view by using terms similar to those of the 18th-century authors (see II.7). Unproductive consumption refers to immoderate and debauching luxury (lecture 27: 480–1). On the other hand, moderate luxury is positive because it stimulates productivity and promotes the education of the masses. That luxury also be extended to the common people is only fair.[19] Baudrillart is a typical author of those lengthy handbooks of the second half of the 19th century: verbose, wise and balanced, terribly banal and conformist.

The concept of unproductive consumption also appears in the dictionaries of political economy, in general with no elements worth mentioning.[20] Emilio *Cossa* (1898: 262–70) listed the Italian economists who used the productive/unproductive consumption distinction (Ciccone, Boccardo, Luigi Cossa) and those who stated, by contrast, that consumption is always productive as long as it satisfies human needs (Majorana Catalabiano, Montanari).

Conclusions

A point emerging clearly at the end of this survey is that classical unproductive consumption was a complex concept. It did not simply mean consumption by unproductive labourers or non-labourers. Many authors also considered consumption above the subsistence level unproductive. One might accept the latter assumption and define unproductive consumption as luxury consumption, but this would mean foregoing the perspective of increasing productivity through increased and more refined consumption. The two definitions are incompatible. This deadlock held the classical authors back from achieving common satisfactory analyses of many crucial issues like underconsumption, technical progress and human capital, as we will see in the following chapters.

Notes

1 See Napoleoni (1962), Zamagni (1979: 27–37) and Perrotta (1998).
2 Lauderdale (1804, ch. 4; —1804a: 59ff).
3 Lauderdale (1829: 79–117).
4 Lauderdale (1804, ch. 2: 39–41; —1804a: 34–47).

5 Lauderdale (1804: 8–10, 39–45, 208–9, passim. —1804a: 20–34, passim). The latter work, which is a rejoinder to his critics, was devoted mainly to this argument.
6 See also Paglin (1961: 118–19; —1962).
7 Malthus (1820, II.1.3: 314).
8 See also *Robbins* (1958: 13, fn. 1).
9 See Quesnay (1766c: 895; —1767: 580). Mirabeau (1769–71, vol. II: 200–3).
10 See, e.g., Houghton (1677: 261–2); Mandeville (1705: 25; —1714: 107ff); Voltaire (1738: 358).
11 Ganilh (1815, I: 315–17; II: 24–5).
12 See e.g. Ganilh (1815, II: 413–44; —1821: 271–9; —1835: 304–18).
13 Ricardo [1951–73, vol 1, ch. 8: 151fn. See also, ch. 26: 348].
14 Ibid, vol. IX: 17, 9-7-1821.
15 Marx (*Capital I*, VII.XXIII.14).
16 Walker (1876, I.IX; —1883, §§ 453–8).
17 J.B. Say (1803, I, 11: 72–3, fn 93; —1820, second letter: 72).
18 This expression is used by Tooke (1823, part 2: 9), Cazaux (1825, III.3: 120), Ganilh (1826: 164–9), Longfield (1833: 164–5), Pautet (1835, ch. 2: 25–6), Sedgwick (1836–39, I: 158–9), Senior (1836: 154–79), Knight (1855: 33, 345–6), etc.
19 Baudrillart (1869, disc. *Luxe et travail*, 53–81).
20 See e.g. Boccardo (1857: 644), Cocqueil (1891: 541b–43a); Newcomb (1886, II.14: 59–61); *Leroy-Beaulieu* (1895, IV: 230–4).

IX Underconsumption and crises

Background

The early 19th century saw periodical economic crises breaking out. This new phenomenon radically changed the economists' attitude. From the major concern over the insufficiency of saving, expressed by Smith (on which he had built his theory of productive/unproductive labour), authors shifted their worries in the opposite direction, to the excess of saving and of investments. These apparently caused the periodical gluts of unsold goods.

The first organic explanation of crises was the so-called underconsumption interpretation. Even today the concept of underconsumption is far from clear-cut. Its exponents distrusted excessive saving and affirmed that capitalism tends to overproduction. However, many classical authors shared this view but did not take an underconsumption approach. The underconsumptionist authors also believed that productive consumption – i.e. the consumption necessary for accumulation – cannot grow beyond certain limits. Consequently, they considered only two remedies to crises: either restraining investments or consuming a growing part of the surplus unproductively.

1. Sismondi: gluts due to low wages

Unlike Lauderdale, Sismondi (1819) – following in the footprints of Smith – saw saving as the only source of accumulation.[1] However, he believed that saving could not absorb the excess of produce. Sismondi anticipated Marx in seeing that capitalist production is marked by a radical, irresolvable conflict between the natural end of accumulation and its actual result. Accumulation, he wrote, aims at happiness, which should derive from the increase of wealth. But no happiness is granted to the producers of wealth themselves. These, by contrast, become poorer and poorer (51). Periodical crises derive from this inconsistency. These crises increase in number and violence since production in the rich countries is determined not by the needs of the people, but by the abundance of capital. Consequently, there is overproduction, on the one hand, and "cruel poverty" on the other.[2]

Sismondi wrote that wages are too low for the workers to acquire the goods in excess to which they were entitled. Thus, the workers do not toil for their needs but for the luxury of the rich. They do not work for the prospect of subsequent rest, but to let others rest.[3] Besides generating unjust distribution, capitalism tends to produce too much; it is not tied to the natural satisfaction of producers' needs.[4] Sismondi powerfully described the process of expulsion of workers from labour caused by the rationale of accumulation. He also explained how they should be protected.[5]

The workers would be able to have luxury goods (namely, comforts) if they could receive a bigger share of the wealth they produce. Necessary goods are limited, while luxury goods have no limits. Sismondi brilliantly suggested the right solution to overproduction and gluts. The latter would be overcome if workers were allowed to consume more. But he also wrote – somewhat contradictorily, and similarly to Malthus – that the problem of gluts can be solved by increasing the number of unproductive labourers.[6]

Later on, Sismondi (1820–27) replied to his critics and outlined a broad picture of capitalist accumulation. In replying to Torrens' criticisms (see IX.3), he attacked Say's law and challenged the idea that crises cannot be general and are only due to disproportions in some sectors. When gluts alternate – he writes – once in one sector then in another, the final result is a permanent excess in production, i.e. a general glut (402–3). He often calls this phenomenon saturation (on saturation, see ch. XX).

Sismondi seems ever to be wavering between two explanations of crises: censuring either the exclusion of workers from luxury consumption or, on the other hand, the very existence of luxury goods. Production and consumption, he wrote, could be equalised if there were only basic goods in the market and people were compelled always to practise the same kind of consumption. But the existence of luxury goods makes it possible for variations to occur in consumption. This, in turn, unbalances the production/consumption relationship (390).

He also attacked the idea – proposed by Ricardo and Say (see XIII.3) – of an indefinite increase in productivity and production. The gluts contradict this prospect. Technical progress is certainly positive, because it shortens labour. But society does not protect workers from the effects of such progress, and in particular from the excess of competition (433). Like Malthus, Sismondi recalls the ancient times, when overproduction – he said – was offset by public works. I admit – he declared – I am not able to provide a solution for the organisation of production, but I am certain the present one is wrong (440–8).

In his last economic work, Sismondi (1837–38) wrote that economists sought to speed up accumulation, whilst he sought to slow it down (2.13: 149). He noted that by then there was redundancy even in intellectual labour. His proposed remedy is decidedly reactionary, contrary not only to the accumulation tendency but also to any civil progress. Society, he said, should discourage low-class people from seeking to get intellectual labour; each should develop his intelligence in proportion to his social status (2.13: 191–2).

In conclusion, Sismondi – as *Barucci* (1975: p. L) notes – is uncertain and unclear about the real tendency of accumulation and the remedies to it. However, despite his own contradictions, he effectively showed the main shortcoming of classical theory, namely the assumption that productive workers could not steadily increase their consumption.

2. Malthus and unproductive consumption

Malthus (1820) showed a certain diffidence towards industry but had great confidence in agriculture. Like Ricardo, he believed that rent increases along with accumulation. But this was due to the fertility of the land, not (as Ricardo thought) to diminishing returns. Land revenue does not fall as cultivation increases (I.3.9: 216–17), while the profit decreases. Land is able to maintain more people than those who work on it (I.3.1).

Malthus criticised Say's law and the authors who supported it, like James Mill, Ricardo and McCulloch (II.1.3: 316ff). He also stated that the subsistence level depends on habits and customs, and so differs in different countries. In some countries, the workers consume only the mere necessary and devote all the surplus to bringing up more and more children; in others, they use the surplus to obtain more comforts.[7] See also *Torrens* (1815: 62–4).

In any case, due to competition among the workers, wages always remain stuck at the subsistence level. Malthus argued that habits change slowly, while accumulation proceeds rapidly. For example, a sudden increase of resources does not lead acquisition of new comforts, but only demographic increase (II.1.3). The remedy that Ricardo envisaged (the surplus will be absorbed by the increase of productive workers, due to population growth) does not hold, according to Malthus, because children do not become workers as soon as they are born, but only at the age of 16 or 18 (319–20). This argument is also to be found in the *Inquiry* (1821: 19–23). Of course, Malthus's rejoinder has no sense in the long run (the proper context of this debate), where demographic variations are a flow. Moreover, Malthus did not consider the fact that increase in population can also be due to falling mortality. On the connection between Malthus's law of population and his theory of growth, see *Sunna* (2004: 52–3).

In this context, accumulation appeared bound to lead to gluts. As *Costabile* (1980) observes, for Malthus the balance between production and consumption is upset by accumulation itself, if the latter is not regulated (115). Moreover, workers tend to be indolent, said Malthus. They are not driven to work harder in order to increase their consumption. On the other hand, if they consume more, profits fall and the incentive to invest vanishes.[8] As *Blaug* (1958) effectively sums it up, for Malthus "saving acts simultaneously to diminish the demand for consumers' goods and, insofar as it is promptly reinvested, to increase the supply of consumers' goods". Against Malthus's underconsumptionist deduction, Blaug objected that this twofold effect does not take place simultaneously. Production takes time to be accomplished; thus, by reducing the cost of goods, it increases the purchasing power of the consumers (86).

Rashid (1977) misinterprets Malthus when he writes that the latter saw the solution to gluts in increased consumption by the workers. Rashid even attributed to Malthus the ambition to redistribute wealth from the rich to the poor by increasing the number of unproductive labourers, such as menial servants. As a matter of fact, according to Malthus, capital accumulation has the *negative* effect of transforming a part of the unproductive workers (he says, workers employed in personal services) into productive labourers. Thus, when accumulation proceeds briskly, it generates a surplus of goods without increasing the demand for final consumption.[9]

Finally, Malthus painted a very effective picture of the supposed causes of underconsumption. Capitalists, he writes, cannot absorb the increase of produce by increasing their own consumption, since they are bound to save and invest. Workers cannot do it either, since higher wages would depress profits. Lastly, the landowners' consumption does not suffice to absorb the surplus. Produce in excess can only be absorbed by the unproductive labourers. Ultimately, accumulation should be slowed down. In contrast with Ricardo, Malthus stated that it is wrong to set no limits to saving and investments. And it is doubtful that man's desires are unlimited. Accumulation cannot keep going at the fastest rate possible.[10] Malthus wrote that Ricardo "frequently speaks, as if saving were an end instead of a means"; but Ricardo denied he ever did so.[11]

Hla *Myint* (1948) devoted a complex commentary to Malthus. He connects Malthus's analyses of value, demand and productive labour with his underconsumption view (3: 34–52). However, Myint's arguments are too far-fetched, implying a deductive rather than empirical approach in Malthus. *Eagly* (1974), too, ascribed to Malthus a formal, coherent model of accumulation (94–100).

Watarai (2015) stresses that, in order to avoid gluts and the subsequent unemployment, Malthus called for a just proportion between productive and unproductive workers (like the physiocrats), or between wage goods and luxury goods (41–2). Even public works, for Malthus, are useful, because they increase the number of unproductive labourers.[12]

Watarai also effectively proves that Keynes's conviction that his own theory revived Malthus's is ill-founded. Not only did Malthus adopt the classical identification of saving and investment (which Keynes sternly criticised), but he also believed that an increase in investment subtracts resources from consumption and brings demand down. On the contrary, for Keynes new investments increase demand because they extend employment. This is why Keynes cannot be said to be an underconsumptionist (8, 20–2). The same interpretation by Watarai had been made by *Corry* (1959: 722–4) and *Barucci* (1972: LXV). See also *Porta* (1998: 73). Unconvincingly, *Graziani* (1980: XLIX) suggests a convergence between Malthus and Keynes.

★ ★ ★

Some years before Malthus, the German *Solly* (1814) also showed a favourable attitude to the influence of unproductive labour in accumulation. But his reasons were opposite to those of Malthus. He wrote that soldiers and menial servants detract from the labour supply in the production sectors (agriculture and industry), and so save the wages of productive labourers from falling (19).

The editor of the posthumous second edition of Malthus's *Principles*, *Cazenove* wrote in 1822 that capital accumulation "does not necessarily diminish consumption … but merely changes the direction of it" from unproductive to productive consumption. Accumulation increases supply "in relation to demand" (2) and leads to a fall in profits. Prodigality, by contrast, increases the demand/supply ratio and boosts profits (3–5). Cazenove, too, advocated a proportion between productive and unproductive consumption. Like the other classical authors, he assumed that necessary goods are simply wage-goods, while comforts are luxuries. Thus, he could not conceive a gradual increase in workers' comfort.

Blake (1823) minutely examined the dynamics of gluts. He set out to show that the only remedy for them lay in public spending and export. As Graham *Tucke*r (1960) shows, the underconsumption authors had different attitudes towards using public spending as a remedy for gluts (175–7).

Finally, it is worth stressing the difference between Malthus and Sismondi (which they themselves seemed not to notice). They both saw in capitalist accumulation an element that deviates from the natural end of production, but Sismondi attributed it to low wages and the scant demand they are able to induce, while for Malthus the unnatural factor consists in the tendency to use all wealth as investment. Consequently, Sismondi favoured moving a part of surplus from profit to wages, while Malthus wanted to see it moved from investment to unproductive consumption and unproductive labour.

3. Say's law versus underconsumption

On crises, J.B. *Say* always repeated that goods and services are exchanged only with other goods or services.[13] Thus, production cannot rise above consumption. An excess of all products at the same time is impossible. "If each produces much, each will consume much", he wrote.[14]

What we now call Say's law is best expressed in the chapter "Des débouchés" (S. 1803, II, 15) and then in the letters to Malthus, particularly the first one (S. 1820). Say's argument, repeated time and again, is that to save is to spend in another way. Permanent overproduction is impossible because the expenditures going into investment generate purchasing power (and thus demand), which is equal, in value, to the goods that the same investment will produce. Thus, crises can only be temporary unbalances between supply and demand, limited to a few sectors of production. Market competition will rapidly eliminate the problem.

James Mill (1808) came up with an extreme (and erroneous) version of Say's law (81–8). He stated that the production of commodities itself "creates a market for the commodities produced" (81). In ch. 4.2, Mill used as title the sentence "That which is annually produced is annually consumed". This is a paraphrase of a celebrated observation by *Smith* (1776, II.3.18). Mill interpreted it as equivalent to Say's law (ch. 4.2–3; for a criticism of this interpretation, see XIII.3.a). James Mill's son (*J.S. Mill* 1844) was later to come up with an even more extreme and indeed superficial version of Say's law.[15]

Contesting Malthus, *Ensor* (1818) compiled an impressive list of public expenditures, which – he wrote – are the very cause of poverty in England.[16] Colonel *Torrens* (1819) criticised Sismondi on the question of the gap between consumption and production (see Sismondi 1820–27, first article). Consumption capacity, Torrens stated, necessarily increases along with production capacity.

The anonymous author of *Inquiry* (1821) put forward a brilliant criticism of Malthus's underconsumption view. A growing investment – he writes – causes an increase in consumption (39–41ff). However, he also criticised Say's law (14–18). The anonymous author also notes that profits tend to drop because the increasing demand for labour raises wages, but accumulation does not slow down. Entrepreneurs simply adapt themselves to lower profits (28–31).

McCulloch (1824) was opposed to increasing public expenditures and invoked Say's law to demonstrate that general gluts are impossible (276b–77a). *McIniscon* (1825) attacked Malthus's argument, observing that one of the remedies to population growth is to diminish unproductive consumption and to use the wealth saved in productive works.[17] *Cardozo* (1826) criticised Malthus's call for unproductive consumption (14–15fn).

Ricardo appears scandalised by Malthus's idea that unproductive workers should absorb the surplus (R. 1820: 234). He commented:

> A body of unproductive labourers are just as necessary and as useful with a view to future production, as a fire, which should consume in the manufacturers warehouse the goods which those unproductive labourers would otherwise consume.[18]

He, too, invoked Say's law: "Mr. Malthus never appears to remember that to save is to spend" (R. 1820: 245); and:

> as I think that demand depends only on supply, the means of obtaining abundance of commodities can never I think be otherwise than beneficial.
>
> (198)

The debate between Malthus and Ricardo on this subject was particularly intense, argued in many letters exchanged between them.[19] In his *Principles,* Ricardo suggested an alternative solution: increase in population will absorb the surplus (R. 1821, 21.5). We have seen Malthus's weak answer to this (IX.2). According to *Paglin* (1961), Ricardo's solution can hold only in the long run (134–50). Moreover, we note that if accumulation proceeds due to increase in population, food resources will also need to steadily increase. And yet this implies that, according to Ricardo's theory, accumulation would be undermined by the diminishing returns on land.

The law of diminishing returns was first formulated by Sir Edward *West* (1815: 2) and endorsed by Malthus,[20] while Ricardo devised the best theorisation of it. The law was effectively challenged by the Rev. Richard *Jones* (1831), who maintained that increase in agricultural productivity overcame that tendency.[21]

Even then, however, the automatic connection between increase in social wealth and increase in population was not considered certain. Against Malthus's law of population, *Torrens* (1808) stressed that Ireland, although much poorer than England, was much more prolific (83–4, note B). In the end, Ricardo himself was not so sure that accumulation would absorb the increase of working population, as emerges from his chapter on machinery (R. 1821, ch. 31).

Say's law was also accepted by *Molinari* (1854), in his criticism of Sismondi (VI.1–2) and in the Dictionary of Léon Say.[22] On the other hand, the underconsumption approach was generally criticised.[23]

4. Late underconsumption theories

However, B.J. *Gordon* (1965) writes that in the 1840s, Say's law came in for a great number of "vigorous and not unintelligent criticisms" (445). Even De Quincey, a follower of Ricardo, was convinced of the danger of over-saving (443).

The denial of structural crises seemed to be contradicted by the constant tendency to overproduction. *Rodbertus* (1851) revived the issue. He started from the thesis – by then commonly accepted – that all commodities are entirely produced by labour. If it is true that there is no income which can be said not to derive from labour (70, 91), then the author's argument was as simple as it was logically strong. The division of labour and technical advance progressively increase productivity. Social wealth grows accordingly, but wages do not follow the growth. The reason is that wages are determined by the relationship between entrepreneurs and workers, in which the latter are the weaker part. Thus, as social wealth increases, wages dwindle, representing an ever-smaller proportion of this wealth.[24]

Rodbertus goes on to contest Say's and Bastiat's argument. These authors maintained that the purchasing power of individuals is determined by their respective contribution to production. Thus, their purchasing power is given by the respective share in relation to the total product (121, 127–31). In conclusion, the growth of productivity, instead of providing prosperity for all, increases gluts and so extends pauperism (131–2).

Rodbertus, who is said – with some reason – to have anticipated some of Marx's theses, remained isolated. In 1898, his tract was rediscovered and translated into English, with an Introduction by John Bates *Clark* (1898), who simply denied any validity to Rodbertus's underconsumption approach, in the name of Say's law. Crises, Clark wrote, cannot be general or permanent; they are due to a temporary lack of equilibrium between supply and demand in some sector.

But in the meantime, most authors had become aware of the tendency of capitalist accumulation to overproduction (see also ch. XIII). Some of these authors interpreted this along underconsumptionist lines. *Lalor* (1852) noted that there is a tendency to create an excess of saving. Thus, not all saving becomes investment. The excess depresses demand and generates gluts in the market (III: 30–4). *Barnes* (1859) wrote that, when the labour market is overstocked, the idle poor should have maintenance in exchange for some work of use for society (172–8). *Nicholson* (1893–1901) stated that overproduction can occur because of the imperfect mobility of labour and capital.[25]

Much later, Charles *Gide* (1931) effectively revived Sismondi's arguments on the close connection between technical progress, unemployment and lack of demand. He was sceptical about the validity of Say's law (121–3) and added that overproduction is clearly due to the frantic progress of industry. It seems inevitable – he prophetically wrote – that this frenetic race will drive us to ruin. Sooner or later these masses of products that flood the market will outdo our capacity for consumption and will no longer be absorbed (127).

Gide thought that overcapitalisation is due to the necessity for big enterprises to foresee future needs and to anticipate investments. This leads to periodical waves in the quantities of products supplied on the markets (129–30). These last observations, however, seem come midway between the underconsumption view and the business cycle approach.

5. Hobson's imaginary underconsumption

Hobson can be taken as an exemplary case of the confusion that the concept of underconsumption can generate if left too vague. Contrary to the general opinion (see e.g. *Richmond* 1978), Hobson can hardly be defined underconsumptionist, at least in the sense we have attributed to this word (see the above *Background*).

Certainly, Hobson was very concerned with excessive saving. *Hobson and Mummery* (1889) stated, in contrast with J.S. Mill, that saving cannot grow indefinitely (ch. 2: 37–55), although they specified that it can in any case be absorbed, provided that there is "a corresponding increase in immediately future consumption" (37).

Hobson's book on machinery (H. 1894) presents the author's overall view. Machinery is "the chief material factor in the evolution of capitalism" (ch. 2.3: 27). It causes overproduction and depression (ch. XI). Saving tends to be excessive (ch. 9.8–9). This fact shows that, in this case, individuals' interests clash with those of society (ch. 11.13). Thus, machinery appears as the cause of the industrial disease, but the real responsibility – Hobson wrote – does not lie in machinery itself, but in consumption. "The root-evil of depressed trade is underconsumption" (288). Hobson criticised Say's law, which denied the possibility of a general oversupply (288–9).

Nevertheless, Hobson's main concern was not excessive saving as such; it was the possible – but by no means unavoidable – weakness of consumption. He notes that, if consumption increases – due to either population growth or the increase of immaterial consumption, machinery does not diminish the demand for labour (ch. 12). Thus, great efforts should be made to boost consumption. The stored-up wealth of the rich should be used to increase wages, for high wages *foster* production (ch. 14.9). This remedy differs from the one proposed by Sismondi (checking production through increase in wages) and is in direct contrast with Malthus's (increasing unproductive consumption).

At this point, Hobson cogently outlined a prospect of growth based on both technical progress and increase in consumption, the latter being based on immaterial goods and their infinite variety (see also XIII.3.b). Improved quality of consumption, he says, is the only guarantee of social progress (ch. 17.13). While machines satisfy routine and standard wants, art satisfies original and personal wants (17.14). Social progress, he added, depends upon the substitution of quantitative methods of consumption with qualitative methods. The latter can transcend the law of diminishing returns (17.15–17).

Moreover, in *Imperialism* (1902), in contrast with *Bleaney*'s observations (B. 1976: 163–7), Hobson not only denied that export is the necessary outlet of the surplus, but forcibly stated the opposite view. In the key chapter (I.II), he first wrote that external commerce involves but a small fraction of national production and then went on repeatedly to stress that the nation has the power to absorb internally any quantity of goods produced (31–3):

> The assumption that home demand is a fixed amount, and that any commodities produced in excess of this amount must find a foreign market or remain unsold, is quite unwarranted. On the contrary, there is no necessary limit to the quantity of capital and labour which can be employed in producing goods for the home market, if the productive power is disposed in industries which meet the rising demands of the consumer.
>
> (32)

Here Hobson even echoes Say's law:

> Whatever quantity of wealth is produced in this country can be bought and consumed in this country, because with everything that is produced a corresponding power to purchase and consume is created.
>
> (32)

And he continues along this line of thought. Thus, if we take Hobson to be an underconsumptionist, it would be all the more reason to include in this category Marx and the other authors concerned with the capitalist tendency to overproduction. And we should also include Keynes and any author who is simply concerned with excess saving.

As a matter of fact, Keynes himself created this misleading view. He cited several 17th–19th-century authors, Malthus and Hobson included, as alleged precursors of his own approach (*Keynes* 1936, ch. 23.VII). Actually, Keynes confuses very different things: the criticism of hoarding by mercantilists like Laffemas, Barbon and Mandeville; the diffidence towards excessive saving shown by many 19th-century authors like Hobson; and finally, the underconsumption view of Malthus and others (see the comment by Watarai, IX.2). These attitudes must be kept separate if we want to understand which elements of the crises the different authors have sought to address.

Actually, among the authors mentioned by Keynes on this issue, Hobson comes closest to him, both being confident that crisis can be overcome through increased consumption. But there is an important difference: Hobson – like Say and Ricardo (see XIII.3.b) – envisioned an alluring prospect of development based on the increasing variation and refinement of goods, while Keynes cherished no such vision.

Conclusions

Classical underconsumption theories implied the conviction that productive consumption cannot grow beyond a certain fixed level. They took to an extreme the classical assumptions that wages are steadily at the subsistence level, and luxury goods, in the sense of goods beyond the necessary, are excluded from productive consumption and accumulation. The majority of classical authors opposed these theories but, as it turned out, were unable to answer the question they raised: where can the growing surplus be employed productively?

Notes

1 Sismondi (1819, 1, I.7: 51, II.4: 90).
2 Ibid., 1, IV.4: 367–8.
3 Ibid., 1, II.3: 78–80. See also Sismondi (1820–27: 396–7).
4 Sismondi (1819, 1, II.3: 75–6. See also —1820–27: 401–2).
5 Sismondi (1819, 2, VII.7–9: 312–68).
6 Ibid., 1, II.3: 77–8.
7 Malthus (1820, I.4.2: 223–31; II.1.2: 311–4; II.1.3: 318–20).
8 Ibid., II.1.3: 314–5; see also: 319–20, 326.
9 Ibid., II.1.5: 360; II.1.9: 398.
10 Ibid., II.1.9: 401–5. See also Paglin (1961: 117); Watarai (2015: 45–6).
11 For both observations, see Ricardo [1951–73, vol. II, respectively: 424 and 288fn].
12 Watarai (2015: 5–7, 27, 56–62; 64, 66). See also Graziani (1980: XLIII–XLIV); Costabile (1980: 123–4). On the influence of physiocracy on Malthus, see Maccabelli (1997: 125–35).
13 J.B. Say (1803, I, XV: 87–8. —1820, 1st letter. —1828–29, III.2: 341–2).
14 Say (1828–29, I: 345; and VII.4; II: 210).
15 J.S. Mill (1844: II.2–5, II.77, passim).
16 Ensor (1818, III.7, 441–87).
17 McCulloch (1824, II: 337, 429).

18 See Ricardo [1951–73, II, fn 284].
19 See at least letters 442–4 in Ricardo [1951–73], vol. IX.
20 See Cannan (1893: 157–61).
21 Jones (1831, VII.2–3: 178–229).
22 See Liesse (1891: 665b–70b).
23 See e.g. Banfield (1845, lecture 1.13: 15); Jevons (1871, V.52–53).
24 Rodbertus (1851: 70–1, 103–8, 123–5, 137).
25 Nicholson (1893–1901, vol. 2, b. III.X: 85–7).

X Technical progress

Background

Technical progress consists in the gradual substitution of labour with natural power processed by men (machines, chemical or biological processes, wind or water energy, heat, etc.). It is pursued to bring down the production costs and raise productivity and profits. Its immediate effect is usually an increase in unemployment and consequent drop in wages. But this is not a permanent effect, because the increase in profits allows for more investments, and so creates new employment.

Industrial technical progress tends to polarise labour. Mass labour becomes increasingly elementary due to more intensive parcelling (technical division of labour), while a relatively small part of the labour force becomes increasingly skilled. Since the times of antiquity, various authors have envisaged man's liberation from the toil thanks to technical progress. In actual fact, the industrial economy saw such liberation granted only to a minority. Finally, thanks to the increase in productivity brought about by technical progress, some workers have been able to turn to more sophisticated types of production. New sectors are born, and our comforts increase. The classical debate on this issue makes particularly interesting reading because, while analysing 19th-century realities, it anticipates most of the main issues of the present economic crisis.

1. Increase of unemployment

In a celebrated passage, *Aristotle* wrote:

> if every tool could perform its own work when ordered, or by seeing what to do in advance, … if thus shuttles wove and quills played harps of themselves, master-craftsmen would have no need of slaves.[1]

In just one sentence, Aristotle brilliantly hit upon the three basic effects of the use of machines: first, it makes some labour redundant; second, it frees men from toil; third, it makes our life more comfortable. Aristotle's aim was to prove that slavery was necessary to secure citizens' freedom and participation in public life. Fortunately, in modern times machines have replaced slaves in freeing humans from toil and enhancing their comforts.

In 1867 *Marx* quoted Aristotle's passage but he also quoted Antipatrus, the Greek poet of Cicero's time, who – on the contrary – extolled the liberation of slaves and the new golden age due to the invention of the water mill. However, Marx noted, as modern economists do not realise, "machinery is the surest means of lengthening the working day".[2] This is another consequence of technical progress, due to the social relationship that governs labour in the capitalist economy. While machinery makes life easier for one part of society, it worsens the life of workers and increases social inequalities. Aptly, *Lowe* (1954) wrote of modern technology in Marx as a "Janus-faced phenomenon" (120).

Later on, *Cournot* (1877) observed that the ideal of the old philosophers was liberation from the toil of material labour. If machines could replace all human labour, Cournot said, we could reasonably look forward to society being much better off (VI.2: 293–6). He recognised the social damage provoked by technical progress but proposed a sort of Pareto optimality: all that saves the toil of some, without diminishing the quantity and quality of production, will benefit some without harming anyone (299). Cournot's forecast has been partly disproved. In fact, it totally neglects the short-run negative consequences of machinery on employment. Nowadays such consequences have invaded the long run: technical progress proceeds at such a rate that unemployment tends to become permanent and, indeed, to go on increasing (see XX.3).

The early classical authors underestimated the impact of investment in machinery on accumulation. *Lauderdale* (1804) – who was anxious to show that value derives not from labour but from utility – maintained that the increase in profits, consequent to investments in machinery, does not imply an increase in labour productivity, as Smith maintained. On the contrary, he stated, it is due to the fact that new machinery replaces a part of labour. On Smith's argument, he writes: "The same process of reasoning would lead a man to describe the effect of shortening a circuitous road between any two given places from ten miles to five miles *as doubling the velocity of the walker*" (185fn). Of course, this is a sophism: producing the same product with less labour clearly means increasing labour productivity.

We have seen (IX.2) that, to counteract increasing unemployment and poverty among the workers, *Sismondi* advocated holding technical progress back and raising wages. *Ricardo* tried to bring technical progress into the analysis of accumulation, but his attempt was weak and uncertain. In the first two editions of the *Principles*, he criticised Luddism because it did not consider that technical progress benefits the workers; it increases profits, and so investments, thus boosting employment (for a similar argument, see *Carrion-Nisas* 1825, 13: 34–5).

In the third edition, however, Ricardo (1821) changed his mind and admitted that technical progress can harm the workers, at least temporarily (ch. 31. – See also *Berg* 1980: 43–74). Ricardo's reasoning runs: an increase in profits and rent, consequent to the increase in productivity, especially in sudden technical changes, can raise net produce, while gross produce shows a relative fall. This can cause the redundancy of some workers, since a part of the previous wage fund can be destined to unproductive (personal) consumption rather than investment. However – Ricardo added, in order to sugar the pill – the more the rich consume in menial servants rather than luxuries, the more workers will be employed in new occupations (31.18–22). *St. Clair* (1957) took Ricardo's arguments to the extreme and ended up by distorting them (chs. 11–13). *Davis* (1989) demonstrated that Ricardo's new line abolishes the social harmony (theorised in the previous editions) that free trade and technical progress should grant.

Ricardo's conclusion is curious. Here he does not seem to share Smith's aversion to menial servants and unproductive consumption in general. Moreover, Ricardo overlooked the fact that also the production of luxuries creates work and that this work even proves productive if its products are sold. In any case, *McCulloch* and *Torrens*, who had shared Ricardo's criticism of Luddism,[3] rejected his new approach.[4] Torrens and *Senior* stressed the positive effects of technical progress on labour. By contrast, *Cayley* (1830), although fascinated by the potentiality of machines, was seriously worried about the decline in labour demand that they caused.[5]

Ricardo's change of mind was consequent to the objection, raised by *Barton* (1817), that employment only grows when investment is devoted to increasing the number of wage-earners. If, on the other hand, investment goes into more machinery, employment will not grow. Barton added that capitalists turn to investment in machines not only when wages happen to be growing (which was an exception), but normally the greater part of investments are made in new machines.[6] Barton's idea was that accumulation normally comes about through technical progress and not through increase in the number of workers. However, his new approach remained unnoticed for 50 years. It was only appreciated by *Marx*.[7]

Schumpeter [1949], while writing on the classical approach, noted: "Replacement of workers by machinery was, of course, not overlooked. But it was treated, except by Marx, as a special case".[8] This neglect caused great difficulties for the classical theory of accumulation. It was also due to the tenacious resistance, both social and intellectual, to the use of machinery in production, well described by *Berg* (1980: 253–314). This opposition, Berg wrote, even extended to Engels and J.S. Mill, who showed a certain distrust (315–42).

Barton [1954] also stands out for his praise of middle-class culture, which is modern and positive, as opposed to that of the aristocracy, which is poor and rhetorical. Enrichment of the middle classes, he wrote, expands social wealth (question 7, 33–7).

A syncretic and insightful view was provided by *Cayley* (1830, above all: 23–57). He rightly observed that the "present race of machinery" was probably fuelled by the first to bring it in, who made enormous profits. This tendency caused a permanent excess of investment and production overconsumption, consequently leading to gluts on the market. While, on the one hand, machinery makes labour increasingly redundant, on the other hand, the excess of supply over demand lowers profits. Nevertheless, declining profits drive entrepreneurs to go on producing an excess supply, despite the gluts, as a remedy to the scant gains per unit of product. Cayley explains: "machinery seems to contain within itself the seminal principle, as it were, of an endless supply of glutted market" (44). All this leads to periodical destruction of physical capital.

This acute analysis perfectly fits the present phenomenon of repetitive goods (see XX.4.a). In Aristotelian (or Sismondian) tones, Cayley concluded: "an insatiable thirst for riches, as the principal good, has supervened contentment with a sufficiency" (45).

Louis Rousseau (1840), in turn, denounced the unemployment and poverty caused by the new machinery. It is true, he said, that machines will eventually free man from oppressive work, but people often speak as if this liberation is happening now. We cannot reject technical progress, but we should be equipped to counter the evil it is causing at present at the social level (20–1, 85–6). By contrast, *Ure* (1835) was a staunch defender of technical progress. Machines, he stated, do actually free workers from the extremely hard toil and from insecurity, which dominated the working conditions of artisans in the pre-industrial period. Instead of attacking entrepreneurs, workers should be grateful to them for technical progress.[9] Finally, *Peshine Smith* (1868), while acknowledging the negative effects of technical progress, believed that it would ultimately prove beneficial to all (V: 137–8).

2. Increase in comfort

The concept of comfort escaped the rigid dualism of the classical distinction between wage goods and luxury goods. Thus, it allowed for a level of analysis closer to reality. Some authors welcomed the increase in comfort,[10] and some associated it with technical progress.

Before publishing his devastating criticism of Ricardo's labour theory of value,[11] *Bailey* (1823) devoted some pages to the question of whether the excessive use of machinery in production might lead to a permanent unemployment (7: 33–7). He recalled James Steuart who had written – in a chapter on the subject – that if innovations which abridge labour are *abruptly* introduced it may have negative effects. But the latter will be temporary, while the advantage of providing new comforts is permanent.

Unlike Sismondi, *Malthus* (1820) acclaimed technical progress and welcomed its main consequence, namely making commodities increasingly cheap (see also *Bonar* 1885: 296). However, he wrote, if technical progress arrives at the point of producing an excess of goods, it lowers profits. In principle, as Smith stated,[12] the increase in machines has no limits, given that comforts have no definite limits; but – Malthus wrote – there are limits to saving and investment.[13]

In defence of employment, *Cazaux* (1826), like Sismondi, was opposed to the uncontrolled introduction of new machines, but his view was less naive. Comfort, said Cazaux, must be encouraged also by introducing new machines, which increase productivity. The production of comfort products not only spreads welfare, but also creates employment. On the contrary, if new machines are applied to the production of luxury items, which are useless for production, we merely spread unemployment without any advantage for welfare. However, there must be a limit to the spread of machinery replacing labour. Otherwise, in the long run we will have all we desire, but unemployment will be rife. This would be disastrous because men need to have jobs if they are to escape degradation (3: 112–8).

Cazaux's book was sarcastically criticised by Charles *Comte* (1827), the founder of modern sociology. On machines, Comte came up with somewhat facile criticism of the enemies of technical progress: I never saw, he wrote, an author who criticises the pen with which he writes his thesis nor the various instruments needed to build the pen, or the printed book, or the plough, etc. (6–8). However, Cazaux's reasoning was not so simplistic, as his answer to Comte confirms (ibid, 51–5).

Also interesting is *Flórez Estrada* (1828). He defended the introduction of machines, maintaining – like Ricardo – that the unemployment they cause will be offset by the new occupations. The latter are spawned by the surplus that the increase in productivity generates (IX: 163–5). Without means of production, he added, a society would be poor, and its occupations would be even fewer (168). Above all, Flórez noted that the increase in productivity through new machines is no different from that obtained through advance in the labourers' skills and education. Both save labour, and both are advantageous to the entire economy (161–2). However, Flórez's arguments against the underconsumption view (169–77) remain somewhat weak.

3. The productive function of "luxury" goods

During the Enlightenment, most economists saw high wages and comfort for the productive classes – workers included – as a form of investment. High consumption on the part of these classes, they deemed, raises productivity thanks to the skills acquired. However, during the industrial revolution, mechanisation made mass labour elementary, and productivity no longer depended on high wages. Thus, in classical economics, the view on high quality consumption (luxury goods) became tautological: luxury goods are non-wage goods, for by definition they cannot be part of workers' productive consumption and cannot enter into the accumulation process. This approach led to a standstill, which made it impossible to take a long-term view of wage dynamics. Consequently, classical theories ended up envisaging a falling rate of profit and stationary state.

Some authors, like *Valeriani*,[14] criticised the increase in comforts, while others expressed more balanced views, opposed to excess, especially in public spending.[15] *Blanc de Volx* (1803) stated that wealth and luxury are both generated by industriousness. Luxury is the necessary spring for the development of a great nation. However, the "luxury" of the workers damages the economy and must therefore be held in check.[16]

Many authors escaped the classical dualism, but their voices remained unheard. Some, like the authors of the Enlightenment, were favourable to increased consumption by the productive classes and took keen interest in technical progress and in boosting productivity. *Boileau* (1811) acutely observed that the term luxury changes meaning in different times and places, according to the level of civilisation. It is a comparative term, because what was luxury yesterday becomes necessity today. However, marked ostentatious luxury is always damaging. Its defenders maintain that it creates employment, but, if that wealth were employed more rationally, much more employment would be created. On the other hand, when luxury is the effect of general prosperity and its production is limited, it stimulates industry. Not poverty, but the fear of poverty is an incentive to labour.[17]

Destutt de Tracy (1817) provided one of the most insightful analyses against the unproductive luxury of the rich. He contrasted the laboriousness of industry and the selfish ineptitude of the landed nobility (165–94). It is not true, he said, that consumption as such is wealth. The defenders of luxury think that it is a source of prosperity, but actually it is only the result of it. Luxury destroys most of the national means for prosperity (182–4). If it is a great evil economically, it is an even greater one on the moral level (193). On Destutt see also V.3.

Cagnazzi (1820) observed that excessive luxury can create disproportion among the different types of manufacture (60). The Brazilian *Silva Lisboa* (1819–20) extolled inventions and research; they make labour much easier and increase productivity and the abundance of goods enormously.[18] Above all, they create artificial (i.e. unnecessary) goods, without which we would have no civilisation.[19]

McCulloch (1824), too, contested the idea that luxury production is unproductive. There is no clear-cut division between necessaries and luxuries, he said. Luxury demand fosters production (273a–74a). He also – somewhat oddly – stated that, if it is true that people can ruin themselves through luxuries, they can also do so through excessive consumption of necessaries.[20] Moreover, on the one hand, he denied that demand as such encourages production while, on the other, he cited Montesquieu and revived the old stereotype (which was already inappropriate at Montesquieu's time) that the consumption of the rich gives work to the poor (276a–77b).

In his *Principles*, McCulloch (1825) criticised Smith's thesis on the unproductive consumption of service labourers and added – like Barbon and Mandeville – that expenditures which are dangerous for an individual can be beneficial for society. However – he admitted – it is dangerous to think that any unproductive consumption should be encouraged because it increases demand for labour. On Montesquieu's position, McCulloch had, by then, some doubts, because – he explained – demand for labour cannot increase significantly without an increase of capital (501–12).

Sanfilippo (1828) condemned ostentatious and frivolous luxury but defended the "unproductive consumption" that aims at comfort (II: 14–16). *Sedgwick* (1836–39) criticised the frivolous goods imposed by fashions and attacked the rich who spend enormous sums on luxuries.[21] *Fuoco* (1825–27) provided an original definition of luxury: it does not depend on the kind of consumption, but on its quantity in proportion to the revenue. Luxury is consumption beyond one's economic possibilities.[22] The vice of luxury is not moral, it is economic. Thus, the remedy does not consist in reducing consumption, but in increasing the productive forces of industry (200–1). Fuoco also observed insightfully that needs do not come before the productive forces but follow them. They emerge thanks to the development of society, which is "coordinated" with the development of industrial forces (197–8). Many authors showed similar approaches – see e.g. *Burton* (1849, 3: 44) – but Fuoco is one of the clearest on this point.

John *Rae* (1834), too, took a dynamic view of luxuries and their relationship with accumulation, although with some contradictions. His view is very close to that of certain Enlightenment authors like Genovesi and the Scottish economists. On the one hand, he censured luxuries and the labour spent on them, as a waste for society (245–76), while, on the other, he saw them as the result of inventions, which progressively increase productivity (132–203). Vanity encourages new inventions and gradually transforms luxuries into necessities (274–5). The wealth of nations, he concluded, is due to inventions (377). Rae's approach is precisely what, in general, the classical authors lack: to formulate a credible view of accumulation in the long run. The classical authors do not usually deny the gradual transformation of luxuries into necessaries, but in actual fact they forget this process, because it contradicts the postulate of wages at subsistence level.

Jobard (1844) wrote a bizarre, lengthy book completely devoted to exalting inventions. Inventors – whom he calls intellectual proletarians – must have the monopoly of their own inventions, against the pretensions of free competition, in order to support development and civilisation (29–32, passim). *Hearn* (1864), too, treated inventions as the driving force of accumulation and civilisation (ch. 4 and 10). He has been accused, with some reason, of having plagiarised Rae (see *Wakatabe* 2001). Charles *Gide* (1883) defined luxury as enjoyments useless for our improvement. The only problem of luxury lies in temperate use of it.[23]

Leroy-Beaulieu (1895) – like others (see XIII.3.b) – wrote of the differentiation of consumption that grows along with the progress of civilisation.[24] Suppressing luxury, he said, would mean suppressing production itself and even the good quality of necessaries. Moderate luxury is the driving force of development; it increases men's productivity (275–84). Leroy insisted that suppressing luxury would lead to a situation of passivity and scarcity, similar to that which would be produced by equality of conditions among all people (293ff). About *Hobson* (1894), see IX.5.

4. Poverty and reform projects

The classical period saw keen debate on how to tackle poverty. The Rev. *Palmer* (1828) maintained that no intervention whatsoever should be made for poor relief or against unemployment, whilst Joseph *Wood* (1832) argued the opposite thesis. Many authors denounced the negative social effects of technical progress. *Senior* (1827) echoed *Defoe* and *Smith*, who maintained that no society can be flourishing and happy if most of the people are poor and miserable.[25] However, he distorted the significance of these fine sentiments. He wrote that a country can be said to be rich only if the workers are provided with the necessaries and "some conveniences of life" and added: England is now rich. Note that he was writing in the 1820s, when conditions for British workers were at their worst.

At the time, the postulate of wages at subsistence level favoured a callous attitude towards the extreme poverty of workers. Bob *Coats* (1967) noted that the classical authors were moved by good intentions towards the labourers and were convinced that individual economic freedom would help them. Of course, Coats added, it was not so, and this facile attitude hid their ignorance of the real situation (177–8).

On the basis of Say's law, *Torrens* (1819) attacked Owen, who had written that technical progress generates overproduction: "The supply of one set of commodities – Torrens explained – constitutes the demand for another" (74). However, *Owen* (1818) did not take an underconsumption view. On the contrary, he had a powerful and positive vision of the future increase in production and wealth (I: 1–15). Owen was also greatly in favour of technical progress and its effect, namely increase of cheaper goods (15). He wrote that England should share its productive knowledge with the other countries, instead of competing with them and making its own workers poor (14). He, however, denounced the enormous inequality of incomes (23). In a previous work, Owen (1815) had expressed appreciation of the enormous enrichment of society due to manufactures but had also complained that no provision was made against the negative social consequences of this progress.

Among the reformers and utopians of the period, it is worth mentioning *Billesby* (1826). He followed Owen but, unlike him, was opposed to machines and any progress in production, because they increased unemployment. He stated:

> Every increase in the *power* of production — under the present systems, actually lessens the *quantity* produced in proportion to the amount of population; and instead of decreasing the number of the needy and their privations, greatly add to both.
>
> (87)

A contrasting view can be found in *Saint-Simon*, the apostle of industrial progress. His polemical target was still the nobility and its parasitism. He stated that the workers (practically all of them: "les industriels") produce all wealth. They are the last in society but should be the first (S. 1824: 1–13). See also his adopted son, *Thierry* (1817: 65, 78). Saint-Simon (1821) called upon the king, Parliament and entrepreneurs to complete the French revolution through industrial development. *Blanqui* (1837–38) wrote that, in the periodical *Producteur*, the Saint-Simonians stressed the importance of the "new trinity" of the religion of love and labour, e.g. intellectuals, industrial entrepreneurs and artists. These authors demanded that social ranks be organised according to productive merits (243–57).

Among the Saint-Simonians, it is worth mentioning père *Enfantin* (1831), who called for a social hierarchy based on merits, abilities and produce (52), and contrasted labourers with the idle (articles VI, VII, IX). See also Fontcuberta, alias *Covert-Spring* (1828–36), edited by *Sánchez Hormigo* (1999). The latter also contains a long essay on Saint-Simonism by the editor.

Another Saint-Simonian is Michel *Chevalier* (1842). This author was committed to free trade and shared his master's enthusiasm over the extension of industrial production and increase in productivity. Both things were necessary to enhance welfare for all (80–124). Increase in productivity is driven by three factors: transport, credit institutions and professional training (VII: 192). See also Chevalier (1844: 5–6). But while he analyses the empirical aspects of the first two factors at length, we find no comment on the third one. On this, see the detailed analysis by Sánchez Hormigo (1999).

Among the utopians of the period is *Fourier* (1808), who severely attacked commerce. Trade has become a source of cheating, corruption, greed and brigandage, due to free competition (311–20). The latter has also caused an excess of commercial and financial agents (352–3) and deconstruction of professions (321–63). It drives lawyers to prostitute themselves with advertising (364–5). Commerce is the natural enemy of manufacture, and public opinion rightly sees merchants as thieves (367). *Roscher* (1854) wrote that also the followers of Fourier attacked commerce and most of the personal services, which they considered unproductive (§ 62fn, 140). However, *Lechevalier* (1834), who followed Fourier, stated that commerce, although unproductive, is necessary (441–4). He also saw education, research and the arts as productive activities (448). Lechevalier rejected the division between the idle (the proprietors) and the producers (proletarians: 438).

Denunciations of extreme poverty and the terrible living conditions of workers were frequent in this period. One of the most noticeable analysers of poverty of the mid-19th century, *Buret* (1840), made a vigorous denunciation of the state of the poor in England and France. He rejected the economists' principle of wages being determined by competition alone (I: 30–2) and praised Sismondi, Saint Simon and Fourier for criticising capitalism (25–9). For an overview of the thought of Owen, Saint Simon and Fourier, see *Paget* (1838). On the poverty related to technical progress in classical thought, see *Coats* (1972).

Finally, *Proudhon* (1846) recalled Sismondi and severely criticised the introduction of machinery in production. Technical progress, he said, degrades material labour, exacerbates the workers' poverty and worsens labour conditions. On the one hand, it creates a great many dependent workers for services, that is serfs, while on the other it creates "scribblers and pen pushers" (IV.2: 160–5).

Conclusions

The classical economists were perfectly aware of the causes and effects of technical progress. However, they found it difficult to reconcile analysis of it with the two main postulates of their accumulation model: wages close to subsistence level and production essentially consisting of elementary goods. Eventually these postulates prevented classical economics from interpreting the new features of the accumulation process.

Notes

1 Aristotle (*Politics*, 1254a; I.II: 17).
2 Marx (*Capital I*, IV. XV.48).
3 See McCulloch (1821: 102–3).
4 See Torrens (1821: xi–xii).
5 Torrens (1834: 33–44). Senior (1836: 170–3). Cayley (1830, I: 17–18, 22–3).
6 Barton (1817: 40–5. See also —1814–17: 182–8). See also J. Hollander (1934: 3–5); Sotiroff (1962–63): xvi–xvii; St. Clair (1957: 226–32).
7 Marx, *Theories*, II, XVIII.B.2.
8 Schumpeter [1949], III.6.5.d: 642–4.
9 Ure (1835, I.1: 7–9; III.1: 279–80; passim).
10 E.g. Vitrolles (1801: 36–7). Schmalz (1808: 5–8, 17ff).
11 See Bailey (1825; —1826). Later, Ricardo's theory was brilliantly defended by De Quincey (1844).
12 See Smith (1776, I.11.59).
13 Malthus (1820: 401–2). See also J. Hollander (1928: xc); Kolb (1972).
14 E.g. in Valeriani (1825–27, I: 96–115).
15 Ressi (1817–19, IV: 556–65). Colmeiro (1859: 508–28).
16 Blanc de Volx (1803, I, V.2: 185–95).
17 Boileau (1811, IV.2: 355–60).
18 Silva Lisboa (1819–20, II, XXII: 238–9).
19 Ibid., III, XI: 46–50.
20 McCulloch (1824: 274a, 275a). See also —1825: 492–501.
21 Sedgwick (1836–39, I: 185–94, 233–6; II.V: 140–73; III.V: 94–111).
22 Fuoco (1825–27, II.6: 191–201).
23 Gide (1883, III.4: 398–402).
24 Leroy-Beaulieu (1895, IV: 244–8, 267–71).
25 Cp. Defoe (1728, I.1: 59–67). Smith (1776, I.8.35).

XI Marx's blind alley on unproductive labour[1]

Background

Unproductive labour is one of the weakest aspects of Marx's economics. As we have seen, the issue was raised in favour of development against all sorts of rent and unproductive consumption (from Petty to Smith). During the classical period, it gradually evolved its nature, until – with Marx – it ended up by excluding, from the development factors, the most important driving force of capitalist accumulation, i.e. investment in human capital in all its aspects (education, skill, science, cooperation, increase in the number of technicians, growth of the service sector in all branches of production).

Despite this failure, Marx's reflection on the subject led to some major advances, including the analyses of mechanisation, the collective labourer and the productive power of science. In the history of thought, Marx provided at least two definitive criticisms: that of Smith's confusion between material production and the production of surplus, and that of the confusion in many authors between exchange with capital and exchange with revenue. Finally, Marx was the first to analyse the productive/unproductive labour distinction in pre-physiocratic literature.[2]

1. Labour productive of surplus value

Marx stressed that productive labour in the general sense and in the capitalist sense are completely different. In the general sense, productive labour simply reproduces what the worker consumes. In the capitalist sense, productive labour is that which produces a surplus value, besides the value of the worker's consumption.[3]

"Labour itself – Marx explained – is productive only if absorbed into capital" (*Grundrisse*: 245–6). What matters is not the specific nature of labour or the final destination of its product, but only the relation with capital. For instance, he writes: "Production for unproductive consumption is quite as productive as that for productive consumption; always assuming that it produces or reproduces capital".[4] Thus, Marx shared Smith's basic principle: labour is productive when exchanged with capital, but unproductive when exchanged with revenue. Unlike Smith, however, by labour exchanged with capital he did not mean any labour activated by investment, but only the labour that *directly* produces surplus value.

On the other hand, Marx criticised Smith for his "second" definition of productive labour, according to which only the labour that adds value to some material object is productive. However – as we will see – Marx put the question in such a way that he ended up by accepting in practice Smith's limitation. All this led Marx to limit the extension of productive labour even more than Smith.[5] We can distinguish the activities Marx considered unproductive in the following categories:

Non-material activities functional to the production process:

(a) Activities which increase productivity through technical progress (scientific research, technology); (b) Non-material labour within the production process (direction and surveillance, assistance, organisation, bookkeeping, etc.); (c) Reproduction and productivity increase of labour-power (household activities, education and healthcare; to which we can add: comfort, culture, entertainment).

Distribution and commerce.

External services and infrastructures (professionals; public sector: services, administration, infrastructures).

Independent material activities (artisans, peasants, technicians of various kinds).

2. Criticism of Smith's twofold definition

Marx advanced the same criticism that Germain Garnier had made to Smith (see IV.4): Smith unwittingly proposed a twofold definition of productive labour. In the first, the right one, he defined productive the labour which "is directly exchanged with capital" (and so yields a profit), while labour directly exchanged with revenue (i.e. which yields a product for personal use) is unproductive. Thus, the same kind of labour can be productive or unproductive according as to whether it is exchanged with capital or with revenue. "Adam Smith here – Marx says – got to the very heart of the matter, hit the nail on the head".[6]

In the second definition – the wrong one – Smith defined as productive only the labour exerted on material objects, upon which it leaves durable modifications. Unproductive labour, on the other hand, is that whose product disappears at the end of the performance, like that of the musician or the menial servant. This definition, Marx objected, gives the concepts productive/unproductive a completely different meaning. He was probably right in saying that Smith was led to this "aberration" partly in order to argue against the physiocrats (i.e. their idea that manufacture is unproductive) and partly under their influence, i.e. their suggestion that only material labour produces value and can be productive. Marx gave many examples of services or intellectual labour that can also be exchanged with capital (Ibid.).

He also writes: "a schoolmaster is a productive labourer, when, in addition to belabouring the heads of his scholars, he works like a horse to enrich the school proprietor. That the latter has laid out his capital in a teaching factory, instead of in a sausage factory, does not alter the relation" (*Capital I*, V.XVI.3).[7] On the other hand, he says, artisan labour is usually exchanged with revenue, in which case it is unproductive.[8]

However, in the same pages, Marx excludes from the productive occupations a long series of activities that concern either the final consumption of workers, or the direction and organisation of production, or education and healthcare.[9] He also writes: "Every productive worker is a wage labourer; but this does not mean that every wage labourer is a productive worker".[10] Finally he adds that it is "a characteristic of productive labourers ... that their labour realises itself in commodities, in material wealth".[11] Contrary to common sense, Marx maintained that capitalist immaterial productions – whether expressed in commodities (like paintings and books) or in services (like private schools, theatres, etc.) – "are so insignificant compared with the totality of production that they can be left entirely out of account".[12]

Thus, Marx corrected Smith in principle but in practice accepted his view that only material labour is productive. *Napoleoni* (1985) commented: first Marx defined productive labour independently of the use value of the product, but then – as in the case of commerce – reintroduced use value as discriminant (66–7). For an insightful analysis of Marx on this issue, see *Gough* (1972). For detailed criticism, see *Ripepe* (1982: ch. 3).

3. Non-material activities functional to production

a. Research and technology

In the previous chapter, we saw that the growing mechanisation of the 19th century caused, on the one hand, mass elementary labour and, on the other, increase of skilled labour for a minor number of workers. The increase of skilled labour generated a growing middle class of technicians and experts. It also caused a change in investment, devoted more and more to the growth of human capital. An increasing part of the final consumption, and consequently of production, was then destined to training, education, comfort and culture.

Marx was well aware of this tendency. He often made mention of the best experts in machinery of his times, especially Babbage and Ure (e.g. in *Capital III*, I.V.67). He himself provided outstanding and detailed analyses of the historical development of machinery and the complex systems of machines coordinated by human labour. Besides, Marx often reflected on science and its influence in production.[13]

In sum, Marx was fully aware that the increase in productivity due to science and to application of it (technical progress) required a great amount of social labour. He also stressed that "science and technology give capital a power of expansion" (*Capital I*, VII.XXIV.57). Nevertheless, he ignored the fact that science and technology are the result of social investments and of social labour. What interested him was private capital. He declared: "Science, generally speaking, costs the capitalist nothing, a fact that by no means hinders him from exploiting it. The science of others is as much annexed by capital as the labour of others".[14] Here Marx reduces the process of development to the experience of individual capitalist.

b. Administration, assistance, organisation, bookkeeping, etc.

Marx noted that Smith includes among the productive labourers "not only the labourer working directly with his hands or a machine, but overlooker, engineer, manager, clerk, etc. [...] whose joint labour (co-operation) is required for commodity production". However, he did not agree with Smith on this point, because these intellectual activities "add their aggregate labour to the constant capital, and increase the value of the product by this amount".[15] Here Marx contradicts his own insightful analyses of the social division of labour and cooperation in production, both external and internal to the production process.[16]

c. Reproduction of the labour-power

The reproduction of labour-power can be divided into two types of activities. One is household labour, for the everyday life, while the other concerns activities that increase workers' productivity: education, healthcare (but we may also add training, comforts, culture, entertainment). According to Marx, these activities – which are bound to either maintain or improve labour-power – are not part of investment and are unproductive. He writes that labour going into everyday life, like cooking, washing, cleaning, etc., is carried out by the working class itself, then costs nothing.[17]

As to education and healthcare, they are just – Marx very often repeats – "*faux frais de production*", i.e. necessary unproductive expenses that add to the cost of production (*Theories*, I, IV.4, 310). Marx tries to bypass this inconsistency by saying that education accounts for a very little part of the production cost of labour-power. Moreover, he maintains that education and the dissemination of knowledge, far from increasing the value of the labour-power, bring wages down because they enable workers to spend less on their purchases (*Capital III*, IV.XVII.53).

Actually, it is precisely the contrary, for education increases the workers' market value. Marx even quoted Petty and J.S. Mill where they asserted the productive nature of learning (*Theories*, I, IV.6.b–c). But he did not change his mind. Smith, he wrote, excludes from productive labour the labour that "produces, trains, develops, maintains or reproduces labour-power". Smith did it "arbitrarily, but with a certain correct instinct—that if he included it, this would open the flood-gates for false pretensions to the title of productive labour" (*Theories*, I, IV.4, 313).

4. Distribution and commerce

Marx drastically ruled out that any of the activities devoted to exchange and circulation of commodities could be productive. Probably influenced by Quesnay – and unlike Smith – he reduced commerce to exchange. The latter must always take place between equal values. He stated that purchase and sale, bookkeeping and transference of money are necessary but unproductive activities (*Capital II*, I.VI.1), however large the scale may be (I.VI.4). Moreover, the independent activities that arise in this field are also unproductive (I.VI.5).

He adds that a man who sells his labour in this sector "works as well as any other man, but intrinsically his labor creates neither products nor values". He belongs to the *faux frais* of production:

> "His services do not transform an unproductive function into a productive one, nor unproductive into productive labor" (I.VI.6). And: "This advance of capital creates neither products nor values. It reduces to that extent the volume of the productive function of capital. It is as though one part of the product were transformed into a machine, which buys or sells the rest of the product. This machine [...] does not participate in the productive process, although it can reduce the labor-power re- quired for the circulation. It constitutes simply a part of the expenses of circulation". (I.VI.7)

The same holds for bookkeeping: "The division of labor, the assuming of independence, does not make a function productive, if it was not so before it became independent". Bookkeeping is a part of capital withdrawn from production (I.VI.10).

Marx made an exception for the activities performed within the circulation process that either maintain the value of the commodities, by impeding their deterioration, like storage, or increase their value, like transportation and packaging (I.VI.2–3). These activities "arise from processes of production, which are continued only in circulation" (I.VI.14). However, while transport of commodities adds value to them, transport of men is a simple service and is therefore unproductive.[18] Again, Marx concedes that some storage activities provide a profit to the entrepreneur; however, they are an unproductive – although necessary – cost for society (*Capital II*, I.VI.14–41).

The same view appears in *Capital III*, where Marx again addresses the issue of the productiveness of commercial capital and labour (chs. 16–18). The problem faced by Marx is how the great realm of distribution and commerce can have its own investments, wage labour and profits without being productive and how it can work thanks only to deductions of a part of surplus value (which is generated in the production sector). In Marx's words: "in the case of merchant's capital we are dealing with a capital which shares in the profit without participating in its production". But he also says: "The merchant's capital, then, plays a determining role in the formation of the average rate of profit in proportion to its pro rata magnitude in the total capital".[19]

Here Marx's analysis appears particularly toilsome. His basic view is that the less developed production is, the greater is the commercial capital, and vice versa (IV.XVI.31). However, this was true in the age of the birth and growth of the modern economy (to which Marx devotes ch. 20). But in the industrial period the contrary holds: the increasing complexity of the economy requires greater investment in the distribution activities.

Marx acknowledged that merchants' capital can "indirectly" contribute in various ways to increasing the production of surplus value (IV.XVI.35). But this can hardly be reconciled with his idea that only the direct production of surplus value is productive. This difficulty appears in Marx's tortuous reasoning:

> "Just as the industrial capital makes profits by selling labor embodied and realised in commodities for which it has not paid any equivalent, so the merchants' capital makes profits by not paying the productive capital for all the unpaid labor incorpo-rated in the commodities…, while in selling it demands payment for this unpaid por- tion still contained in the commodities and not paid for by itself". And soon after: "The unpaid labor of his [the merchant's] clerks, while it does not create any surplus-value, at least appropriates surplus-value for him".
>
> (IV.XVII.32–33)

The conclusion appears rather acrobatic:

> "For the industrial capital, the expenses of circulation appear as dead expenses, and so they are. For the merchant they appear as a source of his profit, which is proportional to the level of the average rate of profit, whose existence is assumed. The investment to be made by the mercantile capital for these expenses of circulation is, therefore, a productive investment. And for this reason the commercial labor which it buys is likewise immediately productive for it" (IV.XVII.56). On the other hand: "The increase of this [commercial] labor is always a result, never a cause of the augmentation of surplus-value".
>
> (IV.XVII.53)

In contrast with Marx, *Bortkievicz* (1906–1907) maintained that commerce is productive (104).

5. Professionals; menial servants; public sector

The unproductiveness of services is the main subject treated by Marx in the *Theories*. In ch. IV, he commented on a long series of authors who essentially criticised Smith's view on this issue. The general view held by Marx is that the bourgeoisie first "adopted a severely critical attitude to the machinery of the State, etc.". But later it realised that an alliance was necessary with the "higher grade" unproductive classes, even the most parasitic, in order to keep its hegemony (*Theories*, I, IV.5). He adds:

> All those who polemise against Adam Smith on the one hand assume a superior attitude to material production, and on the other hand they attempt to justify immaterial production—or even no production, like that of lackeys—as material production.
>
> (IV.8, 364)

Answering to the critics of Smith, Marx stressed that their confusion between labour paid with capital and labour paid with revenue results in social capital coinciding with the sum of revenues. Consequently, the existence of constant capital is neglected (however, Marx – as it is well known – ascribed the neglect of constant capital not only to these critics but to Smith himself).[20] The confusion between capital and revenues drives these authors to conclude that all labours are productive insofar as they produce something useful. Consequently, they reject Smith's distinction. Marx, in his defence of Smith's distinction, even defended Smith's view that only material labour is productive. Actually, Marx was convinced that the only productive sector which carries out accumulation was industry (*Theories*, I, IV.10).

Marx then examined the arguments of these critics of Smith. Some of these arguments are merely based on verbal tricks and fully merit Marx's sarcastic comments. Let us see some examples:

> "According to Storch – Marx writes – the physician produces health (but also illness), professors and writers produce enlightenment (but also obscurantism) … and so on" (I, IV.16, 410). See, also, the comment on Pellegrino Rossi (IV.18, 413, 415). According to Nassau Senior – Marx notes – the Moses who gave the Ten Commandments, like the Dutch and English people who revolted against tyranny, are productive because their "product" is durable. And the doctor who heals a sick child produces a durable result. Marx comments: "Rubbish! If the child dies, the result is no less durable" (I, IV.17). Mind, however, that these notes were written by Marx for his own use, not for publication.

In the *Addenda*, Marx is ironic about the "products" of the criminal, which include "the whole of the police and of criminal justice, constables, judges, hangmen, juries, etc.". Besides, the criminal "produces not only compendia on Criminal Law, not only penal codes and along with them legislators in this field, but also art, belles-lettres, novels, and even tragedies", and so on.[21] Another example is Marx's comment on Chalmers, where the latter insists that priests and the church are productive (IV.19).

In other cases, Marx's sarcasm is inappropriate; for instance, when it is directed against J.B. Say's view that immaterial activities tend to increase beyond the social need and that all labours can be in excess (IV.13. See ch. VII). Although not very consistent, Say at least followed common sense.

Both Smith and Marx believed that public employees are unproductive despite being necessary. Marx disagreed with G. Garnier and Nassau Senior, who considered them productive (IV.7.a, 348; IV.17), because he held that the capitalist logic maintains a distinction between social utility and productiveness of labour. There are useful labours that are unproductive (like the public sector) and productive labours that are useless, like luxury production.[22] Garnier and Senior also criticised Smith's view that the musician is unproductive while the maker of his instrument is productive. Marx's answer to both is that "On this reasoning a man who eats corn is just as productive as the man who produces it".[23] However, these authors were comparing two producers, not a consumer and a producer.

6. Independent producers

Consistently with his approach, Marx stated that independent producers, like peasants and handicraftsmen "belong neither to the category of productive nor of unproductive labourers, although they are producers of commodities". They exchange commodities with revenue, and "their production does not fall under the capitalist mode of production".[24]

These workers can even create surplus value, thanks to the advanced means of production provided by the capitalist system. In such a case, Marx said, they are entrepreneurs (or wage labourers) of themselves. In general, however, they tend to disappear as independent producers and to become either small capitalists or wage-labourers (see also XVIII.1).[25]

7. Neglected potentialities

In rejecting the productive nature of intellectual labour, Smith and Marx precluded for themselves the possibility of forecasting the future of capitalist development. This is a possibility that Marx misses on many occasions, when, in a number of splendid analyses, he outlines different prospects but always concludes by excluding new approaches. Let us take a look at some of his insights.

a. Saving labour

Many of the authors examined by Marx in ch. 4 of the *Theories* maintained that personal services are productive because they help high-level people to save their labour.[26] This argument legitimised the mass of menial servants, which, for Smith, epitomised unproductive labour.

Marx could not accept that view, but he took this occasion to reflect on the division of labour between productive and unproductive activities as a means to increase social productivity:

> If everyone had to perform productive and unproductive labour, and through the dividing up of these kinds of labour between two persons both were better performed, according to Adam Smith this would in no way alter the circumstance that one of these labours is productive and the other unproductive.

However, he concludes that this collaboration does not mean that unproductive labour becomes productive.[27]

b. Historical context

Storch maintained that Smith's productive/unproductive labour distinction is important for the production of material goods but does not hold for intellectual labour. This would mean that material and intellectual products are not, as the other commentators on Smith believed, subject to the same laws. Marx appreciated Storch's observation but objected that material and intellectual production differ in different periods. They and their reciprocal relationship are the product of specific historical processes (*Theories*, I, IV.16). However, this reflection did not lead Marx to admit the productiveness of intellectual labour.

c. Increase in productivity

On the unproductive workers who sell their services on the market, Marx observed that they can be too many in two (opposite) cases: either when wealth is scarce and is appropriated by a few people (as it was in the Middle Ages) or when the system is characterised by high productivity (IV.17). Thus, excess of rent and high productivity have the same result: an excess of unproductive workers. Actually, by increasing profit, productivity allows for the employment of a greater number of productive workers (IV.9, 378), but, on the other hand, it reduces the number of workers needed for a certain amount of production (see ch. X).

On this issue, Marx writes: "A country is the richer the smaller its productive population is relatively to the total product; just as for the individual capitalist". Actually, capital "strives to reduce the norm [the standard] of necessary labour, but [also strives] to employ the greatest possible quantity of productive labour at the given norm" (IV.9, IX.377).

Here Marx prompts a question: do the workers made redundant by the increase in productivity become unproductive? This may seem to be the inevitable outcome, but actually most of them do not. They are shifted from material labour to services. Then, since services foster productivity, these workers are, at the same time, effect and cause of progress in productivity. Marx, on the contrary, answered that the growth in productivity increases the number of workers in some particular sectors (luxuries, commercial middlemen, machine construction, railway, etc.), but above all it increases the numbers of unproductive labourers, like artists, "lawyers, physicians, scholars, schoolmasters, inventors, etc." (IV.9, 367–8). We must bear in mind that for Marx these activities are unproductive even if they are indirectly productive (IV.18, 413).

d. Cooperation and collective labourer

In *Capital I*, Marx writes: "As in the natural body head and hand wait upon each other, so the labour-process unites the labour of the hand with that of the head. Later on they part company and even become deadly foes". However, this does not obstruct the formation of the collective labourer:

> The product ceases to be the direct product of the individual, and becomes a social product, produced in common by a collective labourer, i.e., by a combination of workmen, each of whom takes only a part, greater or less, in the manipulation of the subject of their labour. As the co-operative character of the labour-process becomes more and more marked, so, as a necessary consequence, does our notion of productive labour, and of its agent the productive labourer, become extended. In order to labour productively, it is no longer necessary for you to do manual work yourself; enough, if you are an organ of the collective labourer, and perform one of its sub-ordinate functions.[28]

Here the contradiction with Marx's usual positions is strident. Shortly after, he adds: "Capitalist production is not merely the production of commodities, it is essentially the production of surplus-value" (*Capital I*, V.XVI.3). But this specification does not eliminate the contradiction.

Moreover, in the last sentences of the *Theories* devoted to unproductive labour, Marx openly contradicted his own attitude on cooperative labour in the factories (see XI.3.b): besides the direct producers of the surplus value, he wrote, there are "the unskilled labourers" who have "nothing directly to do with the working up of the raw material", plus the overseers, the engineers, etc. Well, "the *totality of these labourers*" produce a "*common product*". He added:

> All these persons are not only *directly* engaged in the production of material wealth, but they exchange their labour *directly* for money as capital, and consequently directly reproduce, in addition to their wages, a surplus-value for the capitalist. Their labour consists of paid labour plus unpaid surplus-labour.
>
> (*Theories*, I, Addenda, 12.I)

This seems to be an explicit disavowal of Marx's thesis that only the material producers of surplus value are productive.

A similar analysis can be found in *Capital III*, where Marx particularly stressed the function of intellectual labour and research in the formation of the collective labourer and in increase of productivity.[29] All these passages are at odds with the "official" doctrine that "indirectly productive" labourers are unproductive. But they do not change the body of Marx's thought.

e. Labour as measure of value

This last section of what we call "neglected potentialities" continues the previous one. At the end of the manuscript of *Capital III*, Marx writes:

> Although the form of labor, as wage labor, determines the shape of the entire process and the specific mode of production itself, it is not wage labor which determines value. In the determination of value the question turns around social labor time in general, about that quantity of labor, which society in general has at its disposal, and the relative absorption of which by the various products deter mines, as it were, their respective social weights.
>
> (*Capital III*, VII.LI.18)

Here Marx could not be clearer. Value (and surplus value) is given by social, collective labour, not merely by wage labour. Once again, however, he forecloses any larger view of productive labour by stating that social value "is indeed connected with the wage form of labor", as is required by the capitalist system (Ibid.).

* * *

At the end of his notes on productive labour, Marx finally tried to explain why all these promising passages do not lead to more reasonable conclusions than those he invariably arrived at. He began with long "philosophical" explanations. He wrote: "Since living labour—through the exchange between capital and labourer—is incorporated in capital, [...] all the productive powers of social labour appear as the productive powers of capital". Then, he added, "the productive power of social labour" now appears as "*materialised* labour". Here, too, there is a sort of *fetishism*, he says. "The *productivity* of capital consists in the first instance ... in the *compulsion to perform surplus-labour*".[30]

Marx goes on to add that "consequently also science and the forces of nature appear as *productive powers of capital*". Science is "*social labour*", which appears "as *means for the exploitation of labour*" (Ibid., 1317–18). Thus, "the social and general productive powers of labour are productive powers of capital", but they "do not directly affect exchange-value" (12.B, 1320). He explains: these production powers increase productivity but do not affect the relationship between capital and worker. For example, twelve hours of labour produce the same amount of value if the production is without machines or is achieved with high-level technology. "Hence labour as producing value always remains the labour of the individual, but expressed in the form of general labour" (1321).

Later on, Marx expressed the same concept with another example: if I pay a teacher privately to improve my skill, the "costs of education, just as the costs of my maintenance, belong to the costs of production of my labour-power. But the particular utility of this service *alters nothing in the economic relation*" (12.E, 1328).

Here Marx gets involved in the same paradoxes as Ricardo, whose analysis sees value and wealth as going in opposite directions (see *Perrotta* 2015). Moreover, Marx seems to beg the question: he tries to present a postulate as a demonstration. In the end, he ascribes the immense increase in productivity of capitalist accumulation, due to science, education, healthcare, services of any kind, comfort, etc., to the surplus labour time of the material final factory workers (see the analysis of relative surplus value in *Capital I*, part IV). This is hardly credible. Marx himself, in the *Grundrisse*, spoke of "monstrous disproportion between the labour time applied, and its product".[31]

His concern appears in another part of the *Grundrisse* (notebook VI: 639–40), where he observes that the increase in productivity creates more and more "not-labour time", but capital converts it into "surplus labour time of the mass by all the means of art and science, because its wealth consists directly in the appropriation of surplus labour time". However, once "the mass of workers" will "appropriate their own surplus labour" (that is, when capitalism is superseded), then "necessary labour time will be measured by the needs of the social individual", while "disposable time will grow for all".

Conclusions

Marx, like Smith, considered the activities of research, education and healthcare unproductive, although they are the main components of investment in human capital. This can appear explicable in Smith, who conceived the increase in productivity as due solely to the division of labour and conceived accumulation as based solely on the increase in the number of workers.[32] Marx's position is harder to explain, since he was perfectly aware that increase in productivity and accumulation are both due mainly to technological improvement, more efficient services, education and science – in a word, to intellectual labour. Moreover, unlike Smith, Marx even saw commerce and independent producers as unproductive.

Marx had a clear idea of the growth of intellectual labour, the expansion of services and their function in capitalist accumulation. However, he meant to present proof of the exploitation and the oppression of factory workers, and the basic tool he chose was labour time as the only source of value. Probably, he thought that admitting the productiveness of intellectual labour would have weakened his approach.

Today Marx's interpretation appears partly correct, partly not. Disposable time has grown for most of society, even within the capitalist economy, although in very different proportions for the different occupations and social groups. On the other hand, exploitation – in the common sense of the word – continues to oppress most of the workers in the world.

Notes

1 Forty years ago, I published a book on Marx's thought on productive labour (Perrotta 1976, vol. 2), completely different, in all aspects, from this chapter. I thank the discussant, Olivier Rosell, and the participants in the session of the *Storep* Conference (Catania, 2016) where I presented this research. Thanks, also, to Claudia Sunna for her useful comments.

2 *Theories*, I, IV.2; IV.6.b; Addenda, 2.b–c–d, XXII–1346. In the period 1857–63, Marx wrote several thousand pages of notes, in his notebooks. The first of these notebooks formed the basis of *A Contribution to the Critique of Political Economy* (published in 1859). The last part of them forms the planned Book IV of *Capital*, entitled *Theories of Surplus Value*. It was published in 1909, by Kautsky, with a different arrangement. The fourth chapter of this *Capital IV* is entitled *Theories of Productive and Unproductive Labour*. In the *Addenda* to volume 1, there are other reflections on this issue. The central notebooks of the manuscript formed the basis of *Capital I* (published in 1867) and, to a lesser extent, of *Capital II* and *III* (which were mainly written after 1863 and published posthumously by Engels). These central notebooks are known respectively as *Grundrisse* (*Outlines of the Critique of Political Economy*), written in 1857–58, and *Manuscripts of 1861–1863*. They were both published in complete editions in the second half of the 20th century.

3 *Grundrisse*, 208. *Theories*, I, IV.1; Addenda, 12.B, 1320; 12.D; 12.E, 1333 and 1336. *Draft chapter VI*, 480.

4 *Grundrisse*, 302, note of p. 243.

5 See also Blaug (1962: 285–6).

6 *Theories*, I, IV.3; Addenda, 12.D.

7 Please note: in the online edition of *Capital I* that we use, the numbering of chapters after ch. IV differs from that of other editions.

8 *Theories*, I, IV.3; IV.4, 309.

9 *Theories*, I, IV.4, 308–11.

10 *Draft chapter VI*, 481, "Secondly".

11 *Theories*, I, Addenda, 12.G.

12 Ibid., 12.H. See also *Draft chapter VI*, 486.

13 *Capital I*, IV.XV.1–22. *Manoscritti*, 3, gamma, 190–7: 335ff. *Theories*, I, A, XXI–1317, 1320.

14 *Capital I*, IV.XV.22, fn. 23.

15 *Theories*, I, IV.4, at the end of 308.

16 E.g. in *Capital III*, I.V, section I.

17 *Theories*, I, IV.4, 309; IV.8, 362.

18 *Theories*, I, Addenda, 12.K.

19 *Capital III*, IV.XVII.10 and IV.XVII.12.

20 IV.7.a; IV.9, 369; IV.11, 391–2. On Smith, see above all *Capital II*, ch. 19, section 2.

21 Addenda, 11. Similar texts recur in *Grundrisse*, 209; *Manoscritti*, 3.b; *Digression*, 324–6.

22 *Draft chapter VI*, 484. *Grundrisse*, 209.

23 *Theories*, I, IV.7.a. *Grundrisse*, fn. 302.

24 *Theories*, I, Addenda, 12.F, 1328.

25 Ibid., 1328–29. See also *Draft chapter VI*, 482, *Firstly*.
26 See, in *Theories*, I: Garnier, IV.7.a and VIII–347; Schmalz, IV.7: IX–421; Lauderdale, IV.12; P. Rossi, IV.18, 413–15. On this, see *Faucci* (1979: 129–30).
27 *Theories*, I, IV.18, 414–15. See also *Capital III*, I.V, 1.
28 *Capital I*, V.XVI.2. See also *Draft chapter VI*, 481, *Firstly*.
29 *Capital III*, I.V, sections I and V. The issues of cooperation and division of labour – both social and technical – are also extensively discussed in *Manoscritti*, 3.a and 3.b.
30 *Theories*, I, Addenda, 12.A, XXI–1317.
31 Notebook VII: 705. See, about the whole passage, XIX.4.c.
32 See Marx, *Theories*, I, IV.11, at the end of 393.

XII Investment in human capital

Background

The 19th-century economists gradually came round to seeing human capital as a social process that determines accumulation. However, their view remained incomplete, for it contrasted with the assumption that workers' consumption could not grow significantly. Only in the 1960s was this approach fully developed (by Schultz and others, see as follows). However, by then their approach no longer addressed society, but only the individual. With a few exceptions.

N.B. This chapter will prove hard to understand if the reader does not keep in mind the analyses that actually used the concept of human capital, mentioned in other parts of this book (see II.5, II.7; IV.3; V.4; VI.2, VI.4; VII.3; VIII.3; IX.5; X.2–3; XI.7). This chapter moves on from these considerations and will, in turn, find continuation in the successive chapters (see XIII.3, XIV.2; ch. XVIII; XIX.1, XIX.4.c; XXI.2.c–d). All these analyses, taken together, convey an idea of the great efforts made by the classical authors and their successors. They have paved the way to a theory of development based on intellectual labour.

1. The classical approach: investment in human capital as a social process

a. Smith: knowledge and abilities

As we have seen (II.7), some 18th-century authors conceived investment in human capital as individual investment in education to acquire skill. Others saw it as social investment that increases social productivity. Smith's approach contains both aspects. He offered (see IV.3) brief but brilliant insight into the capital of knowledge and abilities that is acquired by individuals and, through them, by society. Such abilities are acquired through "education, study or apprenticeship". The expenditure for them is "a capital fixed and realized, as it were, in his person. Those talents – Smith added – as they make part of his fortune, so do they likewise of that of the society to which he belongs" (Smith 1776, II.1.17).

Smith also examined the different wage levels, where higher wages are repayment for the labour employed in acquiring a skill (I.10.9–10). While the former passage has attracted little attention, the latter raised a great deal of comment, leading many historians to believe that Smith was only interested in human capital as individual investment.[1]

b. Early 19th century: education

At the turn of the century, Jovellanos clearly pointed out the connection between education and labour productiveness.[2] *Dutens* (1804) acutely observed that national wealth increases proportionally to the growth of education and culture (105).

Melchiorre *Gioia* (1815–17), too, associated labour productivity with the level of knowledge. He also very effectively described the toil to achieve scientific knowledge through the education of the new generations. This is an investment made by families (tome III: 81, 195–9). Writing about "spiritual goods" (see VI.3.a), *Storch* (1815) referred to human dexterity, skill, culture, etc. These faculties, which increase workers' productivity, derive from a specific kind of investment, i.e. education and training.[3] In his notes to Storch (1815), Say substantially agreed. On this issue, *Demidov* (1830) followed Storch (28–33). *Bosellini*'s book (1816) is devoted to arguing the productive nature of services (menial servants included) and especially of intellectual labour. Above all, the author insisted that education and culture, when applied to production, bring about growth in productivity. The cultural capital of society, he said, is the best way to increase social wealth.[4]

In a book full of very bizarre and contradictory arguments, the vicomte de *Saint-Chamans* (1824) stated that national wealth includes immaterial goods. The skill of a professional or the talent of an artist are the capital of such people and provide them with an income (4fn, 11, 17). *Agazzini* (1822), a conservative and quirky author, stressed the importance of education in improving production (75–87. See also Agazzini 1834). According to *James Mill* (1824), the education of workers in knowledge and intelligence is necessary both for their happiness and to raise productivity (38–41). *Bailey* (1823), too, called for the education for the poor, following in the footprints of Smith.[5]

Von Thünen also dealt with investment in personal education, but extended the issue to society as a whole. He even tried – as Schultz would do much later – to calculate quantitatively the influence of education on productivity (see *Kiker* 1969). *McCulloch* (1828) effectively argued that Smith's view on productive labour contradicted his own analysis of the division of labour. Moreover, it also contrasted with his observation that an educated and skilled man is like an expensive machine that yields higher profits thanks to a greater investment.[6] Two Sicilian professors, *Scuderi* (1827: 52–3) and *Sanfilippo* (1828: 21–5, 137–41), extolled research, since it supports production. They also included non-material products in social wealth. However, they held that these goods could not be accumulated. Thus, the production of non-material goods was not to be encouraged and must be kept on a smaller scale than that of material objects.[7]

According to *Dunoyer* (1830), non-material products contribute to national capital. They form a sort of fixed capital of customs and knowledge. Dunoyer rightly observed that Smith and Say recognised this, but contradicted themselves by denying the productive nature of such fundamental labour as education, which allows for the accumulation of non-material capital. He concluded by saying that there are no professions that are better than others (16–18, 28–30). On the role of knowledge in production analysed by Hodgskin and John Rae, see *Prendergast* (2010: 424–7).

Hamilton (1830) commended the middle level of consumption practised by the middle classes, as opposed to the luxury of the rich and the poverty of workers. He also advocated relieving the working class from poverty (180–6). Hamilton stressed the importance of skill, which increases productivity (32). He aptly observed that even in the primitive state of society "a desire for convenience and a taste for ornament is congenial" to human nature (23). Thus – he said, like the Enlightenment authors – it is wrong to try to force workers into industry by restricting their enjoyments. Rather, the approach should be reversed (32–3). Also moral education encourages workers to be industrious (186–7). The same idea can be found in *Eisdell* (1839: 75).

De Augustinis (1840) argued that intellectual labour prevails among civilised people (54–5). *Wayland* (1937) maintained the same thesis and attributed great importance to education for the growth of productivity (132–40). On certain bizarre theses of De Augustinis, see *Roscher* (1854, § 62fn: 140).

c. Eisdell and Henry George: wealth depends on high wages

Joseph *Eisdell* (1839) concluded the first phase of the classical reflections of this issue with an outstanding analysis. He not only linked up all the aspects of the question, but offered a final solution to the underconsumption problem. First of all, he extolled science and skill at length as the driving forces of accumulation (I: 74, 77–108). He then complained about the waste perpetrated by the rich in unbridled luxury. This, he affirmed, is the main cause of the wretched conditions of the working class (II: 255–8). Eisdell stated that the great disparity in the distribution of wealth is the very cause that hinders development: "The wealth of a country depends mainly on the skill", but we cannot acquire sufficient skill because the workers are too poor to put their children to study. "The poverty of the lower classes, he added, overburthens and gluts the market with the commonest sort of labour" (264). This is why we have too many unskilled workers, many of them unemployed.

Thus excessively low wages hamper investments in human capital; in turn, the lack of such investments on the one hand hinders growth, while on the other it creates unemployment. In Eisdell, gluts are seen to derive from two conditions: the low level of workers' consumption and the scarcity of skilled workers. Unfortunately, Eisdell's brilliant intuitions remained unnoticed.

Like Eisdell, Henry *George* (1880), from the US, also revived the idea of a positive proportion between wages and productivity (first asserted by the late mercantilists and the Enlightenment authors, Smith included). George's well-known theorem maintains that state spending on public goods (like infrastructures, administrative offices, governance of the environment) increases land rent, and so land value, more than proportionally. Thus all taxes can be reduced to only one, the tax on land, through which all public spending can be financed (today this apparently utopian view has been reformulated by Joseph Stiglitz). Thus, Henry George maintained that, thanks to tax on land, wages could increase.

It is advantageous to raise wages – George continued – because there is a positive relationship between wage level and productivity: "it is but a truism that labor is most productive where its wages are largest. Poorly paid labor is inefficient labor" (IX.2: 398). He adds:

> just as wages are high, so do the invention and utilisation of improved processes and machinery go on with greater rapidity and ease". Thus, the "increase in the reward of labor and capital would still further stimulate invention and hasten the adoption of improved processes.
>
> (399)

George was sure that this would free workers from technological unemployment. When people no longer fear poverty, he wrote, they will cease to strive to become rich (399–400). Unfortunately, this has not been the case in affluent societies.

2. J.S. Mill: education and research for accumulation

J.S. Mill acknowledged that skill, teaching and research increase social wealth, but he stuck to Smith's idea that accumulation can only consist of material goods. This prevented him, first, from coming up with an appropriate solution to the underconsumption question and, second, from envisaging development based on the growth of human capital.

Mill (1844) tried to reconcile Smith with his critics. He wrote that, to be considered productive, labour must produce wealth, i.e. must add to the things that afford utility or enjoyment to man (III.7). However, wealth includes the skill of the productive labourers and also includes infrastructures, although the latter are produced with public expenses and by public workers (III.10–12). Thus, wealth consists not in enjoyment, but in the permanent sources, either material or immaterial, which give enjoyment. Such sources "may be accumulated and stored up; enjoyment itself cannot".[8]

Now, skill is a permanent source of enjoyment (III.26–27). And yet the musician or soprano, etc. are unproductive, because their performances only afford enjoyment and do not increase social wealth. But those who teach them (and, to be sure, the violin-maker) are productive because they produce a permanent source of enjoyment (III.27–28).

Thus, Mill introduced immaterial labour and public labour among the productive activities, while maintaining Smith's principle that labour is productive only when its product is accumulable. However, Mill unwittingly replicated Smith's contradictions: if producing enjoyment directly is unproductive, why should producing it indirectly (through a permanent source of enjoyment) be productive?

Mill also affirmed that the labour of judges, legislators, police officers, soldiers and domestic servants is "partly productive and partly unproductive", because it contributes to the production of useful goods or faculties, but is also directed to promoting enjoyments (III.34–7), while labour that has the sole purpose of enjoyments is totally unproductive (III.39).

In the *Principles*, Mill (1848) appears less tortuous, but only at the cost of returning to Smith and narrowing down the range of productive labour even more. He writes that, "in applying the term wealth to the industrial capacities", we always refer to material products. "A country would hardly be said to be richer" because of "the genius, the virtues, or the accomplishments of its inhabitants". Unless, he added, these qualities become marketable (I.3.10). Surely, however, this is precisely the case of the musician, etc. In the economy, Mill wrote, wealth is "only what is called material wealth", and productive labour is only that which produces "utilities embodied in material objects" (I.3.11). He concluded: "All labour is [...] unproductive, which ends in immediate enjoyment, without any increase of the accumulated stock of permanent means of enjoyment" (I.3.13).

However, Mill remarked, also productive labour can be useless, due to defect of skill or excess of means of production when fewer are needed (I.3.15). This observation suggests an idea of unproductive labour as labour in excess (see XIV.3). In conclusion, according to Mill, besides material labour, the following immaterial labours are also productive: technical teaching; healthcare applied to workers; inventions and the relative theories; but also speculative thought, which often opens the way to inventions (I.2.16–19). Thus, healthcare and education are part of productive consumption, not of luxury (see above, VIII.2).

Mill made no mention of comfort and cultural activities other than education, which indirectly increase productivity. *Bladen* (1974) rightly noted that Mill underrated the effects of better living standards on human productivity. Mill and the authors of his time reduced the whole issue to the education-productivity causal linkage (237). Nevertheless, Mill rejected the idea that productive labour is confined to the production of necessaries. Progress, he wrote, consists precisely in the fact that an ever-larger share of production is devoted to satisfying the wants of the community other than those of mere subsistence (J.S. Mill 1848, I.3.19).

This is the deepest of Mill's contradictions. On the one hand, he maintained the static distinction between necessaries and luxuries, which was the ultimate cause of the classical standstill in the analysis of accumulation. On the other, he saw accumulation as a process, which progressively increases "luxuries", whose consumption is defined as unproductive. In any case, Mill's main concern was much the same as Smith's. He saw the issue in terms of contraposition between the waste of luxury expenditures and saving, the latter being the only source of investment. In his *Principles*, chapters 4 and 5 of book I are devoted to this problem; see especially I.5.16–17.

Many historians have pointed out the difficulty of calculating the gross and net national product on the basis of Mill's subtle distinction (*Cannan* 1893: 3; *Myint* 1948: 11; *Blaug* 1962: 190). *Spengler* (1960) stressed the importance Mill attributed to education for development (229–31) and in general for shaking off the constraint of old institutions. *Becattini* (1978) pointed up the twofold position of the two Mills (father and son) on both productive and unproductive consumption.

In conclusion, despite his contradictions, J.S. Mill asserted the productivity of some important non-material occupations and restated the original sense of the issue: investment versus waste. Because of his great influence on subsequent economic thought, his analysis represents a turning point in the history of the concept of unproductive labour.

Cattaneo (1861) is a tract devoted to proving, with historical arguments, that science and culture constitute the driving force in the accumulation of wealth. Cattaneo was writing against Smith's view of the unproductiveness of intellectual labour. *Roncaglia* (2014) denies that Smith really held this view (20–1). However, this is one of Smith's contradictions.

3. Community and intellectual progress

a. List: the major factor of development

The analysis of Friedrich *List* (1841) is no less outstanding. List complained that Smith, despite being aware that development depends on the skill and dexterity of labour, went on to change his mind and put the division of labour at the basis of accumulation. But it is the productive powers of labour that are responsible for development (II.XII.1–7). However, the attitude of the individual is conditioned by the social context, by customs, institutions, culture, religion and education. In general, the basis for development is the national system, which extends manufactures and transport, increases material capital and improves and coordinates education and skills. Yet, Smith's doctrine "sinks deeper and deeper into materialism, particularism, and individualism" (II.XII.8–9).

List proposed a powerful project for "national division of labour", in which all the moral energies of the nation cooperate for common development. The driving forces of this project were industrialisation and the growth of intellectual capital (see, at least, chs. 13, 18 and 24). He also added further fuel to the arguments about Smith's inconsistencies. "The man who breeds pigs is, according to this school, a productive member of the community, but he who educates men is a mere non-productive" (II.XII.20). Again, he referred to the usual paradoxes: the musician and the maker of musical instruments; the doctor and the pills-maker; the great inventors and the horse (Ibid.). Also, Say's theory of immaterial goods is misleading, because it concerns value in exchange and not the productive powers of immaterial producers (II.XII.21). The theory disregards "the powers of the human mind" (II.XII.21).

Rist interpreted List's approach as a spiritual approach and associated it with Müller.[9] Although he had some reason, List's passionate concern for development is far more reminiscent of mercantilism (which he expressly praised: ch. 29) and Cameralism. Criticising List's protectionism, *Cattaneo* (1843) objected that in an open market the division of labour and competition are much more effective for development than the national association and community of interests that List preferred to them (§ 15: 535). *Trinchera* (1854) insisted on the importance of intellectual labour for economic progress (138–45).

At first, List's influence was confined within the German world. However, later on, his keen interest in the moral and educational aspects of development found great furtherance in Marshall, who admired List.

b. Marshall: industriousness stimulates skill

Marshall (1890) conceived as productive all the labours that yielded some utility. But he was well aware that the key point was the extent to which the various occupations increase the wealth that is stored up.[10] On this basis, Marshall repeated that labourers in excess can be found not only among menial servants but in any sector (see XIV.3). As for productiveness, there is no difference between material and non-material products, and even the difference between what is material and what is not is very "vague and unsubstantial". This is why the expression "productive labour" is a slippery one and should not be used.[11]

At first sight, Marshall does not appear very keen on the constant increase in workers' consumption (which is the necessary way for investment in human capital). Like J.S. Mill, he deemed productive only that consumption which enables workers to perform their labour efficiently (giving less than that, he writes, is not saving, it is a waste). Nevertheless, listing what he considered the conventional necessaries, he also allowed for some moderate luxuries (II.III.9–17). On the other hand, Marshall noted with pleasure that progress increases wages and the incomes of the lower classes (VI.XII.45). He insisted on the virtuous linkage between wage level and labour efficiency (VI.XIII.39–41).

More open to a dynamic perspective is his statement that men tend towards ever newer activities, driven as they are by the desire for excellence in their own labour. It is this tendency that drives men towards increasingly refined consumption, not the other way around (III.II.9–14). Seeing the increase in consumption as the driving force of accumulation, Marshall suggested that wants and consumption eventually become impulsive and no longer derive from increase in productivity (VI.XIII.1–4).

Marshall enunciated a sort of variant of the invisible hand theory: he wrote that moral and intellectual faculties, "on which the progress of industry depends", are not acquired solely for economic interest, but also for pleasure,

> in the same way, that greater factor of economic prosperity, the organisation of a well-ordered state, is the product of an infinite variety of motives; many of which have no direct connection with the pursuit of national wealth.
>
> (IV.VIII.16)

A constant concern of Marshall was that industrial work should be able to develop the faculties of workers (e.g. IV.IX.23). Such faculties depend on custom and natural attitude, but also on training (IV.VI.4–6). On this issue, he distinguished between general and specialised ability (IV.VI.8), with the prospect of improvement in the skills of the new generations (VI.XIII.65). He added:

> The most imperative duty of this generation is to provide for the young such opportunities as will both develop their higher nature, and make them efficient producers. And an essential condition to this end is long-continued freedom from mechanical toil; together with abundant leisure for school and for such kinds of play as strengthen and develop the character.
>
> (VI.XIII.71)

Schultz (1961: 15–6) and *Bowman* (1966: 103) accused Marshall of abandoning the concept of human capital. But this was an impression that depended solely on their conception of human capital as mere individual investment. As we have seen, although he never used the expression "human capital", Marshall was greatly concerned with improvements in productivity through education.

Both List and Marshall had a strong sense of the productiveness of the moral and intellectual faculties and an intense national feeling. They outlined a concept of social capital, but their organicism, associated with a sense of superiority of race, is worryingly close to Müller's *Volksgeist* (the nationalistic "spirit of people"). On the other hand, these authors reflect the common culture of their time. See, for example, F.A. *Walker* (1883, II, § 74). See also *Baudrillart* (1883, chs. 13–14), who devoted several pages to the question of how race affects productivity.

c. *Crisis of the classical approach*

At the turn of the century, various academic treatises of the time reduced the relationship between culture and productivity to an insipid and banal formula. *Cauwès* (1881) is a good example of this (section 226: 368). However, it was from such analyses that the idea of human capital gradually emerged. Shield *Nicholson* (1891) effectively recalled Petty and Smith on the concept of human capital and analysed the importance of this factor for accumulation. Later on, Nicholson (1893–1901) included services, education and intellectual labour in general within immaterial capital.[12]

John *Commons* (1893), the founder of institutionalism, promptly reacted to the tendency with severe criticism of the definition of human abilities as capital. First, he argued, abilities are paid on the basis of the result of labour, not in relation to surplus, as capital is paid. Second, even in the case of abilities acquired through education with the aim of increasing labourers' productivity, it is difficult to separate these abilities from those acquired through general education in the family, at school, etc. Third, Commons conceded that to see abilities as capital is plausible from the viewpoint of production, but deemed it certainly wrong from the viewpoint of the distribution of wealth (II.3: 41–4). "Capital – Commons stated – can be accumulated indefinitely both in quantity and duration, while abilities are narrowly limited" (44).

And yet, all the authors who have an idea of human capital maintain precisely the opposite: the growth of material capital has certain limits, that of human capital has not. On this issue, Commons – despite his acute criticisms – was even more backward than the classical economists. The latter, and Smith, too, saw labour as part of invested capital. Other authors of that period continued to propose excellent perspectives on the growth of human capital along classical lines. See, for example, *Hobson* (IX.5) and *Leroy-Beaulieu* (X.3). *Robertson* (1918) insisted on the importance of the education of workers, for both efficient work and social harmony (ch. 2).

4. Neoclassical approach: individual investment – Schultz

Fisher (1906) can be taken as making the turning point in reflections on human capital. Fisher had an idea of capital as a flow of services (IV.4), which can include skilled human activities. He also wrote expressly of individual self-investment in skill (X.4) and briefly alluded to dissent with Marshall (IV.5: 61). *Schultz* (1961) overrated this dissent and stated that Marshall was responsible for the persistence of the classical approach to the issue (15). With this philologically inaccurate interpretation, Schultz was able to stress the novelty of his analysis. *Bowman* (1966) explained the real position of both Marshall and Fisher (107).

Fallon (1923), while rejecting the idea of unproductive labour, stressed that intellectual labour is enormously more productive than material labour because its results are infinitely reproducible (42). *Walsh* (1935), in a sense, paved the way to Schultz's analysis. He raised the question as to whether education can be defined an investment. He then distinguished between the first years of education and the later years. Gradually, the nature of investment emerges in the later and more specialised education (256–7). His empirical research confirmed that acquired abilities behave like the other forms of capital (apart those of lawyers). Thus, they have to be included as capital in the account of national wealth (284–5).

Theodore *Schultz* (1961) completed the reduction of the concept of human capital to an individual dimension. A Nobel Laureate in 1979, Schultz complained that the concept had long been resisted, because the idea of investing in human beings as capital aroused thoughts of property and slaves. But, he writes, by investing in themselves, men can increase their welfare and arrive at a greater degree of freedom (14). The classical concept saw labour mainly as manual activity, which requires little knowledge and skill, abilities being more or less equal for all. However – Schultz stressed – considering only the number of workers is like considering only the number of machines regardless of their productive capacity (15).

Much of what we call consumption is in fact human capital in which people invest. For example, education, healthcare, migration to seek better opportunities, even leisure time (when employed to improve personal skills and knowledge) are investments. However, such activities do not even enter into the national account, despite the fact that human productive capacity outmatches all the other forms of wealth taken together. This type of investment has grown in western countries much faster than conventional capital (13–4), accounting for a large part of the higher productivity of industrialised countries (16).

Finally, Schultz brilliantly explained the basic principle of his concept: according to the dominant theory, the countries that have a great abundance of traditional capital should employ it more than labour and land. In actual fact, capital is a smaller share of their investment. Schultz takes the examples of the US, of Europe (which rapidly picked up again after World War II, despite the extreme scarcity of the residual physical capital) and of the developing countries, which – he held – are not able to absorb the physical capital they receive as aid (18–21).

Schultz (1968) came up with another finding of great effectiveness: the supposed decline in capital returns, which so much concerns economists, is not actually real. It seems to exist because analyses do not take into account the enormous growth of human capital. The latter should be included in the calculation of the capital/revenue ratio (280). According to a tenacious prejudice, public expenses for healthcare, education and even for retraining, are seen as mere consumption, and not for what they are, i.e. enhancement of people's productive capacity.

Often, a developing country is handicapped because economists place the emphasis on steel rather than investment in human capital. This investment yields both returns and increase in productivity. The input is twofold, given by the income value of its service and the value of capital (282). The two aspects, however, must be kept distinct. We cannot confuse services with the stock (283).

Schultz maintained that Smith, while including human abilities in the concept of capital, did not distinguish inherited abilities from acquired ones.

Only the latter should be included in capital (278–9). Schultz also pointed out that "not all the benefits from schooling that accrue to the student are revealed in his future earnings" (285a). He then returned to an issue already addressed (with some differences) in his article of 1961: these benefits are of three sorts. First, the satisfaction obtained from schooling. Second, the permanent abilities acquired as consumer: for example, the ability to appreciate the fine arts. Third, the increase in productivity. The first two types of satisfaction do not enter into the student's future earnings.

As for food, clothing, housing and even healthcare, Schultz is aware that they are not very productive. Thus, as consumption increases, they tend to lose their productiveness completely and become mere consumption expenditures (23). The contrary holds for education. Even if we consider all the spending on education as investment, the return on such expenses is no smaller than that provided by the expenses for physical capital. If we assume that half of the education expenses consist in consumption, then the return on education is double (25–8).

Another, rather less interesting aspect of Schultz's research is the attempt to measure the return rate of investment in education (Schultz 1963). The same approach was pursued in those years by Gary Becker, Jacob Mincer and others. Over time this line of research has proved sterile, despite many attempts to take it further. It derives from two assumptions, particularly strong in neoclassical economics. One is that an economic analysis can always be expressed in quantitative terms. The other is that, investment in education being an individual action, its return can be calculated at the individual level. However, as Commons and Shaffer noted (see here, 3.c and 5), at the individual level investment in education is subject to too many variables that determine the return rate. Among these variables, there are the different degrees and nature of the following factors: comforts, culture of the social environment, family's culture, quality of social relationships, attitudes, personalities, intellectual abilities, etc.

However, the lack of these (impossible) measurements by no means diminishes the great importance of Schultz's achievement. He was able to get rid of the assumptions that derive from industrial economy: one, productive labour and consumption are confined to elementary labour and consumption; two, accumulation consists mainly of material goods. These classical postulates were substantially shared by the Keynesian, neo-Ricardian and Marxist economics. On the main theorisers of human capital, see also *Spalletti* (2009).

5. Gary Becker to Machlup

Gary *Becker* (1964), too, a Nobel Laureate from Chicago, observed that the US exported labour-intensive products and imported capital-intensive goods. However, these concepts have been challenged by the growth of human capital, and the significance of this kind of import-export is now opposite to that of the past. Labour-intensive production was usually understood as based on low-level technology and low productivity, while capital-intensive production was a matter of high-level technology and high productivity. Subsequently, however, labour-intensive production, being based on skilled labour, was the more productive (59–60).

Becker (1981: 20–1) added another insightful observation: when production relies mainly on human capital, the comparative advantages no longer depend on the different resource endowments, but rather on the infinite variety of goods made possible through skills. This explains why, despite their similarities, the highly developed economies see the volume of their interchange increasing rather than diminishing.

Shaffer (1961) effectively criticised the whole concept of human capital, above all by underlining the difficulties (which Schultz himself, 1961a, admits) in measuring the effect of investment in education. However, he makes the same mistake as Gary Becker and various others, including, to some extent, Schultz, with the belief that the concept holds only with a quantitative support. In 1962, Daniel *Bell* first proposed the concept of "post-industrial society", which is founded on education and services (B. 1973: 143–5). And yet the evident connection of this analysis with that of human capital has been overlooked for many years.

Schmookler (1966) stressed that the accumulation of intellectual capital is much more important than that of physical capital. This issue is central to the theme of development. Schmookler rightly complained that technical progress was viewed as an external, non-economic factor, which comes about like earthquakes or wars (3–6).

The economics of education directly derives from the concept of human capital. According to *Blaug* (1968), the new discipline sought to answer questions like these: how much should a country spend on education? Is education mainly investment or consumption? What is the optimal structure of the educational pyramid? (7). Blaug (1970) examined education as both private and public investment. He tried to calculate the rate of returns on these investments (ch. 2) and then calculated the contribution of education to economic growth in various countries (ch. 3). *Michael* (1972) built up a model to prove that education and, in general, investments in human capital affect consumption efficiency positively. However, it also works the other way around (113, passim). *Quadrio Curzio* (1973) examined the different policies of investment in education and their potentialities.

Bowman (1966) described the spread of the human capital concept as a real revolution in economics. He stressed that most of the studies on the economics of education published up to then came out between 1955 and 1965 (101). It was against this background that Schultz's theory entered the scene. Bowman rightly criticised Keynes for seeing workers as passive agents of production, whose employment only depends on physical capital. Even his followers, although reasoning over the long run, held on to this view (108).

Later on, many authors began to favour the expression "human resources" rather than "human capital". The latter concept, they maintained, is bound up with calculation of increase in productivity, while "human resources" is less rigid and includes the social dynamics of human increase in skill, productivity and welfare: see Leonard *Nicholson* (1980), Werner *Clement* (1980), *Human Resources* (1980). The expression dates back to *Ginzberg*'s writings (1966 and 1976). These two books are concerned not with theory, but with social analysis. Their interest was in the development of human potentialities.

Klaassen and Eizenga (1977) wrote that economists usually see consumption as alternative to investment, and so as opposing rather than supporting growth. A higher level of productivity requires a higher level of consumption, not only of manual labour and food but also of intellectual labour, including education (435–6). These authors – while the Harrod-Domar development model is based only on saving – propose a model in which, until the optimal level of consumption is reached, the increase in consumption contributes to growth more than saving. It is the principle – the authors maintain – already applied by governments when they promote productive consumption, like education, while not promoting other objects of consumption, like tobacco or alcohol. By then, even private enterprises were starting to invest in higher consumption, although the results were not evident in the short run (440–1).

Machlup (1980) is a remarkable work on the economics of knowledge. The author took a neoclassical approach, but far from the strictly individual dimension. Knowledge – he wrote – can be divided into consumption and investment, stock and flow. Its principal difference with goods is that the flow of knowledge from one to another does not reduce the stock of one part at the expense of the other, as is the case with goods (159–79). Even listening and reading can be economic activities, provided that they aim at learning, rather than pleasure (190–2). Machlup stated that the input value of knowledge can be measured in terms of opportunity cost (193).

Smith had already compared the skilled man with the machine (as – we may add – did Marx, Marshall and many others). Since then, Machlup writes, the concept of capital applied to man never disappeared. Today, knowledge can no longer be seen as an independent exogenous variable. We must recognise it as an endogenous variable that depends on input and on the allocation of resources. In this way, we can speak of the productivity of investment in knowledge and consequently of development as being associated with it (5). Finally, it is worth stressing Machlup's observation that most of the production of knowledge is not driven by the market but by the state, which finances public education, research and public broadcasting (155–8).

The 1980s–90s saw the issues of human capital and economics of education very much in vogue, and even now they remain among the overcrowded sectors of economics.

* * *

In general, the Marxist authors seem indifferent to the concept of human capital. *Carter* (1977) criticised it. Also, in this case, he wrote, wages do not depend on increase in productivity but on the cost of production (38–41). However, Carter failed to take into account the fact that labour productivity in turn affects the cost of production of the labour force. Nevertheless, a few Marxist authors do have a theory that can be said to be of human capital, as we will see (XVIII.3).

Conclusions

Some neoclassical economists had the great merit of overcoming the classical standstill on human capital due to the assumption of wages at low levels. However, the individual dimension of their approach hindered complete development of the concept's potentialities. Paradoxically, a social concept of investment in human capital was mainly due to some heterodox economists who were familiar with the classical approach (see XVIII.3–4). However, despite these exceptions, economics has so far lacked a full theory of development based on human capital as a social process. This is the basic impediment to understanding the present crisis and arriving at a strategy to overcome it.

Notes

1 See Bowman (1966: 103–8); Negishi (1989: 86); Schultz (1992: 130–1).
2 See *Llombart* (2012: 116–21).
3 Storch (1815, vol. 1, 136, 208, passim).
4 Bosellini (1816: 9–10, 270–73, 419–25).
5 Bailey (1823, questions 25–26: 113–22).
6 McCulloch (1828, *Notes* to book II.3, 96–7fn). Cf. Smith (1776, I.10.8-12. See also Scialoja 1848).
7 Scuderi (1827: 23–7, 179–81, 196–7). Sanfilippo (1828: 128–31).
8 J.S. Mill (1844, III.21–22). See also Mill (1848, I.3.9).
9 Gide and Rist (1909, II.4, 302fn).
10 Marshall (1890, II.III.5 and fn 34). **N.B.** *We refer to the section numbers of the online edition (see the References), which differ from those of the paper edition.*
11 Ibid., II.III.6–7 and fn 35.
12 Nicholson (1893–1901, vol. 1, I.II.3: 37–44).

XIII Overproduction versus underconsumption

Background

The tendency to overproduction has haunted capitalist accumulation since the beginning of the 19th century. Underconsumption was only one of the possible answers to this new tendency. From a formal viewpoint, overproduction and underconsumption are the same thing. Both terms express the tendency of capitalist accumulation to provide a supply in excess relative to consumption.

However, when we speak of underconsumption, reference is usually to the idea that structural consumption cannot increase. On the other hand, overproduction refers, in general, to more dynamic interpretations of the accumulation process, while acknowledging the excess in supply. In this chapter, we briefly examine the following issues connected with overproduction: the business cycle (a concept that actually bypasses the problem of structural surplus), unproductive capital (which can be considered another form of the underconsumptionist view) and the prospect of indefinite growth.

1. Business cycle, an illusory solution

a. J.S. Mill: short-run process

As we have seen, we owe the first explanation of periodical crises to the underconsumption theories. The latter are long-term analyses and refer to the structure of accumulation (although *Paglin*, 1961: 116–17, did not share this view). John Stuart *Mill* (1844) challenged the underconsumption interpretation with the theory that we now call business cycle. This theory however refers to the short term and is not concerned with the accumulation's structure (see also *Schneider* 2008: 456–7). Nevertheless, over time the new view became dominant and supplanted the underconsumption approach. Mill's followers tended to disregard the inappropriate shift from one type of analysis to the other.

Like his father James, J.S. Mill greatly relied on Say's law, coming up with an even more extremist and tautological version of it. He stated:

> All which is produced is already consumed, either for the purpose of reproduction or of enjoyment. … Consumption, therefore, already takes

> place to the greatest extent which the amount of production admits of" (II.4). He adds: "There will never, therefore, be a greater quantity produced, of commodities in general, than there are consumers for."
>
> (II.5)

Mill concluded his long essay by repeating that

> there cannot be excessive production of commodities in general" (II.76); since "it is produce which constitutes the market for produce"; and every increase in production "creates, or rather constitutes, its own demand."
>
> (II.77)

However, the earlier supporters of Say's law argued that crises are only due to momentary unbalances in the distribution of investments among the different sectors, while Mill admitted that crises can be general. Nevertheless, he said, these crises are only apparent; they are due to a sort of general delusion of economic agents. When demand grows very fast and supply grows after it, prices increase. The dealers then believe they are getting richer and increase supply even more. But in actual fact there is simply a depreciation of money. When the delusion dissolves, says Mill, an excess of commodities appears in the market, and production must be immediately reduced (II.64). Actually,

> when there is a general anxiety to sell; and a general disinclination to buy, commodities of all kinds remain for a long time unsold, and those which find an immediate market, do so at a very low price.
>
> (II.72)

Thus, the superabundance of goods in the market is momentary, due to fluctuations in the adjustments of demand and supply (II.65–6).

Mill added that the source of this cyclical process lies in the very nature of the monetary market economy. When money is introduced, he says, it is no longer necessary for sale and purchase to proceed simultaneously, as in barter. The purchase after the sale can be deferred, and this opens up the possibility of temporary unbalance between supply and demand. However, the unbalance is bound to be eliminated sooner or later thanks to competition in the market (II.69–73). Thus, in Mill's approach, upswings and downswings alternate more or less regularly, and these perfectly normal fluctuations are caused by adjustment between a great number of individual buying and selling decisions. In the end, such crises are both inevitable and temporary.

b. Marx: production of use values or of surplus value

Marx most probably took from Mill the idea of periodical crises as cycles (he sometimes uses this word). And yet they held opposite views. Mill continued with J.B. Say's harmonic conception of the market and accumulation. Marx, on the other hand, saw also in the business cycle the basic "contradiction" of capitalism, i.e. the contrast between production of use values, which is the necessary feature of any production activity, and production of surplus value, which characterises capitalist production. Thus, the link between private motivation and social result of capitalist production, which other authors had seen as a harmonious convergence,[1] is seen by Marx as an unsurmountable conflict.

Marx, however, distinguished between periodical crises, which depend on the market and are temporary by definition, and the tendency to the final crisis of capitalist accumulation, which he analysed elsewhere (see XV.1.a).

The bulk of Marx's analysis of the periodical crises can be found in his extensive critique of Ricardo's theory of accumulation (*Theories,* ch. 17). Here, first of all, Marx rejects the underconsumption explanation. Such crises are normal fluctuations, proper to capitalist accumulation. He accurately described the upswing and downswing phases of the cycle, the breaking point of the former and the starting point of the latter (chs. 17.11–12).

On the other hand, Marx is highly critical of Say's law, since the tension between production of use values (which is limited by the effective social needs) and production of surplus value (which is pursued without limits) tends to depress the final demand to the benefit of profit: "the more developed capitalist production is, the smaller, relatively, will be the part which is directly laid out in wages" (ibid., section 5, [704]). Thus, there is a permanent tendency to the overproduction of constant capital, while consumption

> "from the outset is inhibited, since the majority of the population, the working people, can only expand their consumption within very narrow limits, whereas the demand for labour, although it grows absolutely, decreases relatively, to the same extent as capitalism develops", because of the increase in productivity.
>
> (section 6, [704])

There is a unity and, at the same time, an opposition between purchase and sale, demand and supply, consumption and production. This linkage creates the possibility of a general glut. The unity is forcefully reasserted during the crises (section 8, [711]). Thus, the crisis is "the manifestation of all the contradictions of bourgeois economy" (this is the title of section 10).

Production, Marx added, expands for two reasons: because of the increase in invested capital and "because the capital is constantly used more productively" (section 13, [720]). But the market expands more slowly than production. The growth of the latter is a cycle that increases not as a circle, but as a spiral (ibid.). Finally, Marx states that "the contradiction between the impetuous development of the productive powers and the limitations of consumption leads to over-production". Thus, it is wrong to say that general overproduction is impossible (section 14).

Similar considerations can be found in *Capital III* (IV.XVIII.7–8ff). In another passage of this book, Marx stated (in Malthusian tones) that overcoming of the crisis depends above all on the consuming power of the unproductive classes, because the consuming power of workers is limited by the laws of wages. He adds:

> The last cause of all real crises always remains the poverty and restricted consumption of the masses as compared to the tendency of capitalist production to develop the productive forces in such a way, that only the absolute power of consumption of the entire society would be their limit. (V.XXX.20)

Finally, we have his considerations on the "industrial cycle" (*Capital III*, V.XXX.31ff) and on the overproduction generated by credit and by the consequent increase in prices (V.XXX.37). Moreover, *Capital II* frequently offers reflections on the cycles of the turnover of the various types of capital (ch. 9 is only one example).

Thus, in Marx we find the business cycle and the final crisis of capitalism, nothing else. But the underconsumption theories implied that crises are structural, i.e. that the unbalance between production and consumption tends to become permanent unless corrected with an appropriate policy. Structural crises have nothing to do with the business cycle, nor with the end of capitalism. It is precisely the concept of structural crises that is lacking in Marx.[2]

c. *Mill's approach becomes universal*

All the economists followed Mill's approach. Most authors also accepted its connection with Say's law: they were certain that capitalist crises were fully accounted for with the business cycle theory. Others (Keynesians, Marxists and neo-Ricardians), although accepting the idea of the business cycle, rejected Say's law.

In any case, Mill's approach is appropriate for a harmonious view of economic development. *Fellner* (1848), for example, saw the business cycle as a deviation from the ideal state of equilibrium (II.4) and, on the basis of this approach, re-proposed Say's thesis that crises can be only partial and momentary (II.5–6). *Cauwès* (1893: sections 215–16) expressed a similar view. *Pareto* (1896) interpreted economic crises as a part of the "vibratory changes of the social aggregate", where the initial imbalance, due to changes in economic factors, is greatly amplified by subjective convergent tendencies.[3]

It was, of course, Schumpeter above all who endowed the business cycle with the dignity of a theory. He was followed by Hayek, Robbins, etc. Charles *Gide* (1931) happily grasped the sense of the transition from the term "crisis" to that of "cycle". While the former indicates a pathological situation, the second implies only something like a rhythm (124). *Keynes* (1936) examined underconsumption as a part of trade cycle analysis (ch. 22, I: 196, 202–3). *Haberler* (1937) provided the official version of the theory of crises as business cycle for publication by the League of Nations. He denied that the business cycle was due to underconsumption (118ff) but failed to explain the difference between the two processes. Haberler made it clear that the main issues dealt with by the classical economists, like population dynamics, the increase in stock, technical progress – in a word, accumulation – have nothing to do with the business cycle (121–2). This confirms that the latter is a short-run and non-structural concept. Later economists repeated Haberler's approach.[4]

However, some Italian authors departed from the business cycle approach. *Loria* (1934) criticised the underconsumption view, because – he wrote – a permanent excess of production does not exist. He also criticised the under-remuneration of labour. The purchasing power subtracted from wages goes to the capitalists, whose demand compensates for the lack of demand from the workers. The ultimate cause of crises, Loria stated, is neither sunspots (605–6), as Jevons believed, nor banks; it is the tendency of the profit rate to fall. This drives capitalists to look for gains through speculation, rather than through productive investments. There is a consequent destruction of huge masses of capital. However, eventually this destruction makes investment worthwhile once again (604–9). As a matter of fact, Loria's analysis wavers between the Marxist and the underconsumption view.

Supino (1907) maintained that expansion itself creates the conditions for crises, because prices increase and many consumers cannot cope with the increase. This tendency is aggravated by speculation (VI: 78–9). Supino, too, saw crises as cyclical (ch. VII to IX). Among the remedies for crises, he mentioned extraordinary public works, greater freedom for entrepreneurs, facilities for credit and borrowing, and support for enterprises in difficulties (X: 146–7).

2. Unproductive capital

As was the case with the concept of unproductive consumption (see VIII.2), J.B. *Say* (1803) was also the first to speak of unproductive capital. However, he conceived the latter as a marginal phenomenon, external to accumulation. Unproductive capital substantially means idle capital (*fonds oisifs*), i.e. wealth not employed in production, because it is hoarded or wasted. The examples Say offered were mainly taken from backward countries, with no competition and with luxury expenses either for religious cult or for ostentation.[5]

According to *Cattaneo*, capital is less productive in the case of diminishing returns on land, due to an excess of capital invested, or if it is distributed over all the industrial sectors (as List proposes), without preferential treatment for the more productive ones.[6] *Wayland* (1837) speaks of unproductive capital, meaning not only hoarding but also malfunctioning factories, mistaken investments and uncultivated land (26–8). *Blanch* (1849) – together with Pellegrino Rossi – used this concept with reference to war expenses (pp. XL–XLI). Amasa *Walker* (1866), however, maintained that in principle we can speak of wasted wealth, not of unproductive capital, because capital means investment (II.9: 58–60).

Over time this concept acquired great importance. Many economists revived Say's category to describe the enormous growth of financial speculation. The financial market was born as a service for commerce and production, to speed up the collection of small sums of capital and make them ready to be invested. However, in the second half of the 19th century, it appeared more and more as an independent sector growing with no reference to real wealth. This phenomenon was adroitly illustrated in Émile Zola's novel *L'Argent* (1891). But hostility towards the unbridled financial speculation appeared much earlier. Ambroise *Clément* (1867) took it as an example of unproductive labour when it is not checked.[7] Another example, wrote Clément, is a possible excess of labour devoted to security (188–9).

Marx devoted a chapter of *Capital III* (published in 1894 but written in 1864–65) to "Credit and fictitious capital", with reference to bills of exchange, banker bills, bank notes, cheques, etc. – all the credit instruments that are used to facilitate exchanges, borrowing and circulation. The growth of such instruments, he stated, creates fictitious capital that does not correspond to actual wealth and is dangerous for the normal working of the economy.[8]

Fictitious capital is not the same as unproductive capital. The former concept implies a false wealth, something deceptive, while the latter refers to real – albeit sterile – wealth. In any case, both concepts were elaborated in an attempt to describe the improper use of money through financial speculation. The growth of the latter revealed that Smith and the early classical authors were wrong to identify saving with investment.

Loria (1889) produced a lengthy pioneering analysis of this issue.[9] He established a connection between unproductive capital and unproductive labour and proposed a new, more refined version of the underconsumption approach. Unproductive labour, Loria writes, has the task of limiting capitalist accumulation in order to keep it going. Everything that increases profit without increasing the number of workers drives up the ratio between unproductive and productive labourers (400–1).

Thus, technical progress has negative effects on employment and wages. Echoing Marx, as he often does, Loria attributes the introduction of machines to the deliberate intention to depress wages, through unemployment, in order to preserve profit (III.5. Cp. Marx, *Capital I,* ch. 23.3 on the industrial reserve army). He then adds: unproductive capital is even more effective in limiting accumulation than unproductive labour. The division between profit and financial interest enables the owner to make gains even when the capital he has lent is employed unproductively. The same holds for the profit of the banker. Loria also held, with rather bizarre arguments, that there is competition between productive and unproductive capital. In the end, the latter gains the upper hand. This tendency depresses the rate of profit, raises the interest rate (402–16) and even tends to expropriate the entrepreneurs, whether big or small (417–26). Unproductive capital does not produce any consumable good and pays workers who are unproductive (444–76).

The second book by Loria (1889) examines the issue through the history of capitalism. The author maintains that unproductive capital grows ever more, even in the colonies, while lawyers and commercial intermediaries burgeon.[10] The banks make enormous profits at the expense of production (342). "The orgy of unproductive capital is made more frantic by the excessive bills of exchange" of the banks (344). In consequence, profits tend to drop below the minimum level. By then, the process was driving the economy towards industrial depression (361–72). Loria (1934) concluded his research by observing that unproductive capital is a parasitic employment of capital that yields a profit to the owner but does not increase social wealth. It is made up of loans for private luxury, public unproductive expenses, like military expenses, or speculation, insurance, banking, etc.[11]

One of Loria's pupils, the incredibly prolific Supino, carried on this research. *Supino* (1898) was a very successful book and still enjoys worldwide renown. It is a detailed technical analysis of speculation in the stock exchange. Supino effectively contrasted productive capital, which produces social wealth, and unproductive capital, which simply moves already existing wealth (29). However, the author extended the concept of unproductive capital too far, also including capital yielding any rent or the expenses for mere consumption (32–3). According to Supino, the growth of unproductive capital is the necessary outlet of accumulation, which drives towards financial speculation (37–9). When the state engages in unproductive expenses, it subtracts capital from the productive use of private enterprises, and the effect is devastating (139–58).

According to *Puviani* (1903), unproductive capital consists of all bad public expenses, especially military. Puviani, too, effectively described the keen competition between productive and unproductive capital, which alternates with moments of collaboration (section 74 and Appendix). The Italian stream of thought on unproductive capital also includes Valenti (about whom see XIV.1.a). On the unproductiveness of finance capital, see also Veblen (see XIX.3.c).

Rudolf *Hilferding* (1910), following in Marx's footprints, called bank capital, bank shares and speculative activities fictitious (X: 173–4). Commenting on the monetary and financial crisis that broke out in the US in 1907 (exactly 100 years before the outbreak of the last financial crisis), Hilferding stated that the concentration of banking activities spreads the risk of crisis (20, 291–2). Hilferding was later criticised by Sweezy (1942) for believing that the dominance of financial capital would last for ever. Actually, Sweezy wrote, such dominance only occurs during the transition from competitive to monopoly capitalism (ch. 14.5: 268). On Rosa Luxemburg's analysis of financial speculation and its great influence, see XV.3. *Grossmann* (1919) maintained that unproductive capital is a consequence of over-accumulation (II.7.b).

The interpretation of the growth of unproductive capital as the means to avoid saturation, presented by Loria and to some extent implied by the other authors at the turn of the century, was later used by Marxist authors in the second half of the 20th century as an alternative to Rosa Luxemburg's approach (see chs. XV to XVII).

3. Unlimited needs and indefinite growth

a. Say's law in the short and in the long run

In the early 19th century, a celebrated observation by *Smith* (1776) – "What is annually saved is as regularly consumed as what is annually spent" (II.3.18) – was often quoted in reply to both the critics of excessive saving and the underconsumptionist authors. According to some historians, it suggests a conclusion similar to Say's law.[12] However, there is a sort of sleight of hand in using that quotation, for Smith was certainly not equalising saving and final consumption. On the contrary, he was contrasting them, as pointed out by *Faucci and Pesciarelli* (1976: 57–64). The misunderstanding arises from the fact that in that time there was a "tendency to dissolve investment into another category of consumption", i.e. wages (see *Bleaney* 1998: 486–7), while the importance of investment in physical capital was disregarded.

Duchini stressed that, according to Smith (S. 1776, I.8.43), accumulation can go on – despite the progressive diminution in the rate of profit and the increase in wages – because high wages stimulate commitment to production, and so productivity. On the other hand, Smith acknowledged the tendency of accumulation to create an excess of capital. He wrote that when profits diminish merchants always complain, but they forget that this tendency is due to the general prosperity.[13]

The tract by *Ackoute Smyth* (1828) put the point very simply: "capital may abound beyond the wants of a nation; beyond the discoverable objects for its investment" (42). Thus, Smith did not maintain that demand and supply always equalise. On the other hand, *Meek* (1950) was probably right when arguing that, on the analytical level, Ricardo did not attribute much importance to Say's law.

Several historians have shown that Say's law, in the short run, begs the question.[14] Actually, it seems a false syllogism. Nevertheless, in a perspective of development, Say's law suggests that the growth of consumption and of production can converge. The starting point is the Enlightenment tradition, best expressed by Smith (1776):

> The desire of food is limited in every man by the narrow capacity of the human stomach; but the desire of the conveniences and ornaments of building, dress, equipage, and household furniture, seems to have no limit or certain boundary.
>
> (I.11.59)

Consistently with that view, Say and Ricardo stated, against Malthus (see IX.3), that human needs are unlimited. J.B. *Say* (1828–29) declared: "Until every one is provided of all things, and no one has any more things to desire, it cannot be said that products are in excess". But he added soon after that the fulfilment of needs cannot be limited to elementary needs; it must also involve non-material needs, which are unlimited.[15] On turn, Ricardo unreservedly endorsed Smith's opinion that needs are unlimited. He added that it is the increase in capital that inclines society to "luxuries" of any kind.[16]

b. Diversification of products to overcome saturation

However, no supply can be unlimited unless it continually varies its products. *Comber* (1808) maintained that the only way to increase production lies in the increase of non-necessary goods. This – he says – is the very basis of national wealth (X: 261–71). *Lawson* (1843) suggested the same concept (II: 47–52). Edward *West* (1815) opposed Smith's thesis that accumulation tends to depress the rate of profit. This, West writes, can happen in one sector (due to excess of production) not for the general expansion of the economy (20–1). The same argument was repeated by the anonymous *Inquiry* (1821: 9–13).

Thus, the diversification of goods is the driving force of accumulation. The most insightful argument in this sense comes from a great philosopher, Hegel. The animal, wrote *Hegel* (1821), has limited wants, while man multiplies his wants and means and dissects "the concrete want into parts. The parts then become other wants …" (§ 190: 160). The multiplication of wants and means generates refinement. Such a tendency is due to social relations, which create interdependence and cooperation (§§ 192–5). The process calls for increasing skills and training and thus increasing division of labour. The latter leads to increase in productivity and growing mechanisation (§§ 196–8).

Ricardo and Say were well aware of this process. *Say* (1803) – precisely in the chapter *Dés Débouchés*, where his famous law is best illustrated – stated:

> In order to encourage industry, mere and simple consumption does not suffice. It is necessary to foster the development of tastes and needs, which raise among people the wish of consuming.
>
> (I, XV: 92)

And *Ricardo* (1821) wrote:

> If every man were to forego the use of luxuries, and be intent only on accumulation, a quantity of necessaries might be produced, for which there could not be any immediate consumption. Of commodities so limited in number, there might undoubtedly be an universal glut.
>
> (21.5)

This was a decisive achievement. Later on, it came to be seen as plain common-sense opinion. *Opdyke* (1851) was aware that the increase in the production of wealth progressively "liberates" other levels of needs and demand (I.3: 71–2). *Baudrillart* (1869: 53–81) saw moderate luxury as a factor of progress. He also saw in the unlimited and mobile nature of needs the factor which makes man superior to the other living beings (B. 1883, IX: 120–4). However, this approach took all too long to make itself felt in the analysis of accumulation.

Of course, when generalised this perspective is no longer dependent on Say's law. The latter actually never went beyond short-term analysis. For our time, it is worth mentioning two insightful analyses of this process. *Richardson* (1975) maintained that, in the division of labour, competition and increasing returns do not tend to monopoly. On the contrary, they appear compatible because they both drive towards progressive increase in specialisation and variation of products. Thus, the tendency runs in the direction of skill and interdependence rather than concentration (352–6). Compare *Smith* (1776, I.1.9).

The problem is best clarified by *Pasinetti* (1981). In theory, accumulation has no limits because with time consumers learn to adjust their consumption to the increase of their income, choosing new goods, which either satisfy new needs or better satisfy old needs. Thus, consumers learn to increase their utility much more through this process of learning than through rational behaviour (affirmed by neoclassical authors). This process avoids the danger of saturation, which would only occur if consumers failed to vary their consumption. On the collective level, saturation is definitely avoided thanks to the possibility of shortening daily labour. The only possible limit to accumulation lies in insufficient speed in learning a new behaviour in one of the following cases: expression of new preferences by individual consumers, supply of new goods by enterprises or shortening of labour time by society. The delay in such cases causes temporary crises and technological unemployment.[17] This analysis also applies perfectly to our time.

Conclusions

All three issues discussed were destined for a long life. The business cycle theory remains a pillar of economic theory. But, although it can be useful to explain short-run fluctuations, it is deceiving for long-term analysis of capitalist accumulation, as is evident in accounting for the current crisis. Unproductive capital has been the main tool of Marxist authors to support a new version of underconsumption. But this approach led to confusing human capital investment with parasitism (see ch. XIX).

On the other hand, the prospect of unlimited growth based on the diversification of goods appears the real solution to capitalist accumulation. However, this view remained marginal even among the classical authors who expressed it. Nevertheless, the approach not only clarifies the 19th-century debate on crises but also helps to account for the crisis of the welfare state, which we have not left behind us. Unlimited needs and unlimited growth was also the prospect envisaged by a few Marxist or radical economists of the 1970s–80s (see XVIII.3–4).

Notes

1 E.g. Poggio Bracciolini, Bernard de Mandeville and Adam Smith (for the first two, see Perrotta 2004, respectively, V: 89–90 and XI: 226, 233). See also Smith (1776, IV.2.9).
2 On Marx's view of development and cycle as two aspects of the same process, see *Sylos Labini* (2004: 52–5).
3 Pareto (1896, §§ 927–9. See also —1906, ch. IX, §§ 75–7).
4 See, e.g. Dow (1977); Kates (1998, ch. 6; etc.).
5 J.B. Say (1803, I, ch. 12: 121–2).
6 See, respectively, Cattaneo (1836, § 11: 408–11) and —(1843, § 22: 546).
7 Clément (1867, tome I, I.VII.1: 187–8).
8 Marx (*Capital III*, ch. 25; see also ch. 30: V.XXX.41).
9 Loria (1889, I, IV.4.3–6: 348–476).
10 Ibid, II, V.3.1.a: 332–5.
11 Loria (1934, §§ 98–100: 292–308).
12 E.g. Blaug (1962: 57); Duchini (1971: 106). See also IX.3.
13 Duchini (1971: 109). Cp. Smith (1776, I.9.10. See also I.9.2 and II.4.8).
14 E.g. O'Brien (1975, ch. 8, 3.2: 231); Graziani (1980: XXXII–XXXIII).
15 Say (1828–29, VII.4, tome 2: 210–13).
16 Ricardo (1821, 21.7; —1810–23, letter 16/9/1816: 44–5; —[1951–73], vol IV, *Funding System*: 179).
17 Pasinetti (1981, chs. 4.7–9; 5.7–8; 10.9).

XIV Fall and revival of Smith's distinction

Background

The last authors who continued to apply Smith's distinction rejected two of its essential postulates: the confining of productive labour to material labour and the separation between productiveness and utility. Nevertheless, the distinction practically died out in the first half of the 20th century. But in the 1940s it was revived by the newborn development economics and transformed into a tool for development policy. The nature of the distinction then changed: it also included immaterial wealth, conceived unproductive labour as labour temporarily in excess and saw welfare as the aim of the increase in productive labour.

1. The final crisis of Smith's postulates

a. Productive as useful again

At the turn of the century, the two most important authors who still used Smith's distinction interpreted productive labour as useful labour. Ghino *Valenti*'s (1892) book is entirely devoted to unproductive labour. Its title in English is "Productive Labour and Speculation". Valenti stated that Smith's definition of productive labour is wrong because productiveness is not given by value but by utility. Along with economic progress, the value of goods diminishes while utility increases (232–3).

According to the principle of utility, menial servants are productive, and an impresario can enrich himself through the immaterial labour of entertainers. While it is true that the king, lawyers, the military and civil servants are unproductive, this does not apply to doctors, engineers and even actors (234–8). On the other hand, Valenti contradictorily shared Smith's preference for material products because the latter are accumulable. Learning apart, social productivity is directly proportional to the products' durability (275–6). Valenti stressed the importance of distinguishing between individual and social economy. On this basis, he contrasted productive activities and speculative activities. The latter prosper when free competition is checked. They are productive only for the individual but add nothing to social utilities. They simply move utilities from one part of society to another (XII–XIV, 277).

In his historical survey, Valenti referred to Ortes, in support to his (Valenti's) thesis that not all kinds of individual enrichment become social enrichment (150–3). But the reference is inappropriate: in Ortes's absolutely static economy, enrichment only means a transfer of wealth (see *Ortes* 1774). Valenti also stated that distribution affects social productivity. An unequal distribution, he wrote, generates a proportional number of idle people, either rich or poor (276). Later on, Valenti (1906) came closer to the neoclassical view of the three factors of production. All of them contribute to the production of utility (I: 216–28). This time he stated, like Marshall, that it is better to avoid the expression productive/unproductive labour as source of misunderstandings (225–6).

Taussig (1896), an American author, considered wages to be made up of use values. With this approach, he was able to reject Ricardo's equivalence between workers' consumption and physical productive power (19–33). On the other hand, capital is not made of wages only, as Ricardo assumed (181). Some wages went beyond mere survival, even in Ricardo's times. Workers were therefore able to consume beyond their productive power, and to contribute to production with non-material activities (33–5).

With the increase of non-material labour, the separation between productive and unproductive activities becomes more difficult. Under the influence of Loria, whom he cites, Taussig stated that a large part of the activities of lawyers, financial operators and brokers is not useful for production (34–5fn).

Later on, Taussig (1911), too, reached the conclusion that, to avoid Smith's contradictions, it is better to define productivity in terms of utility rather than value. Taussig made a good point when writing that there are different degrees of utility in different occupations. Nevertheless, this consideration drove him to fall back on the boring casuistry on unproductive activities. In the end, he confined real unproductive activities to the pauper, thieves, swindlers and ne'er-do-wells (I: 16–20), but also to the financial speculators who accumulate huge quantities of wealth with predatory – and so unproductive – activities (25–8).

We must repeat, in conclusion, that such criticisms of Smith about value and utility arose from misunderstanding him. His real distinction is between labour paid with capital, for investment, and labour paid with income, for personal consumption.

b. Distinction rejected

The hegemony of neoclassical economics left hardly any room for the issue of unproductive labour for some decades. Hla *Myint* (1948) wrote that this was due to the general equilibrium principle, which is based on the idea that the allocative efficiency of resources is realised by the preferences of the individual consumer. This approach is incompatible with the concept of unproductive labour because the latter implies that not all paid labour is productive (71–2). *Kirkaldy* (1920) wrote that all labourers are productive, except those in excess and those who harm society morally. He also listed occupations according to the degree of productiveness (64–73). In a collection of essays for the sesquicentennial of the *Wealth of Nations* (*Clark et alii* 1926), none of the economists (Jacob Hollander and Viner included) mentioned the issue of unproductive labour. Passing reference is made by the only non-economist author (Palyi).

Smith's distinction was misunderstood by most neoclassical authors, who tended to criticise it superficially.[1] *Bowley* (1937) maintained that Smith's distinction had generated a great confusion (74fn.). Other authors, while not rejecting the distinction, came up with improbable interpretations of it, philologically and historically unfounded.[2]

Only the American moralists, in this period, still found the concept of unproductive labour appropriate, but they attributed it with a meaning very far from the original. *Carver* (1919) revived the concept of indirectly productive and applied it not only to teachers, artists and public employees but also to menial servants. What matters is not whether the product is sold but whether it contributes to social wealth. That labour whose products is sold to satisfy a vice is unproductive. On the contrary, the preacher is productive.[3] *Bye* (1924) distinguished between individual gain and social wealth in order to declare all dishonest or speculative activities unproductive (81–2). Significantly, this subject disappeared in a later edition (*Bye-Hewett* 1952). However, some other authors adhered to Smith's distinction (e.g. *Marconcini* 1926: 25–32).

Some useful analyses of Smith's distinction were to come later on. John *Hicks* (1965) wrote that Smith considered his chapter on productive/unproductive labour as the central one of the whole book. Hicks aptly described Smith's growth model, which derives from that chapter and pointed out its main flaws. This model implies that capital is reduced to circulating capital (actually: wages); reproduction is strictly confined to the previous product, which excludes variations due to different expectations or the presence of money. The lack of the latter elements, Hicks writes, had disastrous consequences, because it led to the conclusion that saving was necessarily invested (ch. 4). Actually, Hicks failed to examine Smith from the historical viewpoint, which makes his (Hick's) analysis rather obvious.

Joseph *Schumpeter* [1949] wrote that the productive/unproductive labour distinction, formerly a serious question, slipped off later "into futility" (III.6.5.a: 628). He maintained that Smith creates confusion by mixing up people unable to work (children, aged people, etc.), public employees paid out of the taxes and service labourers (628–31). As it happens, however, the first categories are not included in Smith's distinction.

In his note, Schumpeter stated that the matter had, *by then*, become a "dusty museum piece". This graphic expression was taken out of its context by the economists. Subsequently it came to constitute the final blow that discredited Smith's distinction once and for all, even at the historical level. Since then, economists have felt relieved: thanks to Schumpeter's authority, they feel they no longer need to bother about a question whose significance eludes present academic education.

Coontz (1965) mixed the issue of unproductive labour with other analytical questions, with the result of muddying the whole analysis (see, e.g., on Smith: 55–7). Coontz quoted Keynes, who defined unproductive consumption as the consumption that does not increase the labourer's productivity (156–7). This suggests that Keynes, like the classical authors, neglected any positive relationship between increase in consumption and increase in productivity.

2. The endless controversy on immaterial wealth

a. The issue

The issue as to whether wealth consists only of material objects or also of immaterial goods runs through all modern economics up to, at least, the 1960s–70s. We have already examined some aspects of this endless controversy (see VI.3–4, VII.3, XIII.3).

The mercantilists had a balanced idea of wealth as made up of both physical and intellectual elements. The former derive from nature, while the latter derive from labour. Labour, in turn, is both a physical activity, which transforms materials, and an intellectual activity, which directs this material transformation and also produces services (like transport). James *Steuart* (1767) best expressed the traditional mercantilist division between the two components of goods: matter and labour. The greater the labour component is, Steuart explains, the higher is the value and the purchasing power of the good.[4]

Smith used to speak of wealth as "the annual produce of our land and our labour". This expression seems similar to Steuart's, but in fact it is very different. Under the influence of both physiocratic theory and the incipient industrial revolution, Smith actually considered only the physical aspect of labour. His theory of productive labour as confined to material occupations confirms this attitude.

The classical economists were greatly influenced by Smith's view (and, again, by the industrial revolution). Their analyses of accumulation and surplus imply that wealth is an aggregate of material goods. We have seen that many authors admitted the productiveness of immaterial labour. But, with some exceptions (see VII.3), the majority of them conceived of immaterial labour only as support for material wealth. This is the old concept of indirectly productive labour, which has an ancillary role, subordinate to material production.

However, during the 19th century, the alternative view gradually spread: the idea that a part of wealth itself is immaterial and that immaterial labour can be productive *per se*, regardless of material production. This idea developed along with economic progress. The increase in productivity allows for progressive increase of autonomous immaterial labour. Moreover, immaterial goods account for an increasing share of final consumption, in both qualitative and quantitative terms. Finally, accumulation also includes immaterial labour that produces immaterial products. In turn, the latter answer to immaterial needs.

In other cases, we see ever-increasing production of immaterial goods, which are conveyed with material supports – telephone, radio and TV, for example, or information technology and various devices for watching films or listening to music, etc. Not to speak of the traditional material vehicles of immaterial goods, like books, technical drawings, maps, etc. The discussions among classical authors on the productiveness of typographers or watchmakers appear a sort of fetishism, where the intellectual nature of the good is reduced to its physical aspect.

b. The discussion continues

J.S. *Mill* (1844) conceived of wealth as consisting in any source of enjoyments, whether material or immaterial (III.9–11). But later, Mill (1848) changed his mind, stating that he would only treat wealth as consisting of material objects, in which labour embodies utility.[5] *Cannan* (1914), too, thought that – for practical reasons – it is better to confine attention to the concept of material welfare, although the material encroaches upon the immaterial (1–5).

Other authors saw wealth as the sum of exchangeable goods, whether material or immaterial.[6] However, *Clément* (1867) criticised J.S. Mill's definition of wealth as the sum of exchangeable goods. Personal faculties, wrote Clément, are part of wealth, although they cannot be exchanged. In any case, wealth is made of all the valuable utilities, whether represented by material or immaterial elements.[7]

Léon *Walras* (1874) described wealth as the sum of all things, material or immaterial, which yield utility and are scarce (V: 23). For *Pareto* (1896), wealth is given by utilities (§§ 31–3). For *Marshall* (1890), it consists of desirable things, whether material or immaterial (II.II.3). Francis *Bain* (1892) concluded a lengthy analysis observing that wealth is made up of material commodities (I.1–2: 16–34). Charles *Gide* (1883) stated that services are a part of social wealth (II.3: 111). A similar attitude appears in *Del Vecchio* (1908), who offered a detailed analysis of the several forms of immaterial wealth.

Ferrara favoured the utility value approach and Say's law (F. 1857: 248–60), but asserted that immaterial goods do not exist independently of material ones. His argument is that in any intellectual labour it is necessary to use material tools.[8] The alleged immaterial products are in fact a material modification of our organs; and they are not accumulable, because what is accumulated is only their useful effect, not the product.[9] As you can see, Ferrara's arguments are often sophistic. According to *Pareto* (1906), Ferrara settled the dispute over immaterial goods by stating that goods are material if we consider the production of them and immaterial if we consider the effect they cause (V, § 34). Of course, this is not so much a solution as a sleight of hand.

Loria (1934) stuck to wealth as material goods, not including services or moral goods. Consequently, immaterial labour is unproductive, although teachers and professionals are very useful to society.[10] Like Marx, Loria thought that unproductive labourers help proprietors to keep the workers under and hold on to the privileges of upper classes (§ 112: 336–7). However, when the proprietors appropriate too much wealth and leave too little of it to the unproductive classes, conflict breaks out between the two, as has often happened in the past. The unproductive classes then join forces with the workers, and revolution is the likely outcome (§ 113: 340–3).

Crosser (1957) was a surviving champion of the original classical current of thought. He complained that, because of the "unrelenting opposition" to Marx, modern "psychologistic economy" has also destroyed the classical categories (xiii). Crosser blamed Keynes for replacing the classical concept of physical product, which is computable, with the concept of product as flow, which is not computable (278–82). Similarly, Keynes's elimination of the distinction between the monetary and real aspects of production makes it impossible to distinguish the productive from the unproductive use of both human and material resources (262–3). All this led Keynes to reject the classical distinction between investment and consumption, and thus between goods that are productively destined for investment and goods unproductively destined for consumption. In the end, Crosser wrote, Keynes deprives both investment and demand of any social significance.[11]

Bagiotti (1976) persisted with the idea that services are less productive than industry. Their prevalence, he said, is responsible for the tendency towards stagnation (230). In the 1990s, the idea that services are less susceptible of increasing their productivity than material goods was still widespread, despite the decline of the industrial economy, from which this bias derived. But *Delaunay and Gadrey* (1992), having outlined the history of the theories on the productiveness of services (chs. 2–5), go on to demonstrate that the information technologies applied in health services can grow even more than material industry. These new productions also use technologies of an industrial type (ch. 6).

In conclusion, the division between material and immaterial goods is not clear-cut. Along with economic progress, most physical products acquire immaterial features, and their value or utility is increasingly depending on these features.

3. Unproductive labour as labour in excess

J.B. *Say* revived the concept proposed by Petty and other mercantilists (see Chapter II) of unproductive labour as labour in excess. From time to time, this idea crops up again in the classical school (see Chapters V–VII). Say (1803), besides stating that professionals – although productive – should not exceed a certain number (78–9; see VII.2.a), maintained that even the most productive sectors can have an excess of labour. In this case, he states, the part of labour in excess is unproductive. Labour is productive only as long as it increases utility; beyond that point, it is an utterly unproductive activity. In some professions, Say continues, an excessive number of members can even damage efficiency, as in the case of lawyers, who – when there are too many of them – spawn ever more complicated norms.[12]

This marked a crucial advance, which went beyond the Enlightenment authors. The latter were inclined to think that the basic production sectors, like agriculture and manufacture, could not suffer any redundancy. Many authors echoed Say, maintaining that an excess of labourers is possible not only among professionals and the other services, but also among material works. This causes waste.[13]

Roscher (1854) observed that most authors had by then equalised useful with productive labour (§ 62: 139). But – Roscher stated – what matters is the proportion in a society between the different occupations and their respective degree of productivity (§ 65–6: 143–8). Thus, first, the types of labour can be less or more productive; second, the less productive occupations are not to be excluded, but rather must be kept within reasonable limits (as also Genovesi and Say affirmed); third, labourers are unproductive only insofar as their number exceeds the social needs.

Towards the end of the 19th century, as Walter *Eltis* (1984) noted, many authors agreed that it is difficult to make a clear-cut distinction between productive and unproductive occupations. The classical division between a surplus-producing sector and a surplus-consuming sector also disappeared, except among the Marxists (85, 334–5).

In the *Palgrave Dictionary*, Ethel *Faraday* (1899) recalled Roscher's considerations and revived the interpretation of unproductive labour as labour in excess. She acutely observed:

> Productive and unproductive labour differ not in kind but in degree. To the community all labour are unproductive which are maintained to the disadvantage of others which are more necessary.

She referred this principle not only to "the military, clerical, or professional classes", but also to agricultural and manufacturing labour (219a).

Faraday added some wise empirical rules to evaluate unproductive labour (the same rules were applied by Petty): there is not "a hard and fast line between productive and unproductive". We can define productive labour as

> "labour which creates or develops, directly or indirectly, material or immaterial products, exchangeable, and possessing a value not less than the value consumed in producing them. These products may be of every degree of necessity", from daily bread to ornaments, "and every degree of durability". Faraday finally states: "The higher the ground we take, the harder it is to estimate the productivity of any given labour".
>
> (219b)

Othmar *Spann* (1910) confirmed this "new" approach: any addition of labour may or may not increase social wealth. Thus, there can be unproductive labour either among teachers or among peasants (65–6).

Later on, the issue of unproductive labour as excess labour was approached in terms of disguised (or hidden) unemployment. This concept – first used by Joan Robinson (see *Sunna* 2016: 73–4) – was applied to backward agriculture by the authors of development economics, like *Rosenstein Rodan* (1943: 245), *Prebisch* (1949: 495–6), etc. For the 1950s economists, see the accurate analysis by *Boianovsky* (2017a).[14]

These authors held that in backward economies, especially in the agricultural sector, the production of the same quantity of a certain good requires more workers than those employed in an advanced economy. The difference between the two groups of workers expresses the proportions of the disguised unemployment. *Barber* (1967) appropriately saw in disguised unemployment a revival of Smith's distinction (26–7). See also XX.5, where "disguised unemployment" is used to express another concept.

4. Development and welfare

As one of history's little ironies, when Schumpeter got rid of the issue of unproductive labour (see here, XIV.1.b), a revival of Smith's distinction was coming underway again. Hla *Myint* (1948) restored to Smith's distinction the original spirit of commitment to development and linked it to welfare policies, i.e. to increase in workers' consumption. Myint's book is a detailed analysis of the classical theories of accumulation and development, in which the author examines the various theories on the basis of their ability to stimulate increase in productive labour and raise productivity. Myint was inspired by development economics, which was a budding branch in those years. Development analyses were revealing the dual structure of the world economy and the backwardness of the non-western world.

The decisive step in this direction was taken in the outstanding essay by W. Arthur *Lewis* (1954). Lewis noted that classical economics, despite its limits, is better suited than neoclassical thought to explain backwardness and development. In particular, he assimilated Smith's productive/unproductive labour distinction to a two-sector economy, divided between a – more productive – industrial sector and a traditional agricultural sector, with low productivity and low consumption. The latter sector can support the former thanks to its unlimited supply of (cheap) labour. This sector is clearly the realm of disguised unemployment, which is another form of low productivity.

Vincent *Bladen* (1960) reformulated Smith's analysis of unproductive labour in terms of Lewis's two-sector model. Here, Smith's menial servants become the cheap, low productivity labourers afforded by agriculture to the highly productive industrial sector. Bladen (1974) also generalised Myint's model. He noted that in the past personal services had flourished because the upper classes made use of many menial servants. But subsequently the number of servants had been drastically reduced. However, Bladen stressed, with the growth of social wealth these services would again be on the rise, but this time not so cheap or of such low quality. They would show dignity and efficiency. This demonstrates, he maintained, that Smith's concern was not with the low value of services as such, but with the disadvantage of the country when too many people are employed in low-value occupations. In a developed economy, these people could be employed in high-value occupations (66–7).

Bertrand de *Jouvenel* (1957), too, had noticed the change in the importance of personal services. He referred to one of Colin Clark's calculations, according to which nearly one half of national wealth is not accounted for because the GDP only includes services that are paid for in the market. This method, Jouvenel observed, leads to overrating the accumulation progress in developing countries, because the product increase is measured on a smaller basis than the actual one. On the other hand, it underrates the progress in developed economies, where non-market services take on growing importance – for example, free labour.

Jouvenel also repeated Pigou's observation about the possibility that some activities, although yielding a profit, can even reduce social wealth. Such is the case of productions that pollute the environment. He calls these "negative goods". They are not only unproductive but are even harmful, although they produce profit.

In the last few decades, the Smithian concept of unproductive labour has from time to time been revived once again as a useful concept for understanding the economy. It was used by, among others, *Gramm* (1987), *Danielson* (1994: 33–5, 71–2, 130–1, passim) and James Buchanan, in his *Ethics and Economic Progress* (1997).

Conclusions

The perspective opened by the last of the classical analyses leads to the key concept of human capital. In the second half of the 20th century, intellectual and service labour was booming fast in developed economies, and analysis had to shift from the accumulation of physical means of production to the accumulation of immaterial means, i.e. mental resources. The concept of human capital, which Schultz and Gary Becker made popular (see Chapter XII), was centred on individuals. But a concept of social investment in human capital could be much more effective for development.

However, as from the 1960s, authors failed to pay due attention to social investment in human capital. The majority of both neoclassical and Marxist authors proposed rigid and scholastic interpretations of the problems raised by the implementation of the welfare state. At the end of the 1970s, no one was aware of the endless crisis that was impending after the long welfare-state boom. That crisis can be seen as a consequence of the unsolved issue of unproductive labour (see Chapters XIX and XX).

Notes

1 See, for example, G. Gough (1920: 62). Prato (1924–25: 71–2). Ayres (1944: 271–2). Jenkins (1948: 181fn). Rima (1967: 67–8). E. West (1969: 204–5). Routh (1975: 101).
2 See, for example, Bertolino (1938–39, V: 631). Nagels (1974: 44–50). Benetti (1979: 112–26). F. Campanella (1982: 100–5).
3 Carver (1919: 255–61. See also —1924: 140–81).
4 Steuart (1767, II.24: 291–2, 296).
5 Ibid., I.3.11. For details, see Mill 1848, XII.1.e.
6 See e.g. Cournot (1838: 2–3; —1877, II.2: 57–8); Faraday (1899: 219a, in the *Palgrave Dictionary*); Hobson (1914, 1.2: 3).
7 Clément (1867, tome I, I.VII.1: 189–91).
8 Ferrara (1853: 253–89; —1855: 472–3; —1859: 377–8, 413–68).
9 Ferrara (1857: 77–84; —1859: 457–8).
10 Loria (1934, §§ 110–1: 332–6).
11 Crosser (1957, 284–5. See also —1960: 95–6).
12 Say (1803, 39: fn 49. —1828–29, I, 1.5: 91–2).
13 Among these authors, see Bosellini (1816: 5–6), Fuoco (1825–27, II.5: 173), Dunoyer (1830, tome 2, b. 5: 14–15), Mrs. Martineau (1832, vol. I, 1.4: 48–9), Pautet (1835: 26–7), P. Rossi (1836–37: 69a), Ms. Meynieu (1839: 52), Joseph Garnier (1846: 43–7).
14 Boianovsky (2017a: 13–16, 29, 40–4).

XV Crises and underconsumption in Marx and his followers[1]

Background

Marx based his analysis of crises on the contrast between production of use values, common to any production system, and production of surplus value, which is proper to capitalism. This contrast generates a permanent tendency to overproduction, which causes cyclical crises in the short run and a tendency for the profit rate to fall in the long run. Some of Marx's followers interpreted this approach in terms of underconsumption (Luxemburg, etc.), while others saw in it the possibility for capitalist accumulation to go on indefinitely, in economic terms (Tugan-Baranowsky, Hilferding). Yet others contested the idea that capitalism tended towards final crisis (Bernstein). The main stream (orthodox, ranging from Kautsky to Lenin) interpreted Marx's view as a tendency of capitalist accumulation towards depression. But the crucial problem is that Marx did not provide an analysis of structural crises, i.e. of a constant unbalance between supply and demand that can be resolved only through intervention external to accumulation.

1. Marx on capital accumulation

a. Two analyses of crises

In Marx, we find two analyses that explain the nature of economic crises. One focuses on the short run, i.e. on periodical crises. We examined it before (XIII.1.b). The other refers to the long-run tendency of capitalist accumulation. This is examined in the law of the falling rate of profit (mainly in *Capital III*) and in the schemes of enlarged reproduction (in *Capital II*). In both cases, capitalist accumulation in the long run reveals a tendency to relative diminution of variable capital, i.e. labour (see *Capital I*, ch. 23.2).

The short- and long-run analyses in Marx have a common premise: there is a conflict between the need to produce use values for final consumption (which is the natural end of production in any society) and the tendency of capitalists to produce surplus value for their enrichment. In capitalist accumulation, the production of use values is not an end, but simply a means for the "valorisation of value", i.e. for the increase of value through production. This dualism is a major achievement of Marx's economic thought.

Apart from this common aspect, the short-run analysis – as we have seen – adopts the business cycle theory and confines periodical crises to momentary maladjustments between supply and demand, which the market will necessarily overcome. The long-run analysis, on the other hand, aims to show that capitalist accumulation will inevitably end in a final crisis of the system and will be replaced by another system of production.

We have already noted that the third analysis, that of structural crises, is absent in Marx. In these crises, the unbalance between production and consumption is so deep that it cannot be overcome without an external factor (usually the state) to restore equilibrium. Later on, failing to find any such analysis in Marx, the Marxist authors ended up by examining depressions either as harmless periodical crises or as the beginning of the final crisis.

In the following paragraphs, we will examine Marx's treatment of the tendency of capitalist accumulation towards the final crisis.

b. The falling rate of profit

This law is illustrated in chapters 13–15 of *Capital III.* Marx's premise is that competition leads every enterprise to increase its own productivity ever more, in order to reduce the production cost. This is achieved mainly through technical progress, which usually consists in the introduction of new machines. The entrepreneur who first introduces the innovation enjoys a temporary extra-profit. But soon the other entrepreneurs of the sector are forced to adopt the same innovation to keep up with competitive prices.

At the social level, this process leads constant capital (the inanimate section of investment, which does not produce surplus value) to grow steadily due to the continual shift of new portions of investment from the variable capital (i.e. wage labour, the only source of surplus value) to constant capital (machinery). Thus, variable capital diminishes relatively along with the corresponding increase in machines. The process is catalysed by the concentration tendency, which is proper to capitalist competition (ch. 15).

Consequently, social productivity increases (thanks to the growth of constant capital), as does the workers' per-capita production of surplus value, but the share of surplus value in the total value produced diminishes. Now, profit depends on the quantity of surplus value produced, but it is also a percentage of the total investment. Marx stated that growth of the sterile part of investment (i.e. of constant capital) reduces profit. Moreover, increase in productivity reduces the value of the goods produced, which further depresses profit.

Marx also examined the counteracting tendencies in this process (ch. 14). Apart from foreign trade, all of them boil down to one trend: increase in productivity (which he did not take into account in the accumulation scheme of ch. 13). However, his assumption was that increase in productivity never reaches the point of compensating for the relative decrease of variable capital.

Marx did not explain how he could assert that productivity grows less than constant capital. *Shibata* (1934: 73–5; —1939: 60–1) maintained that, contrary to Marx's view, the growth of constant capital increases the rate of profit, rather than reducing it. But many leading authors have noted that it remains undetermined which of the two tendencies prevails.[2] *Blaug* (1960) aptly observed that Marx was aware of the two types of technical progress, one which increases productivity by saving labour and the other which does so by saving capital. However, he attributes more importance to the first type. Actually, in Marx's times, the former type prevailed.

Similar to Blaug, *Pasinetti* (1981) maintained that Marx confuses capital intensity (i.e. the capital/product ratio) with mechanisation (the capital/labour ratio). Increase in the latter implies an increase in unemployment but not necessarily an increase of the "organic composition" (total value of constant capital/total value of labour), on which depends the fall in profit. The increase can leave the rate of profit unchanged (ch. 9.7, fn 11). However here, too, the two types of ratio mentioned by Pasinetti started steadily diverging only in the 20th century (see as follows, sections 4 and 5).

The original version of the law of the falling rate of profit does not relate directly to underconsumption in the strict sense.[3] Joan *Robinson* (1949) maintained that, in *Capital III*, the law is inextricably intertwined with underconsumption theory.[4] But, on the contrary, Marx used the steady expansion of constant capital as an explanation alternative to underconsumptionism. The demand that absorbs the growing surplus – he stated – is given neither by unproductive consumption (Malthus's solution) nor by the increase in population (the first of Ricardo's answers to Malthus), nor indeed by Say's law (Ricardo's second answer). It is given by the growing investment in constant capital. Thus, in Marx, the tendency to overproduction produces two results. In the short term, it causes periodical but momentary crises, which are solved by market itself. In the long term, it leads to the collapse of capitalism.

A great number of commentators have strived and struggled around the law of the falling rate of profit. Actually, the mere tendency of the profit rate to fall along with accumulation had already been assumed by Smith, Ricardo and J.S. Mill. In the last decades of the 19th century, it was generally admitted. On this assumption, a new theory of stationary state was also constructed (see XIX.4). Moreover, *Bronfenbrenner* (1965: 239) stated that the analysis of stagnation consequent to Marx's law is more effective than the analyses proposed by Keynes, Hansen and Schumpeter. James *Becker* (1962) effectively associated Marx's theory of the falling rate of profit with unequal distribution, which he deplored as unavoidable in capitalist economy.

The general acceptance of the idea that the rate of profit tends to fall was in part due to the classical economists' neglect of investment in human capital. The latter tends to hold the rate of profit from falling, since an increasing part of investment goes to raising the workers' productive consumption rather than constant capital. In addition, in the 20th century, innovations became increasingly capital-saving rather than labour-saving.[5] Thus, productivity could grow even when constant capital no longer increased in value and the rate of profit did not fall. Nevertheless, 20th century Marxists took the falling rate of profit as bearings to orientate their analyses.

c. Enlarged reproduction

In *Capital II* (ch. 21), Marx reproduced Quesnay's *Tableau Economique* dynamically. The *Tableau* had described the relationships among the different activities of the general economic process (production, circulation, consumption and reproduction) and among the fundamental social classes (rentiers, farmers and manufacturers). Social classes had, from Quesnay and Smith on, been defined by their respective roles in the production process. On the basis of the *Tableau*, Marx described the succession of cycles of capitalist accumulation. The result is given by the schemes of enlarged reproduction. This process is distinguished in three sections. The largest describes the production of means of production (constant capital), which drives the other two.

The second section (mainly production of wage goods or necessaries) depends on the quantity of surplus value devoted to it, which in turn depends on the number of workers employed in production. It cannot usually grow beyond the workers' subsistence level. The third section is production of luxury goods, i.e. non-wage goods, which do not come within the production process. The consumption of luxury goods is mainly unproductive and is accounted for by capitalists and their "clients" (unproductive labourers). This section can only grow to a very limited extent because capitalists tend to invest the surplus rather than waste it. Of course, this assumption by Marx is highly unrealistic, although none of the commentators has noticed it: enlarged accumulation with negligible growth of non-elementary goods is impossible.

In the enlarged reproduction schemes, Marx's assumption was the same as in the law of the falling rate of profit: constant capital grows much more than both workers' consumption and luxury consumption. Here, too, no room is left for the expansion of productive consumption, nor for investment in human capital. This is probably the weakest point of Marx's analysis. Enlarged reproduction with no growth of per-capita consumption not only contradicts historical experience, even in Marx's times, but is logically unthinkable.

2. Bernstein and others against underconsumption

The controversies of the early followers of Marx often revolved around underconsumptionism. The latter implied that, within a given market, productive consumption cannot grow steadily and so cannot absorb the growing surplus. Many historians have written about Marx's underconsumption view, but in general what they really meant was what we call here overproduction (for other meanings of the term, see *Bleaney* 1976, ch. 1). We will briefly outline the debate that arose in the mid-1890s, soon after publication of

Capital II (1885) and *Capital III* (1894), edited by Engels. Note that we bring in the issues of underconsumption, crises and the falling rate of profit only when connected with unproductive labour.

In 1894, *Tugan-Baranowsky*, a Russian professor, published *Industrial Crises in Contemporary England*, translated into German in 1901. In this work and in Tugan (1905), the author describes capitalist accumulation as a smooth progress that proceeds indefinitely. With regard to Marx's reproduction schemes, he assumes that, even if living labour is reduced more and more, due to technical progress, the growing surplus is absorbed by the first sector (production of means of production) and the relative decrease in final consumption is no obstacle (ch. 9). Tugan-Baranowsky turned out to have a great influence. His first book was commented on by all the German Marxists of the time. Later on, Sweezy (1942, ch. 10.1) complained that all the key figures of German Social Democracy, including Hilferding, albeit with the exception of Rosa Luxemburg, were influenced by Tugan's interpretation.

The most striking case is that of Eduard *Bernstein* (1899), one of the leaders of German Social Democracy. Bernstein criticised the underconsumptionist view that Rosa Luxemburg had meanwhile been proposing in a number of articles. But he also dissented from Marx's conviction that crises were bound to get worse as capitalist accumulation proceeded (ch. 3.d). Relying on a rich collection of data on the German economy, Bernstein maintained that – contrary to Marx's forecast (e.g. in *Capital I*, ch. 25) – the workers' incomes were growing (ch.3.b) and the prices of staple goods were falling (3.d: 96–7). These circumstances, together with the birth of trusts and the growth of producers' associations and labour unions, made crises much less disruptive than in the past.

Bernstein came up with a definitive answer to the question as to where the growing surplus would be employed. It goes to increasing wages, and – even more – to increasing the *middle classes*, the latter by no means being parasites, as Marx suggested. The middle classes are made up of employees, technicians and traders, who are both a consequence and a cause of the increase in productivity and social wealth (3.b: 91–6). The middle classes, Bernstein maintained, like the traditional workers, had enormously increased in number, but the former more than the latter (96fn.). Besides, the small enterprises, far from being destroyed as the *Manifesto* predicted, were growing in number in every field of production (3.c).

This was the real solution to the underconsumption problem, which had troubled 19th-century economics from the outset. Unfortunately, Bernstein's answer was rejected by the orthodox Marxians. It is true that it was over-optimistic and unduly generalised the situation of Germany at the time. Like Marx, the orthodox authors pinpointed and stressed the tendency to depression, which actually prevailed in the 1920s–30s crisis. Nevertheless, failure to take account of Bernstein's analysis left Marxist reflection in a deadlock. Much later, when the depression was left behind and accumulation showed a new leap forward thanks to the welfare state, the Marxists no longer had the tools to get to grips with what was going on.

The most influential author of German Social Democracy, Karl *Kautsky* (1902), known as "the red Pope", put forward a balanced interpretation of crises, faithful to Marx and based on overproduction. Kautsky – like Marx – reduced periodical crises to cyclical fluctuations (271–5) and criticised both the theories of the breakdown (275–80) and Tugan's approach (281–96). He added that the persistent tendency to overproduction would drive capitalism to stagnation, mass poverty and class conflicts. In a word, capitalism would give way, sooner or later, to a chronic depression. This view later came to be shared by *Sweezy*.[6]

Boudin (1907: 201) criticised Bernstein in favour of Marx's forecast. He argued that the artisans and peasants were in fact diminishing in number, because the falling rate of profit left little surplus for them. *Hilferding* (1910), another leader of German Social Democracy, did not share the Tugan's optimism but was inclined to see periodical crises as due to momentary disproportions, rather than to overproduction. He also considered Marx's reproduction schemes as proof that *on the purely economic level* capitalist accumulation could go on indefinitely (ch. 16).

Lenin, in his early economic writings, fiercely criticised the underconsumption view of the Russian "People's Friends" or *Narodniki* (see *Lenin* 1894, —1895, —1897, the last of these also being a critique of Sismondi). The *Narodniki* maintained that capitalist development in Russia was impossible for lack of a modern market and sufficient demand. In reply, Lenin showed that, on the contrary, capitalism was already developing in Russia. These People's Friends were by no means ill-equipped, and Rosa *Luxemburg* (1913) treated them with much respect. She devoted two chapters of her book (19 and 20) to analyse their main exponents of them (Voroncov and Nikolaj-on).

3. Rosa Luxemburg's underconsumption

An underconsumption theory similar to the classical one was cogently expressed by Rosa Luxemburg. She, too, was a leading exponent of German Social Democracy. After World War I, Luxemburg founded the insurrectional Spartacus League, anti-Bolschevik and anti-reformist. She was defeated and killed, her dead body thrown into the river.

Luxemburg (1913) raised what is known as the realisation problem, i.e. the fact that there is not sufficient demand in the market to acquire the surplus generated in production. Luxemburg made it clear that her concern was not with the periodical or cyclical crises examined by Sismondi. These crises do not affect capitalist accumulation in the long run (35). Rather, she was interested in Marx's schemes of enlarged reproduction, where the section of constant capital grows more than the other two (ch. 6). The latter, by definition, cannot absorb the growing surplus value. Wage-goods cannot increase beyond the subsistence level; otherwise, instead of being exploited, the workers would enjoy the surplus they produce. But this, for capitalism, is a nonsense.

As for the third section, a permanent increase in luxury consumption, too, would contradict the capitalist rationale. Unlike rentiers, capitalists do not waste surplus; indeed, they invest it as much as possible (134–6). Thus, the means of production section grows much more and absorbs most of the increase in surplus value (ch. 7). This view – which was faithful to Marx – was later to be endorsed by *Sweezy* (1942: 167).

However, the additional goods, which represent the surplus value, must necessarily be sold and assume the form of money, before entrepreneurs use this money to purchase the new machines. Luxemburg considers entrepreneurs as a whole: they cannot be at the same time sellers and buyers of the surplus value. Thus, the problem is: who will be able to buy these commodities (ch. 8)? No one, inside the capitalist economy, for the reason previously explained. The only solution is to sell these excess commodities to non-capitalist consumers. But every sale of such commodities entails further extension of capitalist relationships. The buyers will soon be transformed into hired labourers for capital or into small capitalist entrepreneurs (ch. 9).

The first purchasers are the independent producers (peasants and artisans), who are inside capitalist society but do not share in capitalist relationships (ch. 29). Once these categories are absorbed, capital must necessarily expand abroad because it needs to conquer new markets, where its surplus can be sold and invested (chs. 27–8). Thus, the process of *proletarianisation* of pre-capitalist categories goes on until the whole world is subjected to capitalist relationships.

At this point, capitalist accumulation no longer has external markets to sell and invest its excess surplus value. Capitalism is destined finally to breakdown. It seeks to divert this trend by exporting financial capital (ch. 30) and above all by producing armaments (ch. 32). But armaments only serve better to conquer new markets through imperialism. Thus, the final breakdown is unavoidable.

Luxemburg summed up her theses in the *Anti-Critique* (1915), her brilliant reply to her critics, in particular to Otto Bauer. For absorption of the growing surplus value, Bauer relied on increase in population. He built up his own model of enlarged reproduction on absurd hypotheses, as *Sweezy* (1942) effectively demonstrated (11.10: 211–12). Even worse, *Grossman* (1919) took up Bauer's scheme, its hypotheses included, and, by extending the timeframe of his calculation from 4 to 35 years, "proved" that capitalism would eventually break down (II.3–4). In Grossmann, however, the breakdown was due above all to the falling rate of profit.

Is Luxemburg's analysis at odds with Marx's view? Actually, it is, despite the fact that she was utterly taken aback when all the key figures of German Social Democracy attacked her book. Her idea that demand is static is incompatible with accumulation itself (on the idea of the economic breakdown of capitalism, see F.R. *Hansen* 1985). Joan *Robinson* (1951) aptly pointed out the technical shortcoming in Luxemburg's approach: her reproduction schemes exclude the possibility of moving capital from the second to the first section and in general from the less profitable sectors to the more profitable ones. The surplus had to be reinvested in the same section (16–17, 25). In the end, Luxemburg forgoes the two principal driving forces of accumulation: increase in wages and technical progress, which are the real remedies for lack of demand (28).

At the scientific level, Luxemburg did not have many followers. *Grossmann* (1919: III.11) repeated her theses regarding armaments as means to counter the tendency to breakdown. *Neisser* (1934) supported the underconsumption interpretation of accumulation. *Corey* (1935) used arguments similar to Luxemburg's (193–219, 460–88), although he seems to come closer to the position Sweezy was to adopt a few years later. Capitalist expansion, Corey rightly maintains, has always been based on increase in luxuries and in the "variety" of goods for the privileged classes (170–2). Increase in workers' consumption is possible, but capitalism does not favour it because it depresses profits (204–5).

In the 1970s, attention to colonialism and imperialism was reawakened, and some authors revived Luxemburg's approach. *Howard and King* (1975) noted that Marx did not consider imperialism a necessary consequence of capitalist accumulation; however, his model excluded both wages growth and increase of luxury goods. This implies that imperialism is a necessity arising from lack of demand (251–2fn). *Carlo* (1975) re-proposed Luxemburg's underconsumption, which he attributed also to Marx (55–93). *Lefebvre* (1977), like Luxemburg, maintained that capitalism needs a third purchaser for its commodities (ch. VI).

In any case, Rosa Luxemburg had a huge influence on Marxist thought in the 20th century. Her ideas about the realisation problem, imperialism and above all the economic role of armaments found vast circulation and was re-echoed by a great many authors. *Bellofiore*'s (2009) collection of essays on Luxemburg is particularly useful.

4. Mixed economy and the new underconsumption approach

In contrast with Luxemburg, the leading Marxist authors, including Lenin, focused on parasitism as the dominant feature of late capitalism. Mature capitalism, they maintained, is characterised by imperialism, the prevalence of monopolies and closer control of the state over the economy.

Lenin (1917) detected a strong association between the monopolistic concentration of late capitalism and imperialism (ch. 7). Monopoly prices, he noted, hinder technical progress due to the lack of competition. This tendency encourages rents and leads to parasitism. The percentage of the productive population diminishes while immigrants pour in from the underdeveloped countries. The superior categories of workers acquire some privileges, and Lenin speaks of a "workers' aristocracy".[7] Some historians date the idea back to Marx (*Capital I*, ch. 23.d), although he never formulated any such concept.

The economic crisis of the 1930s resulting from insufficient demand dramatically showed up the structural weakness of traditional accumulation.

This was due to uncontrolled market conditions and lack of social provisions by the state. The crisis forced governments to intervene heavily, rescuing banks, promoting public works, implementing vast social policies and even creating state-owned big enterprises. State intervention to boost demand was also theorised by Keynes in the same years. All this led Marxist authors to speak of a *mixed economy*, which was replacing the economy founded on atomistic agents and the state as "night watchman".

Paul *Sweezy*'s work *Theory of Capitalist Development* (1942) reflected the new context. It represents a turning point in Marxist economics. As we have seen, Sweezy admitted that the law of the falling rate of profit cannot be assumed as certain. It remains uncertain whether or not the value of constant capital increases more than productivity (6.3: 102–5), although accumulation itself and other factors actually tend to depress profits (105–8).

Sweezy, too, acknowledged that Marx's analysis of periodical crises is very close to the business cycle theory (8.3: 143). He distinguished between crises caused by the tendency of accumulation to depress profits and "realisation crises". The former do not depend on the falling rate of profit but derive from the increase in employment, generated by accumulation. The latter are due to scant demand (8.4).

As to employment growth, Sweezy explained that increase in demand for labour reduces the "industrial reserve army" (made up of unemployed workers). The unemployed press on the wages of the employed through competition between the workers. However, less unemployment means higher wages, and this in turn depresses the rate of profit. The capitalists' reaction to this tendency is to cut investments, but this leads to depression. In turn, depression drives up unemployment once again, then lowers wages and recreates the conditions for return to accumulation. These crises, Sweezy repeated, are actually business cycle crises, i.e. the natural fluctuations of capitalist accumulation (ch. 9).

As for the realisation crises, Sweezy acknowledged that Marx rejected the underconsumption explanation. However, he said,

> the social relations of capitalist production enforce a restriction of consumption and at the same time spur the capitalists on to attempt an unlimited expansion of production.
>
> (10.2: 173)

Nevertheless, Sweezy deems Luxemburg's analysis a failure (178). She interpreted enlarged reproduction as if it were simple reproduction, where consumption cannot increase (204). Sweezy set out to complete Marx's theory on this point. He defined underconsumption as mere overproduction: the tendency of production to expand more rapidly than demand. This can come about either by producing more than is demanded and coming to a crisis, or by leaving some productive resources idle and lurching towards stagnation (180).

Sweezy also shared Lenin's and Bukharin's idea, which did away with the old opposition between crises due to disproportions between sectors and crises due to underconsumption. This alternative had divided Malthus and Sismondi from Say and Ricardo. Lenin and Bukharin saw underconsumption as a disproportion – precisely the disproportion between production and consumption.[8] Of course, this is a sophism (see also Vitantonio *Gioia* 1981: 227–39).

On the other hand, Lenin and Sweezy unreservedly embraced Marx's balanced approach to the underconsumption question. Marx, however, although using the concept of overproduction, never accepted the concept of underconsumption, while Sweezy openly accepted it: underconsumption theory, he wrote, is "one aspect – and a very important one – of the whole crisis problem" (186). Moreover, Sweezy defined underconsumption as "a disease of old age" in capitalist development (189).

While sharing Kautsky's forecast of profound depression, Sweezy also described the forces that counteract the tendency to underconsumption (ch. 12). The most important, in his list, are the last two. One is unproductive consumption. Sweezy scrupulously followed Marx's thesis about the unproductiveness of services, including commerce, but he was uncertain and contradictory about which has the greater influence: the traditional unproductive consumption of rentiers or that of service labourers. In the end, he inclined for the latter and maintained that the expansion of services is a major factor standing in the way of depression (226–31). The second force counteracting underconsumption is represented by state expenditures (except the few that aim at yielding surplus value). These expenditures, too, constitute a major obstacle to the tendency towards underconsumption (231–4).

Services and public expenditures – Sweezy stated – are in constant increase, but meanwhile new industries and growth in population – i.e. the forces that traditionally used to sustain consumption – tend to decline. However, he concluded, now the state is explicitly and effectively acting against the tendency to underconsumption by increasing consumption through inflation. Rising prices depress incomes, but in a context of depression they can also boost purchasing power. Finally, the young Sweezy was uncertain as to whether the state had eliminated Kautsky's prospect of depression or not (234–6).

In conclusion, according to Sweezy, there are two different theories of underconsumption held by Marxists. One, best represented by Rosa Luxemburg (but also including the *Narodniki* and Grossman), had it that capitalism can develop only up to a certain point, because it requires purchasers for its surplus product who are external to capitalist relations. In addition, she held increase of unproductive labour to be unconceivable.

The other theory, Sweezy says, is inspired by Marx's (incomplete) analysis and finds expression through Lenin, Bukharin and Sweezy himself. According to this theory, in capitalist accumulation there is an inherent tendency towards overproduction. Capitalism reacts by promoting public policies to boost demand and restore production-consumption balance. Sweezy is evidently desirous to support his new approach with a noble parentage. However, neither Marx nor his early followers, Lenin and Bukharin included, ever founded their accumulation theory on the economic role of the state.

Nevertheless, Sweezy best interpreted the mood of his time by seeing state expenditures as the solution to the surplus problem. It is now the state that, in the interest of monopolies, *unproductively* absorbs the excess surplus generated by capitalist accumulation.

Maurice *Dobb* (1946) maintained that the crisis of the 1930s derived from the lack of competition, due to the prevalence of monopolies. Monopoly economy holds production costs back from falling, and with them prices, despite the increase in productivity. Thus, monopolies cause both permanent lack in demand and unproductive production costs (321–3). Dobb often repeated that a "fear of productive capacity" dominated the economy (321, 379, passim). Monopolies swing between concern over high production costs, due to competition, and efforts to consolidate their control over the market, which favours an excess in productive capacity (325–6). The mitigation of crises and the "surprising" stability of demand derive from external factors, and above all from government expenditures, especially armaments (332–4). In the end, it is armaments and other public expenditures that keep demand high (354–7ff). In his *Postscript* to the 1963 edition of his book, Dobb did not take into account the birth of the welfare state. In the end, he converged with Sweezy's approach. They both paved the way for a new underconsumption theory.

Joseph *Steindl* (1952) admired Sweezy's book but was not fully convinced by his underconsumption solution. Like Joan Robinson, Steindl recognised the outstanding features of Marx's approach, which sees the economy as a whole, establishes links among the aggregates and builds up general models. As for the Marxists, however, he complained that, instead of showing due appreciation of Marx's method, they persevere with his inevitable mistakes (349–50). On the analytical level, Steindl shows that, according to Marx, in the short term there is a relationship between wages and accumulation opposite to that of the long term. In the short term, the level of wages determines the accumulation rate. Wages in turn are determined by the rate of employment. When wages rise beyond the equilibrium level, the rate of accumulation slows down. This brings employment down, and the reduction in turn drives wages down. This process continues until low wages push investments up and accumulation grows again, following a cyclical trend (355).

By contrast, Marx saw long-term accumulation as based on the tendency of the profit rate to fall. Here it is technical progress that determines all the other factors. However, Steindl observes, at present technical progress is based more on saving constant capital than on increasing it – a tendency that probably also existed in the past (369–70). Nevertheless – he maintains – Marx's law is still valid as a potential perspective: when capitalists realise that technical progress can hinder the rate of profit, they abstain from increasing investment. We cannot tell, he notes, how much this attitude has hindered accumulation in the past (370–2). For this reason, Sweezy's theory of the tendency of accumulation towards underconsumption is not fully convincing: accumulation can be hindered by capitalists themselves, who can invest less and leave a part of gross profit unemployed (375–7).

5. The state as the way to escape crises

In the 1930s, another factor was also going on in capitalist accumulation, namely Taylorism. It was developing in the factories and increasingly weakening the workers' bargaining power. *Sohn-Rethel* (1970), proposing some ideas formulated over the previous decades, denounced Taylorism as the third stage of workers' subordination to capital. The first two stages, described by Marx, were the creation of wage labour in manufactures and its subjection to machines in the factories. In the third stage, Taylorism achieves complete transformation of workers into machines. This is due to the radical opposition between intellectual power, represented by the managers, overseers, etc., and manual work, the latter being by then completely devoid of any critical or intellectual attention (chs. 24–5, 30–2).

We may, however, observe that in the 1950s the assembly line – the main accomplishment of Taylorism – reached its physical limits. Efforts now went into exploring new ways to continue accumulation. The new approach relied on skill and cooperation in production. This started a new wave of innovations. Meanwhile, Keynesian policies and the birth of the welfare state favoured technological advance and gave rise to a prolonged economic boom. Wages increased, education was extended to the masses, information and culture were disseminated on a vast scale and living conditions grew far more comfortable.

Joseph *Gillman* (1957) marks a milestone in the Marxist theory of accumulation. The author maintained, on the basis of some statistics (chs. 4 and 5), that after World War I capitalist accumulation had changed radically. Competition was replaced by monopoly capital; the realisation costs (the costs borne by capital for distribution and sale of products) increased enormously. Above all – Gillman noted, just like Steindl – the application of research to technology and the organisation of production had greatly increased productivity, no longer thanks to the quantitative growth of constant capital, but thanks to better-quality machines. Moreover, the cost of constant capital was no longer growing, but actually tending to fall.[9]

In this new context, Gillman writes, the original version of the law of the falling profit rate no longer applies. However, he prefers to retain the ultimate sense of the law: the demonstration that capitalist accumulation moves towards a final crisis. He maintains that business cycles are only an – increasingly marked – manifestation of downward trend of the profit rate over the long run (163, 167). This is why he insists on the increased costs of distribution. Apparently, he sees such unproductive costs playing the same role previously performed by constant capital, progressively increasing that part of investment which does not produce surplus value, and consequently depressing the profit rate (183).

However, there is a difference. The shift from constant capital to social costs external to the production process leads the author to see accumulation as being oppressed by underconsumption. Unproductive social expenses grow ever more, both as realisation costs borne by enterprises and as state expenditures (ch. 7). The crisis of accumulation is not due to lack of investments, as Keynesians have it, but to the excessive productivity of investments (180). Gillman then lists the various unproductive expenses: loans to consumers and above all war expenses (ch. 9: 183–95). He repeated his theses in Gillman (1965).

However, Gillman seems to have overlooked two obvious facts. First, the author himself mentions the new way of increasing productivity by saving constant capital, rather than spending more on it. But he disregards the fact that this process is due to the growth of skilled labour, research, organisation and experts, and so to the growth of education, division of intellectual labour, etc. Second, what he calls realisation costs are in actual fact new services and new intellectual occupations, which greatly contribute to the surplus production. *Crosser* (1960) shared the Marxists' thesis that state intervention in his time aimed at financing private industry and supporting its productivity (97–9).

Monopoly Capital, by *Baran and Sweezy* (1966), is the most outstanding and influential book representing the new underconsumption approach. Much of the vast debate this book raised focuses on the adoption of the concept of surplus, instead of surplus value. In actual fact, it was a minor change from the viewpoint of the structure of capitalist accumulation. The authors continue to consider accumulation as a private valorisation process, while public expenses still create a parasitic ever-growing sector.

The authors write that Marxist theory has been shaped by the economy of market competition. In the new context of monopoly capitalism, it needs to be remoulded (ch. 1.2). This is why they replace the concept of surplus value with that of surplus. Marx himself – they stated – observed that a large part of surplus value hides in non-profit forms, like the state and church revenues, the costs for transforming commodities into money (the realisation problem) and the wages of unproductive labourers. These forms, which Marx considered of little importance, have now taken on such importance that they cannot be neglected. Surplus, then, is the difference between the entire social product and the total cost of production (1.4).

The authors then go on to explain the features of the new economy following in the footprints of Schumpeter and of Berle and Means. The "giant corporations" are guided by managers, not by the proprietors. They do not tend to maximise profits all the time, but rather aim at satisfactory performance, which minimises costs and yields a constant profit rate (ch. 2). This is a new form of accumulation, which generates a stable dominant class of wealth owners (which Veblen called "the leisure class" and Charles Wright Mills defined "the elite of power").

Due to these oligopolies, "prices tend to be stickier on the downward side than on the upward side" (3.3: 62), like the monopoly prices of the theory. This is why social surplus steadily grows. On the basis of these monopoly prices, the state regulates all other prices to keep them from going too high or too low (3.4). Moreover, the lack of competition brings the production costs down (3.6). Thus, the surplus and consequently investments grow even more. Hence the classical question of the underconsumption approach arises once again: what will absorb the surplus?

In the monopoly context, the authors say, innovations cannot absorb the surplus, because they are slower now and do not create new goods. They are not product innovations, but only process innovations (ch. 4.4.2). The very core of the absorption of surplus consists in government spending, both civilian (ch. 6) and military (ch. 7). The authors underline that public spending is not subtracted from private investments or private consumption. On the contrary, it "pushes the economy nearer to capacity operation". It offers a remedy to the problem that "surplus grows more rapidly than effective demand" (147–8).

Note that the authors also consider spending on the welfare state as mere absorption of the surplus, including public education, roads, healthcare, environment protection, recreation, commerce, housing, the police, justice, and legislative and administrative activities. Only social security, according to the authors, really contributes to welfare (152–3). However, the very factor that prevents stagnation lies in military and imperialist expenses, to which a substantial part of the book is devoted (175–248). It is a conclusion very close to that of Rosa Luxemburg.

Finally, note that the context examined by Baran and Sweezy is much simpler than today's. Examining sales drives as another outlet for surplus (ch. 5), they only consider advertising. They just mention "product differentiation, artificial obsolescence, model changing" (141). But today, these processes have taken on enormous importance (see XX.4.a). Moreover, they see advertising only as a cost for material production. They barely mention the decisive fact that advertising yields profit for a considerable number of enterprises (126).

Conclusions

Thanks to Marx's category of overproduction, the "orthodox" stream were able to take into consideration new phenomena, like depression, growth of monopolies (Marx's process of concentration), the mixed economy, and state expenditures. However, the absence of structural crises in Marx's analysis led his followers into error over the nature of both the 1930s crisis and its definitive solution, namely the welfare state. All state interventions were interpreted as unproductive employment of the surplus, carried out in order to keep accumulation going (a view which converged with the later 19th-century theories of unproductive capital).

Thus, these authors failed to grasp the real nature of the welfare state and the consequent economic boom. Military expenses and welfare expenses were placed on the same level, as evidence of the forthcoming final crisis of capitalism. Eventually, the orthodox view based on depression shifted to a new underconsumption approach (Sweezy, Dobb, Steindl, Baran, Gillman, etc.).

Notes

1 My thanks go to the participants in the session of the Conference "Marx 1818–2018" (Lyon, September 2017), where I presented this research.
2 E.g. Croce (1900, VI: 139–50). Bortkiewicz (1906–7: 89–96). Sweezy (1942, 6.3: 102–5). Robinson (1949, ch. 5: 35; etc.). Steindl (1952, ch. 14: 360).
3 See e.g. *Grossmann* (1919, II.13).
4 *Robinson* (1949, ch. 6: 46). See also, for ex., E. O. *Wright* (1977).
5 See J. Robinson (1948: 18); Steindl (1952: 369–70); Gillmann (1957: 195–200).
6 Sweezy (1942, ch. 11.6; 216).
7 Lenin (1917, ch. 8: 139–47; ch. 10: 167–8).
8 Sweezy (1942: 185–6). Bukharin (1925, ch. 1).
9 Gillman (1957: 58, 110ff, 195–200).

XVI Productiveness of public expenditures

Background

The transformation of the economic role of the state was already underway in the last decades of the 19th century. But it became more radical and rapid in the 1930s when the crisis pushed governments to play a leading part in the rescue of banks and enterprises. New public institutions were created to protect saving and credit, grant investments and provide assistance. The change raised a problem for economists: was this new attitude on the part of the state compatible with or even suitable for the production of social wealth, or was it a degeneration of traditional capitalist accumulation? Neoclassical and Marxist authors were both internally divided in answering this question. Only the Keynesians were unanimous in their positive view of the new role of the state. However, they confined it to the short run.

1. State monopoly capitalism

In the second half of the 20th century, Marxist authors assumed that monopolistic capitalism radically changed the features of accumulation and called it "state monopoly capitalism". Some of them even used the term *Stamokap* (from the German "Staatlich Monopolistisch Kapitalismus"). This concept derives from the close connection established by *Lenin* (1917, ch. 7) between monopolies and regulation of them by the state in the later phase of capitalism. The original expression dates back to Bukharin [see *Jessop* (1982: 33–8)].

Initially the expression referred to the subordination of the state to the interests of finance. In the 1950s, it implied that the new state had the task of absorbing the excess surplus (which otherwise would suffocate the economy) through various unproductive expenses. In France, a large team of authors adopted this approach systematically in a lengthy treatise (*Traité* 1971), written on the initiative of the French Communist Party. For broader analyses, also see *Schmidt* (1977: 66–76), and *Jessop* (1982: 57–63).

According to *Altvater* (1968), we have moved on from state "ideal collective capitalist" (Engel's definition) to state material collective capitalist, which regulates demand to boost employment and production. Thus, Altvater concurs with Baran and Sweezy (27–9). Many other authors also recall Engels' definition to stress the state's subordination to capital.[1]

Mandel (1972) makes it clear that economic growth does not come to an end in late capitalism but, on the contrary, is even faster. However, parasitism and waste also grow. The labouring forces are squandered and ill-used (214–16), and there is increasing difficulty in employing capital productively (293, 387). Mandel adds that the welfare state has inevitably been an illusion. The redistribution of the social wealth it promises would be unbearable for accumulation (483).

Galgano (1974), too, maintained that the mixed economy came about in support of private capital (1–14). The state helps private enterprises through low interest rates, loans and grants, infrastructures, assistance to the unemployed, and subsidies to the underdeveloped areas or sectors. All this is financed by the taxes levied on workers. Thus, there is a huge transfer of wealth in favour of the capitalists. This is another way of extracting surplus value (15–18).

Wolff (1977) tried to verify statistically the assumption of Baran-Sweezy's *Monopoly Capital* for the US between 1947 and 1967. He divides economic activities between productive and unproductive. Although he always refers to Marx's criteria, his classification is in fact much less restricted and more realistic than Marx's. For instance, he includes among the productive activities not only all means of transportation, but also the services related to broadcasting, hotels, healthcare and education, household entertainments, research and development (99). Nevertheless, Wolff sees "a direct relation between unproductive activity and the surplus". They grow together. The result, he says, "does not indicate which is the cause and which the effect", but probably "causation runs both ways" (110).

Wolff believes that unproductive expenditures help capital in dealing with the realisation problem but remain a waste. However, Wolff rejected the underconsumption view: the surplus "could also be absorbed by increased accumulation (and, of course, increased personal consumption by workers and capitalists)" (111). He was not aware that this is precisely what was happening.

2. Public expenditures in mainstream economists

a. In favour of their productiveness

Of the mainstream economists, very few believed in the productiveness of public expenditures, but Alvin *Hansen* (1941) brilliantly explained why they are productive. Public spending, like private investments, can create utilities (such as parks, swimming pools, etc.) or efficiency (for example, soil protection, school buildings, etc.). However, it can also create income because it expands employment. Private expense is said to be self-sustaining, while public spending is not, but this is not the case. No private business could sell without a flow of public expense. The "private sector is not self-sustaining either". During depressions, only the government is able to support income by increasing its expenses (144–51).

Hansen went on to offer an insightful reflection based on an evolutionary approach similar to Genovesi's (see II.5). Those who state that public expenses are maintained by private income are like the physiocrats, who say that industry is maintained by agriculture. Actually, social revenue increased enormously thanks to the part of productive resources that was moved from agriculture to industry. Similarly, today many needs can be satisfied only by public activities. Public services enter into the exchange process and increase the stream of revenue. Nor is it not true that with their surplus some sectors of the economy maintain some other sectors. Every sector contributes to the total stream of revenue. Agriculture does provide the essential goods needed, but this priority is paramount only in primitive societies, where nearly all labour must be concentrated on the acquisition of food. When material productivity increases, it allows for the satisfaction of other possible needs, such as artistic or intellectual needs (151–2).

In another book, Hansen (1951) included public products and services in the NDP (Net Domestic Product 97–100). He writes that private industries are increasingly interested in public services (639). Hansen's view was neglected by all the streams in economic studies, which is a striking example of how much ideological stereotypes can prevail over analysis. Moreover, many authors confuse the actual inefficiency of public labour, due to lack of competition and control, with the basic nature of this kind of labour.

However, Hansen was not entirely alone in his position. *Stone* (1943) denied that public services constitute a loss. Just like private services, they contribute to the social product (63–75). Simon *Kuznets* (1966) explained that many expenses, public and private, that are considered final consumption (such as education, healthcare, etc.) actually belong to intermediate consumption, since they increase final production. He estimated that the exclusion of this intermediate consumption reduces the GDP (Gross Domestic Product) by about 23% (224–34).

Kapp (1950) cast light on another aspect of the issue. Like Pigou, he thought that production costs go well beyond those of private industry. Many costs (like occupational diseases, environmental pollution, unemployment itself) are social costs that are not taken into account. Smith, he says, was aware of these costs, because he considered public works as a necessary precondition for free competition (28–30). However, public works confined to a precondition for "real" production are not the same as the expansion of the public sector in consequence of development.

Not even the supporters of the welfare state believed in the productiveness of its policies. In a tract written for the Fabian Society (*Hughes* 1970), the authors asked themselves whether the state could afford any expansion of education, given the low rate of growth at that moment. They did not conceive that education can be not only the result but also the cause of growth.

According to *Sleeman* (1979), public spending contributes to the national product by providing infrastructures and services. The only difference is that its products are paid for through taxes, rather than directly (38–9). Social services, he said, like school, healthcare and social security, provide more benefits to the private citizen than the traditional state expenditures, like defence (2–3). *T. Wilson and D. Wilson* (1982) restated that the social projects that are financed outside the market can be economically viable. They also criticised the distinction between social and economic targets (15–18).

In the 1960s–70s, the post-Keynesians were in the front line in defence of social spending to increase demand. Of course, they became the main target of the neoclassical critics. However, there was another – less known and more appropriate – kind of criticism of the Keynesian theory, looking to the kinds of demand. *Lekachman* (1966) criticised the lack of distinction between the types of demand. He also criticised Keynes's famous paradoxes, where he affirms the necessity of public spending even when its product is completely useless (104–6).

John *Hicks* (1974) observed that Keynes's analysis of liquidity preference is too negative. The liquidity preference is useful in slowing down hasty decisions regarding any kind of social investment. According to Hicks, Keynes is solely interested in increase in demand. So, he favours increase in investments regardless of their productivity (57). Kalecki's attitude – as described by *Feiwel* (1975: 176–7) – confirms Hicks's view.

b. Against their productiveness

The vast majority of mainstream economists believed that public expenditures are unproductive.[2] According to *Hazlitt* (1969), social expenses drive the nation to ruin (209–10). This idea is taken to the extreme by *Rothbard* (1962, II: 815–17). *Gilder* (1981) comes up with a tirade against the "unproductive sectors", which increase taxes and generate inflation. His list of such sectors is impressive for his total failure to understand economic development. It includes, besides the state sector as a whole, all services like those of lawyers, social workers, teachers, travel agents, rock singers (what about the other singers?), managing consultants, even nurses and computer programmers, etc. (206–16).

Bacon and Eltis (1976) gave rise to a great debate, even among Marxists. Their approach was based on empirical data and valuable expertise. The authors assumed the same principle common to Smith, the early classical authors, Marx and most of the Marxists of the 1970s: the non-market sector is unproductive, while the market sector, i.e. private production of tradable products, produces the social surplus.

The authors maintain that the British economy is overburdened by public expenditures for unproductive activities. This reduces private investment and productive labour while also reducing the social surplus. Consequently, the wages of the productive sector are under pressure, and unemployment grows. The authors state that, if the market sector thrives, the non-productive sector will also fare well. On the other hand, if the latter absorbs a great part of the surplus produced by the market sector, both sectors will decline (77–91). Their implicit target was spending for the welfare state.

3. Public expenditures according to the orthodox Marxists

The majority of Marxist authors did not agree with the idea that public expenditures and public labour could be productive.

This attitude is very clear in *Lenin*'s famous tract *State and Revolution* (1918). In contrast with Kautsky and other orthodox authors, Lenin maintained that, after the revolution, ministers and the public administration itself should not be eliminated (194–202). These functions, thanks to the progressive simplification achieved by capitalism, can be dispatched by the workers through a rotation of tasks and direct democracy.[3] Lenin seemed unaware of the complex intellectual and professional skills required by qualified administrative and organisational labour. The latter is reduced to the directing functions, which moreover are seen as mere command, deriving from the privileges and parasitism of the middle class (87–9, 107–8, passim).

Lenin supported his ideas by referring to Marx's political writings (Marx 1852 and —1871). However, these works contain no such suggestions. Nevertheless, Lenin's ideas to some extent reflected the conviction that skilled labour is per se unproductive. This attitude was prone to degeneration. We find it at its most devastating in two tragic episodes: the Chinese cultural revolution of the 1960s–70s and the Cambodian Khmer Rouge dictatorship of the 1970s.

Moreover, *Calvez* (1956) wrote in his survey of the Soviet economists of the 1940s that they considered the services sold in the market productive but had doubts about the public services since they do not have a market price (83–113).

In his extensive treatise on Marxist economics, Ernest *Mandel* (1962) enlarges – relative to Marx – the sphere of collateral productive occupations, including transport and storage as well as the distribution of gas, water and electricity. Mandel observes that the survival of many services is a sign of backwardness rather than economic progress. The only sector which grows is that of the creative activities, which are, however, unproductive (vol. I: 230–50).

Mattick (1969) did not share the prevailing tendency of his time to interpret state intervention as a consequence of underconsumption. He also repeated Marx's theses without any variations (see *Capital III*, III.XV.15). Mattick declared that the Keynesian attempt to revive capitalism through public spending was doomed to failure, since the downward trend of the profit rate can be slowed down but not stopped (chs. 6–9).

Like the free-traders, Mattick thought that state expenditures can only be financed by subtracting capital from private investments. The vicious circle triggered by Keynesian policies runs: public spending begins because private accumulation tends to diminish, but the state expenditures further diminish private accumulation. Consequently, public production – which does not produce profit – increases once again (ch. 16). The same vicious circle comes about in the case of productivity: the more public production increases, the higher is the need to increase the productivity of the private sector to cope with the dwindling of invested capital.[4] This results in widespread unemployment. It is also the last "contradiction" of capitalist accumulation (254). Therefore, permanent application of the Keynesian policy implies the self-destruction of capitalism (Epilogue: 428).

Mattick (1974) repeated the same thesis: state expenditures cannot overcome crises (150–63). He criticised the new underconsumption view, especially in the version presented in Gillman's and Baran-Sweezy's books. According to Mattick, these books were inspired by Keynesianism, since they affirm that overproduction is caused not by scarcity of surplus value but by an excess of it (149–50). He also criticised Hansen for not distinguishing between natural productivity (which concerns the quantity of goods) and capitalist productivity, which concerns surplus value (142).

Bullock (1974) replied to Gough (1972, see as follows) that public and service labourers cannot be productive because their labour is not exchanged with capital (10–14). According to *Yaffe* (1975), public spending, besides preventing profit from plunging, also has the function of checking the unemployment caused by increase in productivity (10, 14). Yaffe even stated that education and healthcare are almost completely unproductive, since they increase neither workers' productivity nor profit (12–13).

Costa (1979) maintained that, since public expenditures are unproductive and do not increase value, they create inflation and stagnation (28). On the other hand, during the crisis, the state replaces private capital in its function of exploitation. Thus, while capitalism was born thanks to the separation between the state and civil society, it is now the state itself that puts an end to this separation. The welfare state – called by many authors the planning state – is an attempt to control the exploitation process (29–37).

Fine and Harris (1979) criticised Gough, who considers public workers productive because their hired labour is similar to that of the production sphere. They objected that, with the exception of the nationalised industries, public labour is not directly controlled by capital. Often, its product does not even have a market price. Moreover, public labour does not produce value and surplus value, as Gough believes, since they are produced only under the direct control of capital (53). Fine and Harris also maintain that the unproductive nature of public employees and health operators is proved by the fact that these sectors are often subject to cuts (56).

The lengthy treatise by *Drugman* (1979) affirmed that all public expenditures for the welfare state are "non-mercantile" forms which reproduce both the labour-force and capitalist relations. Thus, the state is the representative of collective capital.[5] According to *Elliot* (1980), Marx and Schumpeter concur in holding that the social policies implemented by the state will end up by destroying the basis of capitalism. *Dale* (1981) repeated that the state supports the productivity of the private enterprises.

According to *Driver* (1980), the public sector differs from commerce because the latter is subject to competitive pressure and production of profit.

In any case, both sectors are unproductive. In the public sector, only state enterprises can be productive, unless their production is conditioned by political factors. In this case, there can be surplus labour but no production of surplus value (18–19). Driver also stated that education and healthcare can benefit capital if they are without any cost.

David *Eisenhower* (1982) presented one of the most coherent versions of the underconsumption view, based on public expenditures. He listed many of these expenditures to prove that capitalism seeks to counter falls in the rate of profit, promoting military expenditures, new technologies, electronic devices, automobiles, administration, etc. The production and management of all this give rise to a huge class of unproductive labourers. They have been celebrated as the "knowledge class" of the "new industrial state", but in actual fact they represent "a capitalism which has entered its 'degenerative phase'" (133).

As to Keynesianism, Suzanne *de Brunhoff* (1976), *Erdos* (1977) and *Barcellona* (1980: chs. 3 and 5) are only a few examples of the authors who criticise it. Keynesian policy is an extreme attempt to save capital domination through the state intervention. Paradoxically, these radical critics of capitalism saw limitation (entailed by the welfare state) of unregulated economy as a violation of market rules. Moreover, they hold that this violation dooms Keynesianism to failure. *Jessop* (1982) showed that, once again, Altvater, Sauer, Clarke, etc. were convinced that the only aim of state expenditures was to overcome the difficulties of capitalist accumulation (90–7). On the studies on productive labour and the role of the state of the 1970s, *Rizzello* (1990) provides a useful analysis.

4. Armaments as luxury goods

In response to Bacon and Eltis, *Ietto Gillies* (1978) warned that public services are not luxury goods, in the sense Sraffa attributed to the term. But *Bacon and Eltis* (1978) retorted that it is impossible to draw a clear-cut distinction between basic goods and luxury goods. As they rightly maintained, Ietto Gillies herself considered as basic several goods that were traditionally considered luxuries and were by then changing status (47–8). This observation is a blow to the old distinction between necessaries and luxuries, which has been a bane for so much classical economics since the early 19th century. Actually *Sraffa* (1960) proposed a distinction between basic and non-basic goods. The former enter directly or indirectly into the production of all the other commodities while the latter do not (10). However, the substance of the concept – as far as we are concerned – remains unchanged: like luxury goods, non-basic goods do not enter into the reproduction process.

We have seen that the production of armaments as a good opportunity for (unproductively) employing the surplus dates back to Rosa Luxemburg and was restated by Baran and Sweezy. Many Marxist authors of that period placed armaments in the category of luxury goods. They explained that armaments, like any luxury good, do not enter into the reproduction process, and so the labour devoted to armaments is unproductive.[6]

Mandel (1962, I: 178–85) stated that the growth of armaments and R&D (research and development) is due to the need to limit overproduction.[7] However, armaments, just like luxury goods, yield a surplus value (M. 1972: 288). The same holds for the various expenditures of the state (which is controlled by monopolies): e.g. direct or indirect financial support for enterprises, contracts, public works, provision of raw materials, price regulation – Mandel lists them all with very little analysis (M. 1962, II: 145–63). Overproduction, stated Mandel, is the acme of capitalist contradictions. Automation increases inequalities between economies. Above all, it drives labour out of production, bringing the surplus value down.[8] Overproduction, then, leads to crises. In turn, it results from the falling rate of profit.[9]

Gillman (1965) considered armaments the favoured destination of the unproductively employed surplus,[10] whereas, generally speaking, welfare policies are distrusted by capitalists. Indeed, he wondered what would happen if "peace breaks out".[11]

However not all authors recognise this bizarre connection between armaments and luxury goods. As *Nishikawa* (1965: 26) and *Vaisov* (1971: 134) noted, the consumption that does not help reproduction, like consumption of armaments and luxuries, must be limited in quantity, according to Marx's schemes of enlarged reproduction. *Nagels* (1974) also challenged the idea of armaments as luxury goods. They are simply consumption goods, which contribute to the "realisation problem" (284–5fn). *Gough* (1972) disagrees with Baran and Sweezy's observation that many commercial costs are irrational in comparison with "a more rational economic order". He goes on to point out that this ambiguous attitude towards commerce had already been shown by Marx (62–6). According to Gough, Baran explicitly separates the question of labour productiveness from the production of surplus value (67–9).

Gamble and Walton (1976) were timely in proclaiming the end of the boom and the beginning of the crisis. Following in the footprints of Baran and Sweezy, they ascribed crises to underconsumption. The final crisis of capitalism is delayed through state expenditures. These authors – somewhat oddly – extend the concept of constant capital to the public sector (4: 144).

Boccara (1978) took a rather confused position. He interpreted the "last phase" of capitalism, i.e. imperialism, as being subject to two contrasting tendencies: parasitic and progressive. Among the unproductive sectors, he mentions, besides armaments, the luxury goods consumed by the workers' aristocracy and in some cases by simple workers. To these sectors, he adds as unproductive: hospitals, sports facilities, holidays, cultural activities and even research. However, Boccara notes that these goods or activities are the result of both the workers' social struggle and the need to have more skilled labour (136–40). This also applies to intellectual production, the social production of the labour force, the national healthcare system and social security (143–4).

5. Public expenditures according to critical Marxists

A few Marxist authors tended to believe that the welfare expenditures increase social productivity in general and workers' productivity in particular.

Barratt Brown (1969), addressing the tendency to overproduction, sees a conflict between state and capital rather than a mere subordination of the former to the latter (31–2). In the US, this conflict has been resolved thanks to military expenses (47). Capitalists, while not opposed to armaments, objected to welfare policies because they go to the detriment of profits (64). Barratt Brown (1972) observed that the great infrastructures have been made possible thanks to the collaboration between the state and the oligopolies (48–9). The state, he adds, is neither neutral nor monolithic (68), and recalls that welfare economics was first theorised by Marshall (71). We may note, however, that there is a great difference between the welfare economics based on Pareto optimality and the welfare state of the 1950s–60s.

Gough (1972) wrote that public workers are in general unproductive because their labour is exchanged with revenue, not capital. However, he makes exceptions not only for public enterprises but also for social services like healthcare, education, housing, etc. These services "directly enter the cycle of reproduction" (62–3). Gough (1975) provided a thorough analysis of all the aspects of the issue of state spending. Making reference to O'Connor and Rowthorn, he argued that most of these expenditures are productive because they increase the workers' productivity either through comfort or through education and infrastructures. These benefits have been gained by workers as a supplement to their wages. Productive, too, are the public workers, because the role of the state in production has now grown on a very large scale (especially: 80–5).

James *O'Connor* (1973) – the famous *The Fiscal Crisis of the State* – had a great impact on the Marxist debate. The author did not rule out the function that Baran and Sweezy ascribed to the state, i.e. absorbing the excess surplus unproductively to avoid crises. However, he stressed another aspect. The state, he maintained, has a twofold, sometimes contradictory, role. On the one hand, it facilitates accumulation, while on the other it legitimises capitalist production. In turn, the former action develops in two ways. In one direction, the state engages in social investments, which increase productivity or cut the reproduction cost of labour power (education, healthcare, etc.). In the other, it deploys a vast amount of social assistance for the unemployed, unproductive labourers and disabled people (social security and many other benefits).

The monopoly sector of the economy benefits from both types of public expenditures. Here, productivity tends steadily to increase, and consequently employment tends to decrease. Thus, this sector suffers a permanent tendency to overproduction and so to unemployment. Through public expenditure, the state absorbs the excess surplus and relieves social distress. Moreover, O'Connor adds that, over the last hundred years, the production sectors have become more interdependent and need ever more technicians and administrative employees, infrastructures and social investments (34). All this seems at odds with the author's observation that the state helps accumulation by socialising production costs and privatising gains. However, in the complex policy of the welfare state, also the latter aspect is present.

O'Connor also distinguished between a monopoly sector and a competitive sector. The latter has fewer advantages and a relatively heavier tax burden. This is why there is fiscal crisis of the state: the competitive sector, which has low productivity, shows strong resistance to paying taxes since they go mainly to the advantage of the monopoly sector and the unproductive sectors of the economy. However, O'Connor rejects the idea that all state expenditures are unproductive and all state initiatives are in the interests of monopolies only. He admits the partial autonomy of social provisions (ch. 6). A substantial part of O'Connor's analysis still holds; indeed, it is by now even closer to reality than in the 1970s.

Klein (1974), too, maintained that social expenditures – for example, on roads, education, healthcare, housing, etc. – are productive.[12] *Negri* (1974), recalling Marx's concept of collective labourer, maintained that all public labour is productive insofar as it cooperates in the production of surplus value: not only the labour that boosts the labour-force productivity but also labour that increases "social harmony" (239–40). In her discussion with Bacon and Eltis, *Ietto Gillies* (1978) stated that public education and health services are actually part of wages. If workers had to seek these services in the market sector, they would have to demand higher wages, which would raise inflation (32–3).

Rowthorn (1979) explicitly affirmed that education and healthcare are not unproductive expenditures that serve to consume the surplus; they are investments that increase labour productivity. Like Gough, *Desay* (1979) stressed that social benefits are not a dubious gift of the state; they are the workers' conquests. He writes:

> "Thus in securing health care, unemployment benefits, guaranteed wages, trade union rights, safety at work and so on through government action, the struggle over the past century has quite rightly succeeded". These achievements are not at all illusory.

Finally, *Grassi* (1979) wrote that Marx's concept of cooperative labour and Engels' definition of the state as collective capitalist should by then have convinced authors to update their analyses. Nowadays, he writes, the state is no longer external to the production process, as in Marx's time. It is present in every enterprise in the following three essential aspects: finding capital, choosing techniques and controlling production. Thus, public labour is not always unproductive (85–7).

The post-Keynesians, on the other hand, have no doubts about the "productiveness" of public spending. *Eichner* (1979) wrote that, by then, at least one third of the US national income went through the public sector. Thus, public expenses could determine the rate and the composition of investments (179).

Conclusions

Among the neoclassical authors of the period, the view prevailed (indeed it still prevails) that state expenditures are unduly subtracted from private production, and this impoverishes the economy. The conditions had been created for the rampant neo-liberalism of the subsequent decades. Among the Marxist authors, the balance sheet is equally dramatic. Here, too, the conservative view prevails, seeing state expenditures as unproductive employment of social wealth and a desperate attempt to avoid the final crisis of the system. Even the enormous social benefits of these expenditures had little interest for the majority of Marxists.

Notes

1 E.g. Drugman (1979: 402–10); Finzi (1977: 13).
2 See, e.g., Russell Lewis (1973: 87–115); Freeman (198: 424–34, passim).
3 Lenin (1918: 150, 165, 188, 197, passim).
4 Mattick (1969: 248, 253, 265–6).
5 Drugman (1979: 321–42, 403–10, passim).
6 See, for example, Morris (1958: 194); Gillman (1965: 23, 233–4); Gough (1972: 62–3); Anderlini (1977: 115–17).
7 See also Mandel (1972: 274–309, 484).
8 Mandel (1972: 192–3, 205–10, 240ff).
9 Mandel (1977: 22–33, 78–83).
10 Gillman (1965: 11–16, 108, 144–5, 231–3, passim).
11 Ibid.: 17–18, 182–3, 232–4.
12 Klein (1974: 1–3, 13–17, 81–3).

XVII Productive labour in the 1960s–70s Marxist thought

Background

During the post-war boom, the services and intellectual labour grew enormously. The latter, in particular, could no longer be considered negligible, as Marx had (see XI.2). However, the majority of Marxists (the orthodox) reasserted Marx's principles and tortuously endeavoured to explain the new phenomena with the traditional categories. Other authors tried out innovative paths, but in turn were divided between those who tried to reconcile, to various degrees, Marx's theory with the new processes and those who directly analysed the growth of intellectual labour independently of Marx's perspective (on the latter authors, see XVIII.3).

1. What kind of productiveness

Rubin (1928) is one of the few Marxist authors who addressed the issue of productive/unproductive labour in the first half of the 20th century. He diligently illustrated Marx's ideas on the subject (ch. 19) and stressed the general principle that activities involved in production are always productive (even bookkeeping) while circulation activities are unproductive (218–19). Rubin, however, concluded that Marx should have referred to "labour in production" rather than "productive labour", since the latter expression had been used by other authors in a different sense (221).

Baran (1957a) returned to the issue, although no longer making reference to surplus value but to a new concept: potential surplus. Potential surplus, he said, is the difference between what could be produced in ideal conditions, i.e. production confined to what is really useful, and what is consumed allowing for a decent living. Thus, Baran's comparison is not between actual consumption and actual capitalist production (both of which he considered subject to waste) but between necessary consumption and an imaginary rational system that should radically reorganise production (ch. 2.1).

Baran's criterion is arbitrary. As in premodern culture, he considers all new customs and goods irrational. All activities are unproductive if they produce goods or services deriving not from a "rationally ordered" society but from the capitalist system, such as work on armaments and military activities, production for luxury and ostentatious consumption, public labour, the work of priests, lawyers, experts in evading taxes, public relations experts, advertising, middlemen, merchants and speculators, etc. (ch. 2.3). This is reminiscent of the moralistic classifications of unproductive labours compiled by the authors of the 15th–16th centuries or indeed by many American economists of the 19th–early 20th century.

Other sources of waste include, according to Baran, insufficient use of scale economies and standardisation in production and also failure to employ both human and material resources. Somewhat contradictorily, Baran invokes against capitalism, first, a society with static consumption and, second, a society which optimises its production activities. Naturally, Baran's approach had scant success. Later on, Baran (1959) accepted the division of private labourers – made by the US Bureau of Labor statistics – between production and non-production workers (the latter being interpreted as unproductive). The non-production workers include all occupations in the field of direction, administration, bookkeeping and surveillance, but also workers in sale, healthcare, advertising, research, etc. (201–2, fn 5).

Behrens (1961) examined the question of measuring labour productivity by using Marx's concept of productive labour but failed to reach any appreciable results. According to *Harrison* (1973a) – and indeed to Sweezy – it is not clear what function the concept of unproductive labour has in Marx's analysis. Probably, he writes, Marx was not yet certain about how to use it (79). Following Baran, Harrison tried to apply the concept to examine how much labour is wasted in the capitalist system, meaning by this the labour that would not be required in a more rational system. However, his – at times abstruse – analyses do not come up with useful results. To this, he added Smith's criterion: all labour directly exchanged with capital should be considered productive, insofar as it contributes to the collective production of surplus value. "Similarly, Harrison adds, all constant capital is 'productive'" (81), i.e. it is necessary for the production of surplus value.

On labour exchanged with revenue, Harrison stated that some activities are clearly unproductive (like those of domestic servants or associated with some useless state expenditures). Others are productive, because they either increase productive labour skills (in education, healthcare) or save productive labourers time for their reproductive consumption (housework – See also Harrison 1973b). However, he does not explain why housework is productive while domestic servants are not. After this rather confused treatment, Harrison concludes that the concept of productive labour does not serve to understand "the laws of motion" of capitalism. It "should therefore not be used in political economy" (81).

Berthoud (1974), despite his pseudo-philosophical arguments, tried to shake off scholastic orthodoxy, but the final result is again orthodoxy. However, he made some good points: Marx's concepts of productive-unproductive labour are merely economic; they cannot be mixed up with political analyses (this apt observation would let him in for criticism from *Bidet* 1976: 35–6). The problem is: what effect does a certain occupation have on growth? Marx's classification is not a preamble to class analysis; rather, it opens the way to the law of the falling rate of profit (9–11). However, Berthoud maintained that Marx shifted from productive labour to labour productivity, i.e. from an absolute definition to a relative one, which implies different analytical levels (Ibid.).

Ben *Fine* (1973), commenting on Harrison's rejection of the productive/unproductive labour distinction, admitted that Marx is most unclear about the nature of supervisory work. However, he observes that without that distinction Marx's entire model of production-circulation is at risk. *Offe* (1971–77) affirmed that extension of unproductive labour is functional to capitalism because it stabilises the system (3.I: 67–76. See also Offe 1979).

2. Collective labour

The enormous growth of services, both public and private, and of intellectual labour forced Marxist authors to mitigate the exclusion of these activities from the field of productive labour, decreed by Marx. The main analytical tool for this operation was the concept of collective labour, which was, however, by then being used with a different sense to that attributed by Marx.

We have seen (Chapter XI) that Marx brilliantly illustrated what he called the "collective labourer" in *Capital I* and elsewhere. However, he always took the question of productiveness to apply exclusively to individuals. Thus, being part of the collective labourer does not change an unproductive worker into a productive one or the other way around. For example, according to Marx, technicians and direction labourers within the factories remain unproductive because they are part of the exploiting class. Another example is wage labour in the circulation sector, on which Marx distinguished between individual and social capital. For the individual entrepreneur in the circulation sector, wage labour is productive because it yields him a profit. However, at the social level, that labour is unproductive, because all circulation activities are a cost that is paid with the profit of the industrial sector.

Caught between Marx's view and the growing importance of immaterial labour, Marxist authors reacted – in this case, too – in three different ways. Some of them simply restated Marx's thesis,[1] while others seemed only to pay lip service to it.[2] *Delaunay* (1971) affirmed that research is unproductive although it is part of the collective labourer.[3] *Terray* (1972) conceded that engineers – being part of the collective labourer – partly contribute to material production and partly help capital in bringing forth surplus value (136–7). Thus, they are partly productive and partly unproductive.

Other authors looked for some nominalistic solution to the contrast. For example, *Hashimoto* (1966) thought he could solve the contradiction between individual production of surplus value and the collective labourer in a "dialectical" way. *Carchedi* (1977) treated the problem with Byzantine subtlety. When thinking of surplus labour, he said, we include among the productive labourers only those who produce surplus value. When we think of the general labour process, we extend the productive qualification to all those included in the collective labourer (17). Carchedi pointed out that the collective labourer also includes an extended unproductive sector, like commerce and other circulation services (26–30).[4]

Jacques *Nagels* (1974), too, maintained that intellectual occupations, although unproductive at the individual level, become productive as part of the "collective labour" (which – note well – is different from Marx's "collective labourer"). Nagel explains that the concept of collective labour has been elaborated by many authors in France. He suggests that skilled labourers in the factories, like engineers and technicians, are a part of the productive collective labour. The hierarchy in the factory – he underlines, in contrast with Altvater and Huiskens – derives not only from class domination, but also from the need to organise production.[5]

Nagels maintained that there are two different ways to evaluate productive labour. One is based on the production of use values, the other on the production of surplus value. However, there is a unity between the two. This is why Marx's analysis is twofold and appears different – for example, in the case of services – when referring to individual capitalist or to the whole process of production.[6] However, we must add that Marx's distinction between individual profit and social cost in the circulation sector has nothing to do with the distinction between productiveness expressed in use values and productiveness expressed in surplus value.

Nagels added that there are some borderline areas where the unity between the two types of productiveness does not work. One of these areas lies in the services organised in a capitalist way. Another area is non-capitalist material production, i.e. performed by peasants and artisans (238–9).

Finally, there are a few authors who openly dissent from Marx. *Launay* (1968b: 87–9), for example, stressed that the general development of the economy prevails over the problem whether individual labour is productive of surplus value or not. Mature capitalism needs the contribution of immaterial labour to achieve final production. *Gough* (1972) stated that all the labourers who have a part in the collective labourer are productive. He added: "This would suggest the inclusion nowadays of large numbers of scientists, technologists, technicians and engineers, plus substantial sections of management and white collar workers" (55).

3. Material and immaterial labour

a. Heterodox views

A few authors are dissatisfied with Marx's view. *Calvez* (1956) criticised Marx for the adoption, in practice, of Smith's principle that only material labour is productive (75–7). He also criticised the way of accounting for national revenue in the USSR, where Smith's criterion was adopted (86–7). Justin *Blake*

(1960: 171) and *Gough* (1972: 65) pointed out that the durability of the good produced by productive labour is not physical, but economic: its value is conserved by transferring it to other goods during the production process. Consequently, the labour of teachers and researchers is productive, while luxury goods are the fruit of unproductive labour. According to *Nishikawa* (1965), immaterial labour contributes to the production of material goods, and so is productive (20–5).

A particular case is *O'Connor*'s essay (1975), which is flawed by its political approach. The author based his analysis on the social conflict between capital and labour, implicitly referring to factories. He saw as productive all behaviours that are subordinate to capital and as unproductive all kinds of rebellion to it. For example, the workers' struggle to prolong the production time (in order to reduce profit) with slowdowns or various pretexts is – according to O'Connor – a (positive) increase of unproductiveness in their labour (122–8).

b. Orthodox views

Far more numerous were the authors who adhered to Marx's approach. It is striking that, although they know Marx very well, nearly all of them "forget" Marx's admission that immaterial labour can, in principle, be productive. In order to save his theoretical framework, Marx had promptly added that productive immaterial labour is a negligible quantity in the economy. But the post-war authors could no longer use this loophole.

Pietranera (1955) offered a subtle historical analysis to explain why the material nature of productive labour is required, although Marx criticised it in principle. Apart from this exception, the author never abandoned Marx's view of the issue, even down to the details (130–7). *Minc* (1962) and *Delaunay* (1971) simply stated that, in capitalism, labour in the material sector is productive and in the immaterial sector is unproductive.[7] *Launay* (1968b), too, conformed to Marx and also employed some bizarre quibbles to argue that the hairdresser's apprentice is unproductive (85–6).

Vaisov (1971) came up with a specious argument. For the social product taken as a whole, he said, we cannot distinguish between productive and unproductive labour without reference to the material form. The latter is proper to the production sphere, while immaterial labour belongs to the circulation sphere. Without such a distinction, Vaisov maintained, it is impossible to see the accumulation process as different from the network of simple exchanges. The total social product can only be material. Even increase of immaterial values derives from the increase of relative surplus value in the sphere of material production (124–30).

Terray (1972), too, confirmed that the real productive labour is that of material production (121). Services can only help the latter. Despite his complex taxonomy, Terray flatly echoed Marx on every aspect of the issue. *Pesenti* (1972) admitted that social wealth is also made up of immaterial goods, like education, but all the same he confined productiveness to material production.

The incomes provided by immaterial labour can only derive from the incomes of material labour (I: 184–90). *Cella and Reyneri* (1974) are representative of the mass of authors who believed that only manual workers are "revolutionary" subjects. Like Lenin (see Chapter XV.4), they condemned the "workers' aristocracy", i.e. skilled workers with high wages and major responsibility in the labour process. The 1968 revolt, they wrote, has shown that the protagonist of the revolutionary movement is the mass-worker (327–9). *Illuminati* (1977) followed Marx very closely. He denied that intellectual labour or services can in any way be productive, even when they are necessary.[8] Geoffrey *Kay* (1979) unconvincingly argued that the material nature of the products is a requisite for the production of surplus value (132–4).

The prolix *Bidet* (1976), in contrast with Poulantzas and Bettelheim, reminded them that productive labour *per se* is not confined to material production (3–24, 32–4). However, he rejected the concept of "indirectly productive" as a stratagem to extend the range of productive activities unduly (24). Bidet acknowledged that immaterial production had by then taken on much more importance than in the 19th century. "The labour of researchers or of information technology operators", he admits, "is materialised into the product (whether material or not) and is a part of its value". However, like Altvater and Huiskens (see XVII.5.d), the author eludes the difficulty by stating that "the concept of productive/unproductive outlines a more general dimension of class struggle" (24–5). It is hard to tell what this means. Bidet also maintained that research, although unproductive, is dominated by monopolies (49). Like Marx, he grasps at a straw when he includes in the unproductive *faux frais de production* (false costs of production) services in commerce, bookkeeping, technicians and overseers of the industrial production (56–63). Later on, Bidet (1982) repeated the same ideas.

4. Private services

a. New approaches

Many authors disagreed with Marx on the assumed unproductiveness of wage labour in the circulation sector, or at least tried to water down this view. Henri *Denis* (1957) considered services productive as long as they yield a value to the capitalist. Also, peasants and artisans are productive, including those in the public sector. But professionals are unproductive because value is only generated in standardised labour. Shop assistants, bookkeepers, etc. are unproductive because they do not transform products (94–8). See also Denis (1950: 49–57). *Horie* (1959) maintained that commerce and banking activities are productive because they yield surplus value (44–6).

Driscoll (1963: 96) held that autonomous services are productive only if they surpass the productivity of industrial services, but this is rarely the case. *Salvati and Santi* (1968) stated that, at least in the US, productive labour can no longer be distinguished from unproductive labour. A series of unproductive functions – like promotion, organisation, coordination – are increasingly performed by technicians who, at the same time, get on with their productive work (1122).

Ernest *Mandel* appears uncertain about immaterial labour in general. In M. (1969), he wrote that technological transformations make it increasingly difficult to distinguish between productive manual workers, unproductive employees and semi-productive repair work. The integration of various occupations extends productive activities before and after the production process proper and also involves the types of labour that are necessary for distribution. Mandel also speaks of a growing proletarianisation of intellectual labourers (86–9).

In his valuable *Late Capitalism* (M. 1972), Mandel effectively described the transformations occurring in mature economies. There is an expansion of services, because the growing division of labour requires increase in intermediate functions. Mechanisation, standardisation and parcelling out of labour spread everywhere, even in research, housework, circulation and services. These processes lead to increase in unproductive wage labour. Advertising shows abnormal growth. Mandel noted that the consumption time of products is shortening, while their quality is deteriorating (he cites Kay). Besides overproduction, the enormous expansion of productive forces also brings about increasing cultural needs among workers. But alienation also increases.[9] At this point, Mandel wonders whether the unproductiveness of services still holds, since they are no longer a marginal sector. In the end, however, he sticks to Marx's theses (404–6).

Nagels reported and commented on a book by *Michielsen* (*Neocapitalisme* 1969), written in Dutch, where a chapter is devoted to productive labour. Michielsen stressed the importance of science in production and maintained that commerce and bank services are productive. Also, public labour is an important part of the economic process and is productive. The only unproductive public labour, he held, is that devoted to repression and war.[10] *Pelosi* (1974) made a careful survey of the authors of his time who occupied themselves with unproductive labour. He asserted that also labourers who are defined unproductive can enrich their employers and can be essential to production (134–42).

Lippi (1976) brought together the two most debated questions that preoccupied Marxists and Neo-Ricardians in those years: unproductive labour and the transformation of values into prices of production. He rejected both Marx's idea that wage labour in commerce is unproductive and his solution to the transformation problem by arguing that the labour theory of value is inconsistent. Lippi went on to endorse the validity of Sraffa's approach in determining the rate of profit.[11]

According to *Salvati* (1977), who agreed with Lippi, Marx appeared more preoccupied with examining unproductive labour from the capitalist viewpoint than investigating the waste in accumulation, as Smith had done (149–50). But then Salvati himself acknowledged that Marx meant to highlight the false costs of accumulation, which is precisely the waste due to the capitalist organisation of production (151–3).

Formenti (1980) showed that Marx, in practice, followed Smith on material labour (9–17). However, he pointed out, in information technology the productive network consists in immaterial services, which also boost the global surplus value (16). *Harvey* (1982) is in favour of including circulation activities in the productive field, since they make up part of the total reproduction process (105).

b. The orthodox

The strictly orthodox authors on this issue, numerous as they were, found themselves in some difficulty. *Bénard* (1952), a treatise on Marxist economics, made no mention of unproductive labour. However, *Nagels* (1974: 178) noted that, discussing the national revenue, Bénard placed commerce and banks in the unproductive sector. *Eaton* (1950, VI: 145–6) did the same.

According to *Gillman* (1957), unproductive labour increases along with distribution services. In turn, services grow in proportion with capitalist development. They are necessary because there is no production of value without realisation (sale) of the goods in the market. But they are unproductive (ch. 7: 134–5). Gillman (1965) continued to believe commerce to be unproductive, since it does not change the use value of commodities (?). Jacob *Morris* (1958) substantially agreed with Gillman (1957): monopoly capital entails a relative reduction in productive labour.[12]

The productiveness of services came under discussion rather early in Japan (see *Hashimoto* 1966: 57–8, 68). For example, in 1956 Soeda complained that Marx, besides the definition of productive labour in capitalism, failed to provide a general definition of it (see *Nishikawa* 1965: 2–3).

Some authors discussed this issue in the national accounting (see Nishikawa 1965; *Launay* 1968a). A number of articles (published in 1961, then collected in *Dunlop and Diatchenko* 1964) addressed the complex problems of classifications in the national accounting. For instance, *Fabricant* (1961: 22–3) complained that domestic labour is ignored and education is classified as cost rather than product, etc. *Greenberg* (1961: 53–5) made similar observations. Many such paradoxes are hard to resolve without falling into other paradoxes. This is why other authors took manual labour as the basis of any productive labour (as *Prudensky* 1961: 5–6). However, *Mandel* (1962) noted that the sum of incomes does not express the wealth created (I: 249).

Vaisov (1971) declares unproductive not only the activities for safety and protection, but also healthcare, research, education and finance (130–1). The same thesis is affirmed in two official textbooks, one from the *USSR Academy of Sciences* (1954: 240–3), the other from China (*Wang* 1974: 124–8). Interestingly, *Ofer* (1973) proved that, due to this prejudice about services, the whole sector had grown too little in the Soviet Union. This had created grave inefficiency, not only in the distribution sector but even in production, where administrative operators were all too few.

Nevertheless, the Soviet national accounting was not faithful to Marx. *Kushnirsky and Stull* (1987) noticed that it followed Smith's classification of unproductive activities (which included public and professional services). It differed from Marx also because it considered productive both independent (material) producers and labourers in commerce (99–100).

According to *Nagels* (1974), services in general are unproductive, including capitalist services, which – he says – are negligible (227–36, 245–53). Nagels, like many others, employed some sophisms. For example: in its "profound Marxist meaning", labour is transformation of nature, so it must have a (material) good to form. Thus, properly speaking, in circulation there are no labour processes (254–5). *Balibar* (1974) reaffirmed that the dependent workers of finance, commerce and of the state are unproductive (154). He also maintained that the growth of intellectual labour in some sectors of production implies a decline in skill in other sectors (146–7). *La Grassa* (1977: 103) and *Corallo* (1982: 906), too, maintained that along with technical progress there is increasing polarisation. These authors probably meant that technical progress, while increasing the skill of some workers, renders the work of others more elementary. However, they present this trend as static and inexplicable.

Bravermann (1974) flatly echoed Marx. However, he stressed that, since Marx's time, commerce and independent labour had grown to an unimaginable extent. The hired workers in these sectors, although still unproductive, came much closer to those in industry (284–93). Contradictorily, Bravermann also maintained that the transformation of unproductive labour into productive "is the very process of the creation of capitalist society" (286). Jean *Massoni* (1973: 51), too, noted the enormous increase of services in the production sphere (bookkeeping, statistics, purchase, research, organisation) and in commerce. He saw these services as absolutely necessary yet still unproductive.

Colliot-Thélène (1975) admitted that the problem, as posed by Marx, is unsolvable. If we call the labour producing surplus value productive, wage labourers in commerce and finance cannot be included since they appropriate surplus value produced by others. On the other hand, if we define the labour given in exchange for revenue unproductive, these labourers cannot be included either, since their labour is purchased with capital. This is why authors are forced either to contest Marx's statement or to forget part of it. Colliot-Thélène eludes this antinomy by stating that the question is not pertinent if it is not raised over the proper part of *Capital*: not the one on production in general (*Capital I*) but that part of *Capital III* devoted to the role of wage labourers in commerce (77–9). However, some pages before she had written the opposite: that labour productiveness cannot be discussed in the sphere of circulation (see XVIII.2)! In actual fact, her brilliant analysis leads to a non-solution of the problem.

Gouverneur (1975), following Marx, provided a detailed taxonomy of activities, according to their capacity to produce use values, commodities, value and surplus value (see also Gouverneur 1978: 70–7). In the tertiary sector, he distinguishes the production of commodities (tourism, catering, entertainment, garages, laundries etc.), administration (which includes education, justice, defence, etc.) and circulation (commercial and financial business). The first series of these activities are productive, but not the others (75–6). *Del Monte* (1977) criticised Lippi and Salvati and affirmed the unproductiveness of wage labour in commerce (see also *Jaguin* 1976: 404–10). *Cuyvers* (1978: 71) set out to prove mathematically that Marx was right about unproductive labour. Unfortunately, as often happens in these approaches, Marx's thesis was already implied in the premises (72–4). Thus, Cuyvers could prove that Marx is formally coherent, but not that his thesis is true.

According to *Howard and King* (1975), the labour theory of value would be senseless without the productive/unproductive labour distinction. The latter reaffirms that value is not created in exchange. The authors follow Gough in saying that Marx distinguishes between labour needed in any production system and labour proper to capitalism. Commerce is of the latter type, which is why it is unproductive. However, they add, Marx is inconsistent and fails to provide precise criteria to distinguish exchange of commodities from production proper (141–3, 172fn). This approach, we must say, is absurd. Commerce existed well before the advent of capitalism and is, moreover, not confined to exchange.

Cutler and others (1977) argued against Marx's thesis that dependent workers in the services are unproductive although they yield a profit for their employer (vol. I: 291–9). *Hunt* (1979) did the same (315–8) and concluded that the productive/unproductive distinction can be used "to show the irrational allocation of resources under capitalism" (323).

Fine and Harris (1979), while affirming that the advent of monopoly economy imposes re-examination of the issue of unproductive labour (49–53), restated Marx's thought and criticised the Neo-Ricardians Gough and Harrison. The latter fail to distinguish between the sphere of production and that of circulation. Since they are not concerned with the production of value and surplus value, they see all economic activities as regulated by exchange and the production of profit. Therefore, according to Gough and Harrison, wage labour in commerce is productive because it yields a profit. For Marx, on the contrary, circulation depends on production, and the profit generated in it is simply subtraction of the surplus value produced in the production sphere (49–53).

Driver (1980) argued that commerce depends on the productivity of the industrial sector, not on its own productivity. Thus, its growth is slower (?). Since its output cannot be expanded autonomously, any increase in the market share gained by an entrepreneur of commerce must be subtracted from other competitors in the sector; it cannot derive from market extension. In addition, Driver maintained, contrary to Marx and Engels, that commerce workers (who are unproductive) are better protected during crises than the productive workers of industry because their sector is less dynamic. His bizarre conclusion is that commerce is "uncharacteristic of capitalism" (as Howard and King also hold). Moreover, Driver insists (12–18) that, in commerce, demand is totally inelastic to prices (probably because he thinks that prices are only determined by the cost of production). Driver's analysis is a series of sophisms. Apart the fact that he overlooked the decisive importance of commerce for capitalist development, he forgot that by then the commercial part of the total cost of commodities was even greater than the "industrial" component.

5. Labour which raises labour-force productivity

a. Semi-independent views

In this field, a few authors dared to breach the barrier of the orthodox. *Gillman* (1965: 22) acknowledged that transport, teaching and research are productive because they help material production. *Nishikawa* (1965: 26), like many other authors, stressed the difference between productive and reproductive labour. The former can be non-reproductive and even harmful (as in the case of armaments and luxury goods).

Paul *Bullock* (1973) stated that the activities serving to increase labour power, as J.S. Mill had maintained, are productive, at least for the individual capitalist. Bullock believed he had found some evidence on the productiveness of transport and education in Marx. But *Fine and Harris* (1979) rightly showed that he had misinterpreted Marx (see also XI.4). They also argued that the labour which increases labour power cannot be productive of surplus value because it is not directed by capital (55).

More interesting is the observation by Bullock (1974) prompted by his reading of the *Grundrisse*. Luxury production, he wrote, "will often anticipate future necessity". While this labour is unproductive for capital as a whole, it "will at a later date fall under a productive relationship, if the results of that labour become socially necessary" (3). Here Bullock is referring to the luxuries that gradually become comforts and necessities. However, he soon falls back on Marxian orthodoxy: "Luxury production leaves the value of labour power undisturbed" (4); and "luxury industry employs labour only insofar a surplus value is produced by wage goods workers" (6).

Some authors used the discarded category of "indirectly productive". *Launay* (1968b) employed the expression for teaching, healthcare, research and services, since they increase the productivity of the labour force but do not produce directly surplus value. The expenses for these activities belong to constant capital (87–94. See also Launay 1968c: 102–3). However, he took the cue offered by the *Grundrisse*, affirming that science was becoming much more important for the production of wealth than the direct production of value (94–5). *Habermas* (1973) acknowledged the decisive importance of education and research for the accumulation of his time and defined them as indirectly productive (II.5: 63–4). *Di Matteo* (1979: 11–22) extended this observation to all services, when they serve for the production of surplus value in the "general process of capitalist production". Housework, wrote Jackie *West* (1979: 178–9), can be viewed as indirectly productive.

b. Orthodox authors

Altvater and Huisken (1970) maintained that the enormous apparatus of education and science, which aims at increasing productivity, is only a part of the *faux frais de production*, like all immaterial labour (ch. 3: 43–65). The same thesis is proposed in the essays on education collected by Altvater and Huiskens (1971). Among these, *Bishoff* et al. (1970) and *Hübner* et al. (1970) confirm the unproductiveness of teaching and research. All these writings share the mix – rather widespread by then – of flat orthodoxy and "class analysis".

In that period, the intertwining of economic and political elements rendered many works tortuous and confused. Charles *Bettelheim* (1972) took the confusion to the utmost. He wrote that, on the social level, labour is productive only if it reproduces the material elements necessary to support the exploitation relationships. Thus, research and information are not productive (unlike the work of engineers), although their results may become commodities which yield surplus value to the capitalist. Research products are not reproducible (should it not be the contrary?), like art products. Their price is not determined by their value and bears no relation to labour time. The research product is due to a collective process, whose "price" (?) is not reproduced in further production processes (71–3).

Vaisov (1971: 133) confirmed the tendency towards the diminution of productive workers in monopoly capitalism. He added that workers in excess increase the number of the unproductive or the unemployed. *Delaunay* (1971) came up with an incredibly confused treatment of education as a useful but unproductive activity (225–48). *Lojkine* (1977) saw research and teaching as a necessary but unproductive expenditure (104, 127–8).

Janco and Furjot (1972) appear tempted to admit that the production of software is a productive labour, insofar as it, first, produces a commodity that is part of capital and, second, enables repetitive processes. Thus, the workers in this sector are very close to being productive labourers. However, the authors evidently felt they should bow to Bettelheim's authority and so, in the end, they interpreted the IT (information technology) revolution as a simple value-saving process.

According to *Bidet* (1976), the expenses borne in the reproduction of the labour force belong to the *faux frais de production*. They are unproductive because they do not add any new use value to the product (64–5). This is another sophism, much used in that period.

Finally, *Godelier* (1979) mixes up and often confuses, among the unproductive activities, labour that reproduces labour power, labour that helps exploitation, immaterial labour and labour exchanged with income. He also maintains that intellectual labourers in capitalist enterprises are productive, but are not so when helping exploitation, (69–70).

6. Housework

At the dawn of the feminist movement, the 1960s–70s saw a vast literature on housework flourishing. Here we will mention just a few contributions.

Several authors stressed that housework is to be considered unproductive, because it is external to the market. However, it cannot be considered external to the division of labour.

Harrison (1973b) and Jackie *West* (1979) maintained that the housewife's domestic labour enables the capitalist to pay less for her husband's productive labour. *Bullock* (1974: 12–13), *Howell* (1975, IV.iii) and *Lebowitz* (1976) objected that Marx held housework to be unproductive (but Harrison was not contesting that point).

Seccombe (1974: 6–7) pointed out that the houseworker is separate, not only from the means of production she uses, like industrial workers, but also from the means of exchange. Thus, the housewife is separate "from any direct relation with capital". The breadwinner (the husband) has basic authority over the use of the wage itself (19). Although housework directly contributes to the production of labour power, it is necessary but unproductive labour (8–15). The organisation of this labour remains static, while the tools it uses are constantly improved by technology (17).

Particularly interesting among the various "feminist" critiques of Seccombe's article is the one by Jean *Gardiner* (1975), who investigated the consequences of the "wife's economic dependence on her husband and the power relations within the family" (51). She maintained that "the overall standard of living of workers is not determined just by the wage bargain between capital and labour, as it appears to be in Marx's analysis" (53). Actually, "the value of the labour power is not determined in any straightforward sense" by the subsistence level, but also by the goods and services provided by domestic labour (54). Domestic labour keeps (productive) labour below subsistence level. This is why there are pressures "from a capitalist viewpoint" to keep housework and childcare in the private sphere (Ibid.).

Of the many authors, above all women who analysed the reproduction of human beings, particular mention is merited by Mary *O'Brian* (1981), who stressed that this issue brings out a major shortcoming in Marx's theory of capitalist development. Marx treated it as a natural, non-economic process, although it produces use value and adds to the GNP (163–70).

7. After the 1970s

In the most advanced European countries, immaterial production (services of various kind) had already reached 50% of the total production by the mid-1970s. Yet the general debate on its productiveness continued up to the end of the 1980s. Marxist writings on this issue are still coming out today, but it would be useless, not to say terribly boring, to extend our survey farther. Subsequent to the 1970s, authors have simply continued to re-echo Marx, either in the original version or in the version provided by some of the authors we have examined. Online Marxist periodicals and blogs are full of contributions of this kind (see e.g. *Duménil and Lévy* 2006; *Williams* 2010). Worth of mention is *Wolff* 1987, who saw as productive the labour of the state or non-profit institutions in education, healthcare, transport, electricity and gas, and protection (39).

However, the majority of references to unproductive labour are to be found in empirical studies, where the postulate is assumed that the public administration, finance and insurance activities, and sometimes commerce, are unproductive, while all the traditional industrial activities are productive. Fred Moseley's *The falling rate of profit in the postwar United States economy* (1991) enjoyed wide circulation and was much debated. Moseley expressed in Marxian terms the same thesis as Bacon and Eltis (see XVI.2.b): the fall in the profit rate derives from a huge increase in unproductive spending, which, according to him, includes commercial activities. The article by *Tsouflidis and Tsaliki* (2014) is a good example of this approach. At least, these authors put education and research among the productive sectors (563–5). See also *Sewell* (2014).

Note that this approach is precisely the opposite of the thesis, best expressed by Sweezy and held by the great majority of Marxists in the 1960s–70s, i.e. that public unproductive spending is done to prevent gluts on the market. In any case, this recent literature shows no signs of considering unproductive labour as a major problem of the crisis that hit the developed countries after the welfare state boom.

Conclusions

Most Marxist economists seemed unaware of the revolution in the social organisation of labour of the 1960s–80s. It was a radical change that rendered the traditional opposition between manual labour (usually elementary and exploited) and intellectual labour (usually privileged) obsolete. Obsolete, too, became the respective definitions of productive for the former type of labour and unproductive for the latter.

These authors did not answer the crucial question: who fosters accumulation in this phase? That is, whose labour *now* is *more* productive? No doubt, the answer should have been, as a few authors suggested (see XVIII.4–5), the intellectual labourers, services, research, education and culture. The question can also be put thus: what labour *now* is *less* productive? The answer is, the labour in excess of the saturated sectors of the economy (see XX.1).

Notes

1 See e.g. Vaisov (1971: 123).
2 See Gough (1973: 69) and Nagels (1974: 248–9). See also below.
3 Delaunay (1971: 204–6, 221–2).
4 Cf. Marx (*Capital I*, V.XVI.2–3).
5 Nagels (1974: 190ff, 208, 308).
6 Ibid.: 208, 238–45, 259, passim.
7 Minc (1962, VIII: 168–70). *Delaunay* (1971: 200–3).
8 Illuminati (1977: 76, 83, 85, 98–9fn, passim).
9 Mandel (1972, ch. 12: 383–403).
10 See Nagels (1974: 182–3, 190, 304–59).
11 On commerce, see Lippi (1976: 15–27, 88–92).
12 Morris (1958: 196–7, 206). See also Morris (1960).

XVIII New middle classes and human capital

Background

The analyses in the preceding Chapters XV–XVII imply the idea of the middle classes as a central factor of social organisation. In Marx we find two different processes regarding this issue. One has to do with the decline of small proprietors, small entrepreneurs and independent producers. This decline is traditionally called proletarianisation, i.e. the transformation of the traditional middle classes into exploited proletarians. The other process is a matter of emergence of new middle classes, which Marx saw as unproductive. The Marxist authors of the 1960s–70s had the "mission impossible" of harmonising the fast growth of the new middle classes in the production activities with Marx's view of their unproductiveness. Only a few out of these authors abandoned the previous negative attitude and saw the new classes as the protagonists of development. In this context, the concept of human capital takes on a new role, far more central to development than the previous one. For the most insightful authors, whether Marxist or heterodox, investment in human capital was to be the driving force of the post-industrial economy.

1. Proletarianisation of the old middle classes and rise of the new

The proletarianisation of the traditional middle classes was first illustrated in the *Manifesto of the Communist Party*. In the words of *Marx and Engels* (1848):

> "The lower strata of the middle class – the small tradespeople, shopkeepers, and retired tradesmen generally, the handicraftsmen and peasants – all these sink gradually into the proletariat, …". And, shortly after: "entire sections of the ruling class are, by the advance of industry, precipitated into the proletariat, or are at least threatened in their conditions of existence".
>
> (I: 18, 19)

Thus, proletarianisation is a process in which the old middle classes lose both means of production and economic autonomy, and find their social status deteriorating. The process was real, and the analysis of it an important achievement. As Marx explained later, proletarianisation started during the so-called original accumulation, but it continued after, along with capitalist accumulation. Through proletarianisation, the capitalist economy is progressively reduced to only two classes: the bourgeoisie and the proletariat.[1]

The other process described by Marx is the growth of new types of middle classes. On this issue, he confined his analysis to some scattered observations of this kind:

> What he [Ricardo] forgets to emphasise is the constantly growing number of the middle classes, those who stand between the workman on the one hand and the capitalist and landlord on the other. The middle classes maintain themselves to an ever increasing extent directly out of revenue, they are a burden weighing heavily on the working base and increase the social security and power of the upper ten thousand.[2]

Just before this passage, Marx had explained that technical progress, by increasing productivity, on the one hand increases surplus value while, on the other hand, it replaces a part of wage labourers. The combined effect of this process is that the bourgeoisie can afford to maintain more unproductive labourers, whether in the form of menial servants or as middle classes maintained by capital. Thus, according to Marx, the new middle classes are unproductive, unlike most of the traditional ones.

Note that in Marx's texts the new middle classes have nothing to do with proletarianisation. The association was only made by some Marxist authors of the 1960s–70s. Note, too, that the two processes described by Marx are not incompatible. While accumulation destroys the old middle classes, consisting of small producers, it creates at the same time another middle class, made up of service labourers and other immaterial occupations. C. Wright *Mills* (1951) proved that the two processes coexist and in some cases merge. However, Mill's analysis also shows that, in real experience, the former process is not so straightforward as Marx and Engels had believed, while Marx's interpretation of the second process is actually erroneous.

Eduard *Bernstein* (1899) challenged the former of Marx's theses. He proved that in the Germany of his times small enterprises and independent producers were still flourishing and in agriculture they were even increasing in number (ch. 3.c). Later on, *Pischel* (1946), too, argued that Marx's thesis was excessively radical: the old middle classes had managed to survive (14–19).

At the beginning of the new century, Gustav Schmoller, followed by other non-Marxist authors, stressed the rise of a new middle class, but it was seen as a productive class. It differed from the old one in that it did not rely on ownership of means of production but on skill. The members of this new class belonged to both the public or the private sector. They were professionals, technicians, operators in new services, teachers, researchers, etc. They were often employees, with high qualifications and incomes (see *Gallino* 2004, entry "Classe media"). *Geiger* (1949) analysed along the same lines the "managers' revolution" (IX.5: 196–217); and J.K. *Galbraith* (1967) described the growing importance of teachers and researchers for the "technostructure", which by then had come to dominate capitalism (ch. 25).

Contesting Schmoller and his followers, *Pannekoek* (1909) restated Marx's view of proletarianisation, but he also admitted the existence of a new middle class. *Mondolfo* (1925) noted that, like the proletariat, the new middle class works, but also has some capital endowment, as proprietors. This endowment, however, does not consist necessarily of means of production or means of exchange; it can also consist in skill, acquired through studies. Surprisingly enough, the excellent analysis of the classes in Marx, by *Gurvitch* (1954), paid no attention to Marx's proletarianisation theory, nor to the rise of the new middle class. Gurvitch referred only to a sort of military-technocratic elite (VI: 65–71) to which he claimed to have found some reference in Marx and which evidently is part of the dominant class.

The new middle classes kept on growing in the last century until their number surpassed that of the material labourers. *Gallino* (2004) writes that, at the beginning of the 20th century, in the most developed countries there were no more than two or three thousand types of occupations. Now, he adds, they number over 30 thousand; and more than two thirds of them - according to the specialist literature - belong to the middle classes. The new occupations are also due to the enormous increase of bureaucracy and its ramifications, the increase in educational activities, etc. (entry "Classe media": 111a). A similar consideration is to be found in *Dahrendorf* (1957, I: 92). All the authors define the new middle classes with two features: they have no property and work as employees.

Dahrendorf (1957) divided the previous authors into those who saw the new middle class as an extension of the dominant class and those who saw it as close to the proletariat (95–7). In fact, he transferred this division to the middle class itself: a part of it belongs to the bureaucratic hierarchy, while the other part is closer to common workers (97–100). *Touraine* (1955) acutely described the decline of crafts, due to automation (II.I). Later on, he wrote that the mass employees and technicians produced by automation are weak in both power and influence, dominated by the bureaucrats, who direct social change (Touraine 1969, I: 64–7).

Giddens (1973) noted that Marx's division between productive and unproductive occupations applies to agricultural rather than industrial societies. In the latter, organisational and administrative labour are indispensable to produce wealth (V.3). In contrast with Dahrendorf and the Marxists, Giddens affirmed that the employees had not been divided between a privileged minority and a proletarianised majority. The mechanisation of office labour did not eliminate the differences with manual labour. Moreover, there are some elements of conflict between blue-collar workers and white-collar workers (X.4).

The same process of automation and the consequent growth of intellectual labour gave rise to two – apparently opposite – interpretations. *Wilensky* (1979) noted consolidation in the features of some new professions whilst

Haug (1979) argued that loss of status was suffered by the professionals. Haug added that the attempt to retain the monopoly of knowledge had by then been undermined with the advent of computers, which led to the liberalisation of knowledge.

2. New middle classes as increase of the proletariat

The growth of new occupations and the new middle classes was in sharp contrast with Marx's theses, which created great confusion for the Marxist authors in the 1960s–70s. They tried to squeeze the new classes into one or the other of the two processes described by Marx: proletarianisation or parasitic growth. But the results are by no means convincing. Substantially they described as social decadence a process that other authors described as social advance (see section 3). We can distinguish the positions that emerged as follows.

a. Proletarianisation of intellectual labour

The *Manifesto* view of the issue inspired two different groups of authors. One saw the growth of middle classes as a direct consequence of the traditional proletarianisation, while the other simply ignored the rise of the new middle classes.

The book by Mariuccia *Salvati* (2000) collects the writings of German authors who studied the new middle classes in the 1920s. In the long preface, Salvati wrote that, being close to Marxism, they escaped the Nazi regime by fleeing to the US. Particular attention is merited by the pages of Lederer and Marschak reproduced in Salvati (their book, of 1926, is entitled *The new middle class*). The authors, first, see the new middle class as deriving from the decline of the independent proprietors or producers, then they describe it as due to the extension of the tasks of public administration. These tasks increase along with economic development. Some members of this class, having managerial tasks, are closer to the bourgeoisie, while others are closer to the proletariat (160–71).

Crompton (1976), too, saw no contradiction in the origin of the new middle classes. As Marx himself explained in *Capital III*, these classes derive from both the traditional proletarianisation and the growth in the division of labour. Both processes are the result of capitalist development (414–16). These classes, in the fields of medicine, education and administration, Crompton added, are unproductive, since they are maintained by revenue, but they (as Lederer and Marschak had already observed) are without property and form part of the collective labourer. Thus, their class situation is structurally ambiguous (417–20ff). Later on, *Crompton and Gubbay* (1977) argued that the middle classes have a basic role in capitalist development. Their work is similar to that of the wage labourers, but they are unproductive (75—7ff).

Offe (1979) interpreted the extension of the public sector as traditional proletarianisation (ch. 2: 23–40). By contrast, *Oppenheimer* (1979) saw the proletarianisation of the "white collars" as consequence of technical progress. The latter sharpens the division of labour and so makes intellectual labour simpler and limited to a few tasks. The living conditions of the new middle class deteriorate and so these labourers, too, turn to collective bargaining.

The second group of authors simply ignored the new middle classes while retaining Marx's analysis. They are a good example of ideological blindness. Paul *Mattick* (1969) reaffirmed all the traditional arguments stated by Marx. The increase in number of proletarians derives from the decadence of small proprietors, who were unproductive because they were not exploited. Capitalism, he added, is basically a two-class society, and the proletariat, contrary to a widespread opinion, is taking on growing importance (430–3). *Zitara* (1970) and *Wright and Singelmann* (1982), too, spoke of proletarianisation in the sense Marx attributed to it. According to Wright and Singelmann, there is even an increase in workers engaged in material production and a decrease in quasi-autonomous workers and public employees (201–2). *Camatte* (1964–72) simply restated Marx's view on the unproductiveness of the traditional middle class. The latter included the new middle class (78–86).

b. Growth of unproductive labour

The following authors, contrary to the authors dealt with previously, defined the new middle classes according to the other process described by Marx. They saw mass intellectual labourers as belonging to the dominant class and contributing to the oppression of proletarians, despite the relative reduction of their privileges.

Besides *Grossmann* (1919, III.8–9), also *Calabi* (1972) repeated Marx's thesis that the growing surplus generates an increase in the unproductive middle classes (61–2). *Tomasetta* (1974) devoted a long analysis to maintaining – following in Saylos Labini's footprints – that the traditional proletarianisation is disproved by the data. But, he added, the unproductive middle classes are increasing (307–47).

Poulantzas (1974) focused on the opposition between intellectual and material labour. He criticised Richta, Mallet, etc. (see section 3), for considering the new middle classes as composed of proletarians and for believing that intellectual labour would become more important than material labour in the production of value. Technical progress, he maintained, rather than reducing, increases the gap between intellectual and material labour (234–7). Poulantzas's approach is the opposite of the approach applying the proletarianisation to the new middle classes. The new petty bourgeoisie, he wrote, reproduces both the intellectual/manual labour division and its ideology. Intellectual labour increases in value, while manual labour undergoes a devaluation (259). Thanks to the professional secret and monopoly of knowledge, bureaucratisation grows and increases the distance between intellectual and manual labour (279–81). *Bowles and Gintis* (1980) and *Carbonaro* (1979: 104–6) agreed with Poulantzas.

On the contrary, *Colliot-Thélène* (1975) offered an effective critique of Poulantzas. She pointed out that labour productiveness cannot be discussed in the circulation sphere, because this is precisely the field where the purchase of labour power acquires the illusory appearance of an exchange between individuals who are on the same level. Besides, wage labour can be the result of two different transactions: the purchase of personal services with revenue or the purchase of labour-force with capital. This has nothing to do with the material or immaterial nature of a certain type of labour. Adam Smith, she said, was deceived precisely by this "coarse fetishism" (75–7). In principle, Colliot-Thélène was right, but in fact Poulantzas was closer to the spirit of Marx.

Duménil (1975) described the growth of managers and immaterial labour as an extension of capital dominance. Capital management tends to grow more complex and articulated. The employees engaged in this labour are unproductive. More balanced were the authors of the *Traité* (1971), who described the great increase of intellectual occupations. Most of these increasingly take on the features of repetitiveness and subordination proper to the proletarian labour. Often the intermediate intellectual labourers belong partly to the managing function and partly to the subordinated one. Thus, they are partly unproductive, partly productive (I, III.3: 228–36). In any case, the social relations tend to polarise (I, III.4).

Fay (1968b) proposed a wider-ranging analysis: the workers in the more developed countries or sectors enjoy an addition of surplus value, that they have not produced, in their wages. This addition comes from the workers of the more backward countries or sectors. Even within the same enterprise, this transfer of value occurs between more and less skilled workers. The process causes growing differentiation between workers in skill, power and wage levels. On this basis, we can speak of new middle classes, an expression in continuity – Fay wrote – with the concept of Engels's workers' aristocracy. The upper levels of the wage labourers feel part of the dominant class and defend their privileges, until – in periods of crisis – they are forced to realise that they, too, are exploited and treated like the other workers.

c. Social decline

Some authors used the term of proletarianisation, or similar terms, not in the structural sense but only to indicate the decline – in status and in working conditions – of the skilled immaterial occupations that had once been privileged.

Dobb (1946) was struck by the great increase of administrative and technical employees. He wrote that their working conditions were much like those of the material workers. On the other hand, technical progress tends to transform the workers' labour into control activity (348–53). As to Mandel, see XVII.4.a.

Like Mandel, other authors also used the concept of proletarianisation as a simple analogy, without implying real participation of these categories in the production of value and surplus value. This is why some authors used other expressions, like reduction to wage conditions or suchlike. For example, *Piccone Stella* (1972) carried out empirical sociological research on the "proletarianisation" of the Italian intellectual labourers. It is a process that consists in deterioration of living standards, loss of self-sufficiency in labour, and increasingly precarious labour (ch. 3). *Rettura* (1973) described the situation of bank employees in similar terms but added that the distribution is no longer unproductive since it contributes to the production of surplus value (50–56). *Boccara* (1978) noted the proletarianisation of the white collars in the production sector and the reduction of intellectual labourers to wage labourers (150–1). According to *Fetscher* (1983), Marx's idea – in the *Grundrisse* – that labour will become increasingly intellectual and non-alienated is utopian, because even intellectual labour is alienating (52–3).

By contrast, *Altvater and Huisken* (1970) describe the proletarianisation process as subjection to capital. The authors acknowledge that intellectual and public work are increasingly important for productivity growth and stress the driving force of education and research. However, they consider these activities unproductive (see XVII.5.b), although, they say, the middle classes tend towards proletarianisation. The authors describe the tendency of modern capitalism to dominate labour through the subjugation to the hierarchy of command (ch.2: 23–42). *Altvater* (1967) maintained that education forms part of the state activities in support of capitalist development (147–61).

d. Devaluation

The concept of devaluation also derives from Marx. Accumulation, Marx wrote, through the increase in productivity, brings about a decline in the value of capital both as means of production and as consumption goods. Due to the latter aspect, the labour force is devalued, too (*Capital* III, III.XV.16). Along these lines we find the concept repeated by many authors.[3] According to *Finzi* (1977: 14), capital devaluation is a consequence of overproduction.

Salama (1973) criticised Rosa Luxemburg because she (contrary to Marx) maintained that the growth of the middle classes cannot constitute an outlet for the growing surplus. He also recalled Baran and Sweezy and concluded that the increase of unproductive labour and unproductive expenses slows down the fall of profit rate (260–6). Also, the devaluation of constant capital, due to technical progress, serves to slow down the fall of profit rate.

By contrast, Olin *Wright* (1978) does not interpret capital devaluation in terms of decline of accumulation. He acutely observes that, even if the organic composition (i.e. the ratio constant to variable capital, in value terms) increases, this tendency will be offset by the enormous expansion of services, which are labour-intensive (135–6).

Olin Wright, however, is an exception. Other authors saw, in the tendency towards devaluation – which they curiously call "devalorisation" – the cause of the proletarianisation of the new middle classes. *Tomassini* (1976) applied this approach to students. He sees education as reducing (rather than increasing) the production cost of labour power, while boosting its productivity. This means that the new students form part of the proletariat.

Carchedi (1975) applied deductive analysis to distinguish two types of devaluation of the labour force: one due to the reduction of production cost for wage goods, the other deriving from the de-qualification of labour due to the increasing division of labour. The proletarianisation of the new middle class derives from the latter process (377–92). This holds for the white-collar workers, who increase in number relative to the total industrial population, receive lower salaries and lose their privileges (392–8). It also holds for the technicians, subject to standardisation of projects and the division of labour (398–403). The devaluation of immaterial dependent labour was reaffirmed in Carchedi (1977). The latter work also explained that, while the old middle class consisted of capitalist agents, who owned and managed capital, the new middle class, born in monopoly capitalism, is a mixture of both classes, capitalists and labourers. Thus, it is spurious.[4]

The concept of devaluation, however, is a slippery one. The aforementioned authors did not consider the fact that the fall in the production cost of wage-goods, precisely in that period, was enhancing the labourers' welfare enormously.

3. Marxist authors for human capital

Not all Marxist or radical economists rejected the idea of the benefits of increased productivity and growth in intellectual labour. A number of authors stressed that accumulation is supported by a constant increase in education, comfort and culture. A growing part of social investment goes to human capital because the increase in productivity shifts towards less physical, more intellectual labour. The increase in productivity relies not only on the production of profit, but also depends on collective services of any kind, professional differentiation, research, variations in consumption, etc. Thus, all the occupations related to such processes are to be considered productive.

These authors opposed, or ignored, Marx's view of the growing parasitism of the petite bourgeoisie. They did not use the concept of proletarianisation, because they saw the new middle class as involved in a positive process that pushes one part of the old proletariat up to a higher social status.[5]

Often these authors drew inspiration from the *Grundrisse*, the notebooks of the 1850s in which Marx frequently described surplus value (and the labour theory of value itself) as too small a basis to measure the whole process of development (among the many relevant passages, see *Grundrisse*: 636–8). In these early notes, Marx insisted on the huge increase of social productivity, which is driven by science, education, research and culture. As a matter of fact, he acknowledged the basic importance for development of what we now call human capital. However, in his later writings, as we have seen, while not denying its importance, Marx relegated these crucial activities to the field of unproductive labour.

Karl *Renner* (1953) maintained that, by then, there was a convergence between the class of supervisors and managers, created by capitalism on the pattern of public employees, and the class of skilled workers who controlled machinery. The task of these workers calls for increasing responsibility. In sum, said Renner, many authors "who claim to be Marxists" treat this question superficially. They do not realise that the social basis "has been completely transformed in the past hundred years". "The working class as it appears … in Marx's *Capital* no longer exists" (252).

The Polish author *Ossowski* (1957) provided an outstanding analysis of social classes. For Aristotle, he wrote, the middle class is the fundamental one, while the rich and the poor are negative deviations from it. On the contrary, Marx has a dichotomic conception of classes, while the middle class is something indeterminate between the dominant and dominated classes (3.1: 45–6). It shares some of the features of the former and some of the latter.[6] Marx forecast the disappearance of the middle class, due to the polarisation caused by capitalist accumulation (5.4: 85). He could not know that the thin new middle class of his time, consisting of public employees, technicians and functionaries, would become so important (12.4: 202–4).

Acquaviva (1958) examined in detail the new class generated by automation, which he called the second and more powerful industrial revolution. The new class is made up of people who monitor the new machines and control the rational organisation of production. These labourers need sufficient elasticity to adapt to the new organisation of labour, less rigid and less hierarchical than that of the traditional factory. Thus, this class, besides having specific skill, must have a broad culture and responsibility. Its work is far from being devalued. The new technicians are no longer passively subjected to the traditional bureaucracy.[7] On the other hand, the traditional working class diminishes in number, eventually representing a modest percentage of the total people employed (ibid: 129–30). With the advent of automation, the old working class is less decisive in the social class structure; it counts less than before and is in some respects superseded by the new class (3.i: 133–5).

Löbl (1967) offered one of the most interesting treatments of human capital. Even in the title, his book is centred on the idea that in the advanced economies, intellectual labour is the very source of wealth (Löbl was a Marxist from communist Czechoslovakia. He was tried alongside Slánsky and spent a long time in jail). He noted that, while in Marx's time physical labour dominated the production process, in the 1960s it was intellectual labour, above all science, which determined production. This – he stressed – obliges us to change the economic categories used by Marx for new ones.[8] Wealth is produced in direct proportion to the quantity of intellectual labour employed and in inverse proportion to the physical labour employed (129).

Of course, there is some mental labour that is very similar to physical labour due to routine. On the other hand, in the past, skill often came through practical experience (146–8). Consequently, the borderline between physical and intellectual labour is impossible to determine precisely, nor is it correct to derive the level of qualification from the level of education attained (141–8). The latter observation seems to be an implicit answer to Schultz's and others' attempts to measure individual productivity on the basis of the curriculum of studies (see XII.4–5).

For the same reasons, Löbl added, we cannot say how much labour a single commodity or service contains. For a pair of shoes, for example, we should take into account the contribution of the public administration, the distribution system, transport, the banks and respective institutions, education, research, etc. This means that the idea that prices express values is a nonsense (190–2). What we can say is that, in the formation of the production cost, social labour has a growing importance, from education to healthcare, from science to art, etc. (201).

Löbl's approach appears to be both utopian and enlightened. He concluded that man's aspiration to be free from the constraints of nature and social oppression can be fulfilled only through science. It is science that makes the difference between production in the past, based on empirical thought, and present production. It is the revolution of thought that made the social revolution possible (291–7).

In the same year, Radovan Richta and his numerous interdisciplinary team – they, too, from Czechoslovakia – published a text that came to represent a milestone in this approach (*Richta* 1967). Some of these authors also published a collection of essays written for the Marienbad (Mariánské Lázně) seminar (*Richta* 1968). These works depicted a great vision of economic progress based on the scientific and technological revolution. The latter drives humanity not only towards well-being, but also towards a superior civilisation, based on culture and new human relations. In these works, an enlightened vision emerges of man's liberation through the rational use of research and applied technology. This was the dream of the Prague Spring. These authors imagined a socialist society just and opulent, guided by scientific and technological labour.

On Rosdolsky, see XIX.3.c. Also remarkable is the little-known article by Yves *Barel* (1968), who stresses that it is a great mistake to stick to the concept of the falling rate of profit. The latter cannot be proved and in any case cannot be the decisive cause of the capitalist crisis (65–7). Automation, he writes, increases production without increasing hired labour. Its profit does not come from the exploitation of workers, but from the "general exploitation" of the economy as a whole. On the other hand, capitalists increasingly invest in the "human factor" (skill, education, psychological resilience, etc.). This makes production ever more dependent on "investment in the labour force" and no longer on the means of production (69, 71). Finally, consumption evolves towards collective forms, although the capitalists have some difficulty in accepting such a tendency. Actually, this type of consumption is costly and in part is not reducible to market processes. The increase of collective consumption requires an increase of leisure time and reduction of the gap between intellectual and executive labour (69–70).

Barel acutely concluded that complete development of such tendencies leads to the conclusion Marx came to in the *Grundrisse*, i.e. that the real measure of social wealth is no longer working time, but rather leisure time. This, however – Barel asserted, in utopian tones similar to those of Löbl and Richta – is incompatible with the survival of capitalism. Nevertheless, he added, even when an institution becomes useless, it does not necessarily disappear.

Mallet (1969) wrote a very successful book on the new strategies of the western trade unions. The author has a strong sense of the revolutionary role of intellectual labour in production. He distinguishes between the traditional working class, subordinate to capital, and the new working class, formed by technicians, engineers and skilled workers. The new class leads technological progress and is involved in all the crucial stages of modern production. This class is different from the traditional middle class, for it has no property to defend (15–27). It is superficial to define it with Lenin's concept of the "workers' aristocracy". It is true that the new middle class enjoys a level of welfare much higher than the traditional one, but it has nothing to do with imperialism. The high living standards of its members are due to the high productivity of the factories where they work (94–8).

The novelty of Mallet's approach and the new middle class analyses were soon picked up by Daniel *Bell* (1973: 148–54). *Bottomore* (1973) took a similar view (21–7), but erroneously attributed it to Marx, besides *Nicolaus* (1973: 51–2). Actually, in the 1970s, interpretations of the generation of the new middle class as a progressive process were submerged by the contrary current, described in the previous chapter, with the authors committed to showing up the crisis of capitalism. However, worthy of mention are two interesting works of the early 1980s, which attest to the revival of a critical attitude.

Formenti (1980) showed how Braverman and the other orthodox Marxists completely misunderstood the scientific-technical revolution of that time. According to Braverman, information technology and robotics are only an extreme application of Taylorism; they bring about a degradation of labour, through mechanisation and de-qualification. Due to these processes, Braverman said, the workers are dispossessed of their last decisional function: the regulation of automatic processes. Formenti replied that the new technologies do not destroy the workers' knowledge in the production process. On the contrary, the workers are led to develop their knowledge in order to appropriate the new technologies (18–29).

Cazzaniga (1981) maintained that in all his writings Marx wavers between an extensive and restrictive view of the productive labour concept. The former sees productive labour as not necessarily material. This view prevails in the early manuscripts of 1857–65 (which include *Grundrisse* and *Theories of Surplus Value*). The restrictive view (productive labour as material labour) prevails in the later manuscripts, which include *Capital*. Thanks to this oscillation commentators have felt free to use one of the two types of texts indifferently and to arrive at opposite conclusions. The author mentions Poulantzas as a supporter of the restrictive view and O'Connor as supporter of the extensive one. Marx's oscillation, says Cazzaniga, makes even the most careful interpretations (like that of Gough) unsatisfactory, because they aim at an unequivocal reading (235–6).

In the end, however – the author stated – Marx tended to underrate the processes of differentiation among workers and attributed more importance to the opposite tendency towards standardisation. He saw the division between manual and intellectual labour as decisive for capitalism. Moreover, Marx interpreted antagonism as the subordination of workers, while the latter – says the author optimistically – was only characteristic of one historical period. If we adopt a broader view, we can see crises as a process of liberation and increased social control over production (240–7).

Cazzaniga stressed that the presence of unproductive labour, too, can be interpreted in two ways: either as the inevitable parasitism of the middle classes or as the possibility to overcome scarcity. In actual fact, he writes, this twofold interpretation can be seen in all the theory and practice of the labour movement (248). Cazzaniga's analysis also suggested what he saw as the right way to examine the question of unproductive labour: he warned not to confine class analysis within the production process. Anatomising society is necessary, but "the analysis of society as a living body is another matter" (253).

Cerroni (1983) observed that manual labour itself becomes increasingly intellectual due to the skill acquired to govern the new technologies (304–5).

4. Human capital and indefinite growth

The major advances made by a few Marxist authors on human capital remained outside the general economic debate. However, in the same period we find other outstanding analyses of the classical type on human capital.

These analyses fully confirmed both the Enlightenment view on consumption and Say's and Ricardo's approach to human needs. The former view opposed the pre-modern hostility towards increase in wealth and the Aristotelian canon, which considered new goods unnatural and useless. The Enlightenment authors had shown just how naive that canon was, since all goods have been introduced as "new" at some moment in human evolution. Thus, they make their first appearance as luxuries, but then become useful comforts and finally necessaries (see II.7). On the other hand, Say and Ricardo, then Rae, Leroy-Beaulieu and others, lastly Hobson held that human needs are unlimited and that consequently there are no obstacles to accumulation in this respect (see, respectively, XIII.3; X.3; IX.5).

A similar approach is shown by the expert in political theory, Raymond *Aron* (1962). He explained that, unlike its occurrence in the 1930s crisis, stagnation could no longer permanently hinder accumulation due to certain new developments like scientific progress, increase in expenditures for education, increase of purchasing power and the progressive shift from the production of means of production to the production of consumer goods (217–29).

Like the Enlightenment authors, *Scitovsky* (1976) held needs to be historically determined (ch. 6: 185–6) and, like Say and Ricardo, effectively demonstrated the need to vary consumption. Scitovsky criticised the Puritan

American tradition for privileging production activities to the detriment of consumption. This attitude led to development of our production capacity, but not our consumption capacity (Chapter XI).

The author disproves the stereotypes of mainstream economists, like the correspondence between consumer's choices and real preferences, consumer's perfect rationality, the aim of maximisation and the quantitative measurement of satisfaction (Chapter I). He observes that satisfaction in consumption is given by two different factors: comfort and pleasure. But permanent comfort eliminates pleasure and leaves us unsatisfied. In order to have satisfaction, we need to receive new pleasure, from time to time, by varying our consumption (ch. 4 – See also Marina *Bianchi* 2004).

Pasinetti (1981) described the dynamics of demand composition through the law of Engel (ch. 4.5). In 1857 Ernst Engel found that the proportion of personal income spent on food diminishes with increase in income. Actually, Engel's law only came to international attention at the end of the 19th century (see *Schumpeter* 1949: 961). Pasinetti extended this law to all final consumption. When income grows steadily, the percentage of it going into basic consumption decreases, while the part going into refined consumption increases proportionally. Thus, in the long run, the determinant of consumers' choice is not prices but the level of income (ch. 4.7). There is a positive reciprocal influence between increase in refined consumption and increase in income. Pasinetti implied that human capital is the driving force of development. He confirmed this view when addressing the indefinite progress of accumulation (see XIII.3.b). The author concludes that, in the advanced economies, wealth is not given by material goods but by technical knowledge (ch. 11.16).

Recently, biologists and ethologists have confirmed all these views. *Acquaviva* (1983) showed that primary needs, although determined by our biological plan, undergo continual transformation, which in turn is determined by the evolutive transformation of the brain. This process shows that primary needs are historically determined, i.e. they are cultural (ch. 1).

Kindleberger (1990), too, started from Engel's law. However, he applied this concept not only to final consumption but also to the production factors. In backward economies, he writes, the scarce production factor that affects the value of goods most is land. In the industrial economies, this role passes on to capital, while in the mature (post-industrial) economies the main factor is human capital (p. 5). Here the author implicitly recalls the principle of the classical and Enlightenment economists: new goods usually enter the market as luxury goods, and demand for them shows marked income elasticity. However, with increasing wealth and incomes they become ordinary goods, and eventually necessary goods, and gradually they lose their income elasticity.

Thus, Kindleberger rediscovered the principle (stated in the Enlightenment) that the distinction between necessary and superfluous goods is senseless (7–9). He went on to observe that, given the low-income elasticity of traditional goods, the markets for these goods tend towards saturation.

The author saw the tendency to globalisation as part of the normal dynamics of accumulation. The first reaction to saturation is exportation of traditional goods to the poor countries. However, these countries sooner or later adopt some import substitution policies that limit this outlet. Thus, the only lasting way to avoid saturation is the production of new goods (11–13).

It is innovation that drives growth, both in the form of new sectors of production and in the form of new types of consumption (15–21). Finally, Kindleberger, like Pasinetti, stressed that the private economy is not always able to implement the desired innovation policy. Often state intervention is called for (14). Note that the solution of avoiding saturation through the production of ever new goods was first proposed by Say and Ricardo (see XIII.3). Subsequently, the concept reappeared from time to time, especially in the 1950s–60s among the heterodox Marxists (see the previous section and, later, for Rosdolsky, XIX.3.c). Finally, it was set by Scitovsky, Pasinetti and Kindleberger as the economic basis for indefinite growth.

However, this theorisation came late, when the boom due to the welfare state was already declining. In this case, too, Hegel's metaphor holds: "The owl of Minerva spreads its wings only when dusk is falling", which means that awareness arrives only when events have already occurred.

Conclusions

Our survey of the literature on unproductive labour/consumption ends here. It might seem that this long research has a happy end: the distinction between productive and unproductive labour and consumption not only regains its original flexible approach, but also – thanks to the concept of human capital – allows for a vision of economic progress and civilisation based on increasingly refined consumption. Unfortunately, this is not the case. As we will see in the next two chapters, implementation of the welfare state generated this positive scenario only partially and momentarily. In it, the tendency to innovative investments and new consumption was ultimately superseded by the opposite tendency to freeze the growing wealth in rents and privileges for the stronger social categories. Thus, new kinds of unproductive labour/consumption emerged, and an endless crisis followed.

Notes

1 Marx (*Capital I*, IV.XV.168–9; VII.XXV.46; ch. 30. *Capital III*, ch. 15).
2 Marx (*Theories*, part II, ch. 18, B.1.d: 745–6).
3 See e.g. Grossmann (1919, III.2–6); Mattick (1974: 156); Lojkine (1977: 77–8, 129).
4 Carchedi (1977: 50, 59–66, 135–9).
5 An old work of mine (Perrotta 1976) took the same approach, but – contradictorily – presented this process as proletarianisation.
6 Ossowski (1957, 5.5: 87–90; 10.5: 169).
7 Acquaviva (1958, ch. 3.h: 120–7).
8 Löbl (1967: 9, 102, 127, 141, passim).

XIX The welfare state as investment in human capital

Background

The literature on unproductive labour/consumption we have so far examined shows that economists had cherished the idea of the welfare state since the 18th century. The final goal of capitalist accumulation was precisely that. But once the welfare state was attained, few economists realised its importance. Most Marxist and neoclassical authors interpreted it as an increase of unproductive public expenditures, in support of profits (Marxists) or to the benefit of some particular classes (according to the neoclassical economists). Only the Post-Keynesians defended it, but they were not concerned with productiveness in the classical sense. They were only interested in increase in demand, whatever that was.

Yet the welfare state has constituted one of the greatest turning points in human progress. For the first time, even the lowest social classes could enjoy some constant and substantial benefit from the increase in wealth due to capitalist accumulation. This occurred after one thousand years of economic growth. The welfare state has also represented the greatest investment in human capital ever seen — a sort of new original accumulation which paved the way to the post-industrial economy.

1. "Consumption as investment" revives

As we have seen (II.7), the Enlightenment authors described increase in consumption as an investment that raises productivity. In the aftermath of World War II, the welfare state seemed to be fulfilling that old aspiration: economic development based on the increase in consumption by productive labourers.

What we call the welfare state is the huge, rapid social advance set in motion by mature economies between the second half of the 1940s to the mid-1970s. There was an unprecedented increase in consumption, comfort, life expectation, education and skills, and consequently in labour productiveness and productivity. Governments provided social security for all, unemployment benefits, public housing, healthcare, education, full employment policies, protection of workers by the unions and protection of the unions by the state, as well as social services and protection of the weak categories.

These processes brought about an upward spiral of reciprocal causation between increase in consumption, in productivity and in production. *Tridico* (2014) has shown that the countries that have skimped on their welfare policies saw their growth slowing down, whilst the countries with more generous policies saw better growth performance. Due to these policies, social inequalities were reduced, democracy was universally accepted, and collective participation grew through a great number of intermediate institutions and associations. On this point, too, the welfare state seemed to implement the approach of the Enlightenment authors, who saw economic development as closely bound up with progress in civilisation, in reciprocal causation.

However, this process was misunderstood by many economists. Not only did most Marxist and neoclassical authors interpret it as simply unproductive expenditures, but the consumerist interpretation of the welfare state also spread (see section 3).

The Marxist approach – which saw the increase in social expenditures as a remedy to overproduction and saturation – was effectively criticised by *Strachey* (1956). He quoted Sweezy who had written a long list of social interventions implementation of which – Sweezy maintained – capitalism would never admit. Nevertheless, Strachey noted, such interventions were already being implemented in Great Britain and various other countries, including the US. True, the capitalists opposed these policies, and yet they went ahead.[1] Strachey also noted that Marx was right in saying that capitalism naturally tends to the polarisation of classes and increase in inequalities, but this tendency had been contrasted by the social forces. This contrast had partly disproved Marx's forecast of growing poverty for the proletariat (95–159).

On the other hand, most neoclassical authors saw welfare expenditures as subtraction from private investment (which they considered the only productive expenditure) and thus as impoverishment of the economy (see XVI.2.b). They did not consider that, in capitalist accumulation, crises have usually been overcome thanks to increase in wages, shortening of the working day and better working conditions. These social achievements have countered the tendency to overproduction by raising demand and have driven development forward. Whenever entrepreneurs were forced to these concessions, they protested that they would be facing failure. On the contrary, they were led to reduce costs through innovations, and this raised profits again and fostered development.

2. Affluence, consumerism and anti-consumerism

a. Fear of wealth

The rapid and extended increase in wealth and comfort generated by the welfare state apparently caused more resistance than approval. In the past, too, similar booms of consumption had raised hostility – from the pauperist movements of the Middle Ages to the radical religious sects or the moralists of the 17th century and on to various 19th-century utopians. Then, too, the original spring was the need to expand capitalist production, and the reactions were, for the privileged classes, fear of losing their status, the parallel imitation effect of the lower classes, the envy of the excluded and above all the uncertainty about social and moral values generated by this fast change.

With the boom brought on by the welfare state, a number of authors became critical of the race towards ever new consumption, which they began to call consumerism, although they distinguished it from the increase in welfare. But when the boom declined and was followed by saturation (see next chapter), an enormous literature flourished critical of any increase in consumption, superficially labelled as consumerism.

b. Defence of affluence plus anti-consumerism

The Affluent Society, by John Kenneth *Galbraith* (1958), is the most insightful and influential book on this issue. In the first part, the author effectively criticises the widespread cultural resistance to acknowledging that western societies had finally moved on from poverty as normal condition of human life and arrived at the affluent society. The latter, for Galbraith, is by no means unnatural. However, in the second part of the book, he criticises economic theory and liberal culture for considering it normal to go in pursuit of ever more goods, regardless of the level of satisfaction reached, and for driving production up to the utmost limits (chs. 11 and 13). Moreover, this race for superfluous private goods runs counter to the production of necessary public goods, a situation described by the author as "private affluence and public squalor".

Vance *Packard* (1957) very successfully described the hidden mechanisms of persuasion to get consumers buying more and more. Packard (1960) can be considered the first radical criticism of the consumer obsession. The author incisively analyses the need of enterprises to keep their market growing. Packard also illustrated in various other books the individuals' race to increasing consumption and success, induced by the capitalist system.

Like Galbraith, *Gorz* (1964) criticised superfluous consumption and the poverty of public consumption services (Part I, chs. 3 to 5), whilst *Iraci* (1970) attacked anti-consumerism, Galbraith's version included (56–64, passim). Jean *Baudrillard* (1974, I.III) described the pressure driving consumers into an endless race, which systematically leaves them disappointed. He also produced one of the best analyses of the culture of waste deriving from this attitude (43–51).

Fred *Hirsch* (1976) carried on Packard's analysis just when the welfare state boom began to slow down and the spectre of saturation was appearing. Hirsch insightfully described the false promises of success thrown up by the capitalist system. The latter drives the labourer/customer to strive ceaselessly in pursuit of new goods and higher status. But, again, behind this race lies a delusion, due to two factors. One has to do with positional goods, which actually raise utility and improve the status of the consumer only if they are exclusive, like second houses, cars, etc. The other factor concerns personal services, whose quality is lower when is acquired on the market. Thus, instead of satiating the lust for consumption, consumerism intensifies it (just as Aristotle had observed, summing up the pursuit of enrichment).

Arndt (1978) associated consumerism with the crisis of the idea of progress. The positive view of progress arose along with the economic boom; then it started declining, and criticisms of consumerism increased (84ff). For a useful anthology of classical writings on consumption, see *Di Nallo* (1997).

The turn of the century saw a burgeoning of studies on consumption. Although many of them are valuable, in general they do not add much to our subject, which was aptly summed up by Galbraith as the cultural transition from the economy of scarcity to the economy of affluence. Of course, there are some exceptions; for example, *Cross* (1993) provided a particularly useful history of the culture of consumption in relation to technical progress.

c. *Anti-consumerism as rejection of affluence*

Even during the boom, a number of authors took to denouncing the mushrooming of "useless" consumption. G. *O'Brien* (1948: 72) affirmed that a society of plenty could not exist. *Baran* (1957a) separated "the useful parts" of consumption and the "superfluous parts" (188–9) but wondered who could establish the point of separation between the two. His naive answer is: "objective reason" (ch. 2.2). On this basis, he considers superfluous the consumption, by middle-class families, of gardens, latest model cars, household appliances and trendy clothes (220). Baran (1959) described consumerism as a consequence of underconsumption. Monopoly capitalism, he explains, tends to stagnation (due to lack of competition and scale economies). To avoid stagnation, superfluous consumption is increasingly needed. This explains the enormous growth of advertising, public expenditures, product differentiation and new goods, ever more extravagant, complex and costly (194).

A deep-rooted diffidence about comfort is tellingly evoked by the novelist V. Naipaul, who recounts that, in a 1971 electoral campaign in India, a candidate condemned the introduction of running water in the villages. The virtuous practice of women using wells – he said – would disappear, with who knows what immoral consequences (*la Repubblica*, April 8th, 2004).

Somogyi (1976) tried to reconcile the spectacular increase in workers' consumption with the concept of wages at the subsistence level, which he sees as a necessary component of the Marxist approach (143–5). Of course, his attempt proved impossible. *Kern* (1983) was bent on reviving Aristotle's condemnation of new goods. Consumerism, he affirmed, is degradation of custom.

The later studies condemning consumerism are even weaker. *Latouche* (1995) judged progress and welfare negatively. These, he maintains, do not make us happier or more intelligent; on the contrary, they destroy human relations. According to *Bauman* (2009), capitalism exploits men through useless increase in consumption. *Korkotsides* (2007), in turn, writes of self-exploitation by the consumers to the advantage of capitalism. *Trainer* (2011) would like to see the economy "motivated by a collective effort to work out what society needs" and to produce "only that stable quantity of goods and services that is sufficient for a satisfactory quality of life" (77–8). What all this means on the analytical level is hard to understand.

Recently, the so-called *Economy of happiness* has been in vogue, with a great many studies devoted to it. Often these studies mix up approaches of different kinds: reflections on Easterlin's paradox, Scitovsky's desire for variation, Kahneman's relational goods, the waste of natural resources, even religious diffidence towards the "materialistic" pursuit of abundance, etc. The result of such sloppy mixing up, from the economic viewpoint, is highly unsatisfactory (see also VI.3.a).

Even *Stiglitz* (2008) fails to clarify the problem of consumerism. Through the concept of consumerism, he tries to explain why the stationary state examined by Keynes did not occur in America. He also speaks of repetitive goods (on which, see XX.3), but referring to individual preferences. Finally, Stiglitz examines saturation, but sees it as a consequence of crisis, rather than one of the major causes of it.

d. Veblen's alleged anti-consumerism

Recently several authors of popular essays have pointed to Veblen as the source of anti-consumerism. This view is not convincing.

Veblen (1899) wrote that in "barbarian" societies, along with surplus and private property of land, a dominant class arises which has the predatory attitude of consuming the wealth produced by the lower classes. The latter are devoted to productive activities ("industry"), while the upper class ("leisure class") is engaged in hunting, command, military activities and sports. The main feature of the leisure class is to dedicate itself to activities not related to everyday survival. Its principal values are force and cunning, through which its members appropriate a part of the goods produced by others.

Besides these basic concepts, repeated time and again, Veblen came up with a great many subsidiary concepts, often graphically expressed. These include – to mention but a few – the "invidious" attitude towards wealth on the part of the lower classes (which today is called the imitation or Duesenberry effect); the distinction between "the base and the honourable" in human activities (19); and the division – among the lower classes – between the tasks of personal services for the masters (which are unproductive) and the tasks of independent production (which are productive: 26).

Veblen's crucial idea is that these features persist also in modern society, sometimes partially or in hidden ways. This persistence is at the basis of the opposition – which Veblen describes in later works – between the production of real wealth, governed by engineers, technicians and productive labourers, and the predatory activities of finance. Veblen's picture is based on modern anthropology and is close to *Sombart*'s (1912) analysis of the tendency of the rich to indulge in waste and luxury consumption.

These views are similar to those of Smith and his contemporaries, who condemned the unproductive waste for which the aristocrats were responsible.

This however – as for the 18th-century authors – does not make Veblen and Sombart supporters of anti-consumerism. Veblen's ideal is certainly sober consumption by the productive classes, but it does not imply hostility to increasing in consumption as such. It is true that in Veblen the theoretical difference between luxury as waste and "luxury" as increase in productive consumption is not clear-cut, but he certainly condemns the former while extolling the latter, which is associated with technical progress and the class of engineers.

A similar undetermined distinction is to be found in *Sahlins* (1972), who showed that in primitive societies behaviour indulging in luxury (for example, feasts) and the activities for survival are closely correlated, just like abundance and scarcity. Significantly, Sahlins's first chapter is entitled "The Original Affluent Society". However, both Veblen and Sahlins unduly transfer the anthropological analyses of primitive society to capitalist society.

On the other hand, the desire for superfluous consumption does not derive from the predatory attitude of the leisure class. It has characterised human nature from the very outset. We can even say that it is the driving force of human evolution, as some Enlightenment and classical economists understood it (see II.7, VII.3 and VIII.3). Thus *Baran* (1957b) was right to criticise Veblen for not placing customs in their historical context. Baran, however, wrongly maintained that Veblen condemns any consumption in excess of bare survival.

In the same years as Veblen, *Supino* (1907) examined superfluous consumption focusing on fashion. First, he reports that, for J.B. Say, fashion consumes things before they exhaust their utility. The rapid change due to this attitude impoverishes the country. Supino adds unconvincingly that rapid changes of fashion can cause disruptive crises (16–17). Both Say and Supino seem unaware that fashion, especially in the period of the capitalist take-off and in other phases of fast development, has been the driving force of accumulation.

3. The mirage of the stationary state[2]

To better understand the welfare state as a phase of capitalist accumulation, we should consider the stationary state theories. Many classical economists imagined that accumulation would come to an end once it had produced all the goods and services needed by society. Then the economy would enter into the stationary state, where productive activities only reproduce what has been consumed in the previous cycle. This prospect was clearly linked to the idea of production as being mainly material. However, several aspects of the idea of stationary state turn our thoughts to the welfare state, which seems to prelude the happy stationary state, in the optimistic vision evoked by J.S. Mill and Keynes.

a. Smith to Wicksell

Adam Smith did not theorise a stationary state. He only observed that, when accumulation is underway, capital increases and the rate of profit declines. A part of capital then goes abroad, where there is less capital supply and profits are still high.[3] Some early classical authors – like Malthus, Ricardo, Webb and James Mill – were concerned with the prospect of the stationary state due to the scarcity of natural resources.[4] Ricardo, however, also adumbrated a concept similar to that of J.S. Mill. In a letter to Malthus, Ricardo noted that, when production no longer proceeds because all needs are satisfied, it is improper to speak of stagnation.[5]

J.S. *Mill* (1848) devoted an entire chapter to the stationary state. He saw it as a sort of liberation of the best human qualities (IV.6.3). Mill did not share the ideal of

> those who think that the normal state of human beings is that of struggling to get on; that the trampling, crushing, elbowing, and treading on each other's heels, which form the existing type of social life, are the most desirable lot of human kind.
>
> (IV.6.5)

If we manage, he added, to check demographic growth and eliminate excessive social inequalities, then the stationary state will raise our civilisation to a higher level (IV.6.6). Thus, society can have well-off labourers, "no enormous fortunes", and many more people who will be "not only exempt from the coarser toils, but with sufficient leisure, both physical and mental, from mechanical details, to cultivate freely the graces of life" (IV.6.7).

Mill added that

> "a stationary condition of capital and population implies no stationary state of human improvement. There would be as much scope as ever for all kinds of mental culture, and moral and social progress; as much room for improving the Art of Living". Moreover "industrial improvements would produce their legitimate effect, that of abridging labour".
>
> (IV.6.9)

Note that the welfare state of the 1960s–70s seems like a prelude to Mill's stationary state. In that period, the vast majority of people attained relative affluence, high-level consumption and the possibility to enjoy cultural goods and services. The inequalities, although still considerable, were reduced. Competing for enrichment was no longer the mass ideal, and solidarity became a widespread value. However, the similarities stop here, because struggling and elbowing for profit did not disappear.

Patten (1896), too, stated that mankind is in "a stage of transition from a pain to a pleasure economy" (IV.2: 80). He then developed this prospect with utopian tones (Chapter IV). However, later on, Patten (1899) depicted a situation similar to that of the 1980s–90s, when the welfare state was declining and saturation prevalent. He observed that, due to the law of diminishing returns, diminishing profits would tend to slow accumulation down. Thus, the promised prosperity would be hindered and the economy driven towards a stationary state long before generating a higher civilisation (309).

Wicksell (1901), too, proposed a non-optimistic vision of the stationary state. He acutely depicts a tendency to the prevalence of rent. First, he notes that

> the unprecedented growth of population recently witnessed in Europe, and still more in certain extra-European countries, will certainly, sooner or later - probably in the course of the present century - prepare the way for much slower progress and possibly for completely stationary conditions.

Then, he adds, there will be a fall in the interest rate and capitalists will have a very small profit. "Labour and land alone (or practically alone) will share the product" (1.III: 214).

Such a situation "would be far from desirable in an individualistic society based on private property. So - adds Wicksell - far from disappearing, the gulf between the propertied and the property-less classes would be well-nigh impassable", because land rent would grow enormously. Even now "a large part of apparent annual savings is accounted for by this increase in the capital value of land and is thus not a real increase in wealth at all". Monopolies will also contribute to this increase of rent (214–15. See also *Boianovsky* 2017b).

This brilliant forecast seems to anticipate the recent analysis by Piketty. The crisis of the welfare state can actually be described as the economy over-burdened by parasitic rents.

b. Keynes

Like Mill, *Keynes* (1930) evoked a vision of the future economy full of "great expectations", as Charles Dickens might have put it. Keynes believed that the crisis of his time would drive society to a higher level of civilisation:

> We are suffering, not from the rheumatics of old age, but from the growing-pains of over-rapid changes, from the painfulness of readjustment between one economic period and another. The increase of technical efficiency has been taking place faster than we can deal with the problem of labour absorption.
>
> (p. 1)

Here we find a striking similarity with the last decades of the 20th century, i.e. the strong acceleration of technology innovations and increase in productivity, with the consequent increase in unemployment. Technological unemployment is treated by Keynes in the same way as in Ricardo. It is due, Keynes wrote, "to our discovery of means of economising the use of labour outrunning the pace at which we can find new uses for labour. But this is only a temporary phase of maladjustment". By now, in the long run, thanks to technical progress,

> "*mankind is solving its economic problem.* I would predict that the standard of life in progressive countries one hundred years hence will be between

four and eight times as high as it is to-day" (p. 3). "This means, Keynes explained, that the economic problem is not - if we look into the *future - the permanent problem of the human race*".

(p. 4)

Keynes stressed the great novelty of this prospect: the history of mankind has always been marked by a pressing struggle for subsistence, as in all the biological world. He added an insightful forecast regarding the cultural difficulty of adapting to affluent society. This transition – Keynes wrote – will not be easy. Our nature has been formed by the context of scarcity, and it will be very difficult to assume another self-identity. For example,

> "the love of money as a possession (…) will be recognised for what it is, a somewhat disgusting morbidity, one of those semicriminal, semi-pathological propensities (…)". We will then be able to discard those "social customs and economic practices, affecting the distribution of wealth and of economic rewards and penalties, which we now maintain at all costs, however distasteful and unjust they may be in themselves, because they are tremendously useful in promoting the accumulation of capital".
>
> (pp. 5–6)

The optimistic, and often utopian, perspective of Mill, Keynes and also Marx (see as follows) has been disproved by our experience. After the welfare state boom, there has been a revival of the very harsh profit-driven economy. On the other hand, history tells us that the pursuit of enrichment – rather than a pathology – is one of the primitive components of human nature, together with other contrasting tendencies. It has prevailed in the modern age and, when left unbridled, it has been devastating. But the pursuit of wealth is also the cause of our well-being. In any case, it can be checked and governed in the name of the collective interest. Keynes himself acknowledges so much, when writing:

> There are valuable human activities which require the motive of money-making and the environment of private wealth-ownership for their full fruition. Moreover, dangerous human proclivities can be canalised into comparatively harmless channels by the existence of opportunities for money-making and private wealth, which, if they cannot be satisfied in this way, may find their outlet in cruelty, the reckless pursuit of personal power and authority, and other forms of self- aggrandisement.
>
> (K. 1936, 24.I)

c. Marx and Rosdolsky

Marx, too, was convinced that, in the end, capitalist accumulation would drive us to depression of the profit rate. He had nothing to say about the stationary state because he believed that capitalism would be overthrown, after which a peaceful, non-competitive society would come about. The features of Marx's post-capitalist society are very close to those outlined by Mill, Patten and Keynes (and are equally utopian). In *Capital III*, Marx writes:

> The actual wealth of society, and the possibility of a continual expansion of its process of reproduction, do not depend upon the duration of the surplus labor, but upon its productivity and upon the more or less fertile conditions of production, under which it is performed. In fact, the realm of freedom does not commence until the point is passed where labor under the compulsion of necessity and of external utility is required. In the very nature of things it lies beyond the sphere of material production in the strict meaning of the term.
>
> (VII.XLVIII.13)

Probably these observations derived from a fascinating page of the *Grundrisse* (notebook VII: 704–6) where Marx, although not contradicting his analysis of productive labour, viewed the increase in productivity from a different angle. The development of large industry, he says, makes the creation of wealth "depend less on labour time and on the amount of labour employed than on the power of agencies set in motion". The power of the latter, in turn "depends rather on the general state of science and on the progress of technology" than on the labour time spent in their production. There is a "monstrous disproportion between the labour time applied, and its product".

Marx continues: the worker (i.e. the material worker) "steps on the side of the production process instead of being its chief actor". The keystone of production is now the "social individual". Large-scale industry makes the traditional "*theft of alien labour time*" a miserable foundation. Labour in the direct form "has ceased to be the great well-spring of wealth" and measure of it (705).

Moreover, in these early notes Marx saw increase in needs as the driving force of progress and civilisation (see also *Berry* 1994: 188–95). Finally, Marx even foreshadowed that the industrial economy would be superseded. He says that, when necessary, labour time is reduced to a minimum, "in the time set free" there is a "free development of individualities", engaged in artistic or scientific activities. Capital "posits the superfluous in growing measure as a condition – question of life or death – for the necessary". On the other hand, machines "are *organs of human brain, created by the human hand*; the power of knowledge objectified" (706). For another important page of the *Grundrisse* similar in tone, see XI.7.e.

In commenting these observations, *Rosdolsky* (1968) – who was writing in the middle of the welfare state boom – argued that Marx's dreams

> ... entered the realm of what is immediately possible. Today, for the first time in history, thanks to the development of modern technology, the preconditions for a final and complete abolition of the 'theft of alien labour-time' actually exist.
>
> (ch. 28.2: 427–8)

He added that, unlike conditions in the past, today's increase in productivity is so high that it can liberate man from the torture of the assembly line and monotonous work. Like Richta and Mallet (see XVIII.3), Rosdolsky detected the enormous social potentiality of technical progress of his time.

Conclusions

The views on the conclusion of the accumulation process suggest that something decisive went missing in the experience of the welfare state. Why was transition to the stationary state not accomplished? What lay behind the welfare state crisis?

Instead of trying to answer these questions, in the late 1970s–early1980s, when the welfare state was declining and the neo-liberal reaction was underway, Marxist and heterodox authors were writing on the transition to socialism. A vast literature on this issue appeared, while even the nature of the welfare state remained unknown. This is an exemplary case of intellectual alienation.

The stationary state theories assumed that the bulk of produced wealth was material and destined for individual consumption. Both conditions were implied in the idea that accumulation would lead to complete satisfaction of needs. As a matter of fact, wealth was increasingly becoming immaterial – although often with material support – and collective goods tended to become the major component of consumption. Immaterial wealth puts no limits to human needs on both the demand side and supply side. But the actual experience of the welfare state did not reflect this tendency.

Notes

1 Strachey (1956, ch. 13: 252–62).
2 Some materials in this section had already been used in my essay "The Stationary State: Deadlocks and New perspectives", in G. Bitros and N. Kyriazis, eds., *Essays in Contemporary Economics. A Festschrift in Memory of A.D. Karayiannis*, Springer, 2015. However, the present text has been much enlarged and completely rewritten and rethought.
3 Smith (1776, I.9.10–11).
4 See Schumpeter (1949, III.5.6); Deane (1978: 36–42).
5 Ricardo [1951–1973, vol. IX, letter 444: 25].

XX Saturation

The growth of unproductive labour[1]

Background

Why didn't the welfare state pave the way to the stationary state? After the boom of the 1950s–mid 1970s, the western economies entered into depression, disguised on the surface by the business cycles. The decline occurred because the welfare state had reached a level of both productivity and consumption such that it called for a sharp turn in investments and market organisation. Accumulation should have been channelled towards higher immaterial production and consumption and towards collective consumption. This did not happen, and the welfare state ground down to halt midway; it was never completed.

Stagnation developed in the mature economies, and this was the first phase of the depression. But the great boom of the welfare state could not stop without giving way to degeneration of capitalist accumulation. This became the second phase of the depression, with an endless structural crisis that has nothing to do with the business cycle.

1. Why saturation arrived

As we have seen, the accumulation process needs a continual variation of products, to avoid saturation. So much had been observed by J.B. Say and Ricardo (see XIII.3) and later by the authors mentioned in Chapters XVIII.3–4 and XIX.4. The welfare state dawned as a huge upsurge in the production of material goods, public services and education. However, once the living standard of all the population, including the lower classes, was significantly raised, the domestic market was relatively saturated. It could no longer find other classes to involve in the spiralling of consumption.

Hence the welfare policies needed to vary investments by opening or enlarging other sectors of production. Some of these sectors were traditional but needed to be improved or extended. Such was the case of infrastructures, culture, education, research, healthcare and public administration. Others were relatively new, like information technologies, robotics, biotechnologies, healthcare technologies, personal services, protection and socialisation of the weak categories, renewable energies and activities to reduce environmental pollution (on the latter, see e.g. *Gallegati* 2106), etc.

In sum, it was time for post-industrial economy to take off, but western society, in its entirety, was utterly unprepared for it. The post-war boom still had the basic characteristics of an industrial boom. Economic theory, as we have seen, still concentrated on industrial categories. Entrepreneurs were afraid to allow further increase in wages and social benefits, which were already checking the growth of profit. Workers and their representatives conceived industry as the stronghold of their bargaining power. Even the new categories – like technicians, university students, intellectuals – saw society only as industrial society.

Thus, change in investments was neither implemented nor even encouraged. Only research for certain new technologies was actually promoted. This was due above all to the military research programmes, whose advances – IT included – went later to the advantage of private firms (see *Mazzucato* 2013). Other fields remained underdeveloped and most of the production still showed preference for the usual sectors of material goods for private consumption. To keep their markets open, the traditional goods were infinitely varied, but this did not put an end to the decline of their marginal utility.

The western economies started producing repetitive goods and services with ever-decreasing utility. The families, failing to find new products for the satisfaction of new needs, were forced to enter into this irrational race for useless goods, replaced as soon as possible by other useless variations. This is the process described by many of the authors mentioned in the previous chapter (suffice it here to recall *Packard* 1957; *Galbraith* 1958; *Hirsch* 1976).

Note that most of the new needs were (and are) still very far from being met; that is, a potential demand did exist. Suffice it to consider such needs as efficient public transport, green spaces, a non-polluted environment, urban and rural rehabilitation, efficient administrative services, restoration of monuments, but also a stepping up on education, basic research, alternative energy sources, etc. Moreover, in the first phase of welfare state decline, households still had the purchasing power to buy new goods and services, either directly or indirectly (through the payment of taxes or tickets). It was certainly not like the 1930s, when demand was insufficient because of low wages. This time, demand existed; what was lacking were the new goods.

2. Opposition to the welfare state and degeneration

On top of the general attitude, still basically fixed on the industrial world, various other factors were standing in the way of change. First, change was costly, especially for private enterprises. Conversion entails great financial strain. Moreover, new investments often take a long time to yield profit or are too big for private producers. Finally, although these investments contribute greatly to society's welfare and productivity, they do not always yield enough profit for the private concerns. Thus, new investment should have been supported with strong state incentives.

On the other hand, when full employment was close to being achieved and the bargaining power of the working class grew, the entrepreneurs reacted in a retaliatory way (see *Pollin* 2012, ch. 2). They took advantage of certain abuses perpetrated in the sphere of public assistance (which also disappointed many intellectuals) and accused the welfare state of subtracting wealth from private investments to channel it towards unproductive uses. They obtained freedom to export capital abroad for investment or financial speculation. Eventually the entrepreneurs succeeded in worsening working conditions and so weakening the workers' bargaining power. In the 1980s, the clash ended with the total victory of the entrepreneurs. This belied the confidence shown by *Strachey* (1956) in the smooth reduction of profit power (208–22) and also the illusions of J.S. Mill and Keynes about the stationary state.

Only the stronger categories were able to resist this attack. But this means that, since then, the benefits of the welfare state have gone mainly to the middle classes and even more to the public employees, rather than to the lower classes, and especially the less organised. This was a distortion that caused a structural unbalance in the economy. Social inequalities started growing again, not only between the upper classes and the rest of society but also among labourers. Some categories acquired growing privileges – with the connivance of the unions and the political forces – through social security, small-scale financial or real estate speculation, easy tax evasion and the lack of actual control over their productivity, especially in the public sector.

An increasing part of the surplus, in the hands of the privileged or protected categories, became rent, subtracted from productive investment. In parallel with overprotection of the stronger social groups, new non-protected groups emerged. This opened the second phase of depression, which is still ongoing.

The logic that had hitherto governed accumulation was subverted. In the capitalist system, the continual increase of wealth had gradually reduced social inequalities, due the need to boost demand and sell the growing product. This process saw the supremacy of capitalism over the other economic systems, governed by huge inequalities, privileges and rents. But the crisis of the welfare state was generating a contrary trend in the very core of capitalism, towards increasing social inequalities.

Today, inequalities in the mature economies hinder accumulation on both sides: they encourage hoarding and unproductive consumption on the part of the well-off and prevent the lower classes from exercising sufficient effective demand (see also *Solow* 2008: 92–3). Consequently, productive investments diminish, unemployment grows, and general working conditions deteriorate due to the mechanism aptly described by Marx with the concept of the industrial reserve army. The spread of unemployment and low wages dramatically depresses demand, even for the repetitive goods. The initial stagnation has now turned into uncontrollable crisis.

On the inequality between the rich and the rest of society, *Keynes* (1936) observed: "For my own part, I believe that there is social and psychological justification for significant inequalities of incomes and wealth, but not for such large disparities as exist today" (ch. 24.I). Probably the present inequalities are much worse than those witnessed by Keynes.

The other type of inequality, between the protected categories and the lower class, was analysed by *Kerr* (1969), who wrote of the "inner society" and the marginal society (82ff). This dualism tends to become ever deeper. Inequalities among labourers tend to worsen at all levels: income, property, education, culture, working conditions, wages, human rights, unions' and political protection.

Thus, the old market organisation, functional to the absolute prevalence of profit, is hindering development. Despite the huge shift of knowledge and creative power from external capital (controlled by entrepreneurs) to human capital (i.e. workers), the great enterprises have seen their power of exploitation enhanced thanks to the increase in unemployment.

3. The processes which create unemployment

a. Globalisation

The saturation of the domestic market led capitalists to seek various ways to employ their wealth. One of these was investment abroad. The globalisation policies, decided upon by the western countries in the 1970s, consisted in liberalising international trade, in the hope of extending the traditional advantage of the developed economies in the world market (thanks also to the price policies imposed by western governments).

Contrary to expectations, however, globalisation turned out to be a great incentive for the development of the Asian emerging countries, while proving disastrous for the developed economies due to the huge gaps in wages. Not only were the western markets flooded with the much cheaper goods of the emerging economies, but many western enterprises were, totally or partially, relocated in the emerging countries in pursuit of low wages (see e.g. *Reinert* 2004; *Chang* 2008). Both processes generated unemployment in the western countries.

As early as the 18th century, Daniel *Defoe* (1728) had come up with the right response to the problem of competition between advanced and backward economies. We cannot compete – he wrote – with China and India, because their production costs take advantage of the wretched conditions of their workers. England can only compete thanks to the high quality of her products (36–68). Today, however, Defoe's solution holds only in part. First, the transfer of western manufactures to the emerging countries is too rapid and too extensive. Second, today the emerging countries are able to compete even in the new technologies, based on intellectual productivity. They are rapidly extending education and research as key factors for development. In some fields they are even ahead.

On the other hand, the western economies are oppressed by rents and unproductive capital in search of productive employment. In the very long run, a new trade balance should appear (Chinese wages are already increasing fast), but meanwhile in the western countries manufacture will be dismantled, high unemployment will become permanent and poverty will spread further.

b. New technologies

On the eve of the information technology boom, *Giarini and Loubergé* (1978: ch. 4) wrote, rather imprudently, that there was a slowing down of innovations. In present times, against all evidence, the same view has reappeared in Robert *Gordon* (2012), whose theses have been reproposed in his *The Rise and Fall of American Growth*, 2016. Actually, the current statistics show that technical progress is advancing rapidly while the increase in productivity appears sluggish.

Schwab (2016) explains this effect, observing that statistics do not take into account the increase in productivity which has no market value. This is the case of most of the digital innovations (31–5). This should hold not only for information technology, but also for robotics, nanotechnologies, biotechnologies, 3D printers, etc.

Actually, the new technologies owe their existence to the massive investments in human capital of the welfare policies. The consequent increase in productivity opened the way from the industrial economy to the so-called post-industrial economy. The latter is mainly based on immaterial production and consumption, with education and research as its driving forces. The prevalence of mental over physical labour is radically changing the production processes (see also *De Masi* 1999, ch. 14; *Gualerzi* 2010).

Production can no longer be classified as either capital-intensive or labour-intensive. Today's labour-intensive production does not mean – as was the case in the industrial economy – elementary or backward production, with low productivity. On the contrary, the more productive manufactures now have a higher percentage of human labour. Production is no longer polarised between material capital and human labour. Labour conditions and labour time are becoming much more flexible, differentiated, mobile, entrusted to the worker's responsibility and are often much more creative. Besides, the dividing line between labour time and leisure time is becoming blurred.

We must keep in mind that, with the present technologies, a developed society is able to produce all it usually needs with less than a quarter of its workers. It seems we are approaching the paradoxical situation imagined by Tugan-Baranowsky (see XV.2): in the end, thanks to mechanisation, one worker alone will be able to produce everything society needs. *Rifkin* (2000) maintained that goods, despite the physical skeleton they retain, are being transformed into a stream of services ever changing and improving (V: 117ff). Intelligent machines will replace workers. He foresaw that by the mid-21st century only 5% of the adult population will be employed in the traditional fields of labour (I: 13).

Again *Schwab* (2016) maintains that the "fourth industrial revolution" (i.e. strong empowerment of the digital economy, robotics, etc.) will work in a radically new social context. First of all, since many societies in the world are rapidly ageing, there will be a growing percentage of working elders, thanks to "the ability to work smarter rather than harder" (30–1). Schwab believes that the unemployment due to technical progress will sooner or later be eliminated thanks to the emergence of new occupations. The new technologies, he says, will need people learning how to manage them and other people teaching them. Moreover, competition in immaterial production is less pressing than in traditional industry. However, he admits that the coming technological revolution will make new employment hard to achieve (31–40).

Many experts are by now admitting that the traditional balancing out, in the long run, between lost occupations and new occupations is no longer functioning, because progress is too rapid to be met with the creation of new jobs. Consequently, the growth of human capital, instead of making labour more autonomous and free as had been expected, has made it more precarious and subject to exploitation. In principle, human capital means that capital is increasingly embodied into labour (see also *Hodgson* 1999: 238). In reality, however, the crisis of the welfare state has revived the old oppression of labour by both rents and capital (see e.g. *Kern and Schumann* 1984). Thus, we are in the middle of the problem, foreseen by Keynes, of culturally adapting ourselves to a stationary state (see also *De Masi* 1999: 260). For a policy to address this issue, see XXI.2.b.

4. Growth of unproductive capital/unproductive labour

a. Repetitive goods

Not only production but also consumption have been distorted by the crisis of the welfare state. *Scitovsky* (1976) helps us to better understand the nature of repetitive goods. Not always, he observes, does a mere increase in consumption – indicated by the GDP – mean an increase in satisfaction or utility. This holds not only for elementary goods, but even for refined consumption (ch. 4).

However, the actual growth of repetitive goods is best described by Vance *Packard* (1960. See especially Parts I and II). Repetitive goods – which do not increase our utility – are the consequence of saturation. When supply constantly exceeds demand, entrepreneurs push the consumer to keep buying their products, although he/she does not need them, through advertising, rapid change in fashion, fake improvements, use of less durable materials, etc. Often the increase in productivity has made these products so cheap that it is easier to buy new ones than apply the due upkeep. Of course, the dividing line between repetitive and new, genuinely improved items is not clear-cut.

This spurs the critics of consumerism on the blanket condemnation of any increase in consumption.

The production of repetitive goods exacerbates competition, making it destructive and a large part of social labour unproductive. A parallel malfunction is to be seen in the enterprises with negative balance sheets, subsidised by the state to grant employment to labourers. In both cases we can speak of "new disguised unemployment", in the sense of an excess of labourers in that sector of production. Here, however, the concept of disguised unemployment is different from that used in development economics (see XIV.3). There, the excess of labourers was in relation to the quantity of product, while here it is in relation to the quantity needed of a certain good.

This raises a problem for the concept of repetitive goods: who will decide within what quantity a certain good is useful and when it becomes useless? The obvious answer should be: the market. But repetitive goods are precisely the goods which are on the market despite being useless, or better, despite being less useful than other goods. In turn, these other goods are precisely those mentioned before (section 1), either new immaterial goods and services or public goods. They have a potential demand but cannot be found on the market due to the inadequate organisation of the latter. The presence of repetitive goods implies that often the market does not offer consumers a real alternative (and so-called consumer sovereignty does not hold). In this case, the consumers cannot express a choice on the basis of their real preferences and are forced to persist in buying goods of ever diminishing marginal utility.

As we saw in section 2, enterprises insist on producing repetitive goods because they either cannot afford conversion or have reached an oligopoly position, or otherwise have grown accustomed to public assistance. However, far from relieving unemployment, as might seem the case, this aggravates it, at least in the long run. The market of repetitive goods is by definition rigid and tends to depress the profit rate. It does not encourage investments in new fields and, moreover, does not enhance consumer productivity through improvements in their consumption.

b. Financial speculation

In the last few decades, the difficulty of finding profitable employment for capital has led many operators to turn to financial speculation (see also *Steindl* 1990). Finance, when it grows beyond the needs of the market, tends to render capital unproductive and becomes a source of corruption. So much has been demonstrated in a great number of studies published at the turn of both the 19th/20th and the 20th/21st centuries (on the former, see XIII.2).

In present times, financial speculation has been so widespread as to provoke serious degeneration of the financial system and business ethics. Even now, many holdings and banks are still fooling small savers into acquiring trash bonds or encouraging public administrators to acquire tricky "futures", which burden future administrations with massive interest. In a word, they cheat their own customers. This unprofessional behaviour has been extended to economic activities in general. Many enterprises have found it normal to counterfeit budgets, to bet on hazardous bonds, to grant managers fantastic remunerations even when they ruin their enterprise or to sack or exploit their employees for mere speculative reasons.

The economists of the 17th–18th centuries repeated time and again that, without honest behaviour on the part of economic agents, trust is eventually destroyed and the very basis of the economy is undermined. This is precisely what is happening today. Corruption, the criminal economy, tax evasion and unproductive hoarding, over-exploitation and real estate speculation are increasingly spreading. Savers no longer trust the banks or insurance companies; consequently, saving for investment is lacking in the developed countries. Such are the origins of the 2007 crisis (see also *Gallino* 2011).

While, in the past, financial capital gained from the growth of production, it now often gains from the crises of the weak economies and weak enterprises. It has shifted from investment – which receives a share from profit – to rent, which increases due to the failure of investments. Even the production enterprises show a tendency to transform the core activity into financial strategy (see e.g. *Salento and Masino* 2013). For a survey of the literature on the last financial crisis, see *Moro and Beker* (2016, ch. 8).

Note that this pathological growth of finance is not the cause of the crises, but the effect. It derives from the increasing difficulty of using wealth for productive investments. In turn, financial speculation has been the main element driving social inequalities to a scandalous level (see e.g. *Stiglitz* 2013; *Williams* 2017).

In conclusion, *Stiglitz* (2003) showed the devastating convergence of many unfounded postulates, which seem to have been invented by the richest Americans to dominate the economy to their own advantage. These postulates – proclaimed in the name of freedom – are: deregulation, no state intervention, globalisation, and productiveness of finance in principle, regardless of its proportion to real production.

We may note that all of these assumptions are belied, not only by the present experience (as Stiglitz has effectively demonstrated) but also by the whole history of economics. The experience from the past shows that: the market is an institution, not a spontaneous product of nature, and thus requires rules and regulation; structural crises have usually been overcome through state intervention; free trade often damages weak economies; speculation, if left uncontrolled, tends to transform investments into rents and productive labour into unproductive labour.

Conclusions

The extended unproductive employment of capital and labour in the present phase of accumulation shows that our problem is not – as anti-consumerists hold – that we consume too much but, on the contrary, that we consume too little. More precisely, we consume too many repetitive goods and too few immaterial and collective goods. A key element in depression has been the confusion between productive and unproductive investments, and between productive and unproductive labour.

Another type of confusion that has contributed to depression is between production of profit and production of wealth. There has always been a certain production of wealth without profit. All independent producers, public services, cooperatives and various associations belong to this type of production. The classical economists have always considered this type of production marginal, but it is certainly no longer so. The confusion between profit and wealth stands in the way of recognising saturation and encourages parasitism. Saturation is the future of a significant part of the production based on profit, and social productivity growth will increasingly rely on the production of non-profit activities.

Note

1 Some materials in this chapter had already been used in my essay "The Stationary State: Deadlocks and New perspectives", in G. Bitros and N. Kyriazis, eds., *Essays in Contemporary Economics. A Festschrift in Memory of A.D. Karayiannis*, Springer, 2015. The present chapter has been completely rewritten and rethought.

XXI The future of productive labour

1. Recapitulation

To foster the growth of national wealth, Petty and the other mercantilists tried to find out which production sectors or occupations were more productive of social wealth and which less. They also wanted to show that some occupations suffer an excessive number of labourers and declared the supernumeraries unproductive. The less productive or excessive labourers had to be discouraged, in order to check unproductive consumption, which is a social waste. These authors also implied that the most productive activities were also the most useful.

In the 18th century, economists went deeper into the subject and two tendencies arose. One, headed by Quesnay and Smith, examined the problem with new analytical categories (surplus, capital, investment, labour as measure of wealth). This approach made the productive/unproductive labour distinction more rigorous but also more rigid. Occupations were defined productive or unproductive as such, with no possibility of change. Moreover, usefulness was distinguished from productiveness.

Smith and his followers used this tool forcibly against the huge waste for which the aristocracy were responsible and to ease the conversion of parasitic rent into capital and investment. In support of this conversion, Smith declared that only investment in material production is productive, leaving aside cultural and administrative activities. Over time, this position weakened Smith's approach.

Another current retained the flexible definitions of the origin, but also their generic nature. Given the absence of the new categories, this approach proved unsatisfactory, and so rapidly died out. However, before its extinction, it generated the most insightful perspective on our issue (best expressed by Genovesi), taking in the evolutionary change of productiveness along with development and the progress of civilisation. In this approach, for example, immaterial labour, and especially intellectual and artistic activities, become productive as the production of wealth grows and social needs are increasingly refined.

The first industrial revolution depreciated both approaches. As to Smith, many of his followers rejected the non-realistic idea that intellectual occupations are unproductive. These authors perceived that mechanisation, while rendering mass labour more elementary, also required that other labourers – especially in the immaterial sphere – acquired higher skills. On the other hand, the evolutionary perspective, too, appeared to have been disproved by then. Mechanisation seemed to confute the idea that increase in productivity relies on workers' skill rather than elementary mass labour. Elementary labour required little consumption by workers. Thus, the classical school assumed that wages remain at the subsistence level.

The tendency to overproduction, fostered by the factory economy, generated the first periodical crises. Sismondi, Malthus, Rodbertus, Gide, Rosa Luxemburg, etc. explained crises by observing that productive consumption was unable to absorb the increasing surplus. They thought that productive consumption could not grow structurally (underconsumption view). Say, Ricardo and many others opposed this approach, noting that investment always generates purchasing power able to absorb the surplus (Say's law). However, they failed to realise that their view was at odds with other classical postulates: wages at the subsistence level, luxury goods as *per se* unproductive, productiveness limited to material labour.

The latter assumptions eroded the credibility of classical political economy. In the long run, wages started to grow, although very slowly, and skilled labour spread so much that new middle classes arose and prospered. Many authors acknowledged the growth of social wealth due to technical progress and the increase in consumption by the productive labourers. The concepts of immaterial wealth, investment in education and skill as social capital opened the way to the prospect of development based on human capital.

Marx's attempt to revive the classical approach to productive labour was a failure. Marx was perfectly aware that intellectual labour was the driving force of capitalist development and that new middle classes were growing along with development. However, he confined his attention to the situation of the early 19th century. He also accepted J.S. Mill's explanation of periodical crises as due to the business cycle. However, to this he added the theory of the end of capitalism, based on the falling rate of profit, although many authors, including Sweezy, deemed it non-demonstrable.

The tendency of the profit rate to slow down led some authors to a theory of overproduction (Marx, Hobson) and others to a theory of depression (Wicksell, Kautsky). Loria and, later on, Sweezy elaborated the concept of unproductive capital, which implies the increasing destination of the surplus to unproductive investment and labour. However, the idea that accumulation is based on the increasing unproductive employment of the surplus is untenable.

In the 20th century, all crises were reduced to the business cycle. Keynes apart, no one considered the possibility of structural crises, calling for intervention from outside to restart accumulation. This prevented economists from understanding the nature of the 1930s crisis (and indeed of the crisis that later followed the welfare state boom). Keynes was the only one who treated the crisis as structural, and his followers could thus assert the reasonableness of the welfare policies. But Keynes and the Post-Keynesians did not distinguish between productive and unproductive consumption.

This hampered – and still hampers – their efforts to analyse the welfare state crisis. The latter is not due to scarce demand as in the 1930s, as they believe (see e.g. *Krugman* 2012), but to saturation.

The concept of investment in human capital – which 19th-century authors had long been working on – was finally theorised, but also confined to the individual dimension, by Schultz, G. Becker and others. Only a few authors (including Löbl, Richta, Mallet, Scitovsky, Pasinetti and Kindleberger) elaborated a theory of development based on the unlimited growth of both intellectual labour and immaterial consumption.

On the other hand, most Marxist authors restated the alleged unproductiveness of intellectual labour, services and public expenditures (on the latter, most neoclassical authors also agreed), and so they totally failed to grasp the novelty of the welfare state. Actually, the welfare state – based mainly on state expenditures – was the greatest investment in human capital ever seen. It fostered not only assistance to the lower classes and full employment policies but also the enormous increase in productivity. It was a sort of new original accumulation, i.e. the prelude to the advent of the post-industrial economy and immaterial accumulation.

However, to keep accumulation going, a radical turn was needed towards immaterial and intellectual production and consumption, collective goods, education and research. This turn was successfully boycotted by private capital, anxious as it was to regain the profit levels that the welfare policies had eroded. The revival of profit supremacy also led the middle classes and the stronger categories of the working class to protect the benefits they had gained during the boom.

Consequently, the markets progressively narrowed, and a great part of wealth was unproductively employed in repetitive goods and speculation or invested abroad. *Paradoxically, the revival of the uncontrolled supremacy of profit led to the prevalence of rent, parasitism and an unprecedented flood of unproductive labour.*

2. Reviving productive labour

a. How to finance the new development

In order to restart steady development, we should revive – duly modified – the factors on which the welfare state was organised (see also *Pollin* 2012, ch. 6). This requires great public expenditures for both productive investments and the protection of non-profit production. However, this seems an impossible policy because the western states appear to be poor, their budgets fraught with perpetual difficulties. Moreover, we are by now under the control of world financial speculation, which is ready to strangle national economies – attacking their public bonds – as soon as their economic performance appears uncertain. Of course, the same vested interests that so successfully undermined continuation of the welfare state now claim that there is no money for assistance to the weakest classes or for investments and reforms.

So, where can the money needed for such investments be taken? Let me stress again that, despite the devastating crises of the last few decades, western societies are still enormously rich thanks to the wealth accumulated in the past and the present very high productivity. It is simply not true that there is not enough wealth. The present mechanism channels a great part of the wealth produced into the private hands of the rich or overprotected categories and transforms it into unproductive rent (see XX.1–2).

This happens in many ways. First of all, many taxes have actually become regressive again. Take the case of the enterprises in the field of information technology, social networks, online sale, financial speculation and in general the great multinational enterprises. The higher their profits, the less they pay. Second, widespread tax evasion, illegal employment, exemptions and public support aggravate the public debt to the benefit of the already rich. The state has to reappropriate at least a good part of this wealth.

b. Reinstating civilised labour conditions

The civil conditions of labour that the trade unions conquered with a two-century-long struggle must be reinstated and applied to all labourers (without the abuses that have often transformed protection into privileges). At the same time, the risk that protection of the organised workers might encourage illegal or precarious labour of non-protected workers (young people, weak categories, immigrants, etc.) must be avoided. A sort of *social income* for the unemployed should be implemented, provided that they are ready to accept the work offered, including useful labour for the community. Social income can also support immaterial labour of different kinds, less linked to labour time and more concerned with productivity.

Social income should also rebalance bargaining conditions in favour of labour, as well as supporting competitive capital (start-up enterprises, etc.) against exploitative capital. *We should substantially reduce daily working time* and raise the minimum wages by law. The major effects will be a certain redistribution of working time among the labourers and increase in demand for final consumption.

The objection that shortening working time, raising wages and improving working conditions would leave the western economies even more vulnerable to the competition of the emerging countries is not convincing. Defoe's warning should be remembered (see XX.3.a): if we chase after the emerging countries and worsen conditions for our labourers, we will be destroyed, because we will never compete at this level. We can once again be competitive thanks only to the general quality and intellectual level of our products.

c. Non-profit labour

A new development policy should acknowledge that not all the agents of the mature economies are prepared to face permanent risk and frantic competition to make their fortune. Mill and Keynes had perceived this, albeit with some exaggeration (see XIX.3.a-b). Besides profit production, we should help other types of productive labour to grow. Again, in the capitalist economy not all wealth is produced through profit. There are independent producers, cooperative labour, public production and those who contribute from outside to what Marx called the collective labourer. This component of productive labour rapidly increases in the post-industrial economy.

We are now moving towards an economy in which direct remuneration of labour is not always necessary thanks to extended social remuneration. This tendency goes even beyond predetermined social income. Immaterial skilled labour is increasingly detached from the traditional features of working time. Its real remuneration derives from complex social relations that give rise to various forms of social productivity.

The post-industrial economy has seen a proliferation of types of productive occupations. Along with them, needs have also increased, especially in the fields of new technologies, research and education, healthcare, personal services, environmental antipollution, training in the use of new technologies, civic education, etc. Non-profit labour can meet these particular needs, niche needs or specific variations of them.

d. State investments for productive labour

Investments to meet new needs call for state intervention. The first aim of public intervention must be to shift the present unproductive labour (employed in the production of repetitive goods, in rents and financial speculation) towards the new fields of investment mentioned before which satisfy new needs.

In the history of capitalist accumulation, state intervention has often been responsible for the take-off of modern economy, as in 16th–17th-century England (under the Tudors); 19th-century Germany, from the *Zollverein*, backed by List, up to Bismarck's social policy; a bit later in Japan; in Italy's original industrialisation at the beginning of the 20th century, under Giolitti; of course, under the welfare state (see *Moe* 2007); and, nowadays, in information and other technologies (see *Mazzucato* 2013). Advocates of the state-free economy ignore the lessons of history.

These public investments (on which, see XX.1) can be financed with long-term bonds or taxes tied to particular projects. Private capital can be added to the initial investments. These investments can directly create employment for millions of workers, but their principal function should be to stimulate private investments.

3. A new Marshall Plan

The level of productiveness of a certain occupation depends on the market we refer to and, in particular, on the needs this market shows. What can appear productive in a western market may be of scant productiveness in the context of a backward economy. We feel that curing serious diseases or teaching the illiterate is more productive than activities to lose weight. From this stems an idea of a new Marshall Plan.

The welfare state was initially made possible by the US implementation of the Marshall Plan for the reconstruction of Western Europe, as well as analogous plans for Japan and other areas. These plans required collaboration, in terms of financial effort, on the part of the countries benefited, but undoubtedly the main burden was borne by the US. A point worth stressing is that – whatever the initial motivations – these plans yielded extremely positive results for the economies on both sides (giver and receivers).

The US absorbed much of the domestic unemployment resulting from the end of the war, while the European countries were virtually reborn. In the medium and long run, these investments intensified commerce between America and Europe, supporting the longest boom in the economy of our times. These plans created productive employment for millions of workers and with it a great surge in demand.

The point in recalling this great experience is that it applies perfectly to the present situation of Europe (as donor) and Africa or other developing areas as receivers. In Europe, there are now dozens of millions of unemployed, most of them young and highly educated. On the other hand, Africa needs nearly everything for its take-off, from physical infrastructures to IT networks, from schools and hospitals to juridical and administrative systems and operators, etc.

Probably the main shortcoming of the stationary state authors was to assume that the age of plenty and peace would be realised in the mature economies independently of the rest of the world. However, a large proportion of humanity is still trapped in the vicious circle of poverty. The present immigration towards the western economies – undertaken in the most dramatic and inhuman circumstances – confirms this situation.

On the other hand, today the millions of unemployed in the rich countries are, in one way or in another, being maintained by society unproductively. If these countries make a vigorous effort to employ their unemployed – either at home or abroad – in starting development in the poor countries, the benefits will be enormous for both parties. This new Marshall Plan can increase demand and revive investments in the western economies, developing the backward economies and international trade, while slowing migration pressure down and making it manageable.

This is a typical long-run investment, but in this case the positive results will not take very long. Actually, there is a big difference between the original Marshall Plan and the one proposed here. The former benefited Europe, which had for centuries accumulated not only material wealth, but also vast human capital, consisting in skills, culture, laws, administrative rules, customs and habits. This is why the recovery of Europe was so rapid.

By contrast, the poor countries have never seen real development and have suffered exploitation for centuries. They need to accumulate human capital starting practically from scratch. This means that several decades of aid will be needed. Moreover, the consequences of backwardness in human capital and the devastation wreaked by neocolonialism are to be seen in the all too widespread corruption, tribal wars and instability. Therefore, the money employed in the development projects must be controlled by the donors, in agreement with the receivers.

Finally, the objection that the poor countries should employ their own people for development is no obstacle. These countries need skilled foreign workers in any case to teach people how to implement the various activities, material or immaterial, and how to organise the production and management of all infrastructures. Once again, the core of this collaboration lies in the human capital of both parties. The unemployed (or unproductively employed) human capital of the western countries can be employed in productive labour for the growth of the developing countries' human capital.

4. General conclusions

The dynamic relations between increase in consumption and increase in productivity lie at the very core of the theory of unproductive labour. The economists of the Enlightenment were the first to find a positive connection between these two factors of growth, but – apart from Smith – a clear analysis of accumulation remained lacking. The classical economists formulated both aspects of the issue in appropriate terms: the influence of workers' consumption on accumulation (which entails the problem of crises) and the growth of immaterial wealth (which implies the growth of human capital and the consequent increase in productivity). However, the classical authors failed to complete both analyses due to their postulates of wages close to the subsistence level and wealth as consisting mainly of material goods.

The neoclassical authors did away with these cramping preconceptions, and indeed the classical concept of value (linked to them), with its infinite and unresolvable analytical problems. However, they discarded the concept of unproductive labour and took income as the only measure of productiveness. Since no labour is made without reward, the concept of unproductive labour as well as the concept of social wealth disappear.

On the other hand, the new approach cleared the way to outline a new dynamic interpretation of the link between increase in consumption and increase in productivity, culminating in the concept of investment in human capital. Applied at the social level, investment in human capital may be seen as the real solution to the problems of crises and indefinite growth – in a word, to the problem of accumulation. However, the neoclassical authors applied the new category only at the individual level, depriving it of its great potentialities. Moreover, the individualistic formulation of their general approach led them to disregard the entire complex of problems related to accumulation.

In neoclassical hands, crises lost their classical sense of structural difficulty in balancing demand and supply, which cannot be solved spontaneously by the market. They were reduced to the business cycle, which can only explain short-run fluctuations of no real importance. Incredibly, the concept of the business cycle was applied by the neoclassical authors to analyse the devastating, long crisis of the 1930s and by the vast majority of the economists to analyse the no less devastating and prolonged crisis that broke out in 2007. You can imagine what results they achieved.

Consequently, not only the causes but also the possible remedies to crises remain a mystery for economic theory. To take just one example, so far no one has been able to explain what the difference in productiveness is between a seller of trash bonds and, say, a teacher. Having lost on the way the classical concepts of structural crises and unproductive labour, we are now left with no valid categories, both on the consumption and the production side to explain the present economic situation, with the huge growth of unproductive labour, the transformation of most investments into parasitic rents while inequalities and unemployment burgeon in the mature economies. *Thus, we should recover those concepts.*

Our suggestion is that the depression of the mature economies following after the welfare state boom is due to saturation. In this situation, the persistence in investing in the saturated sectors, rather than opening new fields of investment, has led to rising unemployment, exploitation of labour and poverty. The only way out of this sorry state of affairs is through a comprehensive policy of investment in infrastructures and human capital, i.e. by reviving the strategy of the welfare state, but this time related to both industrial and post-industrial development. Such a policy should first of all reduce the inequalities in incomes and culture both within the mature economies and between them and the poor countries.

References

Acquaviva, Sabino. 1958. *Automazione e nuova classe*. 3rd ed. Bologna: il Mulino, 1969.

———. 1983. *La strategia del gene. Bisogni e sistema sociale*. Roma and Bari: Laterza, 1988.

Agazzini, Michele. 1822. *La science de l'économie politique*. Paris: Bossange.

———. 1834. *Sconvenevolezza delle teoriche del valore insegnate da Smith … Malthus e Say* …. Milano: Fontana.

Alberti, Leon Battista. 1433–40. *I libri della famiglia*. Torino: Einaudi, 1969.

Altvater, Elmar. 1967. "Crisi e critica … lo sviluppo economico e la politica scolastica … ". Trans. from German. In C. Donolo, ed. *Per la critica dell'università*. Torino: Einaudi, 1971: 147–65.

———. 1968. "L'attualità del *Capitale*". In Fay 1968a: 17–31.

Altvater, Elmar and Huisken, Freerk. 1970. *Lavoro produttivo e improduttivo* …. Trans. from German. Milano: Feltrinelli, Opuscoli marxisti, 1975.

Altvater, E. and Huisken, F., eds. 1971. *Materialen zur politischen Ökonomie des Ausbildungssektors*. Erlangen: Politladen GMBH.

Anderlini, Fausto. 1977. *Lavoro produttivo e improduttivo*. Bari: De Donato.

An Essay. 1821. *An Essay on the Political Economy of Nations* …, anonymous. London: Longman etc. Online: Google, from Northwestern University, Evanston, IL.

Appleby, Joyce. 1978. *Economic Thought and Ideology in Seventeenth-Century England*. Princeton, NJ: Princeton University Press.

Aristotle. 1998. *Politics*. The Loeb Classical Library, Aristotle XXI. Cambridge, MA: Harvard University Press.

Arndt, Heinz. 1978. *The Rise and Fall of Economic Growth*. Melbourne: Longman Cheshire.

Aron, Raymond. 1962. *La società industriale*. Trans. from French. Milano: Comunità, [1965].

Arriquíbar, Nicolás. [1764–70]. *Recreación política*. 1st ed. 1779. Reprint Bilbao: Instituto Vasco de Estadística, no date.

Attwood, Thomas. 1817. *Prosperity Restored* …. London: Baldwin etc. Online: Google – Internet Archive from University of California (no division in chapters or others).

Aymone, Fiorella, Ada Sivini Cavazzani, and Giordano Sivini, eds. 1969 *Sviluppo economico e rivoluzione*. Bari: De Donato.

Ayres, C. E. 1944. *The Theory of Economic Progress*. Kalamazoo, MI: New Issue Press, 1978.

Bacon, Robert and Eltis, Walter. 1976. *Britain's Economic Problem: Too Few Producers.* London: Macmillan.

———. 1978. "Marketed Output – Yes, Luxury – No. A Reply to Mrs. Ietto Gillies". *British Review of Economic Issues*, May 1978: 47–54.

Bagiotti, Tullio. 1976. "Per la nuova edizione italiana della Ricchezza delle Nazioni". *Rivista Internazionale di Scienze Economiche e Commerciali*, 1976: 207–33.

[Bailey, Samuel]. 1823. *Questions in Political Economy, Politics, ...* London: Hunter. Online: Google, from Harvard University Library.

———. 1825. *A Critical Dissertation on the Nature, Measures and Causes of Value; ....* London: Hunter.

———. 1826. *A letter to a Political Economist; ....* London: Hunter.

Balibar, Étienne. 1974. *Cinque studi di materialismo storico.* Trans. from French. Bari: De Donato, 1976.

Banfield, Thomas Ch. 1845. *The Organization of Industry.* 2nd ed. London: Longman etc., 1848. Online: Google, from University of Iowa.

Baran, Paul A. 1957a. *The Political Economy of Growth.* New York: Monthly Review Press.

———. 1957b. "La teoria della classe agiata" (review of Veblen 1899). Now in Baran 1969: 213–24.

———. 1959. *Riflessioni sul sottoconsumo.* Now in Baran 1969: 187–204.

———. 1969. *Saggi marxisti* (trans. of The Longer View, 1969, John O'Neill ed.). Torino: Einaudi, 1976.

Baran, Paul and Sweezy, Paul. 1966. *Monopoly Capitalism.* New York and London: Modern Reader, 1968. Online: scribd.com.

Barber, William. 1967. *Storia del pensiero economico.* Trans. from English. Milano: Feltrinelli, 1971.

Barcellona, Pietro. 1980. *Oltre lo stato sociale.* Bari: De Donato.

Barel, Yves. 1968. "Marxismo e sviluppo". In Fay 1968a: 53–77.

Barnes, William. 1859. *Views of Labour and Gold.* London: Russel Smith. Online: Google – Internet Archive from University of Michigan.

Barratt Brown, Michael. 1969. "Il marxismo e lo sviluppo economico del capitalismo". Trans. from English. In Aymone et alii 1969: 23–76.

———. 1972. *From Labourism to Socialism ....* Nottingham: Spokesman Books.

Barton, John. 1814–17. *Population Growth and National Strength.* In Barton (1962–63).

———. 1817. *Observations on the Circumstances Which Influence the Conditions of the Labouring Classes of Society.* Baltimore: Johns Hopkins University, 1934. Jacob Hollander ed.

———. 1954. "Effect of a decrease in the value of money on taste and literature". 1st ed. 1954, in Dalhousie Review. Now in Barton (1962–63).

———. 1962–63 *Economic Writings.* G. Sotiroff, ed. Regina, SK: Lynn. 2 vols.

Barucci, Piero. 1972. *Introduzione to Malthus, Principi di economia politica.* Milano: ISEDI, XI–LXXII.

———. 1975. *Introduzione to Sismondi, Nuovi principi di economia politica.* Milano: ISEDI, XIII–LXIV.

Bastiat, Fredéric. 1850. *Harmonies économiques.* Vol. VI of B., *Oeuvres complètes.* Online: bastiat.org, F.R. Rideau ed.

Baudeau, Nicholas. 1767–70. *Explication du Tableau économique à Mme. de ***.* In Daire 1846: 822–76.

———. 1771. *Première introduction à la philosophie économique ....* In Daire 1846: 657–821.

Baudrillard, Jean. 1974. *La società dei consumi*. Trans. from French. Bologna: il Mulino, 1976.
Baudrillart, Henri. 1869. *Économie politique populaire*. Paris: Hachette.
———. 1883. *Philosophie de l'économie politique (lectures 1852–68)*. Paris: Alcan. Online: Internet Archive from University of Toronto.
Baumann, Zygmunt. 2009. *Capitalismo parassitario*. Trans. from English. Roma and Bari: Laterza, 2011.
Becattini, Giacomo. 1978. "La posizione del consumo nel pensiero degli economisti classici". In T. Bagiotti and G. Franco, eds. *Pioneering Economics … in Honour of G. Demaria*. Padova: CEDAM, 1978: 59–71.
Beccaria, Cesare. 1769–70. *Elementi di economia pubblica*. In Custodi 1803–16, Moderna, vols. 11 & 12.
Becher, Johann. 1668. *Politische Discurs, … dess Auff- und Abnehmens der Städt, Länder und Republicken* …. Reprint Glashütten im Taunus: Auvermann, 1972.
Becker, Gary. 1964. *Human Capital … with Special Reference to Education*. Chicago: University of Chicago Press.
———. 1981. *A Treatise on the Family*. Cambridge, MA: Harvard University Press.
Becker, James. 1962. "Il sistema marxiano e lo squilibrio sociale". Trans. from English. Now in Horowitz 1968, ch. 11 (1971 ed.: 300–25).
Behrens, Friedrich. 1961. "The Concept of Labor Productivity". Now in Dunlop and Diatchenko 1964: 82–92.
Bell, Daniel. 1973. *The Coming of Post-Industrial Society*. New York: Basic Books.
Bellers, John. 1699. *Essays about Poor, Manufactures* …. Reprint New York: Johnson, 1972.
Bellofiore, Riccardo, ed. 2009. *Rosa Luxemburg and the Critique of Political Economy*. Abingdon and New York: Routledge.
Bénard, Jean. 1952. *La conception marxiste du capital*. Paris: SEDES (Soc. Éd. Enseignement Supérieur).
Benetti, Carlo. 1979. Smith. *La teoria economica della società mercantile*. Milano: Etas Libri.
Bentham, Jeremy. 1800. *Abstract … of a Tract Entitled Circulating Annuities* … In B. (1952), Vol. 2: 201–423.
———. 1801a. *The True Alarm. A View of Paper Money* …. In B. (1952), Vol. 3: 61–216.
———. 1801b. *Defence of a Maximum* …. In B. (1952), Vol. 3: 247–302.
———. 1952. *Economic Writings*. W. Stark, ed. 3 vols. London: Royal Economic Society and Allen & Unwin.
Berg, Maxine. 1980. *The Machinery Question and the Making of Political Economy. 1815–48*. Cambridge: Cambridge University Press.
Bernstein, Eduard. 1899. *The Preconditions of Socialism*. Trans. from German. Online, Cambridge: Wordpress, 2016.
Berry, Christopher. 1994. *The Idea of Luxury*. Cambridge: Cambridge University Press.
Berthoud, Arnaud. 1974. *Travail productif et productivité du travail chez Marx*. Paris: Maspero.
Bertolino, Alberto. 1938–39. *Scritti e lezioni di storia del pensiero economico*. Milano: Giuffrè, 1979.
Bettelheim, Charles. 1972. "Informatique et capitalisme". In Janco and Furjot 1972: 71–73.
Bevan, Wilson. 1894. *Sir William Petty*. Baltimore: American Economic Association.
Bianchi, Marina. 2004. "Se la felicità è così importante, come mai ne sappiamo così poco?". In L. Bruni and P. L. Porta, eds. *Felicità ed economia*. Milano: Guerini, 2004: 170–91.

Bidet, Jacques. 1976. *Travail productif et classes sociales: deux études*. Paris: CERM (Cahiers Centre Études Recherches Marxistes), no. 130.
———. 1982. "Production, Travail Productif – Improductif". Entry of Labica 1982: 720–22.
Biffi Tolomei, Matteo. 1792. *Esame del commercio toscano* .... Firenze: Allegrini.
Billesby, Langton. 1826. *Observations on the Sources and Effects of Unequal Wealth* .... Reprint New York: Russell & Russell. Online: Google from University of California.
Bishoff, J., Ganssmann, H., Kümmel, G., Löhlein, G. 1970. "Produktive und unproduktive Arbeit". Now in Altvater and Huiskens 1971: 194–219.
Bladen, Vincent. 1960. "Adam Smith on Productive and Unproductive Labour: A Theory of Full Employment". *Canadian Journal of Economics and Political Science*, November 1960: 625–30.
———. 1974. *From Adam Smith to Maynard Keynes* .... Toronto, ON and Buffalo: University of Toronto Press.
Blake, Justin. 1960. "Jacob Morris on Unproductive Employment ...". *Science and Society*, Spring 1960: 169–73.
Blake, William. 1823. *Observations on the Effects Produced by the Expenditure of the Government during the Restriction of Cash Payments*. London: Murray & Lloyd.
Blanc de Volx, Jean. 1803. *État commercial de la France, au commencement du 19me siècle* .... 3 vols. Tome I. Paris: Treuttel et Würtz. Online: Google from Bayerische Staatsbibliothek, München.
Blanqui, Jérôme-Adolphe. 1825. *Précis élémentaires d'économie politique* .... 2nd ed. 1842. Paris: Guillamin, 1857.
———. 1837. *Historie de l'économie politique en Europe* .... 2nd ed. 1845. Paris: Guillaumin. 2 vols.
———. 1843. Notes added to A. Smith, *Richesse des nations* .... G. Garnier, ed. Paris: Guillaumin.
Blaug, Mark. 1958. *Ricardian Economics*. Westport, CT: Greenwood Press.
———. 1960. "Progresso tecnico ed economia marxiana". Trans. from English. Now in Horowitz 1968, ch. 9 (1971 ed.: 246–68).
———. 1962. *Economic Theory in Retrospect*. 3rd ed. Cambridge: Cambridge University Press, 1978.
———, ed. 1968. *Economics of Education: Selected Readings*. Harmondsworth: Penguin.
———. 1970. *An Introduction to the Economics of Education*. Harmondsworth: Penguin, 1980.
Bleaney, Michael. 1976. *Underconsumption Theories*. London: Lawrence & Wishart.
———. 1998. "Underconsumption". Entry of Kurz and Salvadori eds., II: 486–8.
Boccara, Paul. 1978. *Sur la mise en mouvement du 'Capital'*. Paris: Éditions Sociales.
Boccardo, Gerolamo. 1857. *Dizionario della Economia politica*. Vol. I. Torino: S. Franco.
Boianovsky, Mauro. 2017a. *When the History of Ideas Meets Theory: Arthur Lewis and the Classical Economists on Development*. Center History of Political Economy, Duke University, WP.
———. 2017b. "Wicksell, Secular Stagnation and the Negative Natural Rate of Interest". *History of Economic Ideas*, 2017/2: 37–61.
Boileau, Daniel. 1811. *An Introduction to the Study of Political Economy* .... London: Cadell & Davies.
Bonar, James. 1885. *Malthus and His Work*. 2nd ed. 1924. Reprint New York: Kelley, 1966, online (Questia).

Bortkiewicz, Ladislaus. 1906–07. *Calcolo del valore e calcolo del prezzo nel sistema marxiano*. Trans. from German. In B. *La teoria economica di Marx*. Torino: Einaudi, 1971.

Bosellini, Carlo. 1816. *Nuovo esame delle sorgenti della privata e pubblica ricchezza*, Vol. I, Modena: Vincenzi.

Boss, Helen. 1990. "Theories of Surplus and Transfer". *Parasites and Producers in Economic Thought*. Boston, MA: Unwin Hyman.

Botero, Giovanni. 1589. *Della ragion di stato*. Torino: UTET, 1948.

Bottomore, Thomas, ed. 1973. *Introduction to Karl Marx*. Oxford: B. Blackwell.

Boudin, Louis. 1907. *The Theoretical System of Karl Marx* .... New York: Monthly Review Press, 1968.

Bowles, Samuel and Gintis, Herbert. 1980. "Education and the Long Shadow of Work". In Nichols 1980: 190–9.

Bowley, Marian. 1937. *Nassau Senior and Classical Economics*. London: Allen & Unwin.

———. 1973. *Studies in the History of Economic Theory before 1870*. London: Macmillan.

———. 1975. "Some Aspects of the Treatment of Capital in the *Wealth of Nations*", in Skinner and Wilson 1975: 361–76.

Bowman, M. J. 1966. "The Human Investment Revolution in Economic Thought". Now in Blaug 1968: 101–34.

Bradley, Ian and Howard, Michael, eds. 1982. *Classical and Marxian Political Economy*. London and Basingstoke: Macmillan, "Introduction": 1–43.

Bravermann, Harry. 1974. *Labor and Monopoly Capital. The Degradation of Work in the Twentieth Century*. New York: Monthly Review Press, 1998. Online: caringlabor.files.wordpress.com

Bray, John Francis. 1839. *Labour's Wrongs and Labour's Remedy*. Leeds: D. Green.

[Briscoe, John]. 1696. *A Discourse of Money*. London: S. Briscoe.

Bronfenbrenner, Martin. 1965. "Il Capitale e l'uomo moderno". Trans. from English. Now in Horowitz 1968: 217–45.

Brougham, Henry. 1804. "Review of Lauderdale 1804". *Edinburgh Review*, July 1804, vol. IV: 343–77.

Buchanan, David. 1814. *Observations on the Subject Treated in Dr. Smith's Inquiry* .... Edinburgh and London: Oliphant and Murray. Online: Google from Bodleyan Library, Oxford.

Buck, Philip. 1942. *The Politics of Mercantilism*. Reprint New York: Octagon Books, 1964.

Bukharin, Nikolaj. 1925. *L'imperialismo e l'accumulazione del capitale*. Trans. from German. Roma and Bari: Laterza, 1972.

Bullock, Paul. 1973. "Categories of Labour-Power for Capital". *Bulletin of the Conference of Socialist Economists*, Autumn 1973: 82–99.

———. 1974. "Defining Productive Labour for Capital". *Bulletin of the Conference of Socialist Economists*, Autumn 1974: 1–15.

Buret, Eugène. 1840. *De la misère des classes laborieuses*. Bruxelles: Société Typographique Belge, 1842, 2 vols. Online: Internet Archive (vol. 1).

Burke, Edmund. 1795. *Thoughts and Details on Scarcity*. In B. *Miscellaneous Writings*. Online: Library of Economics & Liberty.

Burton, John Hill. 1849. *Political and Social Economy* .... Edinburgh: Chambers. Online: Google from Bodleyan Library, Oxford.

[Butel-Dumont, George-Marie] 1771. *Théorie du Luxe*. Londres: no publisher, 1775.

Bye, Raymond. 1924. *Principles of Economics*. New York: Crofts, 1931.

Bye, Raymond and Hewett, William. 1952. *The Economic Process*. New York: Appleton etc., 1963.

Cagnazzi, Luca de Samuele. 1813. *Elementi di economia politica*. Napoli: Sangiacomo. Online: Google, from Biblioteca Nazionale di Napoli.

———. 1820. *Saggio sulla popolazione del Regno di Puglia … Parte I*. Napoli: Tipogr. Trani. Online: Google, from Bodleyan Library, Oxford.

Calabi, Lorenzo. 1972. "L'estensione delle classi medie in Marx …". *La Critica sociologica*, primavera 1972: 48–63.

Calvez, Jean. 1956. *Revenue nationale en URSS*. Paris: SEDES (Soc. Éd. Enseignement Supérieur).

Camatte, Jacques. 1964–72. *Capital and Community*. Trans. from French. London: Unpopular Books, 1988. Online: R. Lucas ed., 2006.

Campanella, Francesco. 1982. *Lavoro*. Entry of Dizionario di Economia politica, G. Lunghini ed. Torino: Boringhieri. Vol. 1: 93–148.

Campanella, Tommaso. 1602. *La città del sole*. Milano: Feltrinelli, 1962.

Canard, Nicolas-François. 1801. *Principes d'économie politique*. Paris: Buisson, an X (1801).

Cannan, Edwin. 1893. *A History of the Theories of Production and Distribution in English Political Economy from 1776 to 1848*. London: Percival.

———. 1904. Editor's Notes to the Wealth of Nations (see Smith 1776).

———. 1929. *A Review of Economic Theory*. London: King & Son, 1930.

Cantalupo, Benedetto. 1825. *Breve cenno della scienza del benessere sociale* …. Napoli: Tipogr. La Minerva. 3rd edn?

[Cantillon, Richard]. 1730. *Essai sur la nature du commerce en général*. London: Macmillan, 1931. French and English text.

Carbonaro, Antonio. 1979. *Povertà e classi sociali*. Milano: F. Angeli.

Carchedi, Guglielmo. 1975. "Reproduction of social classes at the level of production relations". *Economy and Society*, November 1975: 361–417.

———. 1977. "On the economic identification of the middle class". *Economy and Society*, February 1977: 1–86.

Cardozo, Jacob Nunez. 1826. *Notes on Political Economy*. Charleston: Miller. Reprint New York: Kelley.

Carey, Henry. 1837. *Principles of Political Economy, Part I*. Philadelphia, PA: Carey etc., Online: Internet Archive.

———. 1858–59. *Principles of Social Science*. Philadelphia, etc.: Lippincot, etc. 3 vols.

Carlo, Antonio. 1975. *Crisi economica e dialettica storica*. Roma: Savelli.

Carrion-Nisas, André. 1825. *Principes d'économie politique*. Paris: Raymond. Online: Google from University of Gand.

Carter, Michael. 1977. "To Abstain or Not to Abstain (Is That the Question?). A Critique of Human Capital Concept". In Schwartz 1977: 36–50.

Carver, Thomas N. 1919. *Principles of Political Economy*. Boston, MA: Ginn.

———. 1924. *The Economy of Human Energy*. New York: Macmillan.

Cary, John. 1695. *Essai sur l'état du commerce en Angleterre*. Trans. from English. Londre: no publisher, 1755.

Catlin, Warren. 1962. *The Progress of Economics. A History of Economic Thought*. New York: Bookman.

Cattaneo, Carlo. 1836. "Interdizioni israelitiche". In E. Sestan, ed. *Opere di G. Romagnosi, C. Cattaneo, G. Ferrari*. Milano and Napoli: Ricciardi, 1957: 361–484.

———. 1843. "Dell'economia nazionale di Federico List". In E. Sestan, ed. *Opere di G. Romagnosi, C. Cattaneo, G. Ferrari*. Milano and Napoli: Ricciardi, 1957: 507–60.

———. 1861. *Del pensiero come principio d'economia pubblica*. Roma: Ed. di Storia e Letteratura, 2014.

Cauwès, Paul. 1881. *Cours d'économie politique*. 3rd ed. Paris: Larose & Forcel, 1893, 4 tomes.

Cayley, Edward. 1830. *On Commercial Economy*. London: Ridgway. Online: Google – Internet Archive from Harvard College Library.

Cazaux, L.-F.-G. 1825. *Éléments d'économie privée et publique* .... Paris: Huzard etc. ... Online: Gallica BNF.

———. 1826. *Bases fondamentales de l'économie politique*. Paris: Huzard, online: Gallica BNF.

[Cazenove, John]. 1822. *Considerations on the Accumulation of Capital* .... London: Richardson. Online: Google from British Museum Library.

———. 1832. *Outlines of Political Economy* .... London: Richardson. Online: Google from University of Chicago.

Cazzaniga, Gian Mario. 1981. *Funzione e conflitto. Forme e classi nella teoria marxiana dello sviluppo*. Napoli: Liguori.

Cella, Gian Primo and Reyneri, Emilio. 1974. "Gli operai comuni come nuovo soggetto rivoluzionario". Now in Strati 1978: 325–30.

Cerroni, Umberto. 1983. *Teoria della società di massa*. Roma: Editori Riuniti.

Chalmers, Thomas. 1808. *An Inquiry into the Extent and Stability of National Resources*. Edinburgh: Oliphant & Brown.

———. 1832. *On Political Economy in Connection with the Moral State ... of Society*. Glasgow: Collins and New York: Appleton.

Chang, Ha-Joon. 2008. *Bad Samaritans*. The Myth of Free Trade and the Secret History of Capitalism. New York etc.: Bloomsbury.

Cherbuliez, Antoine. 1862. *Précis de la science économique* ... r. Paris: Guillaumin. 2 vols.

Chevalier, Michel. 1842–44. *Cours d'économie politique*. Paris: Capelle. 2 vols.

Child, Josiah. 1693. *A New Discourse of Trade*. London: Hodges etc. 1740.

———. 1694. *A Discourse of the Nature ... of Trade*. Now in Ch. *Selected Works*, 1668–97. Farnborough, Hants: Gregg, 1968.

Clark, John Bates. 1886. *The Philosophy of Wealth* .... 2nd ed. 1887. Reprint New York: Kelley, 1967.

———. 1898. *Introduction* to Rodbertus, 1851: 1–18.

———. 1907. *Essentials of Economic Theory* .... New York: Macmillan.

Clark, John Maurice, et al. 1926. *Adam Smith 1776–1926*. Chicago, IL: University of Chicago Press.

Clément, Ambroise. 1867. *Essai sur la science sociale. Économie politique, morale expérimentale, politique théorique*. Paris: Guillaumin. 2 vols. Online: Google from Univ. of Gand.

Clement, Werner. 1980. "From the Human-Capital Approach to a Political Economy of Human Resources". *Human*, 1983, vol. 2: 328–44.

Coats, A. W. (Bob). 1967. "The Classical Economists and the Labourer". Now in his *The Classical Economists and Economic Policy*. London: Methuen, 1971.

———. 1972. "The Classical Economists, Industrialization and Poverty". Now in his *On the History of Economic Thought. British and American Economic Essays*. Vol. 1. London and New York: Routledge, 1992: 186–209.

Cocqueil, Charles de. 1891. "Consommation". In Léon Say and Joseph Chailley, eds. Entry of *Nouveau Dictionnaire d'Économie politique*. Paris: Guillaumin. 2 vols. Vol. I: 539a–47a.

Cole, Charles. 1931. *French Mercantilist Doctrines before Colbert.* New York: Richard Smith.

Colletti, Lucio and Napoleoni, Claudio, eds. 1970. *Il futuro del capitalismo. Crollo o sviluppo?* Bari: Laterza.

Colliot-Thélène, Catherine. 1975. "Contributo a un'analisi delle classi sociali". Trans. from French. In Mingione 1980: 59–79.

Colmeiro, Manuel. 1859. *Principios de economía política.* 2nd ed. Madrid: Martínez García, 1865.

Colquhoun, Patrick. 1806. *A Treatise on Indigence* .... London: Hatchard. Online: Google – Internet Archive.

———. 1814. *A Treatise on Wealth, Power and Resources of the British Empire* ... London: Mawman. Online: Google, from Univ. of Michigan.

Comber, William. 1808. *An Inquiry into the State of National Subsistence as Connected with the Progress of Wealth and Population.* 2nd ed. London: Cadell & Davies, 1822.

Commons, John R. 1893. *The Distribution of Wealth.* New York and London: Macmillan. Online: Google from Harvard University.

Comte, Charles. 1827. *Critique du livre ... par ... Cazaux* .... Paris: Huzard etc.

Condillac, Étienne Bonnot de. 1758–1765a. *Cours d'études ... Histoire Moderne,* partly in C. (1947–1951), Vol. 2.

———. 1758–65b. *Cours d'études ... Histoire Ancienne,* partly in C. (1947–51), Vol. 2.

———. 1776. *Le Commerce et le Gouvernement* ... In C. (1947–51), Vol. 1.

———. (1947–51). *Œuvres philosophiques.* Paris: P.U.F.

Coontz, Sydney. 1965. *Lavoro produttivo e domanda effettiva.* Trans. from English. Milano: F. Angeli, 1973.

Cooper, Thomas. 1826. *Lectures on the Elements of Political Economy.* 2nd ed. 1830. Reprint New York: Kelley, 1971.

Corallo, Jean-François. 1982. "Travail materiel/travail intellectuel". Entry of *Dictionnaire marxiste,* 905–8.

Corey, Lewis. 1935. *The Decline of American Capitalism.* London: John Lane.

Corry, Bernard. 1959. "Malthus and Keynes – A Reconsideration". *Economic Journal,* December 1959: 717–24.

Cossa, Emilio. 1898. *Il consumo delle ricchezze* ... Parte I. Bologna: Treves.

Cossa, Luigi. 1892. *Introduzione allo studio dell'economia politica.* 3rd ed. Milano: Hoepli.

Costa, Tino. 1979. "Stato del capitale e classe operaia". In T. Costa, ed. *Il capitale e lo stato* .... Verona: Bertani, 1979: 17–40.

Costabile, Lilia. 1980. *Malthus. Sviluppo e ristagno nella produzione capitalistica.* Torino: Einaudi.

Courcelle-Seneuil, Jean Gustave. 1858. *Traité théorique et pratique d'économie politique.* 2nd ed. Paris: Amyot, 1867. 2 vols.

———. 1862. *Études sur la science sociale.* Paris: Guillaumin.

Cournot, Augustin. 1863. *Principes de la théorie des richesses.* Paris: Hachette. Reprint Roma: Bizzarri, 1969.

———. 1877. *Revue sommaire des doctrines économiques.* Paris: Hachette. Online: Internet Archive from University of Michigan.

Coux, Charles de. 1832. *Essais d'économie politique.* Paris: Bureau ... défense de la liberté religieuse.

Covert-Spring, Joseph (Josep Fontcuberta). 1828–36. *Escristos saint-simonianos.* Madrid: Instituo de Estudios Fiscales, 1999.

Craig, John. 1814. *Elements of Political Science.* Edinburgh: Blackwood. Online: Google from New York Public Library.

Croce, Benedetto. 1900. *Materialismo storico ed economia marxistica.* Bari: Laterza, 1968.

Crompton, Rosemary. 1976. "Approaches to the Study of White-Collar Unionism". *Sociology,* September 1976: 407–26.

Crompton, Rosemary and Gubbay, Jon. 1977. *Economy and Class Structure.* London: Macmillan.

Cross, Gary. 1993. *Tempo e denaro. La nascita della cultura del consumo.* Trans. from English. Bologna: il Mulino, 1998.

Crosser, Paul. 1957. *Economic Fictions. A Critique of Subjectivistic Economic Theory.* New York: Philosophical Library. Online: Google from University of California.

———. 1960. *State Capitalism in the Economy of the United States.* New York: Bookman.

Cunningham Wood, John, ed. 1985. *David Ricardo: Critical Assessments.* London & Sydney: Croom Helm. 4 vols.

———, ed. 1986. *Thomas Robert Malthus: Critical Assessments.* Reprint London and New York: Routledge, 1994. 4 vols.

Custodi, Pietro, ed. 1803–16. *Scrittori classici italiani di economia politica.* Reprint O. Nuccio ed. Roma: Bizzarri, 1965–69.

Cutler, Antony and Hindess, Barry, Hirst, Paul, Hussain, Athar. 1977. *Marx's 'Capital' and Capitalism Today.* London: Routledge & Kegan Paul. 2 vols.

Cuyvers, Ludo. 1978. "A Mathematical Interpretation of Marxian Unproductive Labour". *Economica,* February 1978: 71–81.

Dahrendorf, Ralf. 1957. *Classe e conflitto di classe nella società industriale.* Trans. from English (revised ed.). Bari: Laterza, 1971. 2 vols.

Daire, Eugène, ed. 1846. *Physiocrates.* Reprint Genève: Slatkine, 1971. 2 vols. in one.

Dale, Jennifer. 1981. *A Marxist Perspective.* Part II of J. Dale and Peter Taylor-Gooby, *Social Theory and Social Welfare.* London: E. Arnold: 141–265.

Danielson, Anders. 1994. *The Economic Surplus.* Westport, CT: Praeger.

Dankert, Clyde. 1974. *Adam Smith. Man of Letters and Economist.* Hicksville and New York: Exposition Press.

D'Arco, Giambattista. 1771. *Dell'armonia politico-economica tra la città e il suo territorio.* In Custodi 1803–16, Moderna, Vol. 31: 11–210.

Davenant, Charles. 1698. *Discourses on the Public Revenues.* In his *The Political and Commercial Works 1771.* Reprint Farnborough, Hants: Gregg, 1968.

Davis, J. B. 1989. "Distribution in Ricardo's Machinery Chapter". *History of Political Economy.* Now in M. Blaug ed., David Ricardo (1772–1823). Aldershot: Elgar, 1991: 209–32.

Dawson, William. 1814. *An Inquiry into the Causes of the General Poverty ....* Edinburgh and London: Anderson.

Deane, Phyllis. 1978. *The Evolution of Economic Ideas.* Cambridge: Cambridge University Press.

De Augustinis, Matteo. 1840. *Elementi di economia sociale.* 2nd ed. No place: no publisher, 1843.

de Brunhoff, Suzanne. 1976. "Crisi capitalistica e politica economica". Trans. from French. In Nicos Poulantzas and others, *La crisi dello stato.* Bari: De Donato, 1979: 111–28.

Defoe, Daniel. 1728. *Plan of the English Commerce ....* Reprint New York: Kelley, 1967.

Delaunay, Jean-Claude. 1971. *Essay marxiste sur la comptabilité.* Paris: Éditions Sociales.

Delaunay, Jean-Claude and Gadrey, Jean. 1992. *Services in Economic thought: Three Centuries of Debate.* Trans. from French. Boston, MA etc.: Kluwer.

Del Monte, Carlo. 1977. "Dal valore lavoro ad un lavoro senza valore". *Monthly Review,* Italian ed., November 1977: 23–28.

De Luca, Mario. 1968. *Gli economisti napoletani del settecento e la politica dello sviluppo*. Napoli: Morano.

Del Vecchio, Gustavo. 1908. *Ricchezze immateriali e capitali immateriali*. Now in Idem, Antologia di scritti, F. Caffè ed. Milano: F. Angeli, 1983: 69–138.

Demarco, Domenico. 1957. "Quello che è vivo nel pensiero economico di A. Genovesi". *Rassegna economica del Banco di Napoli*, 1957: 71–100.

De Masi, Domenico. 1999. *Il futuro del lavoro*. Milano: Mondolibri.

Demidov, Nikolai. 1830. *Opuscules d'économie politique et privée*. Paris: Imprimerie Selligue.

Denis, Hector. 1904. *Histoire des systèmes économiques et socialistes*. Vol. I. Paris: Giard et Brière.

Denis, Henri. 1950. *La valeur: les lois fondamentales du capitalisme*. Paris: Éditions Sociales.

———. 1957. *Valeur et capitalisme*. Paris: Éditions Sociales.

De Quincey, Thomas. 1844. *The Logic of Political Economy*. Edinburgh and London: Blackwood.

Desai, Meghnad. 1979. *Marxian Economics*. Oxford: B. Blackwell.

Destutt de Tracy. Antoine. 1817. *A Treatise on Political Economy*. Trans. from unpublished French original. Reprint New York: Kelley, 1970.

Deyon, Pierre. 1969. *Le mercantilisme*. Paris: Flammarion.

Díez, Fernando. *Utilidad, deseo y virtud. La formación de la idea moderna del trabajo*. Barcelona: Península.

Di Matteo, Massimo. 1979. "Alcune considerazioni sui concetti di lavoro produttivo e improduttivo in Marx". Mimeo, Università di Siena (Fondazione Einaudi).

Di Nallo, Egeria, ed. 1997. *Il significato sociale del consumo*. Roma-Bari: Laterza.

Dobb, Maurice. 1946. *Studies in the Development of Capitalism*. London: Routledge & Kegan Paul, 1950. Online: digamo.free.

———. 1959. "The Falling Rate of Profit". *Science and Society*, Spring 1959: 97–103.

Dorfman, Joseph. 1946. *The Economic Mind in American Civilization, 1606–1865*. Vol. 1, New York: Kelley, 1966.

Dow, L. A. 1977. "Malthus on Sticky Wages, the Upper Turning Point and General Glut". Now in Cunningham Wood 1986, Vol. 3: 208–23.

Driscoll, Robert. 1963. *Capitalist and Socialis Economies*. 2nd ed. Portland, OR: Aardvark. Mimeo.

Driver, Ciaran. 1980. *Productive and Unproductive Labour* .... London: Thames Polytechnic, Thames Papers in Political Economy.

Droz, Joseph. 1829. *Économie politique* .... Bruxelles: Wahlen, 1841.

Drugman, Bernard. 1979. *État, capital et salariat*. Université de Grenoble, Thèse de Doctorat.

Du Bois Aymé, Jean-Marie. 1823. *Examen de quelques questions d'économie politique* .... Paris: Pelicier.

[Dubuat-Nançay, Louis-Gabriel] 1773. *Éléments de politique*. London: no publisher.

Duchini, Francesca. 1971. *L'evoluzione storica degli schemi di analisi della distribuzione del reddito*. Milano: CELUC.

Duménil, Gérard. 1975. *La position de class des cadres et employés*. Grenoble: Press Universitaire. Online.

Duménil, Gérard and Lévy, Dominique. 2006. "Unproductive Labor as Profit Rate Maximizing Labor". Online: https://fr.scribd.com/.../

Dunlop, J. T. and Diatchenko, V. P., eds. 1964. *Labor Productivity*. New York: McGraw Hill.

Dunoyer, Charles B. 1830. *Nouveau traité d'économie sociale*. Then vol. 2 of D., *De la liberté du travail*. Paris: Guillaumin, 1845. 2 vols.

Dupin, Claude. 1745. *Oeconomiques*. Paris: Rivière, 1913. 2 vols.

Dupont de Nemours, Pierre-Samuel. 1815–16. *Correspondance avec J.-B. Say*. In Daire 1846: 394–424.

Dutens, Joseph. 1804. *Analyse raisonnée des principes ... de l'économie politique*. Paris: Courcier.

———. 1835. *Philosophie de l'économie politique*. Paris: Aillaud. 2 vols.

Eagly, Robert. 1974. *The Structure of Classical Economic Theory*. New York, etc.: Oxford University Press.

Eaton, John. 1950. *Economia politica*. Enlarged ed. 1963. Trans. from English. Torino: Einaudi, 1978.

Eichner, Alfred. 1979. "A Look Ahead". In F. Eichner, ed. *A Guide to Post-Keynesian Economics*. London and Basingstoke: Macmillan.

Elliot, John E. 1980. "Marx and Schumpeter on Capitalist Creative Destruction: A Comparative Restatement". *Quarterly Journal of Economics*, August 1980: 45–68.

Eltis, Walter. 1984. *The Classical Theory of Economic Growth*. London: Macmillan.

Eisdell, Joseph. 1839. *A Treatise on the Industry of Nations ....* London: Whittaker. 2 vols. Online: Google, vol. 1, from University of California; vol. 2, from University of Minnesota.

Eisenhower, David. 1982. "Unproductive Labour and Crisis". In D. Johnson, ed. *Class and Social Development. A New Theory of the Middle Class*. London: Sage, ch. 5: 133–53.

Enfantin, Barthélemy (le père —). 1831. *Économie politique et Politique: religion saint-simonienne*. Articles extraits du "Globe". Paris: Bureau du Globe.

Ensor, George. 1818. *An Inquiry Concerning the Population of Nations, Containing a Refutation of Mr. Malthus ....* London: E. Wilson.

Erdos, Peter. 1977. "A Contribution to the Criticism of Keynes and Keynesianism". In Schwartz 1977: 255–82.

Fabricant, Solomon. 1961. "Meaning and Measurement of Productivity". Now in Dunlop & Diatchenko 1964: 12–26.

[Faiguet de Villeneuve] 1763. *L'économie politique*. Reprint Paris: Éd.s d'Histoire Sociale, 1973.

Fallon, Valerio. 1923. *Principii di economia sociale*. Trans. from French. Torino: Marietti, 1946.

Faraday, Ethel. 1899. "Productive and Unproductive Labour". Sub-entry of "Production". In Inglis Palgrave, ed. *Dictionary of Political Economy*. London: Macmillan, 1908. 3 vols. Vol. III: 217–19.

Faucci, Riccardo. 1979. *Marx interprete degli economisti classici*. Firenze: La Nuova Italia.

Faucci, Riccardo and Pesciarelli, Enzo, eds. 1976. *L'economia classica. Origini e sviluppo (1750–1848)*. Milano: Feltrinelli.

Fawcett, Henry. 1863. *Manual of Political Economy*. 4th ed. London: Macmillan.

Fawcett, Millicent Garrett. 1870. *Political Economy for Beginners*, 10th ed. London: Macmillan 1911. Online: Internet Archive.

Fay, Victor, ed. 1968a. *Cent'anni dopo il 'Capitale'. Trans. of En partant du 'Capital'*. Roma: Samonà e Savelli, 1970.

———. 1968b. "Le classi medie salariate". In Fay 1968a: 91–103.

Feiwel, George. 1975. *The Intellectual Capital of Michal Kalecki*. Knoxville: University of Tennessee Press.

Fellner, William. 1948. "Employment Theory and Business Cycle". In ch. 2 of H. S. Ellis, ed. *A Survey of Contemporary Economics*. Homewood, IL: American Economic Association: 49–98. Online (Questia).

Ferguson, Adam. 1767. *Saggio sulla storia della società civile*. Trans. from English. Firenze: Vallecchi, 1973.

Ferrara, Francesco. 1853. *Prefazione a McCulloch and Carey. Biblioteca dell'Economista*. Now in his *Opere complete*, vol IV, Roma (Banca d'Italia), 1956.

———. 1855. *Prefazione a J.B. Say. Biblioteca dell'Economista*. Now in his *Opere complete*, Vol. II, Roma (Banca d'Italia), 1955.

———. 1857. *Lezioni di Economia politica 1856–57*. In his *Opere complete*, Vol. XI, P. Barucci and P. F. Asso, eds. Roma: Bancaria, 1986.

———. 1859. *Prefazione a Dunoyer etc. Biblioteca dell'Economista*. Now in his *Opere complete*, Vol. V, Roma (Banca d'Italia), 1961.

Ferreira-Borges, José. 1834. *Instituçõens de economia politica*. Lisboa: Imprensa nacional. Online: Google from Stanford University.

Ferrier, François. 1805. *Du government considéré dans ses rapports avec le commerce*. Paris: Libr. Perlet.

Fetscher, Iring. 1983. "Tesi sulla crisi del marxismo". In F. Cerutti, ed. *La crisi del marxismo come problema del marxismo*. Milano: F. Angeli, 1983: 48–55.

Fine, Ben. 1973. "A Note on Productive and Unproductive Labour". *Bulletin of Conference of Socialists Economists*, Autumn 1973: 99–102.

Fine, Ben and Harris, Laurence. 1979. *Rereading 'Capital'*. London: Macmillan.

Finzi, Roberto, ed. 1977. *Il ruolo dello Stato nel pensiero degli economisti*. Bologna: il Mulino.

Fisher, Irving. 1906. *The Nature of Capital and Income*. London: Macmillan. Online: Internet Archive.

Flórez Estrada, Álvaro. 1828. *Curso de economía política*. 4th ed. Madrid: Imprenta M. de Burgos, 1835. Online: Universidad de Sevilla.

Flury, Louis-Noël. 1833. *De la richesse. Sa definition et sa génération ....* Paris: Le Normant, etc. Online: Internet Archive from Bibl. Nazionale di Napoli.

Forbonnais, François. 1753. "Commerce". Entry of *Encyclopédie*, Vol. 3, reprint 1966: 690b–9b.

Formenti, Carlo. 1980. *La fine del valore d'uso. Riproduzione, informazione, controllo*. Milano: Feltrinelli, Opuscoli marxisti.

Fortrey, Samuel. 1663. *England's Interest and Improvement*. In McCulloch 1856a: 211–49.

Foster, Richard. 1815. *An Address to the Nation, on the Relative Importance of Agriculture and Manufactures ....* London: Longman, etc.

[Fourier, Charles]. 1808. *Théorie des quatre mouvements et des destinées générales ....* Leipzig: no publisher. Online: Gallica (BnF).

Franklin, Benjamin. 1760. *The Interest of Great Britain Considered*. Passages in Dorfman 1946: 183–7.

———. 1768. *On the Labouring Poor*. Passages in Dorfman 1946: 183–7.

Freeman, Roger. 1981. *The Wayward Welfare State*. Stanford, CA: Hoover Institution Press.

Fuoco, Francesco. 1825–27. *Saggi economici*. Pisa: Nistri. Reprint Roma: Bizzarri, 1969, O. Nuccio ed. 2 vols.

Furniss, Edgar. 1920. *The Position of the Laborer in a System of Nationalism. A Study in the Labor Theories of the Later English Mercantilists*. Reprint New York: Kelley, 1965.

Galbraith, John Kenneth. 1958. *The Affluent Society*. London: Hamish Hamilton, 1960. Online: archive.org.

———. 1967. *Il nuovo stato industriale*. Trans. from English. Torino: Einaudi, 1968.

Galgano, Francesco. 1974. *Le istituzioni dell'economia capitalistica*. Bologna: Zanichelli.

Gallegati, Mauro. 2016. *Acrescita*. Torino: Einaudi.

Gallino, Luciano. 2004. *Dizionario di sociologia*. 2nd revised ed. Torino: UTET.

———. 2011. *Finanzcapitalismo*. Torino: Einaudi.

Gamble, Andrew and Walton, Paul. 1976. *Capitalism in Crisis*. London and Basingstoke: Macmillan.

Ganilh, Charles. 1815. *La théorie de l'économie politique* .... Paris: Deterville. 2 vols.

———. 1821. *De systèmes d'économie politique* .... 2nd ed. (1st ed. 1809). Paris: Treuttel et Würtz. Online: Google from Koninklijke Bibliotek.

———. 1826. *Dictionnaire analytique d'économie politique*. Paris-Brussels: Ladvocat.

———. 1835. *Principes d'économie politique et de finance*. Paris-Strassburg: Levrault.

Garbero, Piero. 1980. *Introduzione* to Idem, ed. *Lavoro produttivo e lavoro improduttivo*. Torino: Loescher: 9–61.

Gardiner, Jean. 1975. "Women's Domestic Labour". *New Left Review*, January–February 1975: 47–58.

Garnier, Germain. 1796. *Abrégé élémentaire des principes de l'économie politique*. Paris: Agasse.

———. 1802. Notes du traducteur. Vol. 5 of *La richesse des nations par Adam Smith*. Paris: Agasse, note XX: 169–201.

———. 1822. *Notes du traducteur*. Vols. 5 and 6 of La richesse des nations par Adam Smith. Paris: Agasse, note XLIX, vol. 6: 120–40.

Garnier, Joseph. 1846. *Éléments de l'économie politique* .... Paris: Guillaumin. Online: Google Bibl. de la Ville de Lyon.

Geiger, Theodor. 1949. *La società di classe nel crogiuolo*. In Idem, *Saggi sulla società industriale*. Trans. from German. Torino: UTET, 1970.

Genovesi, Antonio. 1757a. *Del perfezionamento delle arti*. In Custodi 1803–16, Moderna, Vol. 10: 141–8.

———. 1757b. *Del lusso*. In Custodi 1803–16, Moderna, Vol. 10: 121–34.

———. 1757c. *Ragionamento sul commercio in generale*. In Custodi 1803–16, Moderna, Vol. 10: 7–70.

———. 1765–67. *Lezioni di commercio o sia di economia civile*. Revised ed., 1768–70. Milano: Vita e Pensiero, 2013.

George, Henry. 1880. *Progress and Poverty*. 2nd ed. London: Kegan Paul & Trench, 1882.

Giarini, Orio and Loubergé, Henri. 1978. *La delusione tecnologica*. Milano: Mondadori.

Giddens, Anthony. 1973. *La struttura di classe nelle società avanzate*. Trans. from English. Bologna: il Mulino, 1975.

Gide, Charles. 1883. *Principes d'économie politique*. 4th ed. Paris: Larose, 1894.

———. 1931. *Principes d'économie politique*. Last ed. Paris: Sirey. Online: Université du Québec.

Gide, Charles and Rist, Charles. 1909. *Histoire des doctrines économiques et sociales depuis les physiocrats jusq'à nos jours*. 6th ed. Paris: Larose, 1944.

Gilder, George. 1981. *Wealth and Poverty*. New York: Basic Books.

Gillman, Joseph. 1957. *Il saggio di profitto*. Trans. of The Falling rate of Profit. Roma: Editori Riuniti, 1961.

———. 1965. *Prosperity and Crisis*. New York: Marzani & Munsell.

Ginzberg, Eli. 1966. *The Development of Human Resources*. New York: McGraw-Hill.
———. 1976. *The Human Economy*. New York: McGraw-Hill.
Gioia, Melchiorre. 1815–17. *Nuovo prospetto delle scienze economiche* .... Milano: Pirotta, 6 vols. bounded two by two. Online: Google from Bibl. de la Ville de Lyon.
Gioia, Vitantonio. 1981. *Sviluppo e crisi nel capitalismo monopolistico*. Bari: Dedalo.
Godelier, Maurice. 1979. *Lavoro*. Entry of *Enciclopedia*, Vol. 8. Torino: Einaudi, 1979: 31–82.
Golicyn, Dmitri. 1796. *De l'esprit des économistes*. Brunsvick: no publisher (Fondazione Einaudi).
Gonnard, René. 1921. *Historire des doctrines économiques*. Vol. 1. Paris: Nouvelle Libraire Internationale.
Gordon, B. J. 1965. "Say's Law, Effective Demand, and the Contemporary British periodicals, 1820–1850". *Economica*, November 1965: 438–46.
Gordon, Robert J. 2012. "Is U.S. Economic Growth Over? Faltering Innovation Confronts the Six Headwinds". Working paper of the National Bureau of Economic Research, Cambridge, MA.
Gorz, André. 1964. *Stratégie ouvrière et néocapitalisme*. Paris: Editions du Seuil.
Gough, George. 1920. *Wealth and Work*. London: Philip, 1928.
Gough, Ian. 1972. "Marx's Theory of Productive and Unproductive Labour". *New Left Review*, November–December 1972: 47–72.
———. 1973. "On Productive and Unproductive Labour. A Reply". *Bulletin of the Conference of Socialist Economists*, Winter 1973: 68–73.
———. 1975. "State Expenditures in Advanced Capitalism". *New left Review*, July–August 1975: 53–92.
Gouverneur, Jacques. 1975. *Le travail 'productif' en regime capitalist*. Working paper, Université Catholique de Louvain.
———. 1978. *Contemporary Capitalism and Marxist Economics*. Trans. from French. Oxford: M. Robertson.
Gramm, Warren. 1987. "Unproductive Labour and Unproductive Consumption: Historical Review, Contemporary Relevance". *International Journal of Social Economics*, 1987/3–4–5: 154–66.
Graslin, J. J. Louis. 1767. *Essay analytique sur la richesse et sur l'impôt*. Paris: Geuthner, 1911.
Grassi, Enrico. 1979. *Forme storiche del capitalismo e metodo marxista*. Milano: F. Angeli.
Gray, John (18th c.). 1797. *The essential principles of the Wealth of nations, illustrated in opposition to some false doctrines of dr. Adam Smith and others*. London: T. Becket.
Gray, John (19th c.). 1825. *A Lecture on Human Happiness*. London: Sherwood & Jones.
———. 1831. *The Social System* .... Edinburgh: Tait.
Gray, Simon, alias George Purves. 1815. *The Happiness of States*. London: Hatchard, etc. Online: Google, from Harvard College Library.
———. 1817. *All Classes Productive of National Wealth* .... 2nd ed. London: Longman etc., 1840.
———. 1818. *Gray versus Malthus. The Principles of Population and Production Investigated* .... London and Edinburgh: Longman etc.
Graziani, Augusto. 1980. *Malthus e la teoria della domanda effettiva*, in Costabile 1980: VII–LV.
Greenberg, Leon. 1961. "Productivity Measurement for Economic Analysis". Now in Dunlop & Diatchenko 1964: 45–56.

Gregory, T. E. 1921. "The Economics of Employment in England 1660–1713". *Economica*, January 1921: 37–51.

Griselini, Francesco. 1766. "Pensieri intorno ai modi pratici di rendere ricca e possente una nazione ...". In G. Giarrizzo, et al., eds. *Illuministi italiani*. Vol. VII. Milano and Napoli: Ricciardi, 1965.

Groenewegen, Peter. 1977. "Adam Smith and the Division of Labour: A Bicentenary Estimate". Now in Idem 2002, ch. 22: 388–404.

———. 1994. "The French Connection: Some Case Studies of French Influence on British Economics in the Eighteenth Century". Now in Idem 2002: 125–43.

———. 2002. "*Eighteenth-Century Economics. Turgot, Beccaria and Smith and Their Contemporaries*. London and New York: Routledge.

Grossmann, Henryk. 1919. *Il crollo del capitalismo*. Trans. of *Das Akkumulations- und Zusammenbruchsgesetz des kapitalistischen Systems*. Milano: Jaca Book, 1977.

Gualerzi, Davide. 2010. *The Coming of Age of Information Technologies and the Path of Transformational Growth*. London and New York: Routledge.

Gurvitch, Georges. 1954. *Études sur les classes sociales. L'idée de classe sociale de Marx à nos jours*. Paris: Gonthier, 1966.

Haberler, Gottfried von. 1937. *Prosperity and Depression: A Theoretical Analysis of Cyclical Movements*. Revised ed. Geneva: League of Nations, 1939. Online (Questia).

Habermas, Jürgen. 1973. *La crisi della razionalità nel capitalismo maturo*. Trans. of *Legitimationsprobleme im Spätkapitalismus*. Roma-Bari: Laterza, 1982.

Hales, John [or Thomas Smith]. 1549. *A Discourse of the Common Weal of This Realm of England*. Cambridge: Cambridge University Press, 1893.

Hall, Charles. 1805. *The Effects of Civilization on the People in European States ....* London: printed for the author (Goldsmiths Library).

Hamilton, Robert. [1830]. *The Progress of Society*. London: J. Murray. Online: Google from Oxford University.

Hansen, Alvin. 1941. *Fiscal Policy and Business Cycle*. London: Allen & Unwin.

———. 1951. *Business Cycle and National Income*. London: Allen & Unwin.

Hansen, F. R. 1985. *The Breakdown of Capitalism. A History of the Idea in Western Marxism, 1883–1983*. London and New York: Routledge.

[Harris, Joseph]. 1757. *An Essay upon Money and Coins*. In McCulloch 1856b: 339–429.

Harrison, John. 1973a. "Productive and Unproductive Labour in Marx's Political Economy". *Bulletin of the Conference of Socialist Economists*, Autumn 1973: 70–82.

———. 1973b. "The Political Economy of Housework". *Bulletin of the Conference of Socialist Economists*, Winter 1973: 35–52.

Harvey, David. 1982. *The Limits to Capital*. Oxford: B. Blackwell; Chicago: Chicago University Press.

Hashimoto, Isao. 1966. "The Productive Nature of Service Labour". *Kyoto University Economic Review*, October 1966: 56–71.

Haug, Marie. 1979. "Deprofessionalizzazione: un'ipotesi alternativa per il futuro". Trans. from English. In Tousijn 1979: 137–54.

Hauterive, Alexandre-Maurice, comte de. 1817. *Éléments d'économie politique ....* Paris: Fantin.

Hazlitt, Henry. 1969. *Man versus the Welfare State*. New Rochelle, NY: Arlington House.

Hearn, William. 1864. *Plutology ....* Melbourne & Sydney: G. Robertson. Online: Internet Archive from University of California.

Heckscher, Eli. 1931. *Mercantilism*. Trans. from Swedish. New York: Macmillan, 1935.

Hegel, George W. F. 1821. *Philosophy of Right.* Trans. from German. Kitchener, ON: Batoche Books, 2001.

Heyking, Edmund. 1880. *Zur Geschichte der Handelsbilanztheorie.* Pat 1. Berlin: Puttkammer & Mülbrecht.

Hicks, John Richard. 1965. *Capital and Growth.* Oxford University Press.

———. 1974. *The Crisis of Keynesian Economics.* New York: Basic Books.

Higgs, Henry. 1897. *The Physiocrats.* Reprint Fairfield and New York: Kelley, 1989.

Hilferding, Rudolf. 1910. *Finance Capital.* Trans. from German. London: Routledge & Kegan Paul. Online: Google.

Hirsch, Fred. 1976. *Social Limits to Growth.* London: Routledge, 1978.

Hobson, John A. 1914. *Work and Wealth.* New York: Macmillan. Online: Internet Archive.

Hodgskin, Thomas. 1825. *Labour Defended against the Claims of Capital or The Unproductiveness of Capital proved by a Labourer.* London: Knight & Lacey.

———. 1827. *Popular Political Economy.* London and Edinburgh: Ch. & W. Tait.

———. 1832. *The Natural and Artificial Rights of Property Contrasted.* London: Steil.

Hodgson, Geoffrey. 1999. *Economics and Utopia.* New York and London: Routledge.

Hollander, Jacob. 1928. *Introduction* to David Ricardo, *Notes on Malthus.* J. Hollander and T.E. Gregory, eds. Baltimore: Johns Hopkins Press, 1928.

———. 1934. "Introduction" to John Barton. In J. Hollander, ed. *Conditions of the Labouring class ....* Baltimore: Johns Hopkins University.

Hollander, Samuel. 1973. *La teoria economica di Smith.* Trans. from English. Milano: Feltrinelli, 1976.

———. 1979. *The Economics of David Ricardo.* Toronto, ON: University of Toronto Press & Heinemann.

———. 1983. "On the Interpretation of Ricardian Economics: The Assumption Regarding Wages". Now in Cunningham Wood 1985, IV: 206–12.

Horie, Tadao. 1959. "Towards a Higher Stage of Marxian Economics ...". *Waseda Economic Papers.* Tokyo: Waseda University, 36–54.

Horowitz, David, ed. 1968. *Marx, Keynes e i neomarxisti.* Trans. of Marx and Modern Economics. Torino: Boringhieri, 1971.

[Houghton, John]. 1677. *England's Great Happiness ....* in J. R. McCulloch 1856a: 251–74.

Howard, M. C. and King, I. E. 1975. *The Political Economy of Marx.* Harlow, Essex: Longman.

Howell, Peter. 1975. "Once Again on Productive and Unproductive Labour". *Revolutionary Communist,* 3/4, September 1975. Online: Marxist Writers' Archive.

Hübner, C., Pilch, I. and Riehn, L. 1970. "Produktive und unproductive Arbeit in Kapitalismus". *Sozial Politik,* September 1970: 2–14.

Hughes, H. D., et al. 1970. *Planning for Education in 1980.* London: Fabian Society.

Human Resources. 1980. "Human Resources, Employment and Development". *Proceedings of the 6th World Conference of International Econ. Association,* 1980, 5 vols. London: Macmillan, 1983.

Hume, David. 1752a. *Of Interest.* In H. (1882–86): 320–30.

———. 1752b. *Of Taxes.* In H. (1882–86): 356–60.

———. 1752c. *Of Public Credit.* In H. (1882–86): 360–74.

———. 1882–86. *The Philosophical Works. Vol. III: Essays Moral,* Political and Literary. Reprint Aalen: Scientia, 1964.

Hunt, E. K. 1979. "The Categories of Productive and Unproductive Labor in Marxist Economic Theory". *Science and Society*, Fall 1979: 303–25.

Hutcheson, Francis. [1733–37]. *A System of Moral Philosophy*. 1st ed. 1755. Reprint New York: Kelley, 1978.

Ietto Gillies, Grazia. 1978. "Does the State Produce Luxuries? A Critique of Bacon and Eltis". *British Review of Economic Issues*, May 1978: 25–48.

Illuminati, Augusto. 1977. *Classi sociali e crisi capitalistica*. Milano: Mazzotta.

Ingram, John. 1888. *A History of Political Economy*. Revised ed. Reprint, New York: Kelley, 1967.

Inquiry. 1821. *An Inquiry into those principles, respecting the nature of demand ... lately advocated by Mr. Malthus ....* London: Hunter.

Iraci, Leone. 1970. *Dall'opulenza al benessere*. Torino: Einaudi.

Isnard, Achille. 1781. *Traité des richesses*. Londres: Fr. Grasset. 2 vols.

Isola, Francesco. 1811. *Instituzioni di commercio e di economia civile*. Roma: De Romanis.

Jaguin, Aureliano (Paolo Ramaccioni). 1976. *Il geroglifico sociale. Forze produttive e struttura di classe in Marx*. Bari: Dedalo.

Jakob, Ludwig Heinrich. 1805. *Grundsätze der Nationalökonomie*. 2nd ed. Charcow etc. 1809. Online: Google from British Museum.

James, Émile. 1959. *Storia del pensiero economico*. Trans. from French. Milano: Garzanti, 1963.

Janko, Manuel and Furjot, Daniel, eds. 1972. *Informatique et capitalisme*. Paris: Maspero.

Janssen, Theodore. 1713. *General Maxims in Trade* ... In *The British merchant or Commerce Preserved*. London: Osborne, 1748. 3 vols. Vol. 1: 1–21.

Jenkins, Arthur. 1948. *Adam Smith Today. An Inquiry ... simplified ....* New York: Richard Smith.

Jessop, Bob. 1982. *The Capitalist State*. Oxford: Martin Robertson.

Jevons, Stanley. 1871. *The Theory of Political Economy*. 3rd ed. London: Macmillan, 1888, Online: Library of Economics and Liberty.

Jobard, J. B. A. M. 1844. *Nouvelle économie sociale ou monautopole ....* Paris: Mathias. Online: Google from Bibl. Nazionale di Roma.

Johnson, E. A. J. 1937. *Predecessors of Adam Smith. The Growth of British Economic Thought*. Reprint New York: Kelley, 1965.

Jones, Richard, 1831. *An Essay on the Distribution of Wealth and on the Sources of Taxation*. London: Murray. Online: Google, from Bodleyan Library, Oxford.

Jouvenel, Bertrand de. 1957. "L'economia politica della gratuità". Now in G. Roustang, ed. *La seconda società industriale*. Trans. from French (1967). Milano: Etas Kompass, 1969.

Justi, Johann. 1755. *Staatswirtschaft*. In his *Gesammelte politische und Finanz-Schriften*. Reprint Aalen: Scientia, 1970, 3 vols. Vol. II.

Kapp, William. 1950. *The Social Cost of Private Enterprise*. Cambridge, MA: Harvard U. P.

Kates, Steven. 1998. *Say's Law and the Keynesian Revolution*, Cheltenham: E. Elgar.

Kautsky, Karl. 1902. *Teorie della crisi*. Trans. from German. Partially in Colletti and Napoleoni 1970: 271–96.

Kay, Geoffrey. 1979. *The Economic Theory of the Working Class*. London: Palgrave and Macmillan.

Kern, Horst and Schumann, Michael. 1984. *La fine della divisione del lavoro?* Trans. from German. Torino: Einaudi, 1991.

Kern, William. 1983. "Returning to the Aristotelian Paradigm: Daly and Schumacher". *History of Political Economy*, 1983: 501–12.

Kerr, Clark. 1969. *Marshall, Marx and Modern Times: The Muldimensional Society*. Cambridge University Press.

Keynes, John Maynard. 1930. "Economic possibilities for our grandchildren". Online: from his *Essays in Persuasion*. New York: Norton, 1963: 358–73 (yale.edu).

———. 1936. *General Theory of Employment, Interest and Money*. Online: University of Adelaide.

Kiker, B. F. 1969. "Von Thünen on Human Capital". Now in M. Blaug, ed. *J. von Thünen, A. Cournot, J. Dupuit*. Aldershot: E. Elgar, 1992: 88–92.

Kindleberger, Charles. 1990. *Leggi economiche e storia dell'economia*. Trans. from English. Roma and Bari: Laterza.

King, Gregory. 1696. "Natural and Political Observations … upon … the Conditions of England". In George Chalmers, ed. *An estimate … of Great Britain*. London: Stockdale, 1802: 405–49.

Kirkaldy, A. W. 1920. *Wealth*. Reprint Abingdon: Routledge, 2016.

Klaassen, Leo and Eizenga, Wietze. 1977. "Some Considerations on the Productive Capacity of Consumption Expenditures". In M. Feldstein and R. Inman, eds. *The Economics of Public Services*. London: Macmillan, 1977.

Klein, Rudolf. 1974. *Social Policy and Public Expenditure*. London: Centre for Studies in Social Policy.

Knight, Charles. 1855. *Knowledge Is Power*. London: Bell & Daldy, 1866. Online: Google – Internet Archive.

Kolb, F. R. 1972. "The Stationary State of Ricardo and Malthus: Neither Pessimistic nor Prophetic". Now in Cunningham Wood 1985, I: 235–50.

Korkotsides, Anastasios. 2007. *Consumer Capitalism*. London and New York: Routledge.

Kraus, Christian J. 1808–11. *Staatswirtschaft*. Vol. 1. Königsberg: Nicolovius, 3 vols. Posthumous.

Krugman, Paul. 2012. *End This Depression Now!* New York and London: Norton.

Kurz, Heinz and Salvadori, Neri, eds. 1998. *The Elgar Companion to Classical Economics*. Cheltenham, UK and Northampton, MA: E. Elgar, 2 vols.

Kushnirsky, Fiodor and Stull, William. 1987. "Productive and Unproductive Labour: Smith, Marx, and the Soviets". In D. Walker, ed. *Perspective on the History of Economic Thought*. Aldershot: E. Elgar, for the History of Economics Society, 1989.

Kuznets, Simon. 1966. *Modern Economic Growth*. New Haven, CT: Yale University Press.

Labica, Georges, ed. 1982. *Dictionnaire critique du marxisme*. Paris: Presse Univ. de France.

Laffemas, Barthélemy de. 1597. *General regulation* …. Trans. from French. London: Anthem, forthcoming.

La Grassa, Gianfranco. 1977. "Il processo di lavoro nel modo di produzione capitalistico". In F. De Cindio and P. Sylos Labini, eds. *Saggi di economia in onore di Antonio Pesenti*. Milano: Giuffrè.

Lalor, John. 1852. *Money and Morals*. London: Chapman. Online: Internet Archive from University of California.

Latouche, Serge. 1995. *La megamacchina*. Trans. from French. Torino: Bollati Boringhieri, 2008.

Lauderdale, James Maitland, Earl of. 1804. *An Inquiry into the Nature and origin of Public Wealth* …. New York: Kelley, 1962. Hathi Trust. Online: Google from Univ. of Michigan.

———. 1804a. *Observations by the Earl of L. on the Review of His Inquiry* ... Edinburgh: Constable and London: Longman. Online: Google.

———. 1829. *Three Letters to the Duke of Wellington* ... (on the Sinking Fund). London: Murray.

Launay, Jean. 1968a. "Réflexions sur la mesure de la production dans le conditions du capitalisme monopoliste d'État". *Économie et politique*, Mars–Avril 1968: 125–39.

———. 1968b. "Réflexions sur le concept de production". *Économie et politique*, September 1968: 69–95.

———. 1968c. "Signification du système français actuel de comptabilité nationale". *Économie et politique*, September 1968: 97–104.

Lawson, James. 1843. *Five Lectures on Political Economy*. London: Parker, 1844. Online: Google from Bodleyan Library, Oxford.

Lebau, Auguste. 1903. *Condillac économiste*. Paris: Guillaumin.

Lebowitz, Michael. 1976. "The Political Economy of Housework: A Comment". *Bulletin of the Conference of Socialist Economists*, March 1976: 1–3.

Lechevalier, Jules. 1834. *Études sur la science sociale*. Paris: Renduel. Online: Google from Bibl. Ville de Lyon.

Lefebvre, Henri. 1977. *Il modo di produzione statuale*. Trans. from French (3rd vol. of Idem, L'État). Bari: Dedalo, 1977.

Lekachman, Robert. 1966. *The Age of Keynes*. New York: Random House.

Le Mercier de la Rivière, Pierre-Paul. 1767. *De l'ordre naturel et essentiel des sociétés politiques*. The last 18 chapters in Daire 1846: 445–641.

Lenin, Vladimir. 1894. *What the "Friends of the People" Are and How They Fight the Social-Democrats*. In his *Collected Works*. Moscow: Progress Publishers, online. Vol. 1: 129–332.

———. 1895. *The Economic Content of Narodism and the Criticism of it in Mr. Struve's Book*. In his *Collected Works*. Moscow: Progress Publishers, online. Vol. 1: 333–508.

———. 1897. *A Characterisation of Economic Romanticism (Sismondi and Our Native Sismondists)*. In his *Collected Works*. Moscow: Progress Publishers, online. Vol. 2: 129–266.

———. 1917. *L'imperialismo, fase suprema del capitalismo*. Trans. from Russian. Roma: Editori Riuniti, 1974.

———. 1918. *Stato e rivoluzione*. Trans. from Russian. Roma: Editori Riuniti, 1974.

Leroy-Beaulieu, Paul. 1895. *Traité théorique et pratique d'économie politique*. 5th ed. Paris: Alcan, 1910, 4 vols.

Le Trosne, Guillaume-François. 1777. *De l'intérêt social*. In his *De l'ordre social*. Reprint München: Kraus, 1980: 489–724.

Lewis, Russel. 1973. *The New Service Society*. London: Longman.

Lewis, W. Arthur. 1954. "Economic Development with Unlimited Supply of Labour". Now in A. N. Agarwala, and S. P. Singh, eds. *The Economics of Underdevelopment*. Oxford University Press, 1963: 400–49.

Liesse, André. 1891. "Débouchés". Entry of Léon Say and Joseph Chailley, eds. *Nouveau Dictionnaire d'Économie politique*. 2 vols. Tome I.

Lippi, Marco. 1976. *Marx. Il valore come costo sociale reale*. Milano: Etas Libri.

List, Friederich. 1841. *The National System of Political Economy*. Trans. from German. London: Longmans & Green, 1909. Online: Library of Economics and Liberty.

Llombart, Vicent. 2012. *Jovellanos y el otoño de las Luces*. Gijón: Trea.

Löbl, Eugen. 1967. *Geistige Arbeit. Die wahre Quelle des Reichtums*. Trans. from Slovak. Wien and Düsseldorf: Econ, 1968.

Locke, John. 1691. *Some Considerations on ... the Lowering of Interest ....* In his *Works* [1823], Vol. 5. Reprint Aalen: Scientia, 1963.

Lojkine, Jean. 1977. *Il marxismo, lo stato e la questione urbana*. Trans. from French. Milano: F. Angeli, 1980.

Longe, Francis. 1866. *A Refutation of the Wage-Fund Theory ... as Enunciated by Mill and Fawcett*. London: Longmans & Green. Reprint, J. Hollander ed. Baltimore: Johns Hopkins P. Online: Internet Archive.

Longfield, Mountifort. 1833. *Lectures on Political Economy* ... In his *Economic Writings*. Reprint New York: Kelley, 1971.

Longo, Alfonso. 1773. "Istituzioni economico-politiche". In C. A. Vianello, ed. *Economisti minori del Settecento lombardo*. Milano: Giuffrè, 1942: 292–331.

Loria, Achille. 1889. *Analisi della proprietà capitalista*. 2 vols. In his, *Opere*. Vol 1, Torino: UTET, 1957: 1–656. Vol. 2, Torino: Bocca, online: openbess from University of Torino.

———. 1934. *Corso di economia politica*, 4th ed. Torino: UTET, 1964.

Lotz, Johann F. E. 1821. *Handbuch der Staatswirtschaftslehre*. Erlagen: Palm & Enke. Online: Google from Bayerische Staatsbibliothek. 3 vols. Vol. 1.

Lowe, Adolph. 1954. "The Classical Theory of Economic Growth". Now in his *Essays in Political Economics*. Brighton: Wheatsheaf Books: 107–31.

Lowenthal, Esther. 1911. *The Ricardian Socialists*. New York: Columbia University.

Lüder, August F. 1800–04. *Ueber Nationalindustrie und Staatswirtschaft. Nach Adam Smith bearbeitet*. Berlin: H. Fröhlich. 3 vols.

Luxemburg, Rosa. 1913. *The Accumulation of Capital*. Trans. from German. London: Routledge & Kegan Paul, 1951. Online: Marxists Archive.

———. 1915. *An Anti-Critique*. Trans. from German, 1st ed. 1921. Online: Marxists Archive.

Maccabelli, Terenzio. 1997. *Il "progresso della ricchezza". Economia, politica e religione in T.R. Malthus*. Milano: Giuffrè.

Machlup, Fritz. 1980. *Knowledge and Knowledge Production*. Princeton, NJ: Princeton University Press.

Macleod, Henry D. 1872. *The Principles of Economic Philosophy*. 2nd ed. London: Longmans, etc. Vol. 1. Online: Google from Harvard College.

Mallet, Serge. 1969. *La nouvelle classe ouvrière*, 5th ed. enlarged. Paris: Éd.s du Seuil.

Malthus, Thomas Robert. 1820. *Principles of Political Economy*. 2nd ed. London: Pickering, 1836, online, Google from Bodleyan Library, Oxford.

———. 1827. *Definitions in Political Economy* .... London: J. Murray, reprint Fairfield: Kelley, 1986.

Mandel, Ernest. 1962. *Traité d'économie marxiste*. Paris: Julliard. 2 vols.

———. 1969. "La classe operaia sotto il neo-capitalismo". In Aymone et al. 1969: 77–98.

———. 1972. *Late Capitalism*. Trans. from German. London: New Left Books, 1975.

———. 1977. *The Second Slump* .... Trans. form German. London: New Left Books, 1978.

Mandeville, Bernard. 1705. *The Grumbling Hive, in his The Fable of the Bees*. Oxford: Clarendon, 1924.

———. 1714. *Remarks, in his The Fable of the Bees*. Oxford: Clarendon, 1924.

Marcet, Jane. 1816. *Conversations on Political Economy* .... 6th ed. London: Longmans etc. 1827.

Marconcini, Federico. 1926. *L'economia del lavoro*. Milano: Vita e Pensiero.

Marshall, Alfred. 1890. *Principles of Economics*. 8th ed. London: Macmillan, 1920. Online: Library of Economics and Liberty.

Martineau, Harriet. 1832. *Illustrations of Political Economy*. 2nd ed. London: Fox, 1832–34. 9 vols.

Martyn, Henry. 1701. *Considerations on the East-India Trade*. In McCulloch 1856a: 541–629.

Marx, Karl. 1852. *Il 18 Brumaio di Luigi Bonaparte*. Trans. from German. Roma: Editori Riuniti, 1974.

———. 1859. *A Contribution to the Critique of Political Economy*. Trans. from German. Chicago, IL: Kerr, 1904. Online: gruppegrundrisse.

———. 1857–61. *Grundrisse. Outlines of the Critique of Political Economy*. Trans. from German. Written in 1857–1861. Harmondsworth: Penguin, 1973.

———. 1861–63. *Manoscritti del 1861–1863*. Trans. of *Zur Kritik der politischen Ökonomie. Teil 1*. Written in 1861–63. Roma: Editori Riuniti, 1980.

———. 1863–64. *Draft Chapter 6. The Process of Production of Capital, Draft Chapter 6 of Capital Results of the Direct Production Process*. Trans. from German. Written in 1863–64. Online: Marxist Internet Archive.

———. 1867. *Capital I. Capital, Vol. I: The Process of Capitalist Production*. Trans. from German. 1st ed. Chicago, IL: Kerr, 1906, online, Library of Economics & Liberty.

———. 1871. *La guerra civile in Francia*. Trans. from German. Roma: Samonà & Savelli, 1970.

———. 1885. *Capital II. Capital, vol. II: The Process of Circulation of Capital*. Trans. from German. Written 1865–1870. 1st ed. F. Engels ed. Chicago, IL: Kerr, 1909, online, Library of Economics & Liberty.

———. 1894. *Capital III. Capital, vol. III: The Process of Capitalist Production as a Whole*. Trans. from German. Written 1864–65. 1st ed. F. Engels ed. Chicago: Kerr, 1909, online, Libr. of Economics & Lib.

———. 1905 and 1910. *Theories. Theories of Surplus-Value*, volume IV of *Capital:* Notebooks VI–XV of the Manuscript 1861–63. Trans. from German. 1st ed. Moscow: Progress Publishers, online.

Marx, Karl, and Engels, Frederich. 1848. *Manifesto of the Communist Party*. Trans. from German. Online: Marxists Internet Archive.

Massoni, Jean. 1973. "La place de l'employés dans l'appareil économique". *Économie et politique, julliet*, 1973: 51–64.

Mattick, Paul. 1969. *Marx e Keynes. I limiti dell'economia mista*. Trans. from English. Bari: De Donato, 1974.

Mattick, Paul, et al. 1974. *Crisi e teorie della crisi*. Trans. from German. Bari: Dedalo, 1979.

Mazzucato, Mariana. 2013. *Lo stato innovatore*. Trans. from English. Roma and Bari: Laterza, 2014.

McCulloch, John Ramsay. 1821. "The Opinions of Messrs Say, Sismondi and Malthus on the Effects of Machinery and accumulation …". *Edinburgh Review*, March 1821: 102–23.

———. 1824. "Political Economy". *Supplement of Encyclopaedia Britannica*, 6: 216–78.

———. 1825. *The Principles of Political Economy* …. 5th ed. Edinburgh: A. & Ch. Black, 1864.

———. 1827. "A Review of Definitions in Political Economy by the Rev. T.R. Malthus", S.I., s.n. [Edinburgh] (Goldsmisths Library).

———. 1828. Edition of Smith, *Wealth of Nations*, with Introduction, Notes, etc. 4 vols. Edinburgh: Black & Tait and London: Longman etc.

———. 1845. *The Literature of Political Economy* …. Reprint London: LSE, 1938.

———. ed. 1856a. *A Select Collection of Early English Tracts on Commerce*. London: Political Economy Club.

———. ed. 1856b. *A Select Collection of Scarce and Valuable Tracts on Money*. Reprint London: King, 1933.

McIniscon, John (J.C. Ross). 1825. *Principles of Political Economy and of Population*. London: Sharewood & Jones. 2 vols.

McVickar, John. 1825. *Outline of Political Economy, Being a Republication of the Article* .... [McCulloch 1824]. *Together with Notes* .... New York: Wilder & Campbell. Online: Google from Pennsylvania State University.

Meek, Ronald. 1950. "The Decline of Ricardian Economics in England". Now in his *Economics and Ideology and Other Essays*. London: Chapman & Hall, 1967: 51–74.

———. 1951a. "Physiocracy and Classicism in Britain". Now in Meek 1962: 345–63.

———. 1951b. "Physiocracy and the Early Theories of Under-Consumption". Now in Meek 1962: 313–44.

———. 1962. *The Economics of Physiocracy*. London: Allen & Unwin.

Meoli, Umberto. 1961. *Il pensiero economico di Condillac*. Milano-Varese: Ist. Ed. Cisalpino.

Metz-Noblat, Alexandre de. 1853. *Analyse des phénomènes économiques*. Nancy: Vagner and Paris: Guillaumin etc. 2 vols. in one.

Meynieu, Mary. 1839. *Éléments d'économie politique* (dialogues). Paris: Cherbuliez.

Michael, Robert. 1972. "The Effect of Education on Efficiency in Consumption". New York: National Bureau of Economic Research, Occasional Paper 116.

Mills, Charles Wright. 1951. *White Collar. The American Middle Classes*. Oxford University Press. Online: archive.org.

Mill, James. 1808. *Commerce Defended*. London: Baldwin, online, Library of Liberty.

———. 1821. *Elements of Political Economy*. London: Bohn, 1844, online Library of Economics & Liberty.

———. 1824. *Education*. Entry of the *Encyclopaedia Britannica*, 6th ed., 1824 (signed G.G.).

Mill, John Stuart. 1844. *Essays on Some Unsettled Questions of Political Economy*. 2nd ed. 1874. London: Longmans etc., online, Library of Economics & Liberty.

———. 1848. *Principles of Political Economy with some of their Applications to Social Philosophy*. 7th ed. London: Longmans & Green, 1909, online, Library of Economics & Liberty.

Minc, Bronislaw. 1962. *Economia politica del socialismo*. Trans. from Polish. Milano: Feltrinelli, 1967.

Mingione, Enzo, ed. 1980. *Lavoro produttivo, lavoro improduttivo e classi sociali*. Roma: Savelli.

Mirabeau, Victor. 1769–1771. *Les Économiques*. Amsterdam: no publisher (Fondazione Einaudi). 3 vols.

Mizuta, Hiroshi. 1967. *Adam Smith's Library: A Supplement to Bonar's Catalogue* .... Cambridge University Press.

Moe, Espen. 2007. *Governance, Growth and Global Leadership. The Role of the State in Technological Progress 1750–2000*. New York and London: Routledge, 2016.

Molinari, Gustave de. 1846. *Études économiques*. Partie I. Online: Institut Coppet.

———. 1854. *Cours d'économie politique*. Vol. 1. Paris: Guillamin, 1863. 2 vols. Online: Library of Liberty.

Mondolfo, Rodolfo. 1925. Il problema delle classi medie. Milano: La Giustizia.

Montaigne, Michel. 1580. *Essays. Livre 1*. Paris: Flammarion, 1969.

Montchrétien, Antoine. 1615. *Traicté de l'oeconomie politique*. Genève: Libraire Droz, 1999.

More, Thomas. 1516. *Utopia*. London: Penguin, 1965.

Morini-Comby, J. 1930. *Mercantilisme et protectionnisme*. Paris: Alcan.

Moro, Beniamino and Beker, Victor. 2016. *Modern Financial Crises*. Cham etc.: Springer.

Morris, Jacob. 1958. "Unemployment and Unproductive Employment". Science and Society, New York, Summer 1958.

———. 1960. "Rejoinder to J. Blake". Science and Society, New York, Spring 1960.

Moseley, Fred. 1991. *The Falling Rate of Profit in the Postwar United States Economy* .... London: Macmillan.

Müller, Adam H. 1809. *Die Elemente der Staatskunst*. Berlin: Sander. 3 vols.

Mun, Thomas. [1623]. *England's Treasure by Forraign Trade* .... 1st ed. London: Th. Clark, 1664. Reprint Fairfield, NJ: Kelley.

Muñoz, Antonio (Enrique Ramos) 1769. *Discurso sobre economía política*. Madrid: Ibarra (Bibl. Nac. Madrid).

Myint, Hla. 1948. *Theories of Welfare Economics*. Cambridge, MA: Harvard University Press.

Nagels, Jacques. 1974. *Travail collectif et travail productif dans l'évolution de la pensée marxiste*. Bruxelles: de l'Université de Bruxelles.

Napoleoni, Claudio. 1962. "La posizione del consumo nella teoria economica". *La Rivista Trimestrale*, I.1, marzo 1962: 3–26.

———. 1985. *Discorso sull'economia politica*. Torino: Boringhieri.

Negishi, Takashi. 1989. *History of Economy Theory*. Amsterdam and Oxford: North-Holland.

Negri, Antonio. 1974. "Stato, spesa pubblica, ...". Now in his *La forma-stato*. Milano: Feltrinelli, 1977, ch. 7: 233–69.

Neisser, Hans. 1934. "General Overproduction: A Study of Say's Law of Markets". Now in his *Selected Papers*. El Cerrito, CA: Charlotte Neisser.

Newcomb, Simon. 1886. *Principles of Political Economy*. New York: Harper, online, Internet Archive.

Newman, Samuel P. 1835. *Elements of Political Economy*. Andover, MA: Gould & Newman. Online: Internet Archive – Microsoft from University of California.

Nichols, Theo, ed. 1980. *Capital and Labour: Studies in the Capitalist Labour Process*. Glasgow: Fontana.

Nicholson, J. Shield. 1891. "The Living Capital of the United Kingdom". *Economic Journal*, March, 1: 95–107.

———. 1893–1901. *Principles of Political Economy*. London: Black. 3 vols. Online: Internet Archive – Microsoft from University of Toronto.

Nicholson, Leonard. 1980. "The Whys and Wherefores of Human Resources". *Human*, 1983, vol. 2: 198–208.

Nicolaus, Martin. 1973. *Foreword* to Marx, *Grundrisse*. Trans. from German. Harmondsworth: Penguin, 1973: 7–63.

Nishikawa, Kiyoharu. 1965. "Productive and Unproductive Labour from the Point of View of National Income". *Osaka City University Economic Review*, 1965, no. 1: 1–28.

Oakley, Allen. 1994. *Classical Economic Man*. Aldershot: E. Elgar.

O'Brian, Mary. 1981. *The Politics of Reproduction*. Boston and London: Routledge & Kegan Paul.

O'Brien, D. P. 1975. *The Classical Economists*. Oxford: Clarendon.
O'Brien, George. 1948. *The Phantom of Plenty*. Dublin: Clonmore & Reynolds.
O'Connor, James. 1973. *La crisi fiscale dello stato*. Trans. from English. Torino: Einaudi, 1979.
———. 1975. "Il lavoro produttivo e il lavoro improduttivo". Trans. from English. Now in Mingione 1980: 81–137.
Ofer, Gur. 1973. *The Service Sector in Soviet Economic Growth*. Cambridge, MA: Harvard University Press.
Offe, Claus. 1971–77. *Lo stato nel capitalismo maturo*. Milano: Etas Libri, 1977 (collection of essays published in German from 1971 to 1977).
———. 1979. *Teoria dello stato e politica sociale*. Trans. from German. Milano: Feltrinelli, 1979.
Opdyke, George. 1851. *A Treatise on Political Economy*. New York: for the proprietor, Putnam. Online: Internet Archive from University of California.
Oppenheimer, Martin. 1979. "La proletarizzazione dei professionisti". Trans. from English. In Tousijn 1979: 155–70.
Ortes, Giammaria. 1774. *Della economia nazionale*. In Custodi 1803–16. Moderna, Vol. 22.
Ortiz, Josef Alonso. 1794. "Notes and translation of A. Smith". *Investigación de la naturaleza y causas de la riqueza de las naciones*. Valladolid: Santander. 4 vols. Vol. 2. Online: marxists.org.
Ortiz, Luis. 1558. "Memorial … a Felipe II". *Anales de Economia*, 63, Enero 1957: 117–200.
Ossowski, Stanislaw. 1957. *Struttura di classe e coscienza di classe*. Trans. from Polish. Torino: Einaudi.
Owen, Robert. 1815. *Observations on the Effect of the Manufacturing System*. 2nd ed. London, etc.: no publisher. 1817. Online: Robert Owen Archive.
———. 1818. *Two Memorials on Behalf of the Working Classes*. London: Longman, Hurst, etc. Online: Google from Harvard College Library.
Packard, Vance. 1957. *I persuasori occulti*. Trans. from English. Milano: Il Saggiatore, 1969.
———. 1960. *The Waste Makers*. New York: Ig publishing.
Paget, Amédée. 1838. *Introduction à l'étude de la science sociale …* Paris: Bureau de la Phalange. Online: Google from Cercle de L'Ecu de Genève.
Paglin, Morton. 1961. *Malthus and Lauderdale. The Anti-Ricardian Tradition*. Reprint, Clifton: Kelley, 1973.
———. 1962. "Introduction" to Lauderdale 1804, ed. 1962: vii–xiv.
Palmer, Henry. 1828. *Remarks on the Nature of Value* …. London: Kerby.
Pannekoek, Anton. 1909. "The New Middle Class". International Socialist Review, October 1909. Trans. from Dutch. Online: Marxists Archive.
Pareto, Vilfredo. 1896. *Cours d'économie politique*. Genève: Droz, 1964.
———. 1906. *Manuale di economia politica*. Pordenone: Studio Tesi, 1994.
Pasinetti, Luigi. 1981. *Dinamica strutturale e sviluppo economico* (trans. of Structural Change and Economic Growth). Torino: UTET, 1984.
Pasquier, Maurice. 1903. *Sir William Petty*. Reprint New York: Lenox Hill, 1971.
Patten, Simon. 1896. *The Theory of Social Forces*. Philadelphia: American Academy of Political and Social Science. Online: Google – Internet Archive from Univ. of Michigan.
———. 1899. *The Development of English Thought. A study on the Economic Interpretation of History*. Reprint New York and London: Garland, 1974.
Pautet, J.-F.-Jules. 1835. *Manuel d'économie politique*. Paris: Roret.

Pelosi, Carlo. 1974. *Marx sul lavoro produttivo e improduttivo*. Roma: Istituto Enciclopedia Italiana.

Périn, Charles. 1880. *Les doctrines économique depuis un siècle*. Paris-Lyon: Lecoffre. Online: B. Saint Libère.

Perrotta, Cosimo. 1976. *La proletarizzazione contemporanea*. Lecce: Milella. 2 vols.

———. 1998. "Consumption". In Kurz and Salvadori 1998, I: 188–93.

———. 2004. *Consumption as an Investment. The Fear of Goods from Hesiod to Adam Smith*. New York and London: Routledge.

———. 2015. "Riches and Value". In H. Kurz and N. Salvadori, eds. *The Elgar Companion to David Ricardo*. Cheltenham: E. Elgar, 2015: 489–94.

Pesenti, Antonio. 1972. *Manuale di economia politica*. Roma: Editori Riuniti, 2 vols.

Petty, William. [1644–45]. *Miscellaneous*. In Petty [1927], II.

———. [1647]. *An Explication of Trade and its Increase*. In Petty [1927], I.

———. 1662. *A Treatise of Taxes*.... In Petty [1899] I.

———. [1664]. *Verbum Sapienti*. In Petty [1899], I.

———. [1671]. *Political Observations*. In Petty [1927], II.

———. [1672]. *Political Anatomy of Ireland*. In Petty [1899] I.

———. [1676]. *Political Arithmetick*, posthumous. In Petty [1899] I.

———. [1685]. *Of a Poll Bill*. In Petty [1927], I.

———. [1686]. *Fiant*. In Petty [1927], I.

———. 1899. *Economic Writings*. Reprint New York: Kelley, 1963 and 1964. 2 vols.

———. 1927. *The Petty Papers. Some unpublished Writings*. Reprint New York: Kelley, 1967, 2 vols. in one.

Petyt, William. 1680. *Britannia Languens; or A Discourse of Trade* ... In McCulloch 1856a: 275–504.

Piccone Stella, Simonetta. 1972. *Intellettuali e capitali nella società italiana del dopoguerra*. Bari: De Donato.

Pietranera, Giulio. 1955. "Marx e la storia delle dottrine economiche". Now in Id., N. Bellanca and G. Pala, eds. *Il capitalismo monopolistico finanziario ... Scritti scelti 1947–61*. Napoli: Città del Sole, 1998: 121–37.

Pinheiro-Ferreira, Silvestre. 1840. *Précis d'un cours d'économie politique*. Paris: Garnot.

Pischel, Giuliano. 1946. *Il problema dei ceti medi*. Milano: Gentile.

[Plumard de Danguel, Louis-Joseph]. 1752. *Remarques sur ... France et ...Grande Bretagne par rapport au commerce*. Amsterdam: Changuion, 1754.

Political Economy. 1810. Entry of the *Encyclopaedia Britannica*. 4th ed., Vol. XVII. Edinburgh: Constable: 106–23. The same entry in the 1815 ed.

[Pollexfen, John]. 1697. *Of Trade* .... London: Barker, 1700.

Pollin, Robert. 2012. *Back to Full Employment*. Cambridge, MA and London: MIT Press.

Porta, Pier Luigi. 1998. "Malthus, Thomas Robert". Entry of Kurz and Salvadori 1998, II: 69–74.

Postlethwayt, Malachy. 1757. *Britain's Commercial Interest Explained and Improved*. New York: Kelley, 1968. 2 vols.

Poulantzas, Nicos. 1974. *Les classes sociales dans le capitalisme aujourd'hui*. Paris: Éd.s du Seuil.

Poulett Scrope, George. 1833. *Principles of Political Economy* .... London: Longman etc. Reprint New York: Kelley, 1969.

Prato, Giuseppe. 1924–25. *Lezioni di storia delle dottrine economiche*. Torino: Giappichelli, 1945.

Prebisch, Raúl. 1949. "El desarrollo económico de la América Latina ...". Now in *Desarrollo económico*, 1986, no. 103: 479–502.

Predaval, Luigi. 1807. *Saggio sulla scienza economico-politica* .... Milano: Destefanis.

Prendergast, Renee. 2010. "Accumulation of Knowledge and Accumulation of Capital in Early 'Theories' of Growth and Development". *Cambridge Journal of Economics*, 34: 413–31.

Pribram, Karl. 1983. *A History of Economic Reasoning*. Baltimore and London: Johns Hopkins University Press 1983. Posthumous.

Proudhon, Pierre-Joseph. 1846. *Système des contradictions économiques ou Philosophie de la misère*. Paris: Guillaumin. Tome I, online, Gallica (BNF).

Prudensky, G. A. 1961. "Labor Productivity: Concepts, Factors and Growth". Now in *Dunlop & Diatchenko*, 1964: 3–11.

[Putnam, Oliver]. 1834. *Tracts on Sundry Topics of Political Economy*. Boston: Russell & Odiorne. Online: Google.

Puviani, Amilcare. 1903. *Teoria dell'illusione finanziaria*. Milano: ISEDI, 1973.

Quadrio Curzio, Alberto. 1973. *Investimenti in istruzione e sviluppo economico*. Bologna: il Mulino.

Quesnay, François. 1756. *Fermiers*. Article of the Encyclopédie. In Q. (1958: 427–58).

———. 1757. *Grains*. Article of the Encyclopédie. In Q. (1958: 459–510).

———. 1759. *Essai sur l'administration des terres*. Reprint Milano: Fondaz. G.G. Feltrinelli, 2003.

———. 1766a. *Réponse au mémoire de M. H. sur les avantages de l'industrie et du commerce*.... In Q. (1958: 749–58).

———. 1766b. *Analyse de la formule arithmétique du Tableau économique*.... In Q. (1958: 793–812).

———. 1766c. *Sur les travaux des artisans. Second dialogue*. In Q. (1958: 885–912).

———. 1767a. *Maximes générales du gouvernement économique d'un royaume agricole*. In Q. (1958: 949–76).

———. 1767b. "Despotisme de la Chine". In A. Oncken, ed. *Oeuvres économiques et philosophiques*. Reprint New York: Burt Franklin, 1969: 563–660.

———. 1767c. Analyse du gouvernement des Incas du Pérou. *In Q*. (1958: 913–16).

———. 1958. *François Quesnay et la Physiocratie*. Paris: Inst. National d'Études Démographiques (INED), 2 vols. The vol. 2: 393–1005 collects Quesnay's works.

Rae, John. 1834. *The Sociological Theory of Capital*. New York: Macmillan, 1905 (original title: ... *New principles ... of Political Economy, Exposing the Fallacy of the System of Free Trade* ...).

Ramsay, George. 1836. *An Essay on the Distribution of Wealth*. Reprint Clifton, NY: Kelley, 1974.

Rashid, Salim. 1977. "Malthus' model of general gluts". *History of Political Economy*, Fall 1977: 366–83.

Rau, Karl Heinrich. 1826–27. *Corso di economia politica*. Trans. from German, Vol. 1. Genova: Monni, 1855 (but, a label on the cover says: Garbarino 1864: Fondazione Einaudi).

Ravenstone, Piercy. 1821. *A Few Doubts ... on ... Population and Political Economy*. London: Andrews. Online: Google from New York Public Library.

Raymond, Daniel. 1820. *The Elements of Political Economy*. Baltimore: Lucas, etc. 2 vols. Reprint, New York: Kelley, 1964.

Read, Samuel. 1829. *Political Economy*. Edimburgh, printed for the Author.

Reinert, Erik, ed. 2004. *Globalization, Economic Development and Inequality*. Northampton, MA: Elgar.

Renner, Karl. 1953. "The Service Class". Trans. from his *Wandlungen der modernen Gesellschaft*. Now in T. Bottomore and P. Goode, eds. *Austro-Marxism*. Oxford: Clarendon. 1978: 249–52.

Ressi, Adeodato. 1817–19. *Economia della specie umana*. Pavia: Bizzoni. 4 vols.

Rettura, Francesco. 1973. *Impiegati e proletarizzazione*. Bari: De Donato.

Ricardo, David. 1810–23. *Letters to Malthus*. James Bonar, ed. Oxford: Clarendon, 1887. Online: Internet Archive.

———. 1820. *Notes on Malthus' "Principles of Political Economy"*. J. Hollander and T. Gregory, eds. Baltimore: Johns Hopkins Press. Online (Questia).

———. 1821. *Principles of Political Economy and Taxation*. London: Murray. Online: Library of Economics and Liberty.

———. 1951–73. *Works and Correspondence*. P. Sraffa ed. Cambridge University Press. 11 vols.

Richardson, G.B. 1975. "Adam Smith on Competition and Increasing Returns". In A. Skinner and T. Wilson 1975: 350–60.

Richmond, W. H. 1978. "John A. Hobson: Economic Heretic". *American Journal of Economics and Sociology*, 37: 283–94.

Richta, Radovan. 1967. *Civilization at the Crossroads*. Trans. from Czech. 3rd ed. White Plains, NY: International Arts and Sciences Press, 1969.

———, ed. 1968. *Progresso tecnico e società industriale*. Trans. from the German edition. Milano: Jaca Book, 1975.

Rifkin, Jeremy. 2000. *L'era dell'accesso*. Trans. from English. Milano: Mondadori, 2000.

Riflessioni. 1824. Riflessioni sul trattato di economia del Sig. Say. Napoli: tipogr. Porcelli (Fondazione Einaudi).

Rima, Ingrid. 1967. *Development of Economic Analysis*. Homewood, IL: R. Irwin.

Ripepe, Eugenio. 1982. *I conti col marxismo*. Milano: F. Angeli.

Rizzello, Salvatore. 1990. "Il dibattito francese sul lavoro produttivo, alleanze di classe e ruolo dello stato". *Quaderni di Storia dell'Economia Politica*, 1990/1.

Robbins, Lionel. 1958. *Robert Torrens and the evolution of Classical Economics*. London: Macmillan.

Roberts, Lewes. 1641. *The Treasure of Traffike* .... In McCulloch 1856a: 49–113.

Robertson, J.M. 1918. *The Economics of Progress*. London: Fisher & Unwin. Online: Internet Archive.

Robinson, Joan. 1948. "Marx e Keynes". Now in her Saggi su Marx e il marxismo. Trans. from R. *Collected economic Papers*. Milano: Il Saggiatore, 1981: 3–20.

———. 1949. *Marx e la scienza economica*. Trans. of An Essay on Marxian Economics. Firenze: La Nuova Italia, 1975.

———. 1951. "Introduction" to Luxemburg 1913 (English ed. 1951), pdf version: 13–28.

Rodbertus, Karl. 1851. *Overproduction and Crisis*. Trans. from German. London: Swan Sonnenschein, 1898. Online: Internet Archive from University of Toronto.

Roncaglia, Alessandro. 2001. *The Wealth of Ideas*. Trans. from Italian. Cambridge University Press, 2006.

———. 2014. "Introduzione" to Cattaneo 1861: 5–29.

Roscher, Wilhelm. 1854. *Principes d'économie politique*. Trans. from German. Paris: Guillaumin, 1857. 2 vols.

———. 1874. *Geschichte der National-ökonomik in Deutschland*. München: Oldenbourg.

Rosdolsky, Roman. 1968. *The Making of Marx's 'Capital'*. Trans. from German. London: Pluto Press, 1977. Online: gruppegrundrisse.files.wordpress.com.

Rosenstein-Rodan, P.N. 1943. "Problems of Industrialization of Eastern and South-Eastern Europe". Now in A. N. Agarwala and S. P. Singh, eds. *The Economics of Underdevelopment*. Oxford University Press. 1958: 245–55.

Rossi, Pellegrino. 1836–37. *Corso di economia politica*. Trans. from French. Ferrara: Servadio, 1849.
Rothbard, Murray. 1962. *Man, Economy and State*. Princeton, NJ: Van Nostrand. 2 vols.
Rousseau, Jean-Jacques. 1755. *Économie politique*. Entry of the *Enciclopédie*. Now in his *Oeuvres complètes*. Paris: Gallimard, 1959–69, Vol. III.
Rousseau, Louis. 1840. "Cours d'économie sociale". In *L'Université Catholique*, Tome X, leçons 4 and 5: 7–26 and 85–101. Paris: Bureau de l'Univ. Catholique.
Routh, Gerald. 1975. *The Origin of Economic Ideas*. London: Macmillan.
Rowthorn, Bob. 1979. "Skilled labour in the Marxist System". Now in his *Capitalism, Conflict and Inflation*. London: Lawrence & Wishart, 1980: 231–45.
Rubin, Isaac Ilych. 1928. *Saggi sulla teoria del valore di Marx*. Trans. from Russian. Milano: Feltrinelli, 1976.
———. 1929. *A History of Economic Thought* Trans. from Russian. 2nd ed. London: Ink Links, 1979.
Ruccio, David. 2016. "Bachaqueros and the Distinction between Productive and Unproductive Labor". *Real World Economics Review Blog*, June 13.
Sahlins, Marshall. 1972. *Stone Age Economics*. London and New York: Routledge, 1974.
Saint-Chaman, Auguste. 1824. *Nouvel essay sur la richesse des nations*. Paris: Le Normant père.
Saint-Simon, Claude Henry. 1821. *Du système industriel*. Paris: Renouard.
———. 1824. *Catéchisme politique des industriels*. In his *Oeuvres complètes*. 2nd ed. Paris: Naquet, 1832.
Salama, Pierre. 1973. "Aumento di un particolare lavoro improduttivo e caduta tendenziale del saggio di profitto". Trans. from French. In Strati 1978: 239–67.
Salento, Angelo and Masino, Giovanni. 2013. *La fabbrica della crisi. Finanziarizzazione delle imprese e declino del lavoro*. Roma: Carocci.
Salvati, Mariuccia. 2000. *Da Berlino a New York. Crisi delle classi medie e futuro della democrazia nelle scienze sociali degli anni trenta*. Milano: Bruno Mondadori.
Salvati, Michele. 1977. "Sul programma di ricerca sottostante alla teoria del valore marxiana (e in particolare sul lavoro produttivo e improduttivo)". *Quaderni Piacentini*, April 1977: 145–61.
Salvati, Michele and Santi, Paolo. 1968. "Critiche 'ortodosse' a *Il capitale monopolistico*. Sovrappiù o plusvalore?". *Problemi del Socialismo*, September 1968: 113–26.
Salvucci, Pasquale. 1972. *Adam Ferguson. Sociologia e filosofia politica*. Urbino: Argalìa, 1977.
Sánchez Hormigo, Alfonso. 1999. *Estudio preliminar*, in Covert-Spring 1828–36, pp. XV–CXXXIV.
Sanfilippo, Ignazio. 1828. *Sposizione dei principj di economia politica*. 2nd ed. Palermo: Reale Stamperia, 1839. 2 vols. in one.
Sartorius, Georg. 1796. *Handbuch der Staatswirtschaft* ... Berlin: Unger.
Say, Jean-Baptiste. 1803. *Traité d'économie politique*. 6th ed. Paris: Guillaumin, 1841. Online: Inst. Coppet.
———. 1820. *Lettres à M. Malthus*, Paris: Bossange. Online: Wikisource.
———. 1823–24. *Notes on Storch*, in Storch 1815 (ed. 1823–24).
———. 1828–29. *Cours complet d'économie politique pratique*. 2nd ed. Paris: Guillaumin, 1840 (with notes by his son Horace Say). 2 vols.
Say, Louis. 1822. *Considérations sur l'industrie et la législation* .... Paris: Aillaud.

———. 1827. *Traité élémentaire de la richesse individuelle et de la richesse publique* .... Paris: P. Mongie aîné.

———. 1836. *Études sur la richesse des nations* ... Paris: Renard.

Schatz, Albert. 1907. *L'individualisme économique et social*. Paris: Colin.

Schlötzer, Chrétien de. 1804. *Principes élémentaires d'Économie politique*. Vol. I. Mitau: imprimerie Steffenhagen.

Schmalz, Theodor A.M. 1808. *Économie politique*. Trans. from German. Paris: Bertrand, 1826. 2 vols.

Schmidt, Max. 1977. "Cause, natura e carattere del capitalismo monopolistico di stato". Trans. from German. In A. Martinelli, ed. *Stato e accumulazione del capitale*. Milano: Mazzotta, 1977.

Schmoller, Gustav. 1900. *Lineamenti di economia nazionale generale*. Trans. from German. Torino: UTET. 2 vols.: 1904 and 1913.

Schmookler, Jacob. 1966. *Invention and Economic Growth*. Cambridge, MA: Harvard University Press.

Schneider, Michael. 2008. "Underconsumption". In S. N. Durlauf and L. E. Blume, eds. *The New Palgrave Dictionary of Economics*. 2nd ed. Basingstoke, UK: Palgrave. Vol. 8: 456–60.

Schultz, Theodore. 1961a. "Investment in Human Capital". *American Economic Review*, March 1961: 1–17.

———. 1961b. "The Concept of Human Capital: A Reply". Now in Blaug 1968: 58–64.

———. 1963. *The Economic Value of Education*. New York: Columbia University Press.

———. 1968. "Capital, Human". Entry of the *International Encyclopaedia of the Social Sciences*. New York: Macmillan & Free Press, Vol. 2: 278–87.

———. 1992. "Adam Smith and Human Capital". In M. Fry, ed. *Adam Smith's Legacy*. London and New York: Routledge

Schumpeter, Joseph A. 1949. *History of Economic Analysis*. 1st ed. 1954. London and New York: Routledge, 1997.

Schwab, Klaus. 2016. *The Fourth Industrial Revolution*. Cologny/Geneva: World Economic Forum.

Schwartz, Jesse, ed. 1977. *The Subtle Anatomy of Capitalism*. Santa Monica: Goodyear.

Scialoja, Antonio. 1840. *I principi dell'economia sociale esposti in ordine ideologico*. Napoli: Palma.

———. 1848. *Trattato elementare di economia sociale*. Torino: Pomba.

Scitovsky, Tibor. 1976. *L'economia senza gioia*. Trans. from English. 2nd ed. 1992. Roma: Città Nuova.

Scott, William Robert. 1937. *Adam Smith as Student and as Professor*. Glasgow: Jackson.

Scuderi, Salvatore. 1827. *Principj di civil economia*. Napoli: Stamperia reale. 3 vols.

Seccombe, Wally. 1974. "The Housewife and Her Labour under Capitalism". *New Left Review*, January–February 1974: 3–24.

Sedgwick, Theodore. 1836–39. *Political and Private Economy*. Reprint Clifton, NY: Kelley, 1974.

Sénac de Meilhan, G. 1787. *Considérations sur les richesses et le luxe*. Amsterdam: no publisher, 1789.

Senior, William Nassau. 1827. *An Introductory Lecture on Political Economy*. 3rd ed. London: Murray.

———. 1830. *Three Lectures on the Rate of Wages*. London: Murray.

———. 1836. *An Outline of the Science of Political Economy*. Reprint New York: Kelley, 1965. Online: Mises Institute from Library of Congress.

———. 1847. *A Lecture on the production of Wealth*. Oxford and London: Parker.

———. 1852. *Four Introductory Lectures on Political Economy*. London: Longman etc.

Serra, Antonio. 1613. *A Short Treatise on the Causes that Can Make Kingdoms Abound in Gold and Silver ....* Trans. from Italian. London etc.: Anthem, 2011.

Serres, Olivier de. 1600. *Le théâtre d'agriculture et mesnage des champs*. Paris: Huzard, 1804–05. 2 vols.

Sewall, Hanna. 1901. *The Theory of Value before Adam Smith*. Reprint New York: Kelley, 1968.

Sewell, Rob. 2014. "The puzzle of productive and unproductive labour". In *In Defence of Marxism*, online, 17 July 2014.

Shaffer, H. G. 1961. "A Critique of the Concept of Human Capital". Now in Blaug 1968: 45–57.

Shibata, Kei. 1934. "On the Law of Decline in the Rate of Profit". *Kyoto University Economic Review*, July 1934: 61–75.

———. 1939. "On the General Profit Rate". *Kyoto University Economic Review*, January 1939: 40–66.

Silva Lisboa, José da. 1819–20. *Estudios do bem-commum e economia politica ....* Rio de Janeiro: Impressão Regia. 3 parts. Online: Internet Archive from Bibl. nacional S. Paulo.

Silveira Pinto, Agostinho. 1837. *Prelecçoes preliminares ao Curso d'economia politica*. Coimrra: Universidade. Online: Google from British Museum Library.

Sismondi, Jean Ch. L. Simonde de. 1803. *De la richesse commerciale ....* Genève: Paschoud, an XI (1803). 2 vols.

———. 1810. *Les deux systèmes d'économie politiques ....* In *Pallas*, zweite Jahrgang, 1810: 97–127 and 175–97 (Fondaz. Einaudi).

———. 1819. Nouveaux principes d'économie politiques. 2nd ed. 1827, Paris: Delaunay. 2 vols. Online: I tome: Gallica, BNF; II tome: University of Michigan.

———. 1820–27. *Éclaircissemens relatifs á la balance des consommations avec les productions*, in S. 1819, ed. 1827, tome 2: 369–464 (also includes two articles of 1820 and 1824).

———. 1837–38. *Études sur l'économie politique*. Bruxelles: Société Typographique Belge, 2 vols.

Skarbeck, Frédéric. 1829. *Théorie des richesses sociales*. Paris: Sautelet. 2 vols. Online: Internet Archive.

Skinner, Andrew. 1979. *A System of Social Science. Papers Relating to Adam Smith*. Oxford: Clarendon.

Skinner, Andrew and Wilson, Thomas, eds. 1975. *Essays on Adam Smith*. Oxford: Clarendon.

Sleeman, John. 1979. *Resources for the Welfare State*. London and New York: Longman.

Sleeman, William. 1837. *Analysis and Review of the Peculiar Doctrines of the Ricardo, or New School, of Political Economy*. Serampore, India: Serampore Press.

Smith, Adam. 1776. *Wealth of Nations*. E. Cannan, ed. London: Methuen, 1904. Online: Library of Economics & Liberty.

Smith, Peshine. 1868. *A Manual of Political Economy*. New York: Putnam. Online: Google & Internet Archive from University of Michigan.

Smyth, Ackoute. 1828. *Outlines of a New Theory of Political Economy*. Cork, Ireland: Fergusson printer.

Soden, Friedrich. 1806. *Die Nazional-Oeconomie*, Leipzig: Barth. 9 vols. (1805–24): Vol. 2.

Sohn-Rethel, Alfred. 1970. *Intellectual and Manual Labor.* Trans. from German. Atlantic Highlands, NJ: Humanities Press, 1978. Online: Libcom.

Solera, Maurizio. 1785. *Essai sur les valeurs.* In Custodi 1803–16, Moderna, Vol. 39: 245–363.

Solly, Edward. 1814. *Considerations on Political Economy.* Trans. from German. London: Richardson, 1821. Online: Google from British Museum Library.

Solow, Robert. 2008. "I nipoti di chi?". In L. Pecchi and G. Piga, eds. *Il 21° secolo di Keynes (Revisiting Keynes).* Trans. from English. Roma: LUISS University Press, 2011: 89–94.

Sombart, Werner. 1912. *Luxury and Capitalism.* Trans. from German. Ann Arbor: Univ. of Michigan Press, 1967.

Somogyi, Giovanni. 1976. "Marxismo e crisi dell'economia". In Guido Carandini, et al., *Crisi della teoria economica e crisi del capitalismo.* Quaderni di *Problemi del socialismo.* Milano: F. Angeli, 1976.

Sotiroff, G. 1962–63. "Introduction" to Barton (1962–63).

Spalletti, Stefano. 2009. *Istruzione, crescita e rendimenti nella teoria del capitale umano.* Roma: Aracne.

Spann, Othmar. 1910. *Breve storia delle teorie economiche.* Trans. from German. Firenze: Sansoni, 1936.

Spence, William. 1807. *Britain Independent of Commerce.* In Spence 1822: 1–92.

———. 1808. *Agriculture the Source of the Wealth of Britain.* In Spence 1822: 93–192.

———. 1822. *Tracts on Political Economy.* London: Longman.

Spengler, Joseph. 1960. "La théorie du développement économique". In B. Hoselitz, ed. *Théories de la croissance économique.* Trans. from English. Paris: Dunod, 1970: 197–252.

Sraffa, Piero. 1960. *Produzione di merci a mezzo di merci.* Torino: Einaudi, 1972.

St. Clair, Oswald. 1957. *A Key to Ricardo.* Reprint New York: Kelley 1965 (other editions write St. Claire).

Steindl, Joseph. 1952. *Maturità e ristagno nel capitalismo americano.* Trans. from English. Torino: Boringhieri, 1960.

———. 1990. "Effective Demand in the Short and in the Long Run". *PSL Quarterly Review*, 2012: 187–95.

Steiner, Philippe. 1995. "Quels principes pour l'économie politique? Ch. Ganilh, G. Garnier, J.B. Say et la critique de la physiocratie". *Économies et sociétés*, 1995/1–2: 209–30.

Steuart, James, Sir. 1767. *An Inquiry into the Principles of Political Oeconomy.* University of Chicago Press, 1966. 2 vols.

Stewart, Dugald. 1809–10. *Lectures on Political Economy.* In his *Collected Works.* Edinburgh: Constable. Vols. 8 (1855) and 9 (1856).

Stiglitz, Joseph. 2003. *I ruggenti anni Novanta.* Trans. from English. Torino: Einaudi, 2004.

———. 2008. "Verso una teoria generale del consumismo ...". In L. Pecchi and G. Piga, eds. *Il 21° secolo di Keynes (Revisiting Keynes).* Trans. from English. 2008, Roma: LUISS University Press, 2011: 49–88.

———. 2013. *The Price of Inequality.* New York and London: W.W. Norton.

Stirati, Antonella. 1994. *The Theory of Wages in Classical Economics.* Aldershot: E. Elgar.

Stone, Richard. 1943. "Two Studies on Income and Expenditure in the United States". *Economic Journal*, April 1943.
Storch, Heinrich F. von. 1815. *Cours d'économie politique*. J. B. Say, ed., with notes. Paris: Aillaud etc., 1823–24, 5 vols.
———. 1824. *Considérations sur la nature du revenu national*. Paris: Bossange père. Online: Google from Princeton Univ.
Strachey, John. 1956. *Il capitalismo contemporaneo*. Trans. from English. Milano: Feltrinelli, 1957.
Strati, Antonio, ed. 1978. *Lavoro produttivo, composizione di classe, egemonia*. Verona: Bertani.
Sully, Maximilien de Bethune, duc de. 1638 and [1662]. *Mémoires des sages et royales économies d'Etat...* Vol. I: Amstelredam, Amsterdam: Clearetimelee et Pistariste, 1638. Vol. II: Paris, Courbé, 1662.
Sunna, Claudia. 2004. *Popolazione, sviluppo e benessere* .... Lecce: Milella/Dip. Filosofia-Scienze soc.
———. 2016. "Dual Development Models in historical perspective". In C. Sunna and D. Gualerzi, eds. *Development Economics in the Twenty-First Century*. London and New York: Routledge, 2016: 71–87.
Supino, Camillo. 1898. *La borsa e il capitale improduttivo*. Milano: Hoepli.
———. 1907. *Le crisi economiche*. Milano: Hoepli. Online: Google, from University of California.
Sweezy, Paul. 1942. *The Theory of Capitalist Development*. London: Dobson, 1962. Online: wordpress.com.
Sylos Labini, Paolo. 2004. *Torniamo ai classici*. Roma-Bari: Laterza, 2005.
Tagliacozzo, Giorgio. 1937. "Nota" in Idem, ed. *Economisti napoletani dei sec. XVII e XVIII*. Bologna: Cappelli, pp. XXIX–LXVII.
Taussig, Frank W. 1896. *Wages and Capital. An Examination of the Wages Fund Doctrine*. Reprint London and New York: Macmillan, 1932.
———. 1911. *Principles of Economics*. 4th ed. New York: Macmillan, 1939. 2 vols.
Terray, E. 1972. "Prolétaire, salarié, travailleur productif". *Contradictions*, July–December 1972: 111–49.
Thierry, Augustine. 1817. *L'industrie littéraire et scientifique liguée avec l'industrie commerciale et manufacturière*. Vol. I, II partie: Politique. Paris: Delaunay.
Thomas, Dalby. 1690. *A Historical Account of the Rise and Growth of the Western-India Colonies* .... In *Harleian Miscellany* (1744–46). Reprint London: Dutton, Vol. X, 1810: 403–45.
Thompson, William. 1824. *An Inquiry into the Principles of the Distribution of Wealth* .... London: Longman etc. Online: Google from Österreich Nationalbibliothek.
———. 1827. *Labor rewarded* .... London: Hunt & Clarke. Online: Internet Archive (funding by Microsoft).
Thornton, William. 1869. *On Labour, Its Wrongful Claims and Rightful Dues* .... London: Macmillan. Online: Internet Archive from Bodleyan Library, Oxford.
Tomasetta, Leonardo. 1974. *Stratificazione e classi sociali*. Milano: Il Saggiatore.
Tomassini, Roberta. 1976. "Scolarizzazione di massa e ricomposizione di classe". Now partly in Strati 1978: 368–81.
Toniolo, Giuseppe. 1908. *Trattato di economia sociale*. Online: Storiologia.
Tooke, Thomas. 1823. *Thoughts and Details on the High and Low Prices of the last Thirty Years*. London: Murray. 2 vols.
Torrens, Robert. 1808. *The Economists Refuted*. 2nd ed. in his The Principles and Practical Operations of Sir Robert Peel's Bill of 1844 .... London: Longman, Brown, etc., 1857.

———. 1815. *An Essay on the External Corn Trade*. London: Hatchard. Online: Internet Archive.

———. 1819. *Mr. Owen's Plans for Relieving the National Distress*. in his *The Economists Refuted and Other Early Economic Writings*. P. Groenewegen, ed. University of Sydney, 1984.

———. 1821. *An Essay on the Production of Wealth*. London: Longman, Hurst, etc. Online: Internet Archive.

———. 1834. *On Wages and Combination*. London: Longman, Rees etc. Reprint New York: Kelley, 1969.

Touraine, Alain. 1955. *L'evoluzione del lavoro operaio alla Renault*. Trans. from French. Torino: Rosenberg & Sellier, 1974.

———. 1969. *La società post-industriale*. Trans. from French. Bologna: il Mulino, 1974.

Tousijn, Willem, ed. 1979. *Sociologia delle professioni*. Bologna: il Mulino.

Trainer, Ted. 2011. "The radical implications of a zero growth economy". *Real World Economics Review*, 57: 71–82, online.

Tramontani, Luigi. 1792. *Voto* … (to the Accademia dei Georgofili, Firenze), attached to Biffi Tolomei 1792: 285–96.

Traité. 1971. *Trattato marxista di economia politica: II capitalismo monopolistico di stato* (sponsorship of the French Communist Party). Trans. from French. Roma: Editori Riuniti, 1973. 2 vols.

Tridico, Pasquale. 2014. "Welfare models, inequality and economic performance during globalisation". Roma: Univ, Roma Tre, Dept. of Economics, Working Paper 191. Online.

Trinchera, Francesco. 1854. *Corso di economia politica*. Torino: Pons. Online: Google from Harvard University.

Tsouflidis, Lefteris and Tsaliki, Persefoni. 2014. "Unproductive Labour, Capital Accumulation and Profitability Crisis in the Greek economy". *International Review of Applied Economics*, 2014/5: 562–85.

Tucker, George. 1859. *Political Economy for the People*. Philadelphia: Sherman & son.

Tucker, Graham. 1960. *Progress and Profits in the British Economic Thought, 1650–1850*. Cambridge University Press.

Tucker, Josiah. ca. 1750. *A Brief Essay … with regard to Trade*. 3rd ed. in McCulloch 1859b: 309–425.

———. 1755. *The Elements of Commerce and Theory of Taxes*. In Idem, *A Selection from His Economic and Political Writings*, New York: Columbia University Press : 51–219.

———. 1757. *Instructions for Travellers*. In Idem, A Selection from his Economic and Political Writings. New York: Columbia University Press : 221–80.

Tugan-Baranowsky, Mikhail. 1905. *Theoretische Grundlagen des Marxismus*. Italian trans. of chapter 9 in Colletti and Napoleoni 1970: 303–32.

Twiss, Travers. 1847. *View of the Progress of Political Economy in Europe* … Reprint, Clifton, NJ: Kelley, 1973.

Urbain, Nestor. 1833. *Introduction à l'étude de l'économie politique*. Paris, etc.: Bossange père.

Ure, Andrew. 1835. *The Philosophy of Manufactures* …. London: Ch. Knight. Online: Internet Archive.

U.S.S.R. Academy of Sciences. 1954. *Political Economy*. 2nd ed. Trans. from Russian. London: Lawrence & Wishart, 1957.

Vaisov, Mifhat. 1971. "Sui concetti di lavoro produttivo e improduttivo". Trans. from Russian. *Critica Marxista*, 1971/2: 121–35.

Valenti, Ghino. 1892. *Lavoro produttivo e speculazione* …. Roma etc.: Loescher.

———. 1906. *Principi di scienza economica* …. 3rd ed. Firenze: Barbera, 1921. 2 vols.

Valeriani Molinari, Luigi. 1825–27. *Saggi di erotemi su ... pubblica economia.* Bologna: Masi. 2 vols.

Vanderlint, Jakob. 1734. *Money Answers All Things* .... Reprint Baltimore: Johns Hopkins University Press, 1914.

Vasco, Tommaso. 1773. "Piano di economia politica". In C.A. Vianello, ed. *Economisti minori del Settecento lombardo.* Milano: Giuffrè, 1942: 390–421.

Veblen, Thorstein. 1899. *The Theory of the Leisure Class.* Online: moglen.law.columbia.edu

Venturi, Franco. 1969. *Settecento riformatore.* Torino: Einaudi. Vol. I.

Verri, Pietro. 1771. *Meditazioni sulla economia politica.* In Custodi 1803–16. Moderna, Vol. 15.

Villari, Rosario. 1970. "Antonio Genovesi e la ricerca delle forze motrici dello sviluppo sociale". *Studi storici*, genn.-marzo, 1970.

Villeneuve Bargemont, Alban de. 1841. *Histoire de l'économie politique* ... Paris: Guillaumin, 2 vols. in one.

Viner, Jacob. 1935. Review of Heckscher, *Mercantilism.* Now in Viner 1958: 407–10.

———. 1937. *Studi sulla teoria del commercio internazionale.* In Idem, *Commercio internazionale e sviluppo economico.* Trans. from English. Torino: UTET, 1957.

———. 1948. "Power versus Plenty as Objectives of Foreign Policy in the Seventeenth and Eightennth Centuries". Now in Viner 1958: 277–305.

———. 1958. *The Long View and the Short.* Glencoe: Free Press.

———. 1968. "Mercantilist Thought". Sub-entry of "Economic Thought", *International Encyclopaedia of Social Sciences*, New York: Macmillan-Free Press, Vol. 4.

Vitrolles, Eugène. 1801. *De l'économie publique réduite à un principe* .... Paris: Desenne, an IX.

Voltaire. 1738. *Osservazioni su John Law, Melon e Dutot*, in V., *Scritti politici.* Trans. from French. Torino: UTET, 1964.

Wade, John. 1833. *History of the Middle and Working Classes* .... London: E. Wilson. Online: Google, from Bodleyan Library, Oxford.

Wagner, Johann J. 1815. *Der Staat.* Würzburg: printed by the author.

Wakatabe, Masazumi. 2001. "William Edward Hearn on Knowledge-Based Growth: Innovator or Plagiarist of John Rae?". *History of Economics Review*, Winter 2001, no. 33: 64–80. Online.

Walker, Amasa. 1866. *The Science of Wealth* .... 4th ed. Boston: Little & Brown, 1867. Online: Internet Archive from Cornell University.

Walker, Francis A. 1876. *The Wage Question.* London: Macmillan, 1888. Online: Library of Economics & Liberty.

———. 1883. *Political Economy.* 3rd ed. London: Macmillan. Online: Library of Liberty.

Walras, Auguste. 1831. *De la nature de la richesse, et de l'origine de la valeur.* Paris: Johanneau.

———. 1849. *Théorie de la richesse sociale* ... Paris: Guillaumin.

Walras, Léon. 1874. *Éléments d'économie politique pure.* Lausanne: Corbaz etc. Online: Internet Archive.

Walsh, Raymond. 1935. "Capital Concept Applied to Man". *Quarterly Journal of Economics*, 1935: 255–85.

Wang, George. 1974, ed. *Fundamentals of Political Economy.* New York: Martin Robertson.

Ward, Bernardo. 1762. *Proyecto económico* .... Madrid: Ibarra, 1779.

Watarai, Katsuyoshi. 2015. *The General Glut Theory of Thomas Robert Malthus.* Mimeo, provisional version.

Wayland, Francis. 1837. *The Elements of Political Economy*. New York: Leavitt & Lord. Online: Internet Archive.

West, Edward. 1815. *Essay on the Application of Capital to Land* .... London: Underwood.

West, Edwin. 1969. *Adam Smith. The Man and His Works*. Indianapolis, IN: Liberty Fund, 1976.

West, Jackie. 1979. "A Political Economy of the Family ...". In Nichols 1980: 174–89.

Weulersse, Georges. 1910. *Le mouvement physiocratique en France (de 1756 à 1770)*. Paris: Alcan. 2 vols.

Wheatley, John. 1822. *An Essay on the Theory of Money and Principles of Commerce*. Vol. II. London: Cadell & Davies (the first vol. was published in 1807).

Wicksell, Knut. 1901. *Lectures on Political Economy*. Trans. from Swedish. 2 vols. Vol. 1, reprint Fairfield: Kelley, 1977. Online: Von Mises Institut.

Wilensky, Harold. 1979. "La professionalizzazione di tutti?". Trans. from English. In Tousijn 1979: 113–35.

Williams, Robert. 2017. *The Privileges of Wealth. Rising Inequalities and Racial Divide*. New York and London: Routledge.

Williams, Sam. 2010. "Productive versus Unproductive Labor". *A Critique of Crisis Theory. From a Marxist Perspective*, online journal, May 2010.

Wilson, Thomas and Wilson, Dorothy. 1982. *The Political Economy of the Welfare State*. London: Allen & Unwin.

Winch, Donald. 1966. "Biographical sketch" (introduction to James Mill), *Selected Economic Writings*. London and Edinburgh: Oliver & Boys, 1966.

Wolff, Edward. 1977. "Unproductive Labor and the Rate of Surplus Value in the United States, 1947–1967". In P. Zarembka, ed. *Research in Political Economy*. Greenwich, CT: JAI Press: 87–115.

———. 1987. *Growth, Accumulation, and Unproductive Activities. An Analysis of the Post-war US Economy*. New York University. Online.

Wood, Joseph. 1832. *Right of Labour to Legislative Protection Demonstrated*. London: Ridgway.

Wright, E. Olin. 1977. "Alternative Perspectives in Marxist Theory of Accumulation and Crisis". In Schwartz 1977: 195–231.

———. 1978. *Class, Crisis and the State*. London: New Left Books.

Wright, E. Olin, and Singelmann, Joachim. 1982. "Proletarianization in the Changing American Class Structure". In M. Burawoy and T. Skocpol eds., *Marxist Inquires: Studies of Labor, Class and States*. Supplement of *American Journal of Sociology*, 1982, vol. 88: 176–209.

Yaffe, David. 1975. "The State and the Capitalist Crisis". *Revolutionary Communist Group*, 1978, mimeo.

Young, Andrew. 1841. *Introduction to the Science of Government* .... 5th ed. Albany, NY: Van Benthuysen.

Young, Jeffrey. 1978. *Classical Theories of Value: From Smith to Sraffa*. Boulder, CO: Westview Pr. Mimeograph (Library of the Fac. di Economia, Firenze).

Zamagni, Stefano. 1979. *Georgescu Roegen. I fondamenti della teoria del consumatore*. Milano: Etas Libri.

Zitara, Nicola. 1970. "Il proletariato esterno". Now partly in Strati 1978: 360–7.

Name Index

Subject Index